Denton J. Snider

A Walk in Hellas

Or, the old in the new

Denton J. Snider

A Walk in Hellas
Or, the old in the new

ISBN/EAN: 9783743313835

Manufactured in Europe, USA, Canada, Australia, Japa

Cover: Foto ©Andreas Hilbeck / pixelio.de

Manufactured and distributed by brebook publishing software (www.brebook.com)

Denton J. Snider

A Walk in Hellas

A

WALK IN HELLAS

OR

THE OLD IN THE NEW.

BY DENTON J. SNIDER.

NEW EDITION. TWO PARTS IN ONE.

ST. LOUIS:
SIGMA PUBLISHING CO.,
210 PINE STREET.
1892.

Entered according to Act of Congress in the years 1881 and 1882,
BY DENTON J. SNIDER,
in the office of the Librarian of Congress, Washington, D. C.

CONTENTS.

I. **FROM ATHENS TO PENTELICUS.**
Plan of the Walk. — Equipment. — At Chalandri. — Recinato. — Pentelicus.

II. **FROM PENTELICUS TO PARNES.**
The Monastery and the Parthenon. — Plaisance. — At Kephissia. — The Brigands.

III. **FROM PARNES TO MARATHON.**
The Scotch Lassie. — Helen. — The Three Races in Greece. — At Marathon. — Speech in the Wineshop.

IV. **MARATHON.**
Modern Scenes. — The Ancient Battle. — Its Three Stages. — Its Meaning.

V. **FROM MARATHON TO MARCOPOULO.**
Aristides. — The Great Idea. — The Donkey. — Rain. — Greek Mythology.

VI. **RAINY DAY AT MARCOPOULO.**
Albanians. — Scanderbeg. — Amphiaraus. — Nemesis. — Brigands. — Sundown.

VII. **FROM MARCOPOULO TO AULIS.**
Orient, Hellas, America. — Fording the Asopus. Socrates. — Delium. — The Nestor of Aulis.

VIII. **AULIS AND CHALKIS.**
The Two Shepherdesses. — The Bazaar at Chalkis. — The Schoolmaster. — Iphigenia.

IX. **FROM AULIS TO THEBES.**
The Symbol — Varvouillya. — Corinna of Tanagra. — The Wallachian Village. — Entrance to an Old City.

X. **THEBES AND PLATÆA.**
Oedipus and Antigone. — Pindar. — Plataea and its Battle. — Epaminondas.

CONTENTS.

XI. FROM THEBES TO LEBEDEIA.
The Sphinx. — Thespia. — Helicon. — Hesiod and his Works and Days.

XII. STOP AT LEBEDEIA.
The Town and Nature. — Trophonius. — Hesiod and his Theogony. — A Greek Family.

XIII. FROM LEBEDEIA TO CHÆRONEIA.
The Greek Soldier. — The Chæronean Lion. — Plutarch.

XIV. FROM CHÆRONEIA TO ARACHOBA.
Panopeus. — Daulis. — The Demarch.

XV. NEW LIFE OF OLD PARNASSUS.
Arachoba. — Parnassian Scenes. — The Goddess Pallas.

XVI. TWO WORLDS OF PARNASSUS.
Arachoba. — The Chorus. — Fallmerayer. — Customs.

XVII. POLITICAL PARNASSUS.
Arachoba. — Pappayohanes and Pappakosta. — The Embassy.

XVIII. RAMBLES OVER PARNASSUS.
Arachoba. — Thermopylæ. — The Father of History.

XIX. THE DELPHIC ORACLE.
Arachoba. — Delphi. — Delphic Scenery. — The God.

XX. THE DELPHIC TOWN.
Delphi. — Gymnasium, Stadion. — Theater, Temple, Town-Hall.

XXI. THE DELPHIC NOTE BOOK.
Delphi. — Random Notes of the Traveler.

XXII. THE DELPHIC FAUN.
Delphi. — The Table-land. — The Cave. — Dimitri.

XXIII. THE RELIGION OF BEAUTY.
Delphi. — Its Religion and Art. — Decline.

XXIV. THE GREAT TRANSITION.
Delphi. — From the Heathen to the Christian World.

I. FROM ATHENS TO PENTELICUS.

I propose to give you some account of a trip through Greece in a series of talks. I do not know that I have any thing very new or entertaining to offer; I feel, however, that I may take for granted that you are interested in this journey as friends of myself. It is doubtful whether you would care much to read what I shall tell you in the book of a stranger, but a personal conversation with you may lay some additional claim to your interest. For this reason, too, I shall speak with unabashed frequency in the first person; I have gone through these experiences, and am now telling them to you. There is no disguising the fact; it is I, and nobody else, — though I would like, for the sake of modesty, to hide this *I* in some misty third person, or spirit him away into the roomy editorial *We*, if you were not sure to catch me in the act. Sometimes, indeed, I may try to free myself for a moment of this uncomfortable person; but in general, brazen-faced I shall speak of him with little or no attempt at disguise.

It is not the information, not the statistics, not the so-called hard facts which I propose to give you, but something very different. Can I impress upon you this landscape, these hills and valleys with the sunlight in which they softly repose; can I call up the emotions — the joy, the serenity, the exaltation in which they are forever steeped; can I leave with you an image of this modern

Greek life as it unfolds to the eye of the tourist in humble but spontaneous reality; but, most of all, can I therein impart to you, in its true mood and coloring, some adumbration of that old Greek world on account of which alone modern Greece has chief interest for us to-day? Nothing must be eschewed for the sake of dignity or of conventionality, if I understand your spirit; we are determined to see, to feel, nay, as far as possible, to live this life as it now rises before us, with the assurance that whatever exists has some right to be, and deserves by the very fact of its existing in the world to be treated with sympathetic appreciation.

Moreover, I intend to tell you many things which are small and unimportant. But little matters, if they be chosen with some insight, are the true characters by which we may spell out a nation or an age; small things often most vividly image the greatest deeds, the profoundest thoughts. You know that the key-stone of the arch may be a pebble; the one pithy anecdote may be the concentrated utterance of centuries. And Greece herself is small, very small compared to most countries, but what does she not stand for? Exceeding small she is; still that is just her gift, to make herself with her smallness the abiding image of what is worthiest and most beautiful in the world's history. Small things we shall not despise, when our very theme, Greece herself, is so small.

Nor shall I be very particular about a rigidly consecutive narration. We — all of us, I hope — shall loiter along the wayside, go and pick in the fields a classical flower, ramble through the ruins, turn about often and look at the mountains and the clouds, stop and wash our faces in a clear running brook, thinking that Pericles or some other great man, or even some god may have done the same thing in the same place. Like merry children let loose in the meadows on the first day of spring, we shall wander around this fair Hellas — itself the eternal spring of the world — going pretty much any whither, without any definite purpose, wherever a flower attracts our attention; and then we shall return home with the spoils of the journey woven into a many-colored garland. Such a garland I am going to try to weave now; its string will be my path, stretching through Northern Greece, to Marathon where the struggle between Orient and Occident was decided; thence to Aulis where the Greek heroes shipped for Troy to recover Helen; thence to Thebes storied with tragic destinies; thence to Delphi, home of the God of Light, well-head of prophecy and poesy. Perchance we shall cross the Corinthian Gulf, sweep around the Peloponnesus, and return by the Isthmus of Corinth to Athens, whence all of us together at this moment are getting ready to start. But let not too much be promised beforehand, for the way is long and the thread is slender.

It is indeed a slender thread, but on it I intend to string many a gem and many a pearl, if I can find them; smooth stones and glass beads of very different values shall not be thrown away; — all are to be pierced and threaded just as I pick them up on my path. A variegated string it will doubtless be; — reflections, reminiscences, recinato; men, women, donkeys — all strung together, side by side. But on this modern garland you will see, if I dare think of success, many a shape hinting of antique beauty; nay, the whole of it will, I hope, fall into your eyes with the free and joyous undulations of a Greek outline, rounded off into harmonious unity. *Kalon taxeibodion* — God speed you, my hearers, on your journey; as for me, I am safe, but you may have a hard time of it.

After inquiring in vain for a companion who would like to make the tour of Greece with me on foot, I concluded to set out alone. Everybody whom I consulted, particularly the members of the American colony at Athens, were inclined to dissuade me. The reasons alleged against making such a trip were chiefly two: first, that it was dangerous; secondly, that the traveler would be subject to great inconveniences. It was said that there were still brigands lurking in the mountains and in covert places; some people intimated that the entire rural population were always on the point of turning into a tempo-

rary state of brigandage. There were even Greeks [?] in
Athens who were not free from such apprehensions, [?]
doubtfully shook the head at the proposition of a soli[tary]
walk through the provinces. Such are the warnings [to]
be heard at the capital; the result is that very [few]
travelers penetrate into the more remote, yet by all means
the most interesting districts of Greece. The unfortunate
case of the party of foreign excursionists who were
captured by brigands in the year 1870 not far from Marathon is always cited, and still works vividly upon the
imagination of both tourist and citizen.

But besides the danger, the representations concerning
the state of the roads and the hotels were sufficient to call
up the second thought in the mind of the traveler before
undertaking such a journey. It is true that there are
not many carriage roads in Greece, and that these run
between some of the larger towns only; but mule paths
amply plain and broad enough for the pedestrian are to
be found leading every-where. It is also true that there
are no hostelries in the rural portions of Greece; but the
hospitality of the citizen takes their place; even the
humblest peasant will share with the traveler his loaf, his
wine and his olives. Always I found shelter somewhere;
always too I was greeted, as I entered the rustic cabin,
with the friendliest signs of welcome.

These admonitions, however, repeated to me often
during a stay of nearly three months at Athens, were not
without their influence. I hardly knew whether I had
better undertake the trip or not. I did not like the idea
of being robbed on the highway, or of being captured by
brigands and held for a high ransom which, I felt certain,
they would never get. The question of accommodation
gave me less trouble; the food which the peasant could
plough on, I knew I could walk on,—and the bed which
he could sleep on, I could snore on. But I was growing
dissatisfied with Athens, not because it was an unpleasant
place to live in, but because it was altogether too European, too much of a repetition of the Occident, it was
not Greek enough. Much and memorable had there been
seen and duly noted; above all, its two glorious temples,

still the most perfect remains of antiquity, and to-day the most beautiful architectural efforts of the world. Many an ancient custom had in living reality been caught from the street and the market-place, and had been treasured; all the famous spots of the antique violet-crowned city had been visited and studiously pondered; the serene climate, the transparent atmosphere, the happy blue skies had sunk deep within, and, I might hope, had left a lasting image upon the soul. But the chief thing was, that I had made myself sufficiently acquainted with modern Greek to converse with reasonable fluency on any topic that was likely to arise during a trip through the provinces.

Of the tongue spoken by the Greeks of to-day there are two leading dialects. The first is the language of society at Athens, of the newspapers, of the professors at the University, and of the cultivated people generally; it may be called modern Greek. The second is the language of the common people — Romaic, as they themselves call it. Modern Greek has a continual tendency to approach ancient Greek, on account of the influence of classical learning. Some of the newspapers the visitor will at once pick up and attempt to read; he will laugh, for he will see old Xenophon trying to put on European frock and breeches. The effect is at first ludicrous; the whole print seems like a modern travesty on ancient Greek. Strangely new is the tinge given to old words; still more strangely new are the compounds made up of old words in order to express the needs and relations of modern life. Railroad, steamboat, constitution — here they all come, peeping with sly mockery out of their Greek masks. A comic masquerade of old Greek forms it seems; this is the first impression.

But the Romaic or the popular tongue is more interesting, to me at least; it has that spontaneity which always gushes from the hearts of the people, and which a cultivated language is apt to file away, as being too rude for polished society. It is muddied, you will soon discover, with Turkish and other foreign elements; still it has turns which will carry you back to old Homer. Moreover, it has a vast body of popular poetry, altogether the most original product of modern Greece.

I felt, therefore, that I had not found at Athens altogether what I had come to Greece in search of. It was a feeling of disappointment, not intense, yet not satisfactory. What it was that I missed, what it was that could not be found there, I was not able to tell then, nor do I know that I am able to tell now.

What had I to come to Greece for? Such was the question which began to insist stoutly upon an answer. Manifestly with some very eager and enthusiastic purpose, yet quite indefinite, very difficult to lay down in words. It was some aspiration following down from youth, some image drawn from Greek classic lore, some dream perchance, sent from above by the gods, through the golden lips of that greatest of terrestrial magicians, ancient Homer. It was something or other quite impalpable but very persistent, that is certain — an airy shape, fading into indistinctness; still it never ceased to beckon, and sometimes in unconscious moments to pluck me by the arm, whispering: "Behold, this is not the place, I dwell not here — go further, and you will find me." I could truly answer in skeptical exclamation: "What, still further! I have crossed the ocean, run through Europe with mine eye mainly fixed on that image; still it beckons me forward after such a chase — what if it be but a phantasm? Shall I again follow?" Of course I shall, and at once I pack up two shirts and two books, and set out.

Now if the unrestful but happy wanderer were to give you some word or expression by which you might catch at the enticing form always floating before him, he would perchance say, it is the image of Helen. He is in pursuit of Helen; her above all human and divine personalities he desires to behold, even speak with face to face, and possibly to possess. But who is Helen? You are aware that on her account the Trojan war was fought, that all Greece when she was stolen mustered a vast armament and heroically struggled ten years for her recovery, and did recover her and bring her back to her native land.

Nor is the legend wanting that she is still there in her Grecian home just the blooming bride who was once led away by the youthful Menelaos to the shining palace of Sparta. So the wanderer is going to have his Iliad too — an Iliad not fought and sung, but walked and perchance dreamed, for the possession of Helen — the most beautiful woman of Greece, nay, the most beautiful woman of the world. There she stands in the soft moonlight of fable, statue-like, just before the entrance to the temple of History. Thither the cloudy image, rapidly growing more distinct and more persistent, beckons and points.

It is likely that you will be inclined to ask concerning the material equipment for such an expedition. Of external things, the less you have, the better. One change of apparel in a water-proof knapsack I advise, since you are certain of being overtaken by showers during the winter and spring — and these are the only seasons possible for traveling afoot in Greece. Your body must be thoroughly trained to the use of water in large quantities continuously applied; rains will descend, heavy and protracted, and there are no friendly houses standing at short intervals along the road — the peasants are collected into villages which are usually hours apart; nor is there the hospitable tree with wide-spreading branches to shelter you, for in our American sense of the word, trees do not exist in Greece except in a few remote provinces. One india-rubber drinking cup which you can double up and put in your pocket, do not forget; it should have a long string attached so that you can let it down into a well or cavernous spring. Two good maps — an ancient and a modern one — are very necessary. Take an additional pair of shoes, if you can carry them; for of all countries Greece is the hardest on shoes. It was with the greatest difficulty that I succeeded in keeping myself shod, as I traveled over its rocky pathways.

In regard to the inner equipment, the spiritual outfit of the man, just the opposite principle holds true — the more you bring along, the better. The more you take with you the more you will be likely to bring back; indeed it may be said in this respect that unless you carry a good deal

along, you will fetch but little back. Consider merely
the geography of Greece, from the Homeric catalogue, to
the traveler, Pausanias! You can not afford to leave behind the mythology, history, poetry; here along our path,
under our very feet they sprang into life and took on their
beautiful forms; here is the vessel, but you must furnish
the wine. Every spot is full, provided you bring the
fullness with you. But the chief requisite for the traveler
in Greece is, in my judgment, a deep and passionate
longing to see Helen already mentioned. With her image
hovering before him, he leaps through the valleys and
skims over the mountain tops sandal-winged; the old poetic world rises up before his eyes, robed in its native
colors and enchased in the setting of Nature in which it
came into existence.

Still you must not think, from these driving fancies,
that the benefits of the Greek trip are purely imaginary.
Here too prevails that law which is the law of the whole
spiritual world — a law which was once expressed by a
very high authority in this paradoxical fashion: "Unto
him that hath shall be given, but from him that hath not
shall be taken away even that which he hath." From him
that hath absolutely no classical knowledge or no Greek
enthusiasm, shall be taken away all pleasures of travel,
all comprehension of the Hellenic world; out of his presence will flee all those joyous images which sweetly lend
their company to the true-hearted traveler. In their stead
the soured tourist will notice only crops of stones on his
path — which will make him lose his temper on account
of their bruising his feet; he will behold only petticoated
men wearing fustanellas — which will degrade his lofty
notion of the dignity of his own sex; he will see only bare-
legged women washing at the fountain — which will give
a strong shock to his innate modesty. Alas, he will cry,
where is that Greek ideal, about which somebody said to
somebody else who told me that it was the highest type
of beauty? What monstrous liars are these Greeks, any
how, both ancient and modern! Then he will go home
and write his book. But that other person, so different,
who feels no inner calling to be uncomfortable himself or

to make all posterity uncomfortable with his discomforts carefully set down in writing, who has in his soul some trace of the genuine Greek mood together with some knowledge of the old Greek world, who is filled with an undying love of its beauty and with a genuine enthusiasm in its pursuit — what will he not see? — He will see Helen, or at least he will catch many a new and more distinct glimpse of her.

I felt, therefore, that I must go, notwithstanding the good-natured admonitions of friends, and I concluded to set out alone and afoot. These were the two qualifications for the journey: absence of a companion and possession of a pair of good walking legs. The lack of an associate I at first regretted, but I soon came to believe that this supposed misfortune was a special blessing sent from above against my will by the Gods. For one man will be taken in, when two men will be turned away; two men are company for each other, one man must find his company among the people. These will be inclined to talk to one man, whereas they will usually pass by two. Besides, there is the inestimable liberty of going and staying where and when you please, without having to compromise with a companion who is likely to have different tastes from yourself. As to brigands, I felt somewhat nervous, I confess, but I resolved to proceed with reasonable precaution, and if matters began to look squally, I would put back toward Athens with decent precipitation.

It was on a bright sunny morning — Jan. 28th, 1879, is the exact date — that I started and with a brisk walk passed up the Kephissia road which leads to Mount Pentelicus, the first stopping point in my destined course. The crests of the mountain rise hooded with clouds in the distance before me, while the Monastery of Penteli lies nestled in secrecy under the summits. Recollect, it is mid winter, yet the mild and bracing air has in it nothing severe or inclement. But that sun — of all countries on earth, the sun is most near and dear to Greece. When it passes under a cloud at this season, a chill, raw wind springs up, the temperature sinks rapidly, the landscape is darkened into gloom, and man falls out of the happiest mood into despondency, or is assailed with a feeling of general wretchedness. Never have I been jerked through such rapid changes of spirits by physical mutations as during my stay at Athens. But this morning Helius has risen in full splendor, while the frosty but genial air lifts the body from the earth and bears it along on lightsome wings.

It is quite impossible, I know, to transfer to the vision of a listener, scenes of detail; but I beg you to take my eyes now and look about yourselves as you pass out on that Kephissia road with me slightly to the northeast. Yonder on the right lies Mount Hymettus, rounded off to a beautiful swell along the horizon; through the transparent air that lies between, reach out your hand; you will be surprised that you do not touch it. The top of its ridge is thrown into a wavy line against the mild blue sky; on that line far up there, as in the paths of the Gods, you would fain move with stately tread, to be seen of all the world below. Treacherously near does the mountain seem, distant not more than a good morning walk; but it will take you the better part of the day to reach the summit of that ridge and return to the city. I know it, for I started to walk out thither once before breakfast; noon-day swept over my head in a chariot of fire and watered his steeds in the sea ere I got my supper. Of all the mountains in Attica, Hymettus will grow most dear to you; there is a honeyed caress in its look as it lies up yonder in the sun-beams; then it is never out of view, it is always hanging over you with its smiles. Nor will a close acquaintance lessen its charms; whole days have I wandered over it alone, without feeling solitariness or fatigue. To-day, however, we shall not go there.

Look now to the left; here is Mount Lycabettus, at whose foot the road winds along, and whose rather abrupt peak rises over the city. Its summit and slopes must in antiquity have been covered with statues and colonnades, gymnasiums and temples; now the whole mountain is almost bare, though the modern city is beginning to creep up its sides. On its top is a small Byzantine chapel inhabited by a solitary monk, who lives from the alms of the believers who toil up to the summit, nor will he refuse the pence of the unbeliever. As you saunter along the road below in full Greek mood, you will look up and behold the far-shining columns with frieze and pediment that once lay in sunny repose on the hillside; a forest of glistening marble springs from the slant, and robes the entire mountain in the white folds of beauty. Nor will you fail to see in this neighborhood the Cynosarges and Lyceum, famous haunts of philosophers, for here Thought too built her most enduring temple, and from this spot went forth to conquer the world. The groves of plane-trees, the shady walks, the youths wrestling in the palaestra, Aristotle walking amid a group of eager disciples and talking of the highest themes, you must bring along with you, for they are not here now. But the river Ilissus is here, just at the road-side; yet it is no river, not even a respectable brook; in the summer it is entirely dry, and in the rainy season, as at present, it often has no water. As I go down into its bed, and walk up its pebbly bottom, I can not find water enough in it to wash my hands. Yet the Ilissus is a far more famous river than our Mississippi, and will probably remain so; its name has been forever preserved by beauty in the transparent amber of ancient literature. No such amber has yet been found on the banks of the turbid Father of Waters, notwithstanding his color.

A similar fact we shall notice everywhere here with deep marvel and questioning: all things seem physically small in comparison to their fame and influence. Can it be, then, that spiritual power is submerged and lost in bulk? Streams are small, mountains are not large, towns are small and were so in antiquity, Greece itself is hardly larger than some American counties, Athens in her palmiest days had scarcely half the inhabitants of the city of St. Louis, even according to the last census. It is the nature of all things Grecian, that they seem to be characters in which, though small, we are able to read the Universe. Though the types be little, in them can be seen all, just as well as if they were large. Strange it is that, in the intellectual culture of the world, this small country has played the most important part: more important than Rome, more important than even Judea. Still more strange is this fact, that its influence is increasing to-day, while all other ancient influences are relatively declining. Why is it thus?—why is it thus? we ask ourselves trudging along up this famous little waterless river of Ilissus. The question will often recur on our journey; it is indeed the question for which a Greek journey may well be undertaken; with the right answer to it, much else in this world will be answered.

But turn around now and take a final good look at the city, before we pass the spur of Lycabettus, when it will disappear behind the mountain. While we have been going on the road, often I have turned about and looked back, though I could not tell you so. The palace of King Otho lies yonder on a rising knoll; it is a rather heavy, unwieldy thing, manifestly set down into this light climate from a Northern fog; no genuine Greek brain could ever have conceived that edifice. It is the work of a German architect — an honest work, one may truly say, but ponderously prosy. Then there are palatial residences, built in the latest French style, such as are going up at this moment in the new streets of Paris; stucco and paint on the outside, common brick on the inside; trying their best to look like solid marble with a sort of Parisian grace, trying to seem what they are not — a sham, an architectural lie.

Do you know where is all this unhappy work in building? Right in the presence of the Parthenon. Raise your eyes now out of the German fog and the French glitter; on yonder summit in the background of your view stands the supreme structure of the world. It looks down upon its city with a joyous, tender glance — as a mother leans over her babe and smiles. For twenty-three centuries the Parthenon has stood upon that height, raying its beauty into the world; still it is as happy as on the day it was finished. Robbed by barbarians, battered by cannon, blown up with gunpowder, it is yet the temple of the Goddess Pallas Athena who looks out between its columns with delighted pride and majesty upon her favorite land. It is wonderful how such a shattered building gives a sense of harmony and perfection. The central columns on both sides have been blasted outwards, yet the unmatched unity of the building, even when seen from the sides, is preserved for the eye and the feeling. As long as a single drum of a column is preserved, its beauty will remain; for the fragment bears the image of the whole work. The emotion which this edifice calls forth can not be told, for it is an emotion; you are caught up and absorbed, as it were, into a new sense of harmony, so that if there be any music in you, it will begin playing. You, life, the world turn harmonious in its glance; strife, discord, anxiety are banished in this new attunement of the soul. I should say, if there ever was a song in stone, an architectural hymn of joy and hope, there it is; listen to it, let us catch the note and carry it with us through the entire Greek journey.

But those old Greeks were heathens — Pericles, the Statesman who caused the temple to be built, and supplied the means; Ictinus the Architect, who can make a marble column dance with the grace and gayety of a Greek maiden in the chorus at a festival; Phidias the Sculptor who according to the Greek epigram, actually went to Olympus and brought down its deities and set them up in the pediment of the temple — all these men were heathens, living in the time of the "false and lying Gods." Still I confess I would like to have lived with them for a while, long enough at least to have found out whether the utterance be true which speaks from all their works, that man then was the most harmonious being that he has yet been upon our planet, so far as he has left a record of himself.

Now we must pass on, unwillingly yet with hope, since there is an absolute certainty, if clouds do not thwart, that we shall see the Parthenon again from new points of view; it is the most prominent object in Athens, in all Attica, visible, some say, at a distance of forty miles in clear weather. From every point of the landscape the look moves to it as the center of radiance, and it throws out its smiles in return, scattering them in golden profusion over the plains down to the seas and up to the tops of the mountains.

The eye drops into the road away from the Parthenon, it beholds the Albanian peasant bringing brushwood to the city. He has with him two donkeys and two women; the bundles of twigs are strapped over the backs of the donkeys in a balance like a pair of saddle bags; the women stoop obediently under their burden of faggots which is also strapped to their shoulders; while the lord of creation walks alongside, proudly erect, with majestic stride, but without any burden. There is a look of wild, half-civilized independence in his bearing; his eye drops in suspicion, if you regard him closely. His linen kilt and white leggins are deeply tinged with overmuch usage; out of a belted pouch lashed about his waist peer forth the handle of a long knife and a horse pistol. It is manifest that the women have the worst of the bargain of life in the case before us, their lot is worse than that of the donkeys, for these have the advantage of not being compelled to stoop in bearing their burdens.

Look and let them pass; here comes another group, men and mules laden with green herbs. A mule brushes me with its stores, when I am greeted with a delightful fragrance. Already I had frequently experienced the same pleasurable sensation on my way to and from Hymettus. Certainly neither the man nor the mule gave forth that pleasant odor; it must be the herb. What is it, and for what is it used? I learn that it is a plant of no less fame than the much-sung bucolic thyme which smells so sweet out of the idyls of Theocritus. It grows in abundance on the spurs of Hymettus, and is employed in the kitchen to give its aromatic virtue to cooked meats. Such is indeed the difference between then and now; anciently thyme was taken by the poet to sweeten his verses with its delicious fragrance; now it is used by the cook to flavor a beefsteak.

The city has already passed out of view, still there is on the right hand the cheerful company of Hymettus, famous for its honey, home of the Attic bee. Again note that undulating sky-line, and imagine yourself moving along it to the highest swell and standing there in solitary Olympian majesty. Every point has become familiar to the eye, I may say, friendly. For it is possible to have a deep and lasting friendship for the mountain; it is not fickle, it always gives you the same joyous look, and subtle nod of the head. It lies there in the sun so calm, so gracious, with such a soft light sweep in its outline that it may truly lay claim to a plastic shape. A thin haze casts over it a slight veil of blue and gold, without hiding in the least its form, but heightening its characteristic points by mild touches of color. A few miles to the left lies its Attic companion Parnes, snow-clad; but the white garment disappears about half-way down the side of the mountain; you may say, that the old slumberer has put on his robe of repose for a good long sleep during the winter night.

I leave the road and pass into the adjoining field in search of a ruin; an ancient aqueduct could not have been far from here. Through the field I go into a vineyard; peasants are at work trimming the vines for the joyous nectar of the coming autumn. A group of them see me, and stop their work, looking spitefully; one of them yells at me, saying: "Get out of here — the road was made to walk in." The salutation I thought a little rude, though I felt myself to be a trespasser. I had already experienced in Italy how jealous the peasants were of strangers walking through their vineyards, especially when the grapes were ripe. I shall not soon forget the hearty good-will with which an Italian peasant answered me once when I was taking a tramp through the country near Frascati. I asked him about the way to the nearest village, when he said, pointing to a path through the grape vines: "This way is nearest, but don't take it, for the peasants will think you are a grape-thief and give you a bastonata. Go round by the public road," and I did not hesitate to follow his advice.

In the present case, however, I turned aside from my course, and marched strait up to the group, asking, perhaps a little tartly: "What are you shouting at me in this way for? What do you want?" The peasant who had called out, observing my foreign accent and dress, as well as my manner perhaps, made a lunge, without saying a word in reply, toward an immense wooden canteen, uncorked it and held it to my lips. It was a peace-offering of remarkable power, as well as a sign of hospitable welcome. My slightly ruffled feelings calmed in a moment; I accepted the token with the deepest draughts of gratitude. I admired that humble peasant's profound knowledge of human nature.

After the fluid had ceased its pleasant gurgle, and eternal friendship had been pledged, the peasants began to quiz me about my nationality. Are you a Frenchman? No. German? No. Englishman? No, by Jove. Thus they quite went through the catalogue of nations, I provoking them always to guess again. But they were unable to classify the dubious specimen before them, and at last I told them that I was an American. At this word an old man, with a bright red fez slouched on his head, and wearing a remarkably clean shirt, who had hitherto been silent, came forward, and shook me heartily by the hand, saying: "The Americans and the Greeks are brothers!" I looked at him, and was suspecting that this sudden burst of fraternal affection proceeded from the recinato; but I answered him, affirming with warmth the same sentiment, for I felt no less brotherly than he did, myself.

The old man then recounted how shiploads of clothing and provisions came from that distant America, as it were from another world, during the dark hours of the Greek Revolution; he stated, if I understood him aright, that he was then a soldier and was saved from starvation by the timely arrival of the ship; he added the fact, no doubt important to him, that potatoes were then for the first time introduced into Greece. Thus he spake, and with decided emotion. What could I do under the circumstances, but drink to the freedom and prosperity of Greece? It would have been ungrateful not to have done so, according to all laws of good fellowship and patriotism. Therefore a hearty bumper to fair Hellas was swallowed, when he in return drank a handsome toast to

America, which of course had to be answered. After a pleasant interchange of good wishes, I prepared to start, for that image of Helen suddenly flitted before me toward Pentelicus, disappearing with a wave of the hand into the clouds. Yet not without a final bumper to the company did I break away, skipping off in happy mood, and taking the friendly conduct of these simple countrymen as a good omen of my future journey. Yes, I can truly affirm that I went in better mood than I came.

I believe that this affection for our country among the Greeks is genuine. Every-where I received more friendly attention when I announced my native land. I know that M. About, with his accustomed satirical scoff at all things Grecian, would have us believe that the wily Greek flatters all nationalities in the same manner, that he is thoroughly insincere and mercenary in his friendships. I can only say, such was not my experience. But it is my emphatic experience that M. About in his book on Greece is more desirous of pointing his epigrams than of telling the truth. I found a very discriminating goodwill for the different European nations even among Greek peasants. Unquestionably the people have the most affection for France, because France, of all the Great Powers, has shown for Greece the most disinterested friendship. Also the Greeks and the French have not a few traits in common — and those traits among the noblest of human nature. One may be mentioned: that aspiration after an ideal, above all a political ideal which shall bring unity to nations, and secure to man freedom and social happiness.

On the other hand there can be little doubt that the Greek has at the present time (the period of the Disraeli ministry) small affection for the English. The reason is manifest: England's diplomacy in the East has sacrificed the Greek race on the ground of supposed English interests. Turkey is thought to be the sole bulwark against Russia, and Turkey must be sustained. So the Greek lamb has been thrown to the Turkish jackal. No person will blame the Greeks for their dislike of England; no candid Englishman will blame them.

Threading my way through the vineyard, I came to the small village of Chalandri. The church is the most important edifice of the village; next to the church is the wineshop, which is the only house open to the stranger as a resort or resting-place All the dwellings are walled in, and seem to be hermetically sealed; there is no friendly opening of porches and of doors toward the street, as in an American town. The domestic abode turns away from the outside world, which is suspected and repelled; one walks through the lonely streets enlivened nowhere by children at play or by housewives sewing at the front door; he feels as if shunned and rejected by his kind, condemned beforehand by some unjust suspicion. Oriental seclusion of the family is suggested, perhaps too readily, to the mind of the traveler.

The wineshop has the only open door or window in the town; there I enter. It has no floor; good mother earth takes my wearied feet upon her bare bosom. There is no ceiling overhead to hide the naked rafters, which give support on the outside to the boards on which the tiles are laid. The place has rather a dark, cave-like appearance, forbidding, I should say, were it not for the huge hogsheads which are disposed in a long row on one side of the room, and which contain infinite joys. My hearers will probably think that I had learned enough for one day about the Greek wine-god; but the thirst for knowledge of Greek divinity was not yet stilled. At my call the youth in attendance brought a clear yellow fluid with a slight sparkle, for which he charged me at the rate of one cent a glass.

In passing, it may be remarked that this is a fixed price for many articles in Greece — one cent. You pay for a cup of coffee one cent; I could not judge of its quality, for I never drink coffee; you pay one cent for a glass of wine, often excellent, though it be recinato; one cent for a glykisma or sweetmeat, one cent for a raki, one cent for a masticha. These last two are distilled liquors of which the traveler will frequently be called upon to partake, as they belong to good cheer and hospitality. Of course they are like alcohol the world over when taken to excess: soul-corrupting, body-destroying. Cheap, antediluvian prices still prevail in the rural districts. I recollect that a merchant of Arachova sold me a cent's worth of thread, required on account of the secession of sundry refractory buttons; the generous shop-keeper threw into the bargain a glykisma or fine titbit, and when I offered him an additional cent, he claimed that his profits were sufficient without it.

I must now make you more fully acquainted with a merry companion, who will accompany us throughout this Greek tour and furnish us many a happy moment: his name is Recinato. Everywhere along the road he is to be met with; you will find him in the humblest hut of the peasant, where he takes his place at the hearth in the evening with the guests, lighting up the dark abode with unaccountable flashes. I confess that I was at first shocked by his peculiarities, but when I became used to them, I rather liked him the better for them. He is emphatically Greek, inspires the Greek mood, has within him the Greek exhilaration; Greek subtlety he possesses too, a sly way of creeping upon you with his flattering caresses ere you be fully aware of his presence. Hardly is he to be met with outside of Greece, but here he reigns without a rival in his particular sphere; indeed Greece would not be Greece without him. Strangers often complain of his bad taste; but why dispute about tastes? Faithful to the last degree, in an eternal flow of high spirits, always bubbling over with merriment — such is our jolly rustic Greek companion, Recinato, that is Resinate or resined wine, whom we shall never fail to celebrate with many feelings of gratitude. Do not forget his name — he will be often alluded to.

Dropping now his personality, I may state that this wine is prepared by adding a crude resinous substance to the juice of the grape at a certain stage of fermentation. Along the road the gum can be seen issuing from the pine-trees which have been chipped for this purpose. The taste of the wine becomes like the taste of pitch, or, as some say, of sealing-wax. At the first effort to drink it nature revolts, sometimes revolutionizes; only after much preliminary training and chastising does the rebellious palate suffer the fluid to pass its portal. As it was my rule to eat and drink, or learn to eat and drink what the people of the countries I visited ate and drank, I began with recinato shortly after my arrival at Athens. In two or three weeks I no longer noticed the pitchy taste in the wine, except by a special effort. Other kinds of wines are obtainable in the city, but in the country nothing but recinato is to be found; hence the necessity of a previous training to this drink, if one wishes to travel in the provinces, for he can not do it on water. The reasons given for treating wine in this way were two mainly: to preserve it from spoiling in the hot climate of Greece, and to make it more healthy. The ancients also had this method of treating wine, as appears from Pliny. Such is our friend Recinato, merrily hailing us at every village and sometimes along the road; such too is his abode, the wineshop, called in the dialect of the people Magazi — the most important house, after the church, in a Greek village.

This is an Albanian town, and the youth at the bar informs me that here within five miles of classic Athens, Albanian is the language of the inhabitants. But let there be no further delay; rest and refreshment have attached fresh wings to the body, the pedestrian will fly into the street, bound for Pentelicus, now rising up cloud-wrapped before him — in real clouds, I mean, and not in wine-fumes, as you might suppose. Women in their white smocks — not a night dress here — dart shyly through the streets without looking at him, or take special pains to glance in the opposite direction while he is passing. Folded over their forehead above, and over their chin and mouth below, is a linen covering, intended to hide the grateful portion of the face from the curious eye of the male. The enlightened traveler will again curse the custom as a relic of Oriental seclusion of women. They are mostly stockingless, their bare feet are slipped into a sort of loose sandal; over the dress is sometimes worn a white woolen cloak. On the whole they seem lightly clad for mid-winter; but their white forms moving along in the distance through the clear mild air gives a joyous Greek impression to the landscape, as if it were dotted with living statuary.

Here comes a maiden, on her shoulder bearing water to the village from the spring in a vessel like the ancient amphora. She turns out of the road, looks away from me, and adjusts more closely the wrappage around her chin and forehead; still I peer into her face. Wild irregular features I caught a glimpse of, burnt to dark brown by the sun of the plain. It is manifest from this and other glimpses that Helen is not here at Chalandri, nor is she to be found among the Albanian race. These people, usually considered of Slavic origin, are said to have come into Greece at various times during the Middle Ages, and they still preserve unmixed their blood, their language, their customs; and their physical characteristics.

Thus one trudges forward, leaving the houses behind, and passing by the spring, from which the maiden came who was carrying water to the village. Washers too are here, women with undraped limbs, standing in the cold stream snow-fed from the mountains; there they twist and writhe in deadly conflict with soiled garments. A momentary glance the traveler will cast at them for the sake of the antique, and then modestly turn away. Something else is calling which must be followed; a good road leading directly up to Pentelicus will not permit him to stray from his goal.

Into this road let us enter; a brook with a most pleasant babble meets us, and keeps us company, having flowed all the way down from Pentelicus for this special purpose, as we may believe, for it never deviates a moment from the side of the road where we are walking. There is a Greek mood in its transparent merry flow; one feels eager to trace it to its very source and there imbibe of the happy waters to see if he may not be able to catch the secret of its eternal joys. Two peasants I come upon, stretched along its bank asleep on the stones, without the protection of bush or passing cloud; their mule is turned loose in the fields. This natural way of taking repose is reposeful even to others; their sleep is as refreshing to the beholder as to themselves.

Now I beg you, bring before the mind's eye the pedestrian as he not very rapidly winds up the ascending road; in one hand he holds a staff, in the other a small bundle tied together by a strap; he steps lightly through the air, though his wings be but the flaps of his mantle playing in the stiff northwest wind. Often he turns around and stands, glancing at the ranges of mountains which bound the horizon at many different distances; at last he will stop and sit on a stone, looking with a long stare full of wonder and delight at the golden sport off yonder between the clouds, the peaks, and the sunbeams. Peer into his face; whatever else you may say about him, good and bad, you will say that now he is happy. So I imagine, every other human being would be, were he alone and afoot, going up Pentelicus this hour.

What a harmonious day, he is continually repeating to himself, a truly musical day in which all the elements of Nature are joined in sweet concordant strains with the soul! It is a day which the old Greek artist would set to music in a poem, in a statue, in a temple. The sun comes out warmly, but the wind from the snows of the northern mountains brings along the spurring freshness of the season and never suffers the energies to droop from their full yet easy tension. With the rays cut off by a passing cloud, Boreas has no modifier and may become a little rough — but this discordant note lasts but a moment, and then heightens by contrast the outpouring harmony of the returning sunbeams. The summits line after line swoon away in the distance into a blue ethereal dream; far off to the left they sink down into the sea whose hazy purple can be dimly discerned holding in tender embrace its azure-girdled nymphs, the islands, fairest of whom, you will say, is Salamis, with a thin blue veil over her form floating on the waters. No thought of peril from brigands introduces a jarring moment into the melodious hours — but another danger has arisen — worse than brigands: that plain, heavy-shod pedestrian is positively in danger of turning sentimental. Who would have expected that of the hard-headed son of Utility?

But let him run his course, there is no curbing him now

upon this spot, since his and our main occupation here as elsewhere in Greece is to fill these deserted fields with the forms of the Past; for all this nature through which we move is but a frame holding an ancient picture, now quite invisible from accumulated dust and mould; yet if we rub it with some patience, shining faces will come to light, of divine power and beauty. Yon white clouds still wrap the top of Pentelicus, who refuses to uncover and salute the stranger approaching; but below on the side of the mountain can be seen large white spots which are not clouds. They are the old quarries of Pentelic marble, some of which have again been opened in recent times; King Otho's palace, for instance, was built of this marble. Thus the quarries lie there, glancing afar — the bright eyes of the mountain you may call them, through glistening tears begging to be made again into forms of beauty. Nay, the whole Pentelic range lies there, a thing of nature waiting for a new transformation — for a regeneration out of nature into a thing of spirit, that it may thus reach the highest end of its existence.

The wonderful works of Athenian Art — temples, public buildings, thousands of statues and monuments — found their material in this mountain. About the middle of the fifth century B. C. the activity here must have been at its height, though it continued, doubtless, for ages. At that period the Athenians must have been quarrying marble for the Parthenon, the erection of which had been resolved on. Along this road, over these fields, what a busy throng! The teamsters with their vehicles in a line quite extending to Athens; the workmen of all kinds, the overseers, the architects with their central figure, Ictinus — here they all come and go with incessant din, sometimes not without conflict, and always with great outpouring of Attic volubility. Nor will the traveler, growing thirsty and hot with the long and high-strained quest, forget the wineshops, which then marked every turn of the road, with merry publicans dispensing the joyous nectar, without which, as a very foundation, the temple of Pallas Athena, Goddess of Wisdom, could not have been built.

But with the physical eye no human being is now visible along the way; no wagons, heavy-laden with blocks of marble pass you; all is silent, deserted, and the white quarries are still as the bones of a graveyard. You have to bring your people with you, and all your objects down to the ox-cart; your winehouse, too, has to be supplied by the imagination. As you go through the fields, your foot will, perchance, stumble against a stone; you will pick it up and nick the edge of it; observe that it is a very old remnant of a piece of marble, in fact, a chip from a block. So you may put on this spot a workshop of Phidias where the material of his statues was dressed in the rough. As you look sympathetically at the fresh break with its crystalline grain, it sparkles and smiles in your eyes, like a broken Greek satyr laughing in its fragments.

But, after all, the most interesting figure which you can see flitting mid these solitudes of stone is that of Socrates, the Attic philosopher, at the time of the building of this temple not a philosopher but a young sculptor, hunting here for good blocks of marble, out of which to make his group of the Three Graces. Long afterwards this work of his could be seen in the Acropolis; of its artistic merit nothing can now be definitely affirmed. But behold him, the mighty, heaven-compelling ghost, for the sake of that which he is to become! In outward appearance he seems to pay little attention to the Graces; wrapped in the careless folds of his himation or blanket, in low sandals or possibly bare-footed the pug-nosed Greek shuffles along, scenting some far-off modern world, yet quite unconscious that he is to begin the revolution which will not only break to pieces the Three Graces, but hurl down all the Gods of Olympus. So in the very bloom of things is the germ of their decay; here with Phidias the great revealer of the Gods, moves Socrates having in his head the ripening thought which is to destroy them.

Thus the rock underfoot still glistens with graceful smiles; the huge boulder will show its origin by its capricious seams; the bed of the brook is marked in its zigzag course through the fields by a line of white, glancing pebbles. Every stone speaks, and points up to Pentelicus, declaring that it is still full of harmony, full of Parthenons, if the man were only here to make it give forth its treasures. In its night lies the most beautiful of Goddesses, the sleeping Venus, she that once was awake in the old Greek world; — who will rouse her again? In its depths still sits Olympian Jupiter, the God who hurled the dark brood of Titans into gloomy Tartarus, but has now in his turn been imprisoned by ancient Chaos in adamantine fetters — where is the Phidias to release him and bring him out to sunlight once more? In the olden time these rude Pentelic blocks were transported to Athens, where they found breath; and men there were able to make them give forth the highest utterances. Of all the great deeds of Athens one is inclined to set this down as the greatest: that for a time it seemed to make this whole Pentelicus, rough chaotic mountain, leap into temples, into the forms of Great Men, Heroes, and Gods. But the man is certainly not here now who can do this; Pentelicus, though, is here, silent, in expectancy; but it vails its summit in a white cloud, out of shame perhaps, unwilling to look upon even that solitary pedestrian who is now loitering up its side not far from the cloud-line, into which, you doubtless think, he has already entered.

But he has not, I affirm; he still can see and can be seen distinctly with a good pair of eyes, though it may now be necessary to strain them just a little for a moment to meet an unaccustomed demand upon them. Look upward, then, once more to those quarries; the earth is slightly moving and has laid bare its white Pentelic bosom. They rise — innumerable sculptured forms — they spring out of the sides of the mountain and hurry past towards the city. One by one, in silent glimmering procession down the slope they move, or at times by groups they march; each is wearing some mighty thought in his shape, or is filled with some mighty deed. One would like to question them as they sweep by in Olympian majesty, in Bacchantic joy, in Niobean sorrow; but thousands on thousands they hasten, bent on their weighty errand. The plain below is now full of their white shapes, they line the hills, they reach to the shores of the sea; still they are moving forth from rocky beds of Pentelicus.

But listen! What sound is that? It echoes through the little vale, it creeps down the slant of the mountain, and spreads far and faintly over the plain. But with its vibrations that whole army of bright plastic shapes is swept away, and disappears into thin air, like a vast throng of sheeted ghosts. Only the empty slopes and the naked fields can now be seen, — but the sound continues. There! it smites the sides of Pentelicus again rudely, as if to drive off the demonic powers: what is it? It is the bell of the Monastery of Penteli; before the edifice we are now standing, on firm ground, it may be hoped. But with the stroke of that bell we drop through 2000 years into a new world; the beautiful Greek life, smitten by the keen sound, vanishes into a dream; instead of the white folds of some sweet nymph sporting over the summits or wading in the brook, yonder in the landscape moves a dark shape — it is a Greek monk, with melancholy stole swashing about his legs as he hurries to his prayers. It is indeed a new world, and we have to confess to the truth of that later medieval legend which affirmed that the ringing of the bell of church or cloister had the power of putting to flight the old Gods. But we belong to our own time, let us enter the Monastery.

II. FROM PENTELICUS TO PARNES.

The Monastery of Penteli is situated in a beautiful dell surrounded on all sides by mountains, with the exception of the narrow pass which leads us into the sacred inclosure. Streams of clear water play through the grounds, and are conducted in artificial channels mid a grove of fine plane-trees; then they gather into a single current and dash off into the vall y below, through the passage up which we have just come, turning in their course the wheel of an old mill. The entire locality bears the impress of some large fountain head which lies in the spacious bosom of the mountains, whence it sends its benignant streams and overflows the thirsty plains. Nature in her very conformation suggests here the inward gathering, the contemplation of the soul, and also its outpouring of charity and blessing upon the world.

The building which incloses the court looks neat and unpretentious; but the first and most satisfying impression is the perfect repose of the spot. It is a quiet green cradle of Tranquillity set down between these rugged summits which overlook it not without a touch of rude tenderness. The rills, the trees, the verdure are always refreshing to the human eye, but here they seem to have a new virtue as being an offset to the wild towering rocks. The hospitality of the Monastery is offered to the stranger; something to eat and a place of rest for the night are now at his disposal; they will be accepted if Pentelicus will but clear up his cloudy brow.

No monks are to be seen just now; they are at prayer in their cells, and all around the building as one makes the circuit of it, can be heard the low mumble of reading and of devotion. They are indeed at work, at their work in this world. Now, of all questions which arise in the mind surveying the scene, this question is uppermost: What means this Monastery here amid these hills? Fifteen men, as I learn on inquiry, dwell in it, of able body and sound mind, separated from all society and domestic life, divorced from the institutions of the world — what business has such a thing to be? Here they remain, passing their lives in this secluded nook, manifestly doing two works with great assiduity: whitewashing their house, and praying. Praying for what? For dear life, at least, if one may judge by that confused multitude of low voices which now float on the air up toward the summits.

They have made this little vale a delightful spot, a beautiful thing amid ruggedness, and the eye rests upon it with joy; so much is a manifest gain. Also they give to the weary traveler and to the poor beggar hospitable shelter and food; — but is this all? This could be done without prayer, or at least without such an organized quantity of it — and without such a life. A little city they have built with its walls and cells for houses; a little world, indeed a spiritual world they have here all to themselves. Why, one asks again, has this thing appeared in the course of time, and why does it remain with us still? Having such a problem in his soul, the reflective traveler turns away, and begins to climb the mountain slowly; then he will stop and look around at the old structure again, calmly nestled there in the dell mid the plane-trees. For what purpose, then, is it here?

This problem rays out in all directions, and embraces many other problems. Here is Pentelicus, there is Athens; now this Monastery, rude, helpless, barbarous edifice, though it be tidy enough — has it any thing to do with yonder Parthenon which one can see in full distinctness from this slant, resting upon its sunny elevation in happy repose and perfection? Yes, there is a connection, indeed the one is a descendant of the other, remote, degenerate, but still a descendant. This is the question then: to derive the Monastery from the Parthenon, by an inner spiritual genealogy, which is written down in Architecture as in any book. Not merely the structures are to be traced, one from the other, — they are only the outermost shell, — but the spirit which resides in them, which built them, and which vivifies them still. Both have been erected for the dwelling-place of divinity; both therefore express what is strongest and deepest in man; both give some utterance to the spiritual principle which animated their builders.

It is on the ideal side that we must connect the modern Greek world with the ancient. There is still here an ideal realm of striving, of hope and faith. But the modern Greek, smitten with the curse of Turkish supremacy, perhaps above all other Christian peoples, has flung the real side of life to the winds. Earth, man, comfort, even cleanliness, he too often casts away as unnecessary externals belonging to this world. *Anthropos einai skolex* — man is a worm — continually repeated my sometime humble bedmaker, pious Spiridion. How different the old Greek! Instead of man being a worm, for him the Divine entered the human body, trained it to supreme perfection by all sorts of exercise, and made it beautiful. With him divinity came down to earth, entered even this Pentelic marble, and molded it into forms that revealed the Highest. Thus there was the happy union, the complete equipoise between the Real and the Ideal, such as has been seen the one time upon our Earth. All became harmonious, beautiful; herein ancient Greece educates the human race to-day.

But short was the festive May-day of that old world; Time soon split the happy unity into a warring dualism. The Ideal overbalanced the Real and cast it out; flesh became sin, the Earth became the abode of the Devil, Parthenon fell into ruins, and there arose the Monastery. And what is still the doctrine of the Monastery? Man has his home not on Earth but in Heaven; the Ideal belongs not here, but beyond; what, therefore, is the use of a comfortable, not to speak of a beautiful house, when we have to move out of it so soon, and pass into an infinitely better one? The Monastery represents this indifference to the sensuous appearance in which Art reveals itself; the world is not indwelt of the divine, but of the diabolic.

Also we have prayer here, incessant prayer — which is the soul's aspiration and indeed momentary elevation into that realm beyond. To this solitary spot human beings have retired where they live wholly for their Ideal, live in a prayer, sometimes in an ecstasy which almost raises the body into the heavenly Beyond. Thus the break between the Real and the Ideal is pushed to its extreme consequences, and is still further manifested in the fact, that the most aspiring and often the most noble natures flee from the world and deliver it over to Satan, who in such case is quick to take possession. That ancient Greek instinct which sought to form both the State and the Individual, nay the whole Universe, into an harmonious work of Art, is now lost in the devilish reality.

Everywhere in Greece these monasteries are to be found; every district of any extent has one of them.

They doubtless answer a need of the human heart, also a need of the community. The Ideal must have some place of protection, some refuge when it is driven out of society and institutions by Turkish oppression or other untoward visitation, else man himself would relapse into savagery. It is a very important matter, this preserving the Ideal to a nation. As long as even a corrupt and subjugated people retain it, there is in them the seed of regeneration. Many and curious are the ways in which it seeks to preserve itself. Often it flees to literature, to poetry, to romance, to the construction of imaginary commonwealths in which it sits upon its own throne, and reigns triumphant, far away from the miserable reality around it. Often, too, it goes to the cloister and there prays. In this way, every large community has, we may justly affirm, its idealists locked up and thus preserved — for they are the seed of the good time coming, and an example of renunciation for the sake of the Beyond. In turbulent periods, as in the Middle Ages, the monastery is the calm green island amid the tossing and tenebrous ocean, where upon a firm foundation a light-house may be built; but in halcyon days it too often attracts the idler, who, sure of his dinner, gazes slothfully into vacuity. Modern society also drives some lofty spirits to monasticism, but its general tendency is to call them back into life where they are sorely needed.

One is at first surprised to learn that there were far more monasteries in Greece under Turkish rule than at present, and that they were then more encouraged. Yet the second thought will show us that this is simply the fruit of tyranny. In such a wretched reality as the Turkish, men were doubtless very eager to quit the world; the better the men, the more ready to preserve their Ideal in the only way possible. Institutions were the instrument of oppression; who would not seek to get away from them and pass life in the shady retreat of a cloister? Likewise it was to the interest of the Turkish oppressor to furnish some outlet for the more aspiring as well as some shelter for the more timorous of their enslaved subjects. So monasticism has flourished in the Greek provinces of Turkey, it culminates in Mount Athos or Holy Mountain in Macedonia, where the monks burrow all over a range of mountains, like a vast colony of prairie dogs. To such a state has the Greek Ideal come! Not a woman is allowed to set foot upon that Holy Mountain; Helen herself, instead of causing a Trojan war for her restoration would now be banished from the ideal realm, were she to appear there, in all her antique beauty.

Therefore we must turn aside from Penteli, with no ill feelings for it, yet with the fervent hope that the state of society which rendered monasticism a necessity and a blessing will rapidly pass away. Come out, ye mountain hermits, and again, as of old, be conciliated with the Real; put a little of your idealism into the world — into society, into politics, into dress, and above all into Art, and build us, if you can, another Parthenon, hew us out another Jupiter Olympius. Here at your very sill lies Pentelicus, praying, if I mistake not the voice, to be made into things of beauty once more; long enough has the old mountain sighed with the imprisoned forms of Gods shut up in its chaotic dungeons. Set them loose, and be reconciled with us, the outsiders — give to us, wallowing in Satanic mire, a breath of your hope and ideal striving, not for Heaven's sake, but for Earth's sake.

From the spur of the hill where I am standing, I can see another house, of imposing magnitude for this region, but at the present time deserted and falling to ruin. It is situated on a beautiful spot overlooking the plain below, which extends across to Mount Parnes and is dotted with frequent villages. Above the door can still be read the name Plaisance. I asked a peasant about it, he said simply that it was the palace of the Duchess. She, though long since deceased, yet haunts, it is said, the spot where she once dwelt and worshiped in her peculiar way. Combining what I have seen in a book with the legends respecting her, I am able to give you the following account.

The Duchess of Plaisance seems to have been one of those strong female characters for which European Society has hitherto not found any outlet in a rational vocation. One frequently finds them stranded in the oddest places and in the most outlandish ways. This woman was the daughter of a minister of Napoleon, was married early and unhappily, was divorced, when she set out on her wanderings. After many an adventure and fierce tempest, she came to Athens to spend her remaining days. She possessed a large income which enabled her to indulge in colossal caprices; these chiefly took a turn for building; one of them was the edifice before us. Here she lived with five or six huge dogs, the favorite one of which, rumor says, was sometimes invited to table with her guests.

But the most remarkable fact in the career of this remarkable woman was the religion which she was going to found. Seeing that all the great systems of belief were old and somewhat effete, she resolved to confer upon the world the blessing of a new one. Exactly what its tenets were has never been known, and they were perhaps but dimly conceived by herself. But some of its more definite doctrines turned on the institution of marriage, as was natural to a faith founded by a woman; though unable to manage her own marital matters, she could tell all about it to others, even settle it by religious precept. A great altar she constructed, or was going to construct, somewhere on Pentelicus, from which she was to consult Deity and receive responses. The altar may be a myth, but here before our eyes is the house with her name upon it, built right at the mouth of the defile which leads up to the monastery. It is just in the spot to catch every monk and ecclesiastic who might enter this passage, seeking the way to the religious retreat. I imagine that the old spider put her web at this place in order to net the whole church, or the younger monastic portion thereof, as they passed by toward an ascetic life. A strong character she was at any rate, strong enough to have her own God.

Such are the three houses with their associations which Pentelicus has, somehow or other, woven into our narrative: the Parthenon, the Monastery, and the Belvidere of the Duchess — the ancient, the medieval and the modern; each of them is characteristic of its inmates, each designates epochs and religions.

I turned around and again looked up toward the summit of the mountain; it still has that close-wrapped turban on its head. All day have I watched the bank of clouds, resting there defiantly on the top and sides; it is thick, growing thicker; its boundary now is so definite, that it seems to be a part of the mountain — a white marble precipice rising aloft to the heavens. On the other side lies Marathon, which one will be eager to get a glimpse of, though it be only in the dim distance. On that spot our Western world opened; the sight of it, along with what it signifies, must still possess some great virtue, one may well imagine. But I may never be able to reach there on account of the brigands; so a view of it must be sought, even under difficulties.

I go up into those new mountains — those foggy crags piled on Pentelicus reaching to the skies; the almost solid boundary I pass, and enter the lofty realm of cloudland. Nothing can be seen, every outline is lost, I lose myself. But, as you may know, I have been lost before in the clouds; also I have been often supposed to be lost by the people below, who were unable to see me, while I was really enjoying the clearest of sunlight which lay tranquilly over the summits. In the present case, however, as in all similar cases of fog, the way out is not difficult, one has only to follow straight down the slope of the mountain, when he will come into clear day on the low plains. Not as fair nor as far-reaching is this light as that above; but on foggy days what else can one do?

Accordingly I came down, and crossed again into sunshine. Scarce had I passed the cloud-wall, when I heard not far from me a cracking of bushes followed by the bark of dogs. Very soon a man with a gun came to view creeping through the brushwood; his outward appearance was chiefly made up of a wild unshaven face, shaggy capote, and dirty fustanella. What did I think of at that moment? Brigands, you will easily guess. He had a flintlock and two large dogs, I had no weapon. There was no use of trying to avoid him, so without hesitation I advanced straight towards him; to my surprise he did not raise his gun. His dogs fiercely rushed at me, but he even went so far as to pick up a stone and drive them off. Leaning on his old flintlock he calmly awaited my approach, and then at a distance of about five paces saluted me in the most friendly manner. I returned the salute, and asked him quickly where was the road to Kephissia. He pointed it out to me, nay, he went a mile out of his way to put me into the best path. In the meantime, we chatted, asked and answered the questions which were natural under the circumstances, and soon were on terms of intimate friendship.

Of course the man might have robbed or murdered me with impunity, had he been so disposed. Yet he showed only kindness, only the most generous endeavor to befriend me. At separation he warmly shook my hand with the best wishes, and raised to my lips his flagon of recinato. My thought of the man was then changed; I believed that under his shaggy capote made of coarse goatshair, there beat not only an honest but a warm heart. He was a shepherd, he told me, and his flock was feeding at that time on the other side of the mountain. It is true that he slept out of doors the whole year round, that like these shepherds generally he could not live in a house without getting sick; it is also true that he ought to have put that fustanella of his to soak in a brook some weeks, if not months ago; — still he was a man, a true man, not a brigand, not even a rude boor. This incident was an important turning-point in my journey; with it much of my anxiety passed away; and I could not help laughing a little to myself at a certain person, who, I am sure, if he had seen this shepherd half a mile distant up the mountain among the brush, would have run off to Athens and said that he had seen a brigand out on Pentelicus. In some such way that scare has been kept up.

So, in musing mood, accompanied by the declining sun, I walk over the fields to the road and soon enter the village of Kephissia. It was famous in antiquity for its pleasant rills and agreeable air, and it is still a great resort during the summer; the diplomatic body generally adjourn hither from the intolerable heat of Athens. It is dusk, I pass through the main street, which always leads to that shining beacon of the Greek village, the wineshop. The hunger and thirst of the weary traveler can here be stilled. This was my first Greek lunch in the country, so it may be of interest to tell you what it was composed of. Recinato, of the best quality and in the greatest abundance at the smallest prices; dark bread, coarse, of unbolted flour, but well-baked and good; such were the two staples, bread and wine. For something by way of luxury I called for goat's cheese. This cheese is brought in little granulous balls which easily crumble and then it looks like our dry hand-cheese. It is made by the shepherds on the mountains in a not very tidy way; one ingredient is often found scattered through it, the reason for which I never learned — namely, the goat's hairs. I always picked them out of mine, thinking that they had no business there, but it must be confessed that they are pretty generally included in this cheese and seem to share in the very idea of it.

Butter, in the occidental sense of the word, is not to be found in Greece; yet I am always afraid that you will think of the pun, and will try to confute me by pointing triumphantly to oleomargarine. But this last article I do not think has yet come into Greece, even though it may sometimes have come out of it. Butter-eating Thracians certain barbarians were anciently called with contempt, in contrast to the oil-consuming Greeks, civilized men. To be sure there are a few cows here; Bocotia and Euboea have fine cattle. But the small picking from the mountains will not produce butter; only goats and sheep yield milk from such slender nourishment. For sheep are milked in Greece, and their milk is made into various products of the dairy. Nothing will better illustrate the extreme economy of this country than the fact that sheep are milked. The American farmer has never heard of such a thing, and sheep's cheese and butter, brought into an American market might possibly be sold as rare curiosities.

There is quite a detachment of soldiers stationed in the town, for the purpose of guarding the road to Marathon, lest timid excursionists get a fright. As it is a holiday, the most of the soldiers are gathered into the wineshop, and are quite merry. They are singing Romaic songs with that jolly whine peculiar to Greek music. All the talk is about the treaty of Berlin, the new boundary of Greece, the prospect of war with the Ottoman. The keeper of the wineshop is flourishing a huge knife, showing the manner in which he is going to sever the Turkish head from the Turkish body, should he only get a chance. Patriotic exhilaration does indeed prevail, but there is no drunkenness, according to the American conception of the word and the deed. The Greek certainly deserves his reputation of being the most temperate of men; for he is not intemperate even in his temperance.

A soldier observing me sits down on the bench at my side and talks with me; he speaks Italian well, and, as it seems, to me, likes to show off his beautiful acquirement to his astonished comrades. He is a good patriot, not a grumbler; he is willingly serving out the time of his conscription, though with privation and pecuniary loss as he affirms, and as one may well believe. But his dear Hellas can have his time and his life, if necessary; he is full of her glories, though he deeply laments her weakness and her small territory. Still he thinks that she has performed wonders of progress during the short period of her independence, and he believes that she is destined to be the bearer of light and liberty to the East. She is to rule the Orient once more, her goal is Constantinople.

Thus thinks the common soldier, representing, in my opinion, the average intelligence and character of the Greek. For in his character there is still a high aspiration, an ideal striving after improvement, although the reality may be discouraging. I hail him as a comrade, and tell him that I too was a soldier and give him a short bit out of my campaigning. He ends by inviting me to bunk with him that night in his quarters — an invitation which I gladly accept. I wanted to see how the Greek soldier fared; I felt perfectly able to endure whatever quarters he had to bestow, even to sleeping on the feathery side of a board, though I confess that I have been a little enervated in recent years by the luxury of a bed.

The bugle blew, my soldier had to go to roll-call; he said he would return in fifteen or twenty minutes, and conduct me to my place of repose for the night. But he did not come back so soon; I was sleepy and tired, and could not wait; accordingly I went off to a large hotel which has been built here for the purpose of accommodating the high guests of the summer; but at the present season it has only an excursionist now and then from the city. I need not say any thing about this hotel except that when you enter it, you step out of Greece into Western Europe. You will get there a fair bed and a fair meal in quite the same fashion as in other parts of the world. It is arranged on the principle of causing the traveler to live quite in the same manner that he lives at home; so that in this way he may travel over the whole world without experiencing any thing of it, substantially without going out of his own house. My regret is that I did not get to bunk with that soldier, and to take a little glance at the inside of things in his quarters, all of which would help to fill up the picture of Greek life. In return for which I can now only tell you that I obtained a bed and a beefsteak -- both of them doubtless old acquaintances of yours that need not be further described.

But as soon as I was comfortably seated in my chair before the fire, who, do you think, came in from a belated journey? None other than my friend Achille, the gay Frenchman, a native of Paris, with whom I had become acquainted at Athens. A merry mocking fellow, of exhaustless pleasantry; he had no faith in any God except Voltaire, the mocker of all Gods; for Achille, the scoffer at authority, delighted nevertheless to call himself a Voltairian. One other authority indeed he recognized as supreme; his Parisian cook. I had before noticed that Achille always snarled at his dinner, and then fell to and ate it with a relish. It seems that he had taken to-day a short excursion from Athens to the country, and that, missing the road, he had been compelled to dine with a peasant on black bread, salted olives, an oil fry, with re-

cinato. Good luck! we shall now have a merry evening,
I exclaimed on seeing him; but Achille at once began to
swear violently, employing his customary French oath:
By the twenty-five names of God! What is the matter,
heroic Achille? He told his story; all Greece, what she
is now and what she was in the past, her literature, art,
history were on the spot judged and condemned in the
light of that dinner. He even went back to old Homer
and damned him and his Helen, whereat I was touched,
and attempted to reply about as follows, according to my
recollection:

"My dear friend, why do you lay so much stress upon
what goes into your stomach, when you exhibit such contemptible brain work as the final outcome of digestion?
Socrates had quite the same kind of food as you have had,
probably not so good with Xanthippe as cook — yet what
a remarkable difference between him and you! Indeed
Plato himself fared no better in all likelihood, yet the
sweetest philosophy of the world he extracted therefrom,
while you extract the sourest. But think of Homer
whom you calumniate — he could have had only bruised
barley-meal, bruised between two stones in a sort of mill,
and a little occasional meat at some festival of the
Gods, with wine, likely enough just this recinato; yet out
of his bruised barley-meal, and meat roasted before the
fire on a spit, together with the wine he has constructed
the most beautiful of all poetical worlds — a world which
stands a good chance of being the most enduring as well
as the most beautiful. I ask, has any man like him come
out of Parisian cookery? Take the old Greeks — what a
glorious result they produced from their oil, olives and
barley! Man is what he eats is your favorite saying;
then give me the food of those old Greeks — and it will not
hurt you to take not one but many dinners of it. Therefore be not so particular about what you put into your
mill unless you can improve the flour. I tell you whom
you most resemble — that crazy man who once thought
Jupiter had descended from Olympian heights and
was seated on a throne in his stomach. Only too many
such lunatics are running loose in these days — people

who have their God in their bellies. Achille, let us now go to bed, in the morning you may turn back to the city for your dinner, but I am going to continue the journey and the pursuit; to-morrow I shall ascend some Greek mountain and look from its clear heights, or possibly march with the old Hoplites to Marathon."

But Achille long continued his satirical banter; particularly my enthusiam for Helen was the theme of his infinite mockery. Under his hand her story was transformed into a modern French novel of illicit love; her character grew tenfold more dubious than I had ever dreamed of, as he poured into it with subtle piquancy all the details of the latest Parisian scandal. Thus with no small skill and with very manifest relish he told her tale anew, bristling now with keen points of ambiguous ribaldry. Nor did he spare me; he more than intimated that I had come to Greece to play the part of Paris, and was now going up the country to run away with the wife of some peasant Menelaus. Overwhelmed with his jibes, I could only answer: O Achille, thy name is deserved, thou art indeed the French Achilles.

I set out early the next morning, long before Achille my tormentor was awake; about sunrise I was in full walk for some further destination, having resolved to go on; the anxiety from brigands, too, had quite subsided. I know of nothing more exhilarating than a morning walk at this season of the year in Greece. There is some secret intoxication in the air; every mental and physical energy sports of itself in frolicsome mood, yet in full tension. The body seeks for its wings, every step is an attempt to fly, man has become a festival of delightful sensation. That morning still lives in memory, with its exuberance of happy music within, its symposium of joyous moods. Yet it all was about nothing in particular; I can only recollect how easily my feet were raised in the air, and how hard it was to bring them down to the earth again.

Pentelicus, not far from whose base the road winds along, is still capped with a cloud which rests on it with adamantine stubbornness. There is no use of trying to go to the summit; you can see nothing and will lose yourself in addition. But on the other side of this valley, distant but a few miles lies Mount Parnes; not a cloud dares touch its tops; the snow glistens from its peaks with an unusual keen brilliancy which cuts through to the eye, as it glances that way. Now solve for me this riddle: Why is Pentelicus always covered with a cloud while Parnes stands forth free and shines with unsullied splendor? Locality, height, configuration cannot account for the difference; there is some secret which nature whispers to set you at work in a deeper vein. Then answer this other question of a spiritual kind: Why are some men's brains wrapped in an eternal fog, while at a much greater elevation other men's thoughts rest in everlasting sunshine? It is so because it is; at any rate I am done with foggy Pentelicus, for I now intend to cross over to Parnes where it is clear on the highest height.

Thither I shall try to take you along with me, if you think the company good, shall let you have a fresh breath of the mountain air, furnish you the exhilaration of climbing the sides of the steep, but above all give you a look from the top over this Attic land; for a look from the top of a mountain in Greece is the best way of seeing the country as a whole and of feeling its highest characteristic influence. Thus we can to a certain extent look down into this honeycomb of mountainous walls and green valleys which constitutes the physical individuality of Grecian territory; thus too we behold through the transparent atmosphere, the gently swaying curves and outlines which Nature, the first Greek Artist, has toned down into tender lines of beauty.

But here I pass by the bridge of Pekirmes, small and insignificant, yet its name has been printed in every language of Europe. Near it was committed that famous act of brigandage which has done more than any thing else to give to the Greeks of to-day a bad name throughout the civilized world. As it is the chief text from which all detractors of the Greeks preach, as it has deterred and still deters the majority of tourists from leaving Athens or its immediate vicinity, as it was the main

FROM PENTELICUS TO PARNES.

cause of my hesitation in regard to this trip, I shall deem it worth while to give a little account of it here, and to introduce it hereafter on suitable occasion. For we shall find the affair still lives among the peasantry, in the most vivid recollection, and with many a mythical addition which recalls the ancient heroic legend; everywhere along our path we shall see it bubbling up spontaneously and demanding some notice from the observant traveler.

Near the spot where we have arrived, on the 11th day of April, 1870, a party of English excursionists composed of Lord Muncaster and wife, Mr. Herbert and Mr. Vyner, Mr. Lloyd with wife and little girl, Count De Boyl of the Italian embassy, were passing in two carriages, on their return from a visit to Marathon. Two cavalrymen rode before them, two behind them, for the purpose of escort. Suddenly there was heard a discharge of fire-arms, the two troopers in front fell from their horses dangerously wounded. The carriages were then halted, and the company found itself surrounded by twenty-one armed men who at once hurried their captives up the mountain into the brush with many demonstrations of joy at the successful capture. After a rapid walk of two hours the brigands stopped on the top of the mountain; they sent back to Athens the two ladies and little girl as being obstacles to the sudden and speedy marches in prospect.

The ladies were bearers of notes from the prisoners, announcing the ransom demanded by the brigands — $160,000; which sum was afterwards reduced to $125,000 with new conditions of a harder kind than even gold. Also a threat was sent to the Greek government that in case of pursuit the lives of the prisoners would be at once taken. Not without a touch of gallantry coupled with audacious avarice were these wild men of the mountains. When the ladies set out for Athens, the chieftain asked for some precious reminder of the event; he preferred a gold chain which the lady could buy and send from the city. She on her part with a coquettish dash worthy of the ballroom, asked of the chieftain a souvenir of their agreeable intercourse. Being a pious man, he gave her a religious token: an ornament of silver wrought with the head of the

Virgin. The chain was in due time transmitted to the brigand, who sent it back by the same messenger, stating it was not heavy enough.

On the third day after the capture, Lord Muncaster himself appeared at Athens, having been released on parole to arrange for ransom or free pardon of the offenders; such was the alternative which he brought. There was little question which of the two things ought to be done; the money, $125,000 in gold, was soon packed in boxes, ready for transport to the mountains in proper business fashion. Behold, however, a new turn given to the proceedings by the arrival of another message from the chieftain who now insists upon ransom and pardon; amnesty is his new word, that is, forgetfulness — forgetfullness of this and all his past crimes and those of his band, during a life of outlawry. Clearly brigandage has become a power, a Great Power, and is claiming recognition among the governments of the world. The chieftain also demanded the release of several members of his gang who had been previously captured and who were then in prison at Athens.

So a new European Power has suddenly sprung up on the declivity of Pentelicus, and is determined to treat with the other Great Powers on terms of equality. Beside the Greek government, the English and Italian embassies send messages, and all the other embassies at Athens take a hand in the game, sending representatives to the court of Takos Arvanitika, King of Pentelicus. The diplomats have got the matter in their toils; what hand will now be able to disentangle the complication? Like all diplomacy, the affair becomes a highly intricate kitten-dance; the employment of the diplomatic kittens being chiefly to run after their own tails — perchance to catch the same in their mouths, and then let go again. During this play of the kittens, otherwise harmless and even amusing at times, who can hope for any serious rat-catching, now imperatively needed? You may perhaps ask: Who would expect such work from kittens anyhow? The point seems well taken.

Meanwhile the prisoners are roughing it out on the

mountain — sleeping on bushes, eating black bread and goat's cheese, with occasional roast lamb or roast goat, and drinking that horrible recinato which tastes like a mouthful of sealing-wax. Well-fed Johnny Bull has certainly a good reason for making wry faces at such a meal. Think of him out there as he squats down to his repast in the open air, with that fat face of his, through which the red fibers run as through a thick beefsteak. We would like to help him though we laugh at him a little; for everybody says that there is no danger, and the first London newspaper has called the whole affair a comedy, at which the world is supposed to have the right of being merry.

One of the party, let us give thanks, is safe; Lord Muncaster did not return to the chieftain, though he had promised to do so. There is no man of a generous soul who will not be glad, if the noble Lord shall be able to find some moral peg stout enough to hold that violation of his parole. I have heard of two such pegs: first, that the brigands changed their terms after he had been sent and had obtained the money, thus fulfilling his part of the agreement and being thereby released from his word. Another peg not so strong apparently: that the brigands had changed their locality in his absence while he had promised to return only to a given spot. Query: ought he to have returned anyhow? You, my hearers — each one of you — what would you have done? Would you have gone back, like Regulus to Carthage, or would you have cried: Alas, I am no hero, I am not anxious for posthumous fame among unknown future generations!

Here we shall have to leave the prisoners exposed to the raw weather of Pentelicus, complaining of the hard fare and of the cold rains. One of the brigands has to sleep close to young weakly Mr. Vyner to keep him warm, out of compassion, we hope, and not for fear of losing his ransom through his death. Not a desirable bedfellow, one thinks, is that dirty fustanella. The affair must struggle on in the diplomatic web till some outside power brush the obstacle away. Meanwhile we shall trudge forward, at our customary slow gait, yet often stopping to look over the pleasant landscape, wholly dismissing the problem concerning what we should do if such a band of wild men should suddenly pounce down upon us from the mountain. We shall repeatedly cross the track of these brigands with their captives; then we shall tell something more about them, as one thread of our little novel here interwoven, being careful not to tell all at once, for that would destroy curiosity.

We have already crossed over the intervening valley watered by the Athenian Kephissus, and have begun the ascent of Parnes. Let us take a long step uphill, and set our feet down at Tatoe, ancient Dekeleia, which was fortified by the Lacedemonians during the Peloponnesian war. From this mountain nest the enemy darted down and laid waste the Attic territory, at the same time controlling important roads leading to Athens. In recent years the King of Greece has built a summer residence here, with beautiful grounds and well-made roads. The royal family is at present in the city, but the grounds are open to the visitor. To the rear of the dwellings are the barracks of the soldiers who are here to guard the persons of their majesties. I am sorry that I shall not have an opportunity of introducing you to King George and Queen Olga with their interesting group of children. Still I cannot help whispering to you my doubt about having such an opportunity, even if they were here. Notice these broad, thick-soled shoes, this knapsack and knotted staff, this long stride of the pedestrian; clearly there is not dignity enough to appear before royalty. Notice, too, this unceremonious narrative, defying all conventionality; quick, let us get out of these royal grounds, so regular, so rectilinear; let us mount, through nature's brushwood and boulders, to the rugged top of old Parnes.

But here quite a large company passes — twenty persons or more — on an excursion from Athens. They are English chiefly, and are carefully guarded by a platoon of soldiers. Let them pass rapidly, for their rear is brought up by a Scotch lassie, straggling at her own sweet will, and quite independent of the rest of the company; then I follow, at some distance at first, but gradually approaching, with the intent of finding a pretext for getting acquainted. All strangers thrown together in a foreign land have a natural right to acquaintanceship without an introduction, subject of course, to the refusal of either party. This is my unwritten law, at least, and I am trying to obey it now.

Why should I recount to you all the details — the first glance, the first little act of attention, the first little word — the English word spoken in a strange land to a native ear sympathetically attuned to its sweet sound? But do not expect too much, my hearers; nor should you love gossip. The Scotch lassie is a hard-headed, imperturbable person, who is going to fight her own battle, and just now she is going to climb this mountain in her own fashion without any assistance from anybody. Plump, with red-faced energy, she grapples the shaggy sides of the old monster determined to ride him and not be thrown. Not much poetry there is in her, but there is plenty of raillery; over the mountain rings her merry laugh which reveals rows of teeth overlapping each other like Scotch granite. Under her very laugh you can see granitic virtues of many kinds.

As we gradually ascend, the country unrolls before us. All the mountain ranges can now be distinguished; even the high peaks of Euboea we behold running along and finally gathering into one highest summit, like the hunchback of a dromedary. The Scotch lassie tugs up through the bushes, puffing, growing redder; she is sometimes caught and held fast in the arms of a rude bramble as if an old satyr, hidden there, had reached out from the twigs and sought to embrace her, the rascal! She refuses all assistance, she can help herself, and takes pride in showing it, as she clambers up the rough sides of a rock, getting down on all fours. Yet she can not be said to be unfriendly; does she not point out to me the scenery which changes every moment with the change of the clouds and sunshine — now light, now dark, in hurrying patches over the landscape? She does indeed want somebody to enjoy along with her: so much of human frailty she still dimly reveals.

Under a strong wind a dense cloud drives against the

side of the mountain where we are standing; we see it approaching and covering us with thick folds; it sheds upon us a little of its moisture, then like a huge ball it is rolled topsy-turvy up the slope, over the summit, and disappears on the other side, leaving the summit as bright as ever. Parnes manifestly will suffer no obscuration, but Pentelicus yonder still sullenly wraps its head in fog.

Finally we arrive at the top where are the foundations of an ancient temple. What a beautiful situation for a religious edifice, to be seen from afar, shining up here in white Pentelic marble! Every old Greek into whose eye it fell from this high spot, as it were from the Heavens, would experience a new joy at its quiet beauty, as he looked up at it from yonder valley. From the summits of the highest mountains these temples must have spoken to the man below of aspiration, of the labor of attaining the end, of the beautiful harmony when that end is attained. Let the aim be high — behold it can be realized, if he but climb. Hither he laboriously toiled up to worship — the ascent being a part of his devotion, the toil being a part of his prayer. Else why is this temple placed up here?

The Scotch lassie is not satisfied to go back with me into the old structure, build it anew, and worship with me there — she is a rigid Scotch Presbyterian. Instead of enjoying these ancient serene harmonies, she wishes to struggle up higher, and points to the top of a very steep precipitous cliff which even overlooks the site of the temple. That rock seems to be the last and strongest convulsion of Parnes in the ancient of days — there it quivers upward in an agony frozen to stone, jagged, distorted, unfriendly. Thither accordingly we go; upon the point of a rocky splinter she sits down and seems for the moment to be happy. I straighten myself up beside her.

Now, my hearers, imagine me perched up there on the very highest peak of the last throe of Parnes; on tiptoe I stand, looking down into the plain of Kephissus — what do you think I behold? Far to the right I can see Athens; the Parthenon rises to view there; even from this distance its whole plan and character can be grasped and felt.

There it lies in the sun, small but joyous as ever; though no larger than your hand it produces the same happy, harmonious impression as if you stood on the Acropolis itself. I believe this to be a supreme characteristic of that edifice: its proportions can not be obliterated by distance. Nor forget, ere it passes out of sight, another distinction which it possesses above all structures: it is not a mathematical measurement, but it has the spontaneity of a lyric, it is an impulse in stone.

But there is something else which I see, and see very distinctly, though the Scotch lassie laughs at me when I try to point it out to her. Yonder just across the valley a long line of men is marching round the base of Pentelicus; the line extends down the road toward Kephissia; those men have evidently come from Athens within the last few hours. The shining helm and buckler flash across the vale; the spears in serried ranks with sharp brilliant points glitter above their heads; fair youths on plunging war-steeds bring up the rear. Rapid is their tread; those men are manifestly in a great hurry, yet they set their feet down on the earth with a firmness that makes old Parnes quake to the very top. But behold another miracle: the clouds lift from the sides of Pentelicus and slowly vanish into the clear sky above; there is revealed beyond it the plain of Marathon. Innumerable beings are swarming there like ants; thousands of white sails are making pale the sparkling face of beautiful blue Euripus. Still the Scotch lassie laughs, laughs contemptuously, and calls me a dreamer.

Nevertheless, the line of men continues marching with steady tread, I affirm, for they have a purpose, indeed rather the greatest purpose in the world's history. Several persons who might be named, can be distinguished from this distance; still their names are often rehearsed as a sort of sacred symbols of the race. But incontestably the first man of them all, — the embodiment of his nation, the bearer of Europe's hopes — is marching yonder at the head of that column. See, now they have turned around Pentelicus, and are wheeling toward the Euboic Straits. Who are they, do you ask? They are Miltiades and his 10,000 Hoplites, hastening to the plain of Marathon. Not long ago the news arrived at Athens that the Persian had landed there; the trumpet sounds, the soldiers rush to arms, the command is given: Fall in and close ranks — march! In six hours from Athens, with a sharp gait, we shall meet the foe.

What shall I do, what would you do, standing tiptoe on the top of Parnes and seeing that body of men pass up the valley not far away? I at once bid good-bye to the Scotch lassie, leaping down from my position, and hastening along the bushy slope; I do not believe that Helen herself could have kept me there any longer. I am going to follow those soldiers round the spur of the mountain whither they have gone, with as little delay as possible; of all soldiers that have marched in our world, they are most worthy of being followed. Next then is the campaign to Marathon, and I see that you all — every one of you, if my vanity does not blind me — have taken your places in the ranks and are eager to march. Forward, then, to Marathon.

III. FROM PARNES TO MARATHON.

When you last saw me, I had hurriedly started down Parnes to Marathon, with the design of taking you along, if I could. It was a sudden spurt of enthusiastic haste, not wholly consonant with the golden leisure of this Greek trip; nor did the time allow, for the Sun had already turned his face away from his Oriental home, and was then casting his full effulgence somewhere on the Atlantic seas. Accordingly we may resume our customary gait and saunter along the road till night-fall, when we shall seek some shelter provided by the Gods.

Unceremoniously I took leave of the Scotch lassie — so I think as I glance back with a little longing up the mountain. But such friendships made during the hours of travel are usually dissolved as quickly as they are formed; they are the most evanescent feature of the landscape. Still, travelers on the whole will do well to obey that unwritten law which has before been announced: to consider themselves acquainted without the formality of an introduction. Thus several hours rapidly fly with pleasant talk, and the two faces having come from the uttermost corners of the earth to peer into each other, and even to exchange sympathetic glances, again flit into infinite space — sometimes not without a mutual sigh. So the Scotch lassie's life-road with its manifold turnings and windings crossed my rather crooked track of existence out here on Parnes; for four hours or so our two paths ran together with gentle intertwinings, then separated to all eternity, probably. But who can tell? Perhaps like that Greek nymph Arethusa, nymph of the fountain, she may disappear in Greece, but may invisibly pass underground across continents, nay, across oceans, and suddenly come to the surface again in far-distant, unexpected places? At any rate let the pleasing phantom now vanish — with one last glance at the red cheeks and wreathed smiles, and I cannot help adding, with a renewed look at those layers of Scotch granite slightly overlapping each other, well-polished but somewhat awry, always seen but more strongly felt beneath her very laugh. She is not unlovely, but made of adamant that is a little crooked. She, with that round visage and those granitic virtues is not Helen — though she may justly be called, I have no doubt, a better woman.

And here, since we have contemplatively resumed our ordinary slow gait, a reflection has intertwined itself in the strand of our experiences. This conflict between the Moral and the Beautiful — where does it begin and where does it end? One fact seems to be well certified: Art and Morality have a tendency to become mortal enemies; they have been in a death-grapple since the time of ancient Homer at least, with much fluctuation of victory from one side to the other. Can they be reconciled? That is one of the most serious questions of the human soul. There is doubtless a limit within which they may exist in harmony, indeed may be helpful to each other. But every person is inclined to place this limit at his own discretion, and often to place it quite out of being. Certainly the extremists on both sides are always in unappeasable conflict. Rigid Puritanism would destroy Art root and branch; it has no solution for the Senses of man except the most violent repression. Such a view may prevail for a time, may even come to govern nations; but then follows the fierce revolt of the Senses with tenfold retaliation for the wrong done them. In such a debauch both Art and Morality perish by the same licentious excess.

But Art, on the other hand, is inclined to cultivate the sensuous nature of man and neglect the moral. Consider those old Greeks, the supreme artistic people of the world, in their chief fable. Did they not cross the sea and fight ten years in order to bring back Helen, not because she was a good woman — good women they had at home in abundance and had left behind — but because she was the most beautiful woman. It is only a legend, let it be granted; therefore it is truer than history, and it reflects more purely and adequately than history the spirit of that people who created it. Then, too, what a large number of good women were sacrificed for the sake of Helen, represented in Iphigenia the innocent virgin, Andromache the devoted wife! Thus it has been with men ever since, more or less; they make long pilgrimages across the world in search of Helen, when there are plenty of good women, indeed better women than Helen at home. What is the meaning of it all, has been a great query with the traveler, and it is also a question of considerable importance to those who have been left behind.

Man would not be man, could not exist as a living being, had he not these passions and senses; they can not be rooted out, ought not to be rooted out, which deracination the ascetic view of morality would have us attempt. What then shall we do with them? They may become the sources of the purest pleasures or the scourge of the direst vices: get rid of them we can not. Here Art steps in where the rigid moralist has failed; it says: Preserve the passions and senses, but elevate them; allow them not to batten on themselves, but give them the spiritual world to feed upon; thus they will be satisfied and saved, for they have attained the Beautiful, and in that realm become sharers in what is truly divine. Helen simply as the runaway wife is not beautiful, nor did the old Greek think that she was, hence his tremendous effort to rescue her from her ugly condition. But Helen, repentant, self-accusing, longing for restoration, as she appears in the Iliad; still more, Helen restored, living in happy unity with her family in the Spartan home of Menelaus once again, as she appears in the Odyssey — this Helen, showing the long struggle overcome, is beautiful, though morality still shakes the head, and will not admit her to good society. Always jealous of her beauty, it seeks to discredit her present life by her past.

Indeed if we scan the legend a little more closely we shall see that it contains the conflict which we speak of and its solution. What caused Helen to err, or what, at least, was the occasion? It was Beauty in its sensuous manifestation; the blooming young wife of the Spartan King, the fairest woman of Greece, breaks the ethical injunction, abandons her husband, and flees with the handsome Asiatic. It is thus the eternal theme: the sensuous element of Beauty in conflict with morality. But what did the old Greek do in presence of such a problem? Did he banish her entirely to the world of sensuality, and thus damn her forever? Did he even let her quietly go and remain in her alienation? No, that he could not do with his consciousness; restoration is his watchword. Helen the Beautiful must be able to live in the family, though it cost ten or twenty years' war, though we have to sacrifice Iphigenia and many other good women, though we immolate our greatest national hero, the youthful Achilles, and many other mighty and worthy men in the enterprise. This must be accomplished — this return of the beautiful woman to the family, this harmony of the sensuous and ethical nature of man; otherwise the Greek people can not be, have no business to be. It was their problem in this world, and manfully they fought it out, producing the typical figures for all time — those heroic characters after which mankind instinctively models itself or finds itself already modeled.

And then what a harmonious world resulted! The living man became the first work of art which afterwards could be embodied in everlasting marble. There is the happy balance between the real and ideal, between the Senses and Morals of men, between Art and Virtue. Homer is indeed not the most rigidly moral of books; it would not be worth much if it were; but of all artistic books it is doubtless the most moral. Ulysses, for example, always trying to harmonize his outer and inner life, seeking to make a complete man of himself through the most violent contradictions, is still the best development of character in this realm. How the two sides gradually fell asunder in Greece itself, how morality became ascetic and art became licentious, how the philosophers assailed poetry — even Plato banished Homer from his imaginary republic — how the Ideal was, on the one hand, utterly destroyed in this world by the hard-headed, practical Roman, and, on the other hand, was relegated into the Beyond by the prayerful, spiritual Christian — all these matters belong to History, — and even our slow and pensive gait will not allow us to pick them up and string them on our variegated thread.

Yet do not think that this change from the ancient world to the modern is, on the whole, to be regretted; it is indeed an advance. Do not imagine that I wish to restore the old Greek life; vain would it be for any mortal with combative spirit to turn his face against the World's History. Let no man with puny hand undertake to grasp the reins and wheel about the mighty steeds of the sun-chariot, now rushing at the top of their speed toward the West, in their swift career around the world. They have swept over the ocean; almost within the memory of living men they have sped from the Atlantic to the Pacific; still with increased rapidity and fiery vigor they are whirling onward their light-dropping chariot. No longer can those steeds be turned out for quiet pasture on the sunny hills of pretty little Hellas. Yet for us that is still the world of beauty and of sweet idyllic rest; we are still in need of its soothing harmonies, and we have to go back to its perennial fountains for refreshment and repose.

Therefore let no Scotch lassie appear any longer in Greece with her granitic beauty and more granitic Scotch Presbyterianism. Personally she commands our highest respect, but in the country of Helen we would ask: "What art thou doing here, thou specter from the land of mist and snow, here in the sunlit fields of Apollo? In the regions of adamant and ice is thy home; there too is thy meed."

I have already intimated that it is too late to go to Marathon this evening, however much enthusiasm may goad the drooping limbs; accordingly I stay at Tatoe over night. Early the next morning I set out across the valley, following those ancient soldiers whom I had seen yesterday, and whom I hope you beheld. It is true that there is now and was in antiquity another road from Athens to Marathon, over which some of the soldiers may have passed to the field of battle, but the bulk of the army went up this road; for did we not see them? 'Tis all imagination, some of you may cry out: be it so. But I maintain that the great eternal fact of this spot and of this whole valley is the march of the Marathonian band. Look up to the hill-tops and ask: has there ever been any thing else here but that one event, which posesses any vitality? Look up once more and question the landscape: is there any thing now here but the green fields, the low brush, the stream Kephissus — and that marching line of old Athenian soldiers? I would never have been on Parnes, you would never go thither, no tourist would ever be passing contemplatively up the valley, were it not for the presence of those old Hoplites. I tell you, the most distinct, the most enduring, the most real thing in all these parts at this moment is the march of that Marathonian band; in fact there is nothing else here.

I am free to say that, when I am on the road again, I do nothing but think of them, the heavy-armed, with steady silent tread winding around the spur of the mountain before me; with the low dull thud of many feet they tramp along the causeway, and I with knapsack on my shoulder, fall into their measured gait and march along, keeping their regular steady step, bound for Marathon.

In reflective mood, I should say the most of them were, as the soldier usually is when going into the uncertain combat. But what one of them had the remotest thought of that which he with his companions was doing — of the place they were filling just at that moment in the history and destiny of our planet? Thus are we all, could we but see; each individual is some unconscious earth-sustaining Atlas. For man, every man, is the instrument of an almighty power which brings him here and makes him a link in the chain which supports the All. Alas, poor mortal, with the full burden of his weakness upon him, he must aid in holding, or rather as a link he must actually hold up the whole Universe.

But to drop a little down the stream of Time: there is another vivid image darting through the air and vanishing amid the brushwood just in the locality to which I have now come; another man passed up the road in recent years whom I would not care to meet at present in this solitude. It was Takos Arvanitaka, the brigand chief with his band, also to be called Marathonian, whom not long ago we saw installed as King of Pentelicus. Somewhere here he passed across the valley to and from Tatoe, guarding savagely his English captives, as we find in a small diary kept by one of them; he also went to Stamata, the next village, where we shall arrive in due season if some successor of his does not capture us too. Those brigands, dragging their unhappy prisoners through the bushes, dodging the Greek soldiery in pursuit, tiger-fierce with continuous alarm and in one case preparing to shoot their prisoners in cold blood, present quite a contrast to that ancient line of heroic shapes rounding in solid tread the mountain. The wretched picture let us not try to fill out, it is too melancholy, it will obscure the brightness of our Greek mood, which we must preserve in the joyous sunlight of Hellas, through which we move as through a thick rain-fall of golden dreams dropping from the skies.

We may, however, at this point introduce a short account of these brigands. They, except two, were subjects of Turkey and did not live in Greece at all, but in Thessaly. They had crossed the Greek frontier in January preceding the capture, had previously had at least two brushes with the soldiers of the Greek government, in which the band had lost seven men. They were tracked from place to place but finally gained their mountain fastnesses. Though they belonged to the Greek church, and spoke Greek, yet their nationality was not Greek, but Wallachian.

Diplomacy during all this while continues spinning, spinning, with little purpose except to delay; in the meantime the brigands encouraged by their friends and elated by success have risen in their demands until they ask for that to which no government can accede without absolute self-annihilation. They now insist upon a full pardon for all their crimes, to be granted before condemnation and indeed without trial. Good advice is cheap after the event, but there was only one logical course for a government to pursue: to hunt down the offenders and bring them to justice, for which purpose government exists among men. If it do not that, it has no right to be at all. Still they negotiated; the Greek ministry permitted too much outside control, particularly from the English embassy as the party most deeply concerned. By vigorous pursuit the prisoners might perhaps have been killed at once by the brigands, perhaps not; at any rate murders of foreigners have occurred in London without the fault of the English government or of the English people. Let us not then abuse the Greeks for a crime which was not done even by native villians, but by a band of foreign miscreants whom the authorities had tried to drive away from Greek soil.

But the unfortunate fact still remains that, to the eye of the traveler, as he goes up this valley on the way to Marathon, in the present year of grace, the form of Takos appears with startling vividness alongside of Miltiades. Nor can it be denied that they may be taken, to a certain extent, as the representatives of their respective epochs. The one is clearly the product of Turkish disorder and oppression — bravery driven out of society and turned brigand; the other is the offspring of free Athenian institutions, and is now marching out to their defense, at the head of heroic companions, whose adamantine tread around these hills thunders still through the ages down to this very hour.

Another most remarkable fact which you cannot help thinking of on this spot, is, that each of these men could, in all probability, have understood the other, had the two spoken together here. Indeed of all facts connected with human speech, by far the most notable one is this immortality of the Greek language. Not as a mummied tongue, preserved only in books does it exist, but it still pours out of the hearts of the people as a vital fountain of utterance. At the same time it preserves more than any dead tongue; it contains more of the treasures of written speech than any other language; in it are to be found the great works of heathen culture and the Christian New Testament.

As one turns around the mountain he will stop and take the last view of the Parthenon now about to pass out of sight. It has been a faithful happy companion of his trip; always when he sits down to rest on some stone, he will seek a place which brings that temple into his eye, for it never fails to send a wave of delight and fresh energy through the fatigued members. It hands a drink from a divine source to the distant thirsty wayfarer, who starts again on his path with new hope. Now we must bid it good-bye, as it sends to us its graceful benediction from the blue distance; we shall behold it no more, till it suddenly rise up before us again, returning from our journey over the Athenian hills.

Thus I move along on the track of the Marathonian men, sometimes passing by a small orchard of olives, though there are not many in this locality. Of all the trees in Greece or Italy the olive is my favorite; it has the prodigal sparkle of youth and the full joyousness of the Greek climate. Then I crouch through the underbrush by a narrow winding path; often gliding among the bushes the Wallachian shepherd can be seen in attendance upon his flocks. At this season of the year these shepherds are found every-where in Greece. They are a nomadic people whose home during the summer is in the mountains of Thessaly, chiefly in the Pindus range. In winter when their native heights are covered with snow, they pack up their families and drive their herds southward to the mountains of Greece, whose sides are covered with abundance of green browsing.

But when summer comes, the hills here are parched by drouth; vegetation is burnt up in the fierce glare of the Sungod who, the old Greeks fabled, smote the earth with his burning arrows; the arched heavens overhead are heated like an immense bake-oven raying down its caloric upon the roasting earth. Then the Wallachian shepherd flees to the North where his own mountainous altitudes furnish in their turn verdure and a cool climate. Thus he passes and repasses between the two countries, enjoying the happy season of each. For the use of the pasturage he pays to the Greek government a certain sum, according to the number of his flocks. But he must not encroach upon the cultivated land — the field of grain or the vineyard; hence his presence is always required to watch his charge, there being no fences in Greece.

His black herd of goats and white herd of sheep now spot the sides of Pentelicus, as you look up; the low continuous tinkle of their bells is the only sound that reaches the ear on the sunny air; absolute quiet you find here into which that incessant tinkle chimes with a sort of idyllic refrain. No factories, no railroads; no smoke, not a wagon, not even a house — nothing but sunshine and pastoral repose. Now and then a shrill whistle may be heard from the shepherd when some goat passes toward the tilled field; sometimes he will throw a stone at it for a warning to keep off; sometimes he utters a word, calling it by name, for like the shepherds of Theocritus he seems to have a name for each member of his flock.

More seldom you will hear the notes of a flute or panspipe — very simple music indeed, but in a wonderful harmony with the life here, with these sunbeams and this tranquillity of the hills.

You will see the shepherd holding a long staff in his hand with a peculiar crook at the end of it — from time immemorial the symbol of his calling as well as that of the Christian Pastor. But with him it is not a symbol, he does not know what a symbol means probably, but it is for use. You will be highly entertained to see him employ it. Some refractory ewe must be caught for milking; he seeks at first to grasp her by the fleece, once, twice, thrice, and fails; but this time, as she tries to run by him in sheep fashion, he throws that hook under the hind leg and she is fast and perhaps capsized. With no small dexterity is the feat accomplished; then he flings her upon his shoulders and carries her off with head dangling down his back.

Wrapped in shaggy capote made of goat's hair and impervious to rain he stays out in the mountains day and night, defying all changes of weather, living in the simplest harmony with his surroundings, the veritable child of Nature. Yet he is not without a tinge of education, often he speaks and writes Greek. The blazing camp-fires seen on the distant hills in the chill of the evening are his; there he gathers his herd for the night, drinks his whey and eats his curds, and on some holy festival he may roast a lamb in honor of the Saint. The women and children he leaves at the Wallachian village, which is constructed mainly of poles and branches, and has to be built anew every year. Close to some spring or run he dumps his family down when he arrives in Greece from his Northern home; there they remain or move about from place to place till ready for departure again the following spring. But the shepherd does not stay in the village with his family, but drives his herds into the hills, where he dwells with them in solitary delight. Some twenty-five hundred years ago an ancient bard took his picture, in magnified outlines yet true to this day, and called him Polyphemus.

The language of the Wallachians is not Greek, but a daughter of the Latin, and cognate with other Romanic tongues. It is often said in the country here that they speak Italian, but this is a mistake. They were an ancient Roman colony and have derived their speech from old Rome. Originally it is supposed that these Wallachians came from the regions about the Danube known as Wallachia, or ancient Dacia where most of them still dwell;

but in the great migration and displacement of nations during the Middle Ages, a fragment of this people was stranded on the mountains of Thessaly, where they have remained ever since with their primitive nomadic habits. They are not by any means a ferocious race, though some of them become brigands, as Takos.

They constitute one of the three distinct peoples which are found at present in Greece. This fact you should carefully remember: not a homogeneous population but three different peoples are now living on Hellenic soil. These are the Greeks, Wallachians and Albanians — each having distinct customs, language and character.

Almost in a straight line from Parnes to Marathon lies Stamata, a small village which I now approach. Just outside of it is a little Byzantine church which I stop to look at for a few moments; the structure is of a pristine rudeness, yet the yard shows the hand of care; it is not devoid of interest, for the humblest religious edifice has always a significant legend written on its stones. A dog sees me and giving a yelp starts towards me down the little hill from the village; this yelp is the signal for every dog in the neighborhood; here they come, a dozen or more, with hair crawling in bristly folds on their necks, snapping their teeth, rushing up behind and in front, with unearthly barking and gnarling. I at once ceased my contemplation of Byzantine architecture, and began shouting at the fiends. I flourished my staff, retreated against the fence of the church-yard, and succeeded in keeping them at bay till I was relieved from my purgatorial position by two hunters who were coming along, and by a youth from the village who pelted the dogs off with stones.

This was the second unpleasant experience with dogs; for the tourist afoot they are clearly a problem. But I found out, after some trials of him, that, though the Greek dog be a great blusterer, he is really a coward. His chief terror is a stone, which if he sees in the hands of the person whom he assails, he will keep at a safe distance and in lively motion. Often he remains perfectly quiet till you pass, then he treacherously slips up behind you and tries to snap a piece of flesh out of your calves.

Or, he will come rushing upon you with hair erect, looking like a lion; but if you reach for a stone, he will bring himself to a stand at once, or quickly turn back. Often he will ferociously run after the rock which you throw, and bite it, as if that hurt you. He is hard to hit, being an excellent dodger and in continual practice. A little bit of malice one has a right to feel against him; so, after I had learned his character, I took delight in overreaching him in this way: when I stooped for a stone, I would pick up two or three, fling one at him which he would run after, then when his attention was turned away from me, I would pepper him to the extent of my ability in projectiles. If you are as much interested in this subject as I am, you will be glad to learn that I often succeeded in sending him over the fields, howling, sometimes limping. Once or twice I came near getting into trouble on account of the excellence of my aim. Every shepherd and every peasant has two or three such dogs, and not always the owners take the trouble of calling them back when they rush out at the stranger.

The Greek dog has usually a wolfish appearance, as if but a step or two removed from a wild animal; a large black dog, somewhat like a mastiff, is also seen; the breed, however, is mixed with many varieties. But he is cowardly, blustering, treacherous — even for a dog; I confess that I have a prejudice against him on account of this affair at Stamata. His strictly vegetable diet may have something to do in modifying his courage. So much for dogs, which in addition to other things were represented at Athens as one of the terrors of a tour afoot in Greece. The pedestrian can now manage them, and may find some satisfaction in punishing their impudent bluster, while defending himself.

One of the hunters invites me to go with him to his house in the village — an invitation which I gladly accept, passing through many a snarl of the large canine colony, which seemed in no hospitable mood toward me. It is a poor hamlet; like all Albanian villages — for the people here are Albanians — it is built on a very wide street or public place, fronting which the huts are erected in two rows, one on each side. In this way a sort of inclosure is formed which may be used for the herds of the village and will probably contain them all. Here they could be shut up in case of an emergency and protected. Thus the form of the village hints to the traveler of ancient unsettled times, when the people had to be ready to defend themselves and their own against the sudden foray of the robber; still the habit of building remains, though the danger be past. What a different history is revealed in the shape of the typical American town!

Guided by my friendly host, I enter his hovel; in one corner is a fire made of brushwood; there is a small chimney supplemented by a hole in the roof, but both chimney and hole do not succeed in enticing the smoke to the outside, for the room is now full of it. I soon get used to it, however, though it makes me cough and even weep a little at first. There is no window with glass panes, but a simple hole in the wall with a sliding board; this board shoved aside admits fresh air and some light. Still with this opening it is rather dark in the room and I can hardly see, but the pupils of the eyes soon expand and every thing becomes visible, nay, luminous. Happy Nature is always ready to adjust herself harmoniously to her surroundings. There is no floor but the earth, no ceiling but the naked tiles above. This room may be called the parlor of the house, to enter which one has to pass through an adjoining room which is the stable; there a little donkey now stands munching his fodder; he will turn around his big head and look at you as you enter, pricking up his long ears at the strange appearance; near him his little gear hangs on a peg.

I am offered the chair of honor, namely a three-legged stool by the fire, while my host squats down on a mat. Recinato is first brought, with which we drink to each other's well-being; then black bread and olives are placed before me, and he insists upon my eating — which I proceed to do without delay, as it is about noon and walking in the Greek morning air whets to a razor's keenness the appetite. Also he takes the trouble of bringing two eggs from a neighbor's and in honor of his guest roasts them in the hot ashes. So we banquet there before the fire, certainly to my great satisfaction. Citizens having heard of the new arrival, call one, two, three in succession; they first come to that hole in the wall, shove the board aside, thrust in their kerchiefed heads, and give a friendly salute; then they go around, and enter by the door, and when seated on the mat drink a bumper of wine to the health of a stranger, who is not slow to respond to such kindness.

In the conversation many a little hint of their ways of thinking and of their condition is brought to light; there is no school in the place; no priest lives here, one comes from another village to hold service; nobody can either read or write, nor does there seem much ambition to change this state of things. Of the other sex only one old woman and two little girls show themselves. A picture of the Virgin hangs on the wall, before which a small oil lamp is kept burning. This sign of devotion greets the traveler pleasantly; here, too, in this humble cabin there is a recognition of something higher than self, a belief in punishment for the wicked deed and in reward for the good deed. That is assuredly a protection; yes, the Virgin holds her shielding hand over thee too, unbeliever, who art wandering alone through Stamata. Think of it.

I have already told you that the inhabitants of the village are Albanians, and that this name was applied to one of the three different peoples which are at present scattered over Greece. They came from the North, doubtless from ancient Illyria, pressed hither partly by migrations of the great tribes during the medieval troubles, and partly allured by the lands of Greece, which must have been largely depopulated at that period. Their language is usually said to belong to the Slavonic group, and themselves to be Slavs, but the point is stoutly disputed; recently they have been held to be even of Celtic stock. I have no judgment upon this matter; but I confess I would like to think with some learned men that they are ancient Pelasgic remnants.

The Albanian is tall, slim and wiry, rather taciturn and dull, and I thought a little inclined to suspicion, often looking slyly out of the corner of his blinking eye at the stranger. He is the sole agriculturist in these parts, and stands in contrast to the Wallachian who is the shepherd, and to the Greek who is mainly a tradesman. Though he be the ploughman, the Albanian loves the gun far more than the plough; he usually goes armed, carrying a long knife in a belt around the waist and sometimes a pistol. He makes an excellent soldier; the bravest champions of Greek independence were the Albanians of the islands; the best soldiers of the Turkish empire are to-day the Albanians of Albania proper or ancient Epirus. There is not a person of Greek blood in this village; and the same statement is true of the entire rural population of Attica and Bœotia, with a few scattered exceptions. The women are not handsome, often sun-burnt and wrinkled, often stooped with hard outdoor labor. Indeed one is inclined to despair of ever seeing Helen as he goes through these country towns. But we shall continue our quest; this air and sky make amends for much that is wanting; the Greek mood never wanes. The image is still hovering before us and beckons; we still have faith that we may yet catch a glimpse of the reality somewhere in our travels.

So I rose to go; two hours more to Marathon it is said. My hospitable friend conducted me out of the village — very necessary guidance through the double line of snarling dogs. I pressed into his hand a few decaria — a copper coin worth about two cents — enough to pay him, yet not enough to spoil him for the next pedestrian. He refused at first, but finally took them upon my urging him; for it should be a principle with the tourist afoot to pay the people a reasonable price for all that he receives, under the just supposition that he is quite as able to pay as they are to give. I do not pretend, however, that my liberality was extravagant; I never forgot that some of you might be my successors. My host put me into the road to Marathon and added many directions which I imperfectly understood, and should have forgotten, had I understood them. A friendly farewell and we separate. Good luck! I am again on my way with lively hopes and joyous images — best of company here in Greece.

But soon the road forked — which branch to take I could not tell; a forking road is a great perplexity to the traveler in a country without sign-boards. He takes one way at random, then concludes that he is wrong, goes back and takes the other, only to find at last that he was right the first time. Such was my fate now. I took one of the branches, but soon imagined that I had made a mistake, and tried to cross over the intervening field to the first branch, but this had dwindled to a small path which I followed till it lost itself in still smaller paths running in every direction through the mountains.

Where am I now? Such is the question which I find myself asking with some bewilderment. Yonder is Parnes and yonder is Pentelicus running in ranges nearly at right angles to each other; with their aid I can keep the direction; so I start straight across the hills and ravines toward Marathon. Not a human habitation can be seen, not a shepherd, not a flock — nought is there but blank solitude. A thick growth of underbrush covers the ground; one has to push through it by main strength, being caught sometimes and held fast by the secret arms of a wood-nymph reaching out of her tree. Underfoot the crystalline grain of marble can be noticed in the rock which is nicked; minerals now and then can be picked up. From some dense copse a woodcock will rise at times with sudden whirr, which startles the solitary wanderer. Thus I go forward, down valleys, across gulleys, up the steep hill-sides, following a path where it can be followed, with the belief that it must lead somewhither. Signs of a vacated camping spot appear, coal pits are burning off yonder, but I see nobody. So for three hours I wander up and down through the brambly and uneven solitudes; it is not easy traveling, I begin to grow weary, the sun too is getting dim in afternoon decline. What if I should have to remain out all night in the mountains?

Still, courage! Parnes and Pentelicus, with a glance at the map, show you that you are right, going directly to Marathon; then forward, without delay! Miltiades met and overcame a much greater obstacle not far from here; you too must meet and overcome a little one. Consider what lies just before you — it is Marathon! Thus I buoy myself up, keeping my mood persistently Greek. As I push through a clump of bushes, suddenly I stand upon the edge of an enormous chasm; the precipice descends hundreds of feet straight down; cascades can be heard below in the abyss, leaping and dashing, but can not be seen from the summit. The scenery is wild in the extreme; colossal boulders have been broken off from mountain tops and flung half way down in gigantic confusion; some rock battle it was of the old Titans. Three immense gorges come together into one gorge still more immense — three throats of the monster at the entrance to Hades, an adamantine triple-necked Cerberus, guard of Hell. After shuddering at the view for a moment, this thought breaks up through the terror: shall I now have to turn back? for there is no getting down this place; or perchance remain out all night in the mountains? I skirt along the edge of the abyss carefully, fearing lest another precipice may cut me off in this new direction also.

But as I turn around a little thicket and emerge on the other side, behold! The whole valley, green with alternate patches of shrubs and grain-fields, gracefully narrow and curving, stretches out before me. Through it a silvery ribbon of water is winding brightly along — it is the river Marathon. Toward the further end of the vale is a pleasant village lying quietly between the hills in sunny repose — it is the village Marathon. In the distance through the opening between two mountains, following with the eye the course of the stream I can behold a plain spreading out like a fan, and stretching along the blue sparkling rim of the sea — it is the plain of Marathon. The whole landscape sweeps into the vision at once from the high station; something struggles within the beholder, wings can be felt growing out of the sides — let us fly down into the vale without delay from this height.

Accordingly I start, not with pinions however, for I must have walked, inasmuch as I stepped on a long slanting slab of stone, all the while casting my eyes below into the valley, and not looking where I should place my feet, which I imagined I had dispensed with. I slipped, gradually falling my whole length along that slab, not falling hard enough to hurt me, but, as it were, being laid down tenderly by some God who knew better what I wanted than I did myself. For I now experienced what a luxury it was to lie there after such a fatiguing walk and to look over that landscape. All anxiety about having to sleep out in the mountains has passed away; just below I notice a path which leads to the main road running along the stream to the village. Thus I lie on the rough slab in full enjoyment of the scene — then I take out my note-book and write pretty much what you have just heard. But what note-book can carry this view across the ocean, and show it to friends — or transfer the atmosphere of memory and emotion which envelops it! Still think of me, my hearers, lying there on a stone and looking over Marathon, while I jot down a note for you here. What next is in store for us anyhow?

But the Sun refused to stand in the Heavens and gaze along with me, to gaze even upon Marathon; he is sighting me now with waning eye just across yonder peak, in five minutes he will drop behind it. Get up then, and be off for the final stretch, though you be a little stiff from much racing to-day. I pass down the mountain, easily, by the path to the road, and come to the pleasant Marathonian stream, not large, but now leaping along its white marble bed with many a joyous gush and babble. The roads run just at the side of it so that it keeps me company; in one spot the smooth basin filled with a dancing transparent flow of ripples is too tempting; I stoop down, wash hands and face, then pull off shoes and stockings, and wade into the cool pellucid waters — I, the undignified man, right along the public road. But it was delicious refreshment to the foot-sore traveler; the cool stream healed the feverish members bruised by the long stony journey — and I was ready again for the march and the battle.

Just as I was prepared to start once more, a new appearance I notice coming down the road; it is the traveling merchant with his entire store of goods laden on the back of a little donkey. His salute is friendly, his manner is quick and winning; we go along together toward the village talking of many things. He tells me that he is from Oropus, a town on the Attic border, famous in antiquity, that his name is Aristides, that he is going to Marathon and will show me a place to stay during the night. There is something new and peculiar about this man the like of which I have not yet seen in these rural portions of Greece. He walks with a quick alert step, he has a shrewdness and brightness of intellect, a readiness and information which are remarkable in comparison to the ordinary intellectual gifts found in the country; his features and his physical bearing, his keen dark eye and nervous twitch distinguish him in the most striking manner from the stolid Albanian peasant. He is a Greek of pure blood, he tells me — manifestly we have met with a new and distinctive type.

I enter the village of Marathon with Aristides, who brings me to the chief wineshop, where lodgings are to be had as well as refreshing beverage. First a thimble full of mastic, a somewhat strong alcoholic drink, with my merchant, who then leaves me and goes to his business. A number of people are in the wineshop, they are the Albanian residents of the village; all look curiously at the new arrival. The merchant soon passed around the word that I was from America — a fact which I had imparted to him on the way. But of America they had very little notion. The strangest sort of curiosity peeped out of their rather small eyes; the news spread rapidly through the town that a live American had arrived; what that was, they all hastened to see. So they continued to pour in by twos and threes, till the spacious wineshop was nearly full. Not a word they said, but walked along in front of the table where I sat, and stared at me; they kept their kerchiefed heads drawn down in their shaggy capotes, being dressed in tight breeches like close-fitting drawers, with feet thrust into low shoes which run out to a point at the toes and curl over. Thus they move before me in continuous procession; when they had taken a close survey of me, they would sit down on a bench, roll a cigarette in paper, strike fire from a flint, and begin to smoke. A taciturn, curious but not unfriendly crowd — I called for recinato.

Presently a man clad in European garments appeared among them, and in courteous manner addressed me, talking good Greek but very bad French; it was the village school-master whom the people familiarly called Didaskali. I hailed him joyfully as a fellow-craftsman in a foreign land, and lost no time in announcing to him that I too was a school-master in my country. Professional sympathy at once opened all the sluices of his heart, we were friends on the spot. He was not an Albanian, but a Greek born in the Turkish provinces; I do not think he was as bright as my merchant Aristides, though he was probably better educated. I took a stroll with him around the town; he sought to show me every possible kindness, with the single exception of his persistency in talking French. One neat little cottage I noticed; it was the residence of the Dikastes or village judge; but the most of the houses were low hovels, with glassless windows, often floorless. Women were shy, hiding forehead and chin in wrappage at the approach of a stranger, who perhaps was too eager in trying to peer into their faces — as if in search of some visage lost long ago in this valley. Still human nature is here, too, in Marathon, for I caught a young girl giving a sly peep through the window after we had passed, which she had pretended to close when she saw the stranger approaching.

But it is growing dark; I have done a pretty good day's work; I must put off the rest of the sight-seeing till to-morrow. Only half a mile below is the Marathonian plain, which one can see from the village, but it must now be turned over to darkness. At my request the Didaskali goes back with me to the wineshop, when he excuses himself, promising soon to return. There I had a supper which was eminently satisfactory after a day's walk: five eggs fried in goat's butter, large quantities of black bread, and abundance of recinato at one cent a glass — good-sized glasses at that.

While I sat there eating, the people began to assemble again. The Papas, the village priest came and listened, the untrowsered man, with dark habit falling down to his heels like a woman's dress, and with long raven hair rolled up in a knot on the back of his head, upon which knot sat his high stiff ecclesiastical cap; the Dikastes or village judge came, an educated man, who had studied at the University of Athens, and who dressed in European fashion, possessing in noticeable contrast to the rest of the Marathonians, the latest style of Parisian hat; a lame shop-keeper came, a Greek of the town, bright, full of mockery, flattering me with high titles in order to get me to hire his mules for my journey, as I had good reason to suspect; finally the school-master and the traveling merchant appeared again, both in excellent humor and expecting a merry evening. There was no doctor present, I asked for him; they told me that there was none in the valley, though it is scourged with malarial fever in summer; one man in particular complained of the health of the place. All the representative citizens of Marathon were before me, looking at me eating in the wineshop on a wooden table. Some one asked me about my native language. "This is the language that I understand best," said I, raising a mouthful of egg and bread to my lips; "you seem to understand it too." This jest, for whose merit I do not make any high claims, caused all the Albanians to laugh and set the whole wineshop in a festive mood. It is manifest that this audience is not very difficult to please.

Finally my long respast was finished — long both on account of the work done and on account of the continued interruptions caused by question and answer. The people still held out — there they were before me, more curious than ever, now with a laughing look on account of that one sterile jest, laughing out of the corner of the eye, and with head already somewhat drawn out of the shaggy capote from expectation. What next? I was on the soil of illustrious Marathon, expectant gazes were centered upon me; what had I, as a true American, to do for the honor of my country? My duty was clear from the start,

I must make a speech. I would have been unfaithful to my nationality, had I not done so at Marathon. Accordingly I shoved the table aside, pulled out my bench, and in the full happiness of hunger and thirst satisfied — perhaps too a little aglow with the golden recinato — I began to address them as follows: —

Andres Marathonioi — Ye men of Marathon — at this point I confess I had to laugh myself, looking into that solid Albanian stare of fifty faces, for the echo of the tremendous oath of Demosthenes in which he swears by the heroes of Marathon, rung through my ears and made the situation appallingly ludicrous. Still, in spite of my laugh, you must know that I was in deep earnest and full of my theme; moreover, there were at least four persons before me who could understand both my Greek and my allusions. As to my Greek, I affirm that Demosthenes himself would have understood it, had he been there — though he might have criticised the style and pronunciation. But I resumed:

Ye men of Marathon, I never was gladder in my life than I am to be with you to-night. I crossed over the mountains on foot from Stamata; every step that I took was lighter with thinking of Marathon. When from yonder summit, I first caught a glimpse of your village and valley and gave a distant peep into the plain beyond to the sea, I had to shed tears of joy. Your name is indeed the greatest, the most inspiring in all history. In every age it has been the mighty rallying cry of freedom; nations oppressed, on hearing it, have taken hope and risen, smiting to earth their tyrants. It has been the symbol of courage to the few and weak against the many and strong; the very utterance of the name inspires what is highest and noblest in the human breast — courage, devotion, liberty, nationality. Under a banner inscribed with that word Marathon, our Western civilization has heroically marched and fought its battle; here was its first outpost, here its first and greatest triumph — and the shout of that triumph still re-echoes and will go on re-echoing forever through history. But Marathon is not merely here; it has traveled around the world along with man's freedom and enlightenment. Among all civilized peoples the name is known and cherished; it is familiar as a household word, nay, it is a household prayer. In the remote districts of America I have often heard it uttered — and uttered with deepest admiration and gratitude. There, in my land, thousands of miles from here, I first learned the name of Marathon in a log school-house by the side of the primitive forest; it fell from the lips of a youth who was passionately speaking of his country. It had in its very sound I can still recollect, some spell, some strange fascination, for it seemed to call up, like an army of spirits, the great heroes of the past along with the most intense feelings of the soul. There you can hear it among the people in their little debates; also you can hear it from great orators in senate-halls. Marathon, I repeat, is the mightiest, most magical name in history, by which whole nations swear when they march out in defense of their Gods, their families and their freedom. By it too they compare their present with their past and ever struggle upwards to fulfill what lies prophetically in their great example. Now I am in the very place; I can hardly persuade myself that it is not a dream, and that you are not shadows flitting here before me. In that log school-house I did not even dare dream of this moment; but it has arrived. I have already had to-day a glimpse where the old battle-field reposes in the hazy distance; to-morrow I shall visit it, run over it, spend the whole day upon it, looking and thinking; for I desire to stamp its features and its spirit into my very brain that I may carry Marathon across the ocean to my land and show it to others who may not be able to come here and see it for themselves. Nor shall I refrain from confessing to you a secret within me: I can not help thinking that I have been here before; every thing looks familiar to me; I beheld yon summit long ago, the summit of old Kotroni; I have marched down the Marathonian stream as I marched to-day; I seem to be doing over again the same things that I have done here before; I made a speech on this spot ages ago in Greek — a much better one, I think, than I am now making. And further let me tell you what I believe — I believe that I too fought along at Marathon, that I was one of those ten thousand Athenian soldiers that rushed down yonder hill-side and drave the Oriental man into the sea. I can now behold myself off there charging down a meadow toward a swamp, amid the rattle of arms and the hymn of battle, with shield firmly grasped and with spear fiercely out-thrust, on the point of which, spitted through and through, I can feel a quivering Persian."

At this strange notion and still more at the accompanying gesture made in a charging attitude, the mirthful Greeks could hold in no longer, but burst suddenly into a loud and prolonged laugh, in which the Albanians joined: they all laughed, laughed inextinguishably, like the blessed Gods on Olympus, and the whole wineshop was filled with wild merriment. Whereat the speech was brought to a close which may be modestly called a happy one: thus let it be now.

IV. MARATHON.

As soon as the speech had come to an end, I rose and looked out of the wineshop, desiring to take a short stroll before going to bed, in order to catch a breath of fresh air and to see a Greek evening in the Marathonian vale. Though long after sunset, it appeared light out of doors every-where; that vague flicker from the sky it was which gives a mystical indefiniteness to the things of Nature and produces such a marked contrast to the clear plastic outlines of day-time. The schoolmaster went along, and we walked up the stream of Marathon, which often gurgled into a momentary gleam over the pebbles, and then fell back into darkness. The mountains on each side of us were changed into curious fantastic shapes which played in that subtle light; caprice of forms now ruled the beautiful Greek world, as begotten in the sport of a Northern fancy; Hecate with her rout of witches and goblins had broken loose from her dark caverns in the earth and was flitting across glimmering patches of twilight up and down the hill-sides. Below the peaks the dells and little seams of valleys running athwart one another were indicated by lines of darkness so that their whole figure came to resemble a many-legged monster crawling down the slant; while above on the summits was the dreamy play of light with the dance of the fairies. But these shapes let us shun in Greece; we may allow them to sport capriciously before us for a few moments in the evening, though in truth they belong not here. Let us then hasten back to the wineshop and await to-morrow the return of Phœbus Apollo, the radiant Greek God, who will slay these Pythons anew with his shining arrows and put to flight all the weird throng, revealing again our world in clear clean-cut outlines bounded in his soft sunlight.

When we arrived there, we still found the priest — the long-haired, dark-stoled Papas, though nearly every body else had gone home. He began to catechise me on the subject of religion, particularly its ceremonies; of which examination I, knowing my weakness, tried to keep shy. But he broke out directly upon me with this question: Were you ever baptized? Therein a new shortcoming was revealed to myself, for I had to confess that I actually did not know; I did not recollect any such event myself, and I had always forgotten to ask my father whether the rite had ever been performed over me when an infant. The priest thought that this was bad, very bad — *kakon, polù kakon* was his repeated word of disapprobation; then he asked me if I never intended to be baptized. This question, here at Marathon, drove me to bed; I at once called for a light. But it was only one of the frequent manifestations that will be observed in modern Greece, of a tendency to discuss religious subtleties. The ecclesiastical disputes of the Byzantine Empire — Homoousian and Homoiousian — will often to-day be brought up vividly to the mind of the traveler. Especially the ceremonies of the Eastern Church are maintained with much vigor and nice distinction in a very finespun and consequently, very thin tissue of argumentation.

After excusing myself from the Papas, who in company with me performs a slight inner baptism of himself with a glass of recinato as the final ceremony of the day, I ask to be conducted to my quarters, and am led to an adjoining building upstairs. The room is without furniture; in one corner of it lies a mattress covered with coarse sheeting and a good quilt, on the floor — for in Greece bedsteads are not much in vogue. They are considered to be in the way and to take up unnecessary room; so the bed-clothes are spread out on the floor along the hearth every evening and packed away every morning. This bed was considered a particularly good one, intended for strangers who might visit Marathon and who had to pay for it two francs a night. Indeed, during a great portion of the year in this hot climate, the bed is not only unnecessary but a nuisance in which one can only roll and swelter; hence the family bed has no such place in the Greek as in the Northern household.

The light which is left me is also worthy of a passing notice. It consists of a cup two-thirds filled with water; on the water lies half an inch of olive oil; on the surface of the oil is floating a small piece of wood to which a slender wick is attached reaching into the oil; the upper end of this wick is lighted, and painfully throws its shadowy glimmer on the walls. A truly pristine light, going back probably to old Homer, thinks the traveler, by which the blind bard could have sat and hymned his lines to eager listeners around the evening board; an extremely economical light, burning the entire night without any diminution of the oil apparently and giving a proportionate illumination — it is a hard light to read by, still harder to write by. There is no tallow in the country for candles; the little wax which is produced is used for tapers in the churches. There is no desk or chair in the room; one must write on the floor in some way, if he wishes to send a line to the dear ones, or take a note.

Accordingly the traveler goes to bed, props himself upon his elbow, opens his book on the floor near the light — but the eyes swim for a moment, the head totters, back it falls upon the mattress: that is the end of one day's adventure; he will rapidly descend into Lethe, where, though in dreams he fight the great battle over again alongside of Miltiades at one moment, and the next moment argue the question of baptism with the Papas, he will lie in sweet unconscious repose, till the Sun-god rising from his bath in the ocean stretch his long golden fingers through the window, gently open the eyelids and whisper to the slumberer who will hear though half awake: "Rise, it is the day of Marathon." Thereupon the traveler leaps from his couch, for he knows that it is the voice of a God and he dares not disobey; if he have any winged sandals, he now puts them on, for to-day he will have to make an Olympian flight; if he have that staff of Hermes with which the Argus-slayer conducts departed souls out of Hades and into it, he will seize the same and sally forth, for to-day he will have to call up from the past many mighty spirits — those colossal shades which still rise at Marathon.

When I came out of my high-sounding chamber in the morning, I met my good host with an ewer of water which he proceeded to pour upon my hands for the purpose of ablution; unpoetical washbasins do not exist, or were refused me, perchance on account of my Homeric habits. After a breakfast quite like the supper on the previous evening, I begin the march for the battle of Marathon, having filled a small haversack with a piece of black bread and some cheese for luncheon, and having slung around my shoulder a canteen of recinato. Nor do I forget my chief weapons — two books and the maps, which I hold tightly under my arm. Thus equipped, I tread along, with becoming modesty I trust, yet with no small hopes of victory.

But there is no hurry, let the gait still be leisurely. As I pass down the road through the village which is spread out on the banks of the stream, I meet many an acquaintance made the evening before at the wineshop; each recognizes me by a slight nod of the head with a pleasant smile. All of them seemed still to be laughing at the idea of my being an ancient Hoplite now revisiting former scenes of activity. Such friendly greeting on every side together with the genial sunshine of the morning puts the traveler into a happy mood, slightly transcendental perhaps. Whatever he now does is an adventure worth recording to future ages; whatever he now sees is a divine revelation.

Passing along to a shelving place in the stream, he beholds the washers — one hundred women or more at work with furious muscle, pounding, scouring, rubbing, rinsing the filth-begrimed fustanellas of their husbands, brothers, sons. There is a strength, vigor, and I should say, anger in their motions, that they seem animated by some feeling of revenge against those dirty garments, and in my opinion with good reason. One Amazonian arm is wielding a billet of wood, quite of the weight and somewhat resembling the shape of the maul with which the American woodman drives wedges into the gnarled oak. Upon a flat smooth stone are laid the garments, boiled, soaped and steaming, when they are belabored by that maul. None of our modern machinery is seen, even the washboard is very imperfect or does not appear at all. Somehow in this wise the ancient Nausicaas must have blanched their linen at the clear Marathonian stream; one will unconsciously search now with eager glances for the divine Phæacian maid to see whether she be not here still. At present the washers are strewn along the marble edge of the water for quite a distance, dressed in white, bare-armed, mostly bare-footed and bare-legged, in the liveliest, fiercest muscular motion, as if wrestling desperately with some fiend. Look at the struggling, wriggling, smiting mass of mad women — Maenads under some divine enthusiasm — while the sides of old Kotroni Mountain across the river re-echoes with the thud of their relentless billets. A truly Marathonian battle against filth, with this very distinct utterance: "For one day at least we are going to be clean in Marathon."

But it is impossible to look at the washers all the time, however fascinating the view; indeed I had almost forgotten that I am on my way to the field of the great battle — which does not speak well for an ancient Hoplite. I still pass along the stream with its white lining of marble through which flows the current pellucid; — what! are the eyes deceived, or is the water actually diminishing in the channel? Yes, not only has it diminished, but now a few steps further it has wholly vanished, sunk away into the earth, leaving merely a dry rocky bed for the wildest torrent of the storm. Thus that crisp joyous mountain stream which gave us such delight in its dance down the hill through the valley when we looked at it coming to Marathon, now disappears with its entire volume of water, to rise again in the marshes beyond or perchance in the sea.

This phenomenon is not unusual in Greece, and like all occurrences of Nature in this country, has been stamped with a spiritual impress. Rivers sink away, pass through a channel underground, then come again to the surface, possibly to vanish, and to rise a second time in like manner. There is a special Greek word to designate such a subterranean passage: it is called the catabothron. Many a stream, therefore, has its catabothron, and this fact always gave origin to a pretty fable which was elaborated by the poet of the neighborhood and through him passed into the mythical treasures of the people. A beautiful stream of water ripples down from the mountain and sinks away; it is the fair nymph Marathonia who is ravished by Seismos, the land-heaving Earthquake, rising out of the ground, as she is bathing in her rivulet and revealing her beauty; but after long struggle and flight, she is rescued by her mother, the far-sounding Amphitrite in the bosom of the sea. Thus each little locality of Greece had its fountain of poetry, incessantly welling up into legend and song.

But this is not all. Why did the Greek seize upon Nature and weave out of her hints that wonderful texture of fable? It was just he who did it with supreme beauty, just he and nobody else; manifestly he wrought from some deep need of expressing himself, he had to utter what was within him, his spiritual life and also the life of his community. Nature lay there before him and was profoundly sympathetic with his utterance; into her forms he wrought his experience, his intellectual stores, his history. For instance, a village migrates, a colony is sent out, a religious rite is introduced from abroad, a political institution is transplanted — what is it but a spring, a stream, a water-nymph, disappearing at the one place and rising at the other? Before his door is the river, it does the same thing and becomes the expression thereof; let him but narrate its course and he has the deep poetic hint of his own life, and it may be, of the life of his whole nation and race. Perhaps the best known of these legends is that of Arethusa, the beautiful nymph of Elis, one of Diana's choir, who beloved of the river-god Alpheius, fled under the sea, still pursued by the god, when finally she rose in the fountain Arethusa in Sicily. A cup thrown into the river Alpheius in Greece would be cast up at the Sicilian fountain; the blood of sacrifice which flowed into the river during the great Olympic festival would ensanguine the waters of fair Arethusa over the sea. A poetical people we behold, always grasping Nature and making her the voice of their deed, the expression of their spiritual revolutions. There was a great colonization of Sicily from Greece in the 7th and 8th centuries B. C., a transference thither of Greek customs, institutions, language; must there not be some utterance of that important event from the hearts of the people, taken directly from that which they see before themselves every day?

Such an utterance, however, becomes a legend — an expression of all similar occurrences: hence it is truly a symbol and lasts forever. Thus the Greek has created the symbols, at least the most beautiful symbols of the race, for they are employed to-day by Art and must be eternally employed. This is the supreme significance of Greek mythology. Notice once more that it comes from Nature, yet it is not merely natural; nor, on the other hand, though it bears the impress of Spirit, is it merely allegorical; it is the perfect blending of Nature and Spirit, their happy interpenetration; thus a brook, a thing of Nature, leaps up into the human shape, while a revolution, a thing of Spirit drops down into the subterranean course of the brook.

With such thoughts I pass by the Marathonian catabothron, see the waters swoon away into the earth; then I have to ask myself: where will it rise next? Not in the Euripus yonder, I say; not even across the sea in Sicily — it has already gone much farther. The Marathonian stream is certain to pass beyond the Pillars of Hercules, wind its way under a great ocean, worm through the cavernous passages of a continent, rise up once more on the banks of the Father of Waters, with whose turbid current it will mingle, and add thereto a little of its quiet transparent beauty. Can you not see it rising already?

So one saunters down that short neck which attaches the village to the plain, joyously attuned by the climate and trying to throw himself back into that spirit which created the old Greek Mythology, determined to see here what an ancient Greek would see. Nature begins to be alive, she begins to speak strange things in his soul and to reveal new shapes to his vision; an Oread skips along the mountain with him, while the Naiads circle in a chorus round the neighboring fountain. Such company he must find, if he truly travel in Greece. Not as a sentimental play of the fancy, not as a pretty bauble for the amusement of a dreary hour, but as a vital source of faith and action, as a deep and abiding impulse to the greatest and most beautiful works, will the loyal traveler seek to realize within himself these antique forms.

But that shape at yonder spring drawing water, — what can it be? Clearly not a Naiad; dark eyes flashing out from blooming features that lie half hidden among her hair falling down carelessly on both sides of her forehead, a short dress drooping over her luxuriant frame in romantic tatters of many colors, under which the bosom swells half exposed, cause the white water-nymphs to vanish into viewless air and leave a seductive image behind, which will long accompany the traveler in spite of himself, rising at intervals and dancing through his thoughts even at Marathon. It is the Wallachian maiden who has come down from her mountain lodge for water, which in two large casks she puts on the back of a donkey. A wild beauty, fascinating on account of wildness, not devoid of a certain coy coquetry; she seems not displeased to have attracted the marked attention of that man in Frankish garments who is passing along the road, for her dark eyes shoot out new sparkles from under the falling tresses, tempered with subdued smiles. She has nothing to do with the villagers of Marathon, she is a child of the mountains, she belongs to a different world. Slowly she passes out of sight with her charge into the brushwood; looking back at the last step she stoops and plucks a flower; then she springs up and vanishes among the leaves.

It is a slight disappointment, perhaps: but look now, in the opposite direction, and you will behold in the road going toward the plain a new and very delightful appearance; three white robes are there moving gracefully along through the clear atmosphere and seem to be set in high relief against the hilly background. Three women, evidently of the wealthier people of the village, for their garments are of stainless purity and adjusted with unusual care, appear to be taking a walk at their leisure down the valley. Their dress is a long loose gown flowing freely down to the heels, all of it shows the spotless white except a narrow pink border. Over this dress is worn a woolen mantilla, also white with a small border. At the view there arises the feeling which will often be experienced in other localities of Greece with even greater intensity: the feeling of a living plastic outline which suggests its own copy in marble. No costume can possibly be so beautiful and so distinct in this atmosphere; there they move along, as if statues should start from their pedestals and walk down from their temples through the fields. Why the white material was taken by the old artists for sculpture, becomes doubly manifest now; here is the living model in her fair drapery, yonder across the river is the marble, Pentelic marble, cropping out of the hills. Unite the twain, they belong together, both have still a mute longing to be joined once more in happy marriage. I have not the least doubt that the ancient Marathonian woman in the age of the battle paced through this valley in a similar costume, producing similar sensations in this bluish transparent air.

But the three shapes draw near, one will look into their faces as they pass, they are Albanian women, not beautiful by any means, not with features corresponding to their costumes, you will say. Therefore we must add something very essential to bring back that ancient Greek woman, for she had brought body into the happiest harmony with dress, if we may judge of those types which have come down to us. Still this is a delightful vision of antique days, passing in stately gait through the clear sunlit landscape;—forms of white marble in contrast to the many-colored tatters of the Wallachian maiden, who, having no sympathy of dress with the climate shows that she does not belong to Marathon.

Now we have arrived—if you have succeeded in keeping up with me—at the point where the bed of the river passes into the plain, in full view of which we at present stand. It sweeps around almost crescent-shaped, like the side of a vast amphitheater cut into the mountains; the line from tip to tip of the arc is said to measure about six miles. That line, seen from the spot where we now are, has a beautiful blue border of sparkling water—the Euripus, which separates the mainland from the island Euboea. There is upon the plain but one tree worthy of the name—a conifer which rises strange and solitary about in the center of it, and looks like a man, with muffled head in soldier's cloak standing guard, still waiting for some enemy to come out of the East. The plain is at present largely cultivated, vineyards and fields of grain are scattered through it, but the ancient olives are wanting. At the northern horn of the crescent is a large morass running quite parallel to the sea; a smaller one is at the southern horn. Into the plain two villages debouch, both having roads from Athens. There is a beautiful shore gradually shelving off into deep water with a gravel bottom; here the traveler will sit long and look at the waves breaking one after another upon the beach. This coast, however, is but a narrow strip for several miles; just behind it lies amid the grass the deceptive marsh, not visible at any considerable distance. This morass and its conformation will explain the great miracle of the battle: namely, its decisiveness notwithstanding the enormous disparity in the numbers of the two contending armies. For the morass was the treacherous enemy lurking in ambuscade at the rear and under the very feet of the Persians.

In regard to the battle of Marathon we have only one trustworthy account — this is given by Herodotus, the Father of History. It is short and omits much that we would like to know, indeed must know in order to comprehend the battle. Still, a view of the ground will suggest the general plan, with the help of the old historian's hints and of one contemporary fact handed down by the traveler Pausanias. The battle was a fierce attack in front, aided by the enemy in the rear — the morass, which had a double power. It, on the one hand, prevented the foe from getting assistance, which could only come from the ships by a long detour round the narrow strip of coast easily blocked by a few soldiers. On the other hand, broken or even unbroken lines being forced into the swampy ground would become hopelessly disordered, and would have enough to do fighting the enemy under their feet.

Imagine now this line of coast with the vessels drawn up sternwards along the shelving bank; then comes the narrow strip of shore on which a portion of the Persian army lies encamped; then follows the marshy tract, then the plain upon which another portion of the Persian army is drawn up; still further and beyond the plain is the slope of the mountain where with good vision you can see the Athenians arrayed in order of battle. At the mouth of one of the two villages, doubtless near the modern hamlet of Vrana they have taken position, since they could easily pass round the road and protect the other valley, if a movement should be made in that direction by the enemy. Single-handed of all the states of Greece they stand here; they had sent for aid to the Spartans who refused to come on account of a religious festival. Still the suspicion lives and will forever live through history that this was a mere pretense, that the Spartans would gladly have seen their rival destroyed, though at the peril of Greek freedom.

But who are these men filing silently through the brushwood of Mount Kotroni, in leather helmets and rude kilts, hurrying forward to the aid of the Athenians? They are the Plataeans, a small community of Boeotia, in all Greece the only town outside of Attica that has the courage and the inclination to face the Persian foe. One thousand men are here from that small place — a quiet rural village lying on the slopes of Kithaeron; the whole male population, one is forced to think, including every boy and old man capable of bearing arms is in that band, for the entire community could hardly number more than three or four thousand souls. Yet here they are to the last man; one almost imagines that some of the women must be among them in disguise — as to-day the Greek women of Parnassus often handle the gun with skill, and have been known to fight desperately in the ranks alongside of their fathers and brothers. But think of what was involved in that heroic deed; the rude villagers assemble when the messenger comes with the fearful news that the Persian had landed just across at Marathon; in the market-place they deliberate, having hurried from their labor in the fields, in coarse rustic garb with bare feet slipped into low sandals; uncouth indeed they seem, but if there ever were men on the face of this earth, they were in Plataea at that hour. No faint-hearted words were there, we have the right to assume — no half-hearted support; no hesitation; every man takes his place in the files, the command to march is given and they all are off. Nor can we forget the anxiety left behind in the village; the Greek wife with child on her arm peers out of the door, taking a last look at that receding column winding up Kithaeron and disappearing over its summit; there is not a husband, not a grown-up son remaining in Plataea. What motive, do you ask? I believe that these rude Greek rustics were animated by a profound instinct which may be called not only national but world-historical — the instinct of hostility to the Orient and its principle in favor of political autonomy and individual freedom. Also another ground of their conduct was gratitude toward the Athenians who had saved them from the tyranny of Thebes, their overbearing neighbor; now their benefactors are in the sorest need, patriotism and friendship alike command, there can be no hesitation. So those thousand men on a September day wind through the pines and arbutes of Kotroni with determined tread, are received with great joy by the Athenians and at once take their position on the left wing ready for the onset. Let any village in the world's history match the deed! Well may the Athenians after that day join the Plataeans with themselves in public prayers to the Gods, in whose defense both have marched out.

Scarcely have these allies arrived, we may suppose, when the moment of battle is at hand. Doubtless it was the most favorable moment, and as such eagerly seized by Miltiades; why it was so favorable no one at this late day can know. Perhaps the much-feared Persian cavalry were absent on a foraging expedition, perhaps the enemy were negligent or were embarking, or, as Herodotus says, because it was Miltiades' day of command; — alas, who can tell? At any rate the order to charge is given, down the declivity the Greeks rush, over the plain for a mile. The deep files on the wings of their army bear every thing before them; but the center is defeated for a time and driven back, for it had apparently been weakened to strengthen the wings. Such is the first fierce attack.

Now comes the second stage of the struggle, the battle at the marshes. The front of the enemy, pressed by the Greeks and consolidated into a mass of panic-stricken fugitives bore the rear backwards; thus the whole hostile army pushed itself into the swamp. Whoever has seen a regiment of infantry in a morass, reeling, struggling with broken lines, sinking under their equipments, soldiers extricating one foot only to sink deeper with the other, cursing their stars and damning the war, that is, a complete loss of all discipline and a sort of despair on account of the new victorious enemy underfoot — such a person can imagine the condition of a large part of the Persian army after that attack. The Greek lines stood on the edge of the marsh and smote the struggling disordered mass with little or no loss to themselves. They also prevented succor from coming round the narrow tongue of coast till the battle at the morass was over, wholly victorious for the Greeks.

The narrative of Herodotus omits entirely this second stage of the conflict, and modern historians have slurred it over with little or no separate attention. Thus, however, the whole battle is an unaccountable mystery. Fortunately this struggle at the morass and its result are vouched for by an authority at once original and cotemporaneous — an authority even better than Herodotus who was a foreigner from Asia Minor. It was the picture in the Poekile at Athens painted not long after the battle. Of the details of that picture we have several important hints from ancient authors. Says Pausanias, evidently speaking of its leading motive, it shows "the barbarians fleeing and pushing one another into the swamp." There can be no doubt that this was the salient and decisive fact of the battle: the barbarians fled and pushed one another into the swamp. By the fierce onset of the Greeks the front lines of the enemy were driven upon the rear, and the whole multitude was carried by its own weight into the treacherous ground, numbers only increasing the momentum and the confusion. Such was the conception of the artist painting the battle before the eyes of the very men who had participated in it; such, therefore, we must take to be the contemporary Athenian conception. The picture may well be considered to be the oldest historical document we have concerning the fight, and as even better evidence than the foreign historian. The ground, moreover, as we look at it to-day, tells the same story. A skillful military commander of the present time, other things being equal, would make the same plan of attack. Thus, too, the great miracle of the battle — the defeat of so many by so few and the small loss of the victors — is reasonably cleared up.

The third stage of the conflict was the battle at the ships, while the enemy were embarking. This, to be successful, had to take place, partly upon the narrow strip of shore to which the Greeks must penetrate at a disadvantage. In their zeal they rushed into the water down the shelving pebbly bottom in order to seize the fleet; still the faithful traveler visiting the scene will, after their example, wade far out into the sea. Seven vessels were taken out of six hundred, the enemy making good their embarkation. Many Greeks here suffered the fate of brave Kynageirus, brother of the poet Æschylus, who seizing hold of a vessel had his arms chopped off by a Persian battle-ax. In general, the Greeks were repulsed at the battle of the ships; but this third stage, since the enemy were leaving, is the least important of the whole conflict.

Not a word does Herodotus say about the numbers engaged on either side — a strange, unaccountable omission. Yet he must have conversed with men who fought at the battle, with the leaders possibly, and he gives with the greatest care the loss on both sides — 6400 Persians, 192 Athenians. The omission leads to the conjecture that he could not find out the true figures; yet why not at Athens, where they must have been known? It is a puzzle; let each one solve it by his own conjecture, which is likely to be as good as anybody else's.

Ancient writers much later than the battle give to the Persians from 210,000 to 600,000 men; to the Athenians and Plataeans 10,000 men. Modern writers have sought through various sources to lessen this immense disparity, by increasing the Athenian and diminishing the Persian numbers. Indeed Marathon became the topic of the wildest exaggeration for the Greek orators and rhetoricians — 300,000 were said to have been slain by less than 10,000; Kynageirus already mentioned is declared to have had first the right hand cut off, then the left hand, then to have seized the vessel with his teeth like a wild animal; Callimachus, a brave general who was slain, is represented to have been pierced by so many weapons that he was held up by their shafts. It was the great common-place of Athenian oratory, thence it has passed to be the world's common-place. Justly, in my opinion; for it is one of the supreme world-events, and not merely a local or even national affair; thus the world will talk of its own deeds. Do not imagine with the shallow-brained detractor that rhetoric has made Marathon; no, Marathon rather has made rhetoric, among other greater things.

Far more interesting than these rhetorical exaggerations of a later time are the contemporary accounts which come from the people and show their faith — the legends of supernatural appearances which took part in the fight. For there was aught divine, the people must believe, at work visibly upon the battle-field that day. Epizelus, a soldier in the ranks, was stricken blind and remained so during life, at the vision of a gigantic warrior with a huge beard, who passed near him and smote the enemy. Theseus, the special Athenian hero, Hercules the universal Greek hero were there and seen of men; no doubt of it, the heroes all did fight along, with very considerable effect too. Nor were the Gods absent: the God Pan, regardless of slighted divinity, met the courier Phidippides on the way to Sparta for aid and promised his divine help if the Athenians would neglect him no longer. Finally Athena herself, the protecting Goddess of the city, in helm and spear strode there through the ranks, shaking her dreadful ægis, visible to many, nay, to all Athenian eyes.

Even a new hero appears, unheard of before; in rough rustic garb, armed with a ploughshare he smote the Oriental foe who had invaded his soil. After the battle he vanishes — who was he? On consulting an oracle the Athenians were merely told to pay honors to the Hero Echetlus. On the whole the most interesting and characteristic of all these appearances — the rustic smiter he is, who reveals the stout rude work put in by the Attic peasant on that famous day. Indeed all who fell were buried on the sacred ground of the battle and were worshiped as heroes with annual rites. Still in the time of the traveler Pausanias, about 150 years after Christ, the air was filled at night with the blare of trumpets, the neighing of steeds and the clangor of battle. Says he: " It is dangerous to go to the spot for the express purpose of seeing what is going on, but if a man finds himself there by accident without having heard about the matter, the Gods will not be angry." Greece was at the period of Pausanias extinct in Roman servitude, yet the clash of that battle could be heard, loud, angry, even dangerous, over six hundred years after the event. Still the modern peasant hears the din of combat in the air sometimes; I asked him, he was a little shy of the matter; the noise, however, has become to him comparatively feeble, still there is a noise. But long will it be, one may well think, before that noise wholly subsides.

So the Heroes and Gods fought along with the Athenians at Marathon, visible, almighty and in wrath. Thus it has been delivered to us on good authority; thus I, for one, am going to believe, for the event shows it; far otherwise had been the story, if the Gods had not fought along on that day. There would have been no Marathonian victory, no Athens, no Greek literature, for us at least. But now Theseus, the deserving Hero, will have a new temple, beautiful, enduring, at this moment nearly perfect, after almost twenty-four centuries. Athena also will have a new temple, larger and more beautiful than any heretofore, still the unattained type of all temples; it shall be called, in honor of the virgin Goddess, the Parthenon. Attic song will now burst forth, Attic art too, celebrating just this Marathon victory; that long line of poets, orators, philosophers, historians, will now appear — all because the Gods fought along at Marathon.

For can we not see the Divine at once springing into artistic utterance at Athens? There in the Poekile or Painted Porch was a large picture representing this battle; prominent were the forms of Miltiades who commanded, of Callimachus whose slain body was held upright by the piercing spears, of Kynageirus seizing the vessel, of Epizelus struck blind by the spectral warrior. But among these mortal heroes the shapes of Hercules, Theseus, Echetlus stood out in that picture; above all, however, the supreme figure was painted there, the warlike virgin Athena, clad in divine armor, moving in the midst of the combat with death-dealing glances from her awful-gleaming eye. Look up yonder at the Acropolis;

there too she stands, or will soon be made to stand — Athena Promachos, Athena the Forefighter, in full panoply towering toward the skies, looking off on the sea in proud defiance at the East. Manifestly the Gods were fighting for their people; let it be imaged before all eyes: then we have Art, which is the Divine appearing in our material world to the senses. Many a regret rises that one can not see how those ancient Artists brought the Goddess down from Olympus and revealed her to men after beholding her at Marathon.

The most prominent object on the plain of Marathon is an artificial mound, perhaps thirty feet high at present; upon it is growing some low brushwood. It is generally considered to be the tomb of the 192 Athenians who were buried on the battle-field and had there a monument on which their tribe and their names were written. To the summit of this mound the traveler will ascend and sit down; he will thank the brambles growing upon it that they have preserved it so well in their rude embrace from the leveling rains. He may reasonably feel that he is upon the rampart which separates the East from the West. Yonder just across this narrow strait are the mountains of Euboea, snow-capped and loftily proud, yet they stooped their heads to the Persian conqueror. All the islands of the sea submitted, Asia Minor submitted. But here-upon this shore defiantly facing the East, was the first successful resistance to the Oriental principle; its supporters could hardly do more than make a landing upon these banks, when down from the mountains swept fire and whirlwind, burning them up, driving them into the sea. Here then our West begins or began in Space and Time, we, might say upon this very mound; that semicircular sweep of hills yonder forms the adamantine wall which shut out Orientalism. Regard their shape once more; they seem to open, like a huge pair of forceps, only in order to close again and press to death.

Strange is the lot of the men buried here, the unconscious instruments of a world's destiny, nameless except two or three possibly. Yet they had some mighty force in them and back of them; one is quite inclined to think that they must have remotely felt in some dim far-off presentiment what lay in their deed for the future, and that such feeling nerved their arms to a hundredfold intensity. Here upon the mound this question comes home to us before all others: What is man but that which he is ready to die for? Such is his earthly contradiction: if he have that for which he is willing to give his life, then he has a most vital, perdurable energy; but if he have nought for which he would die, then he is already dead, buried ignobly in a tomb of flesh.

But what is this Greek principle which Marathon has preserved for us against the Orient? It is not easy to be formulated in words, to anybody's complete satisfaction. Politically, it is freedom; in Art, it is Beauty; in Mind, it is Philosophy; and so on, through many other abstract predicables. Perhaps we may say that the fundamental idea of Greece is the self-development of the individual in all its phases — the individual state, the individual city or town, the individual man. Henceforth the task is to unfold the germ which lies within, removed from external trammels — to give to the individual a free, full, harmonious development. Thus will be produced the great types of states, of men, of events; still, further, these types will then be reproduced by the artist in poetry, in marble, in history and in many other forms. This second production or reproduction, is, indeed, of all Grecian things, the most memorable.

The battle of Marathon is itself a type and has always been considered by the world as a supreme type of its kind, representing a phase of the spiritual. Athens from this moment has the spirit of which the Marathonian deed is only an utterance. Soon that spirit will break forth in all directions, producing new eternal types, just as Marathon is such a type in its way. Athenian plastic Art, Poetry, Philosophy are manifestations of this same spirit and show in a still higher degree than the battle, the victory over Orientalism. The second Persian invasion came, but it was only a repetition of the first one; it too was defeated at Marathon, which was the primitive Great Deed, the standing image to Greece of herself and all of her possibilities. Hence the use of it so often by her writers and speakers, as well as by those of the entire Western world.

With Marathon, too, History properly begins; that is, the stream of History. Now it becomes a definite, demonstrable, unbroken current sweeping down to our own times. Before Marathon, indeed, there is History, and much History, but it is in flashes, short or long, then going out in darkness. The history of Greece itself before Marathon is merely an agglomeration of events quite disconnected. The head waters take their start at Marathon; Oriental bubblings there are in abundance, but no stream. In fact it could not be otherwise, such is just the character of the Orient: to be unable to create this historical continuity. But the West has it, and it was won at Marathon, marking the greatest of all transitions both in the form and in the substance of History. Moreover the historic consciousness now arises; History for the first time is able to record itself in an adequate manner. If you now scan him closely, you will find that man has come to the insight that he has done in these days something worthy of being remembered forever. But where is the scribe to set it down? Behold, here he comes, old Herodotus, the Father of History, with the first truly historical book, in which he has written together with the rest of the Persian War the noble record of just this great Marathonian deed. Thus with the worthy action appears the man worthy of transmitting its glory.

Still the traveler remains upon the top of the mound, asking himself: Why is Marathon so famous? Other battles have had the same disparity of numbers between the two sides, and the same completeness of victory, while they have had the same principle of freedom and nationality at stake. The battle of Morgarten with its 1600 Swiss against 20,000 Austrians is often cited, and is sometimes called the Swiss Marathon. But Morgarten to the world is an obscure skirmish, it is not one of the heroic deeds which determined a civilization; it is not one of the hallowed symbols of the race. This then must be the cause: Greece has created to a large extent what we may call the symbols of our Western world — the typical deeds, the typical men, the typical forms which are still the ideals by which we mould our works and to which we seek, partially at least, to adjust our lives.

Marathon therefore stands for a thousand battles; all other struggles for freedom, of which our Occident has been full, are merely echoes, repetitions, imitations to a certain extent of that great primitive action. And Greece is just the nation in History which was gifted with the power of making all that she did a type of its kind. The idea of the West she first had, in its instinctive form, in its primal enchanting bloom; most happily she embodied that idea in her actions making them into eternal things of beauty.

That is, all the deeds of Greece are works of Art. In this sense the battle of Marathon may be called a work of Art. Grandeur of idea with perfect realization is the definition of such a work, and is that quality which elevates the person who can rightly contemplate it into true insight. It fills the soul of the beholder with views of the new future world and makes him for a time the sharer of its fruits. Marathon is only that single wonderful event, yet it is symbolical of all that are to come after it — you may say, embraces them all; it tells the race for the first time what the race can do, giving us a new hope and a new vision. So indeed does every great work of Art and every great action; but this is the grand original, it is the prophecy of the future standing there at the opening of History, telling us what we too may become, imparting to us at this distance of time a fresh aspiration.

One step further let us push this thought till it mirror itself clearly and in completeness. The Athenians were not only doers of beautiful deeds, they were also the makers of beautiful things to represent the same — they were artists. Not only a practical, but an equal theoretic greatness was theirs; in no people that has hitherto appeared were the two primal elements of Human Spirit, Will and Intelligence, blended in such happy harmony; here, as in all their other gifts there was no overbalancing, but a symmetry which becomes musical. They first made the deed the type of all deeds, made it a Marathon; then they embodied it in an actual work of Art. They were not merely able to enact the great thought, but also to put it into its true outward form, to be seen and admired of men. Their action was beautiful, often supremely beautiful, — but that was not enough; they turned around after having performed it, and rescued it from the moment of time in which it was born and in which it might perish, and then made it eternal in marble, in color, in prose, in verse.

Thus we can behold it still. On the temple of Wingless Victory at Athens is to be seen at this day a frieze representing the battle of Marathon. There is still to be read that tremendous war poem, the *Persae* of Æschylus, who also fought at Marathon; the white heat of this first conflict and of the later Persian war can still be felt in it through the intervening thousands of years. Upon the summit of the mound where we now stand, ancient works of Art were doubtless placed; the stele inscribed with the names of the fallen is mentioned by Pausanias. Only a short distance from this tomb ancient substructions can still be observed; temples and shrines, statues and monuments must have been visible here on all sides; to the sympathetic eye the whole plain will now be whitened with shapes of marble softly reposing in the sunshine. The Greeks are indeed the supreme artistic people, they have created the beautiful symbols of the world; they have furnished the artistic type and have embodied it in many forms; they had the ideal and gave to it an adequate expression. Moderns have done other great things, but this belongs to the Greeks.

So after the mighty Marathonian deed there is at Athens a most determined struggle, a supreme necessity laid upon the people to utter it worthily, to reveal it in the forms of Art and thus to create Beauty. Architecture, Sculpture, Poetry spring at once and together to a height which they have hardly since attained, trying to express the lofty consciousness begotten of heroic action. Philosophy too followed; but chiefest of all, the Great Men of the time, those plastic shapes in flesh and blood, manifesting the perfect development and harmony of mind and body, rise in Olympian majesty and make the next hundred years after the battle the supreme intellectual birth of the ages; — and all because the Gods fought along at Marathon and must thereafter be revealed.

But let us descend from this height, for we cannot stay up here all day — let us go down from the mound resuming our joyous sauntering occupation, let our emotions, still somewhat exalted, flow down quietly and mingle once more with the soft pellucid Marathonian rill. The declining sun is warning us that we have spent the greater part of a day in wandering over the plain and in sitting on the shore and the tumulus. Let us still trace the bed of the river up from the swamp; everywhere along its bank and in its channel can be seen fragments of edifices. Here are ancient bricks with mortar still clinging to them; there is the drum of a column lying in the sand, half-buried; pieces of ornamented capitals look up at you from the ground with broken smiles. Remains of a wall of carefully hewn stone speak of a worthy superstructure; the foundation of a temple of Bacchus was discovered here a few years ago, together with a curious inscription still preserved in the town. The fragments scattered along and in the channel for half a mile or more tell of the works once erected on this spot to the Heroes and Gods of the plain, and which were things of beauty. The traveler will seek to rebuild this group of shrines and temples, each in its proper place and with suitable ornament; he will fill them with white images, with altars and tripods; he will call up the surging crowd of merry Greek worshipers passing from spot to spot at some festival.

As one walks slowly through the fields in the pleasant sun, a new delight comes over him at the view of the flowers of Marathon. Everywhere they are springing up over the plain, though it be January still — many of them and of many kinds, daisies, dandelions, and primroses — looking a little different from what they do at home, yet full as joyous. The most beautiful is a kind of poppy unknown to me elsewhere; so let me call it the Marathonian poppy. In most cases it wraps its face in a half-closed calyx, as the Greek maiden covers forehead and chin in her linen veil; still you can look down into the hood of leaves and there behold sparkling dark eyes. Some of the flowers, however, are entirely open, some only in bud yet; then there is every variety of color, red, purple, and blue, with infinite delicate shadings. One tarries among them and plays after having gone through the earnest battle; he will stoop down and pluck a large handful of them in order to arrange them in groups passing into one another by the subtlest hues. So, after being in such high company, one gladly becomes for a time a child once more amid the Marathonian poppies.

If it were in me, I would like to manifest a little sentiment over the name of the flower in modern Greek. It is called *loulouthi* — the most beautiful word for a beautiful thing that I know of in any language, particularly if it be spoken low from tender lips and be reached by gentle fingers from bosom throbbing visibly faster. The ancient Greek word was *anthos;* herein the voice of the daughter far surpasses that of the mother, to my ear at least. And there are other names in Modern Greek of which the same complimentary thing can be said, but there are some designations concerning which just the opposite must be affirmed. At the mention of that word *loulouthi*, as I recollect, the face of the speaker lights up, the eye kindles, the voice grows softer, indeed the whole appearance is transformed, while the image of the thing and the music of the word unite in producing one delightful melody in the soul. Such are my associations with the name that it speaks of green fields, and wavy slopes, of transparent rills running through olive orchards, with the song of maidens gathering the fruit, all in Greek sunshine — making together a harmony which seems to be uttered only by that one word — *loulouthi.*

Out of the field of poppies I pass into the narrow neck which led me early this morning from the village into the plain. As I turn back and look again at those lunar-shaped hills, they seem to glance more fiercely than ever towards the East, inviting the foe into their retreating folds in order to envelop and crush him. The first shadow of evening lies upon the plain; the conifer towers up in the middle of the level expanse; it is still the sentinel standing there, now more deeply muffled in his war-cloak, but looking out watchfully upon the sea as if the enemy were yet expected there and he was ready to shout the warning to the hills. The mound, too, can be seen in the distance, slightly swelling above the surface of the plain, but soon its outline has mingled with the shadows. After going forward a little further I turn around once more and look, it is the last view of the plain of Marathon — I bid it good-bye and resolutely set my face in the other direction.

At the entrance to the village I met the schoolmaster, cordial as ever, and apparently waiting for my return. I asked him to take me to the school-house, though the school had been dismissed an hour or more. It was not a palace, yet it was one of the better houses of the place; pupils' benches were very low, teacher's desk very high. As you pick up a text-book you will find essentially the ancient idiom written in the ancient letters; it were not hard to imagine some old Greek pedagogue trouncing his boys on the spot. The youth of the village can still read of the great actions here in the same tongue in which they were first recorded — the great actions performed upon this soil by men whom the Greek people still delight to call their ancestors. Yet when I asked the schoolmaster whether he had ever read Herodotus' account of the battle, he replied that he had not. But he had written poetry, like some other schoolmasters, and he began to recite me his verses. Great pleasure it gave to see that the Muses still continue to hover delightfully around Marathon.

As I come out of the school-house in the late dusk of the evening, large fires are blazing up at various points on the mountains. One thinks of those ancient war-signals that leaped from peak to peak rousing the people to resist the invader. Now it denotes the presence of a different race — the Wallachian shepherd who has driven in his herd and kindled his camp-fire around which he is to repose for the night. It is quite chilly, while the day has been very agreeable on account of the sunshine; I would not like to be in his place, though yesterday evening I thought that I might have to seek his company with the warmth of his fire and of his bed of leaves. Under the almond tree the Didaskali walks with me in pleasant chat, the tender almond blossoms of mid-winter drooping over our heads in the soft twilight.

I come back to the wineshop feeling as if I had fought a day at Marathon — wearied, yet full of triumphant joy like a returning soldier. After supper my audience was again before me, ready for a speech which I did not make; but they were equally eager to hear strange stories from the other world, whose inhabitant in their presence they curiously gazed upon. One of the Albanians, observing that I talked French with the schoolmaster and Greek with the rest of them, while I said that my native tongue was English, asked me how many languages I knew. I gave him the number with which I had more or less occupied myself at different times of my life, when he crossed himself on his breast rapidly, took off his headkerchief, and made a long profound bow, muttering a prayer not to me but to the Virgin, as I understood him. What he meant by all this ceremony, I do not know; but I imagine that he only intended to pay his respects to what he considered the biggest fib he had ever heard in his life. I do not propose to repeat to you the number which I mentioned, lest you may go through with some gesticulations like the Albanian.

The Papas, that long-haired Achaean, was also on hand, and again introduced the subject of baptism, most discordant theme at Marathon. I shifted quickly to the answer of another question which led me to tell of the city where I lived; — St. Louis among her other virtues is capable of being translated into tolerable Greek. I spoke of her commerce, of her great river, of her railroads with their enormous distances yet speedy transit. I spoke of her population, now a tragic theme, alas! too deep for tears. Five hundred thousand at least she had, I said, and I do not believe that I stopped there. Little did I then think that a plague would so soon sweep over our fair city, a plague worse than war, worse than cholera, and at one fell swoop would carry off hundreds of thousands of our best citizens — that plague of a census. Utter astonishment there was on those Albanian faces, but the ideas must have been vague, for one of the men asked me whether Greenland was near my city — whereat the schoolmaster sharply reproved the questioner. But for many minutes I continued the encomiastic vein, and I cannot but think that Agios Loudophikus will remain in memory a little while at Marathon. Such was then, the bright vision of our home, beheld in the far distance through Marathonian gleams.

But will this city ever mean to the world the thousandth part of what Marathon means? Will it ever make a banner under which civilization will march? Will it ever create a symbol which nations will contemplate as a thing of beauty and as a hope-inspiring prophecy of their destiny? Will it rear any men to be exemplars for the race? Alas! no such man has she yet produced, very little sign of such things is here at present; we are not a symbol-making people, do not know nor care what that means; our ambition is to make canned beef for the race — and to correct the census. St. Louis has some fame abroad as a flour market, but she is likely to be forgotten by ungrateful man as soon as he has eaten his loaf of bread or can get it from elsewhere. A great population she has doubtless, greater than Athens ever had; but I can not see, with the best good-will, that in the long run there is much difference between the 350,000 who are here and the 150,000 who are not, but were supposed to be. Marathon river is often a river without water, but will turbid Mississippi with her thousands of steamboats — stop! this strain is getting discordant, at Marathon should be heard no dissonance, least of all the dissonance of despair. Yes, there is hope; while the future lasts — and it will be a long time before that ceases — there is hope. The Marathonian catabothron is certain to rise here yet, with many other catabothrons and form with native rivers a new stream unheard of in the history of the world. Who of us has not some such article of faith? When this valley has its milliard of human beings in throbbing activity over its surface, we, all of us I doubt not, shall look back from some serene height and behold them; we shall then see that so many people have created their beautiful symbol.

V. FROM MARATHON TO MARCOPOULO.

The first stage of my trip was now accomplished. When I left Athens on foot, you will recollect that I was not certain of reaching Marathon; but Marathon now lies behind me a conquered territory, and I am resolved to push forward to some other destination; where it is, I do not exactly know, but I am going to follow the image. Up the Euripus lies Aulis, the port where the hosts of Agamemnon embarked for Troy; perchance some ancient shapes may still haunt the spot; thither accordingly let us turn our steps. It will be a fair walk of two days; at the end of the first day is a convenient town called Marcopoulo, where there is reported to be a *khan* or Greek inn. Aristides, the merchant, is going part of the way; him we shall accompany with fresh delight.

So favorable had the trip been thus far that all thought of danger from brigands had quietly passed out of mind. There was an unconscious assurance on every side that the country was perfectly safe; people were seen at work everywhere, and people who work are not robbers and will not tolerate robbery. Men were manifestly the same here as in other parts of the world — just as honest and just as orderly; it would have been a contemptible piece of cowardice to have felt insecure any longer.

A little after daylight I rose — daylight does not come too early at this season — and took my position before the wineshop, observing the people pass to their labor in the fields. All were hastening toward the plain — men, women, and children; it was the season for trimming the vines and picking the olives; every hand could find something to do. The long-haired Papas went by with his pruning-hook, leading a little girl whom he in fatherly pride showed to me as a future Cleopatra; his wife, with a babe in her arms and a large grubbing-hoe on her shoulder, passed, adjusting more closely her head-wrappage as she approached. Also the Dikastes the village judge, went by, bearing an implement of labor, dressed to-day in his old clothes, yet keeping on his Parisian hat. It was a working day at Marathon.

Soon the merchant appeared with his store upon the back of the little donkey; from the small company which had gathered before the wineshop we started on our way up the valley amid friendly farewells. The pleasant waters of the Marathonian river met us with the incessant babble of a baby, and a baby river it is. The village slowly recedes; one turns around often and looks at the houses lying along the banks of the stream and sending up blue wreaths of smoke in idyllic tranquillity. Beyond the village let us glance once more into the plain where the battle was fought, and whither groups of peasants are now moving; still further beyond let us catch at intervals the faint blue sparkle of the surface of the sea. But look at the skies yonder; clouds are gathering over the plain, sullen squadrons of them are hurrying along, preparing for a Marathonian battle of the elements. Yet one must pass on, though hesitatingly; there is a peculiar emotion as one separates from this historic spot; he has a feeling of weight, the weight of a mighty past, which, though departed forever, still casts a dark outline upon the soul; it is a monument whose very shadow is heavy and burdens with its presence.

But not ancient story alone is found here; some traces are left of intervening times. Yonder at the entrance to the valley is the ruin of a Turkish tower erected for the purpose of watching this region. Is is now wholly deserted, but it stands as one of the mementos of centuries of hateful oppression. The merchant tells me that three hundred Greeks were murdered there during the Revolution by the Turks. It is a spot haunted and accursed — shunned by the country people who in that locality can still hear at the middle of the night the curses of the infidels, with the groans of dying men. Now it is left to decay — the sign of odious tyranny which also has fallen to ruin ; and the prayer which the traveler puts up, as he passes it, is, that never again this or any other tower may watch over an enslaved Marathon.

At the turn of the road the town disappears, though the chattering stream is still leaping merrily along at our side. But the clouds which all morning have threatened village and plain, now overtake us and begin to dash down large drops of water into our faces. This was at first regarded merely as a sportive sprinkle from Zeus, but the matter continued to grow more serious, and it soon became manifest that the God was in earnest, if not in anger. My great coat became saturated and very heavy, so my obliging companion loosened from his pack a shaggy capote and handed it to me for a change. This garment is very useful for such weather ; it is made of goat's hair so compactly woven that it sheds rain. It has joined to it at the top a pointed cap of the same material, into which the head is thrust and protected. My friend also insisted upon taking my bundle and laying it on the back of that poor heavy-laden donkey, but I protested and continued to carry it myself.

I have already told you that my companion is called by the classic appellation of Aristides ; he informs me that he has an uncle at Oropus, who is a schoolmaster by the name of Aristoteles. The ancient designations are not without their effect ; I rejoice that the Marathonian name Aristides still lingers here and seeks my company, having returned to its former haunts ; for ancient Aristides, called the Just, was in the battle of Marathon and notably commanded a detachment of Athenians. So I walk along with a veritable Aristides, talking Greek to me, and revealing, one will think, certain spiritual outlines of his great namesake. But he is a man of business and herein has a decided modern tinge ; his main characteristic is brightness, coupled with a youthful manner which is peculiarly Greek, though he be over thirty. A quick nervous action accompanies all his movements, showing a spirit restless and struggling with its limits; of steady patience he has but little, particularly for his patience-trying donkey. His friendliness is unbounded, yet not ostentatious; he has already invited me to put up with him. at Oropus and see his uncle Aristoteles the schoolmaster, who, he claims, is no unworthy representative of the illustrious name.

At this point we may notice an honorable trait of the modern Greek: it is the desire of inheriting the greatness as well as the fame of his ancient kinsmen. Hence these names of the distinguished worthies of antiquity are very common at present; sometimes they make an incongruous impression. One meets with Plato in baggy blue breeches and pointed red moccasins carrying greasy oil-skins; one beholds Demosthenes in fez and fustanella belaboring his refractory mule; in a country town I saw two women engaged in furious combat, using their distaffs as weapons — they were Penelope and Clytemnestra.

Also my friend Aristides, like his ancient namesake is a true patriot with a keen insight into the evils and dangers of Greece. The smallness of her territory, her dependence on the whims and interests of the Great European Powers, her lack of internal development, her manifold governmental ills are subjects of the sharpest regret; still, he has hope and thinks that in the fifty years of independence she has done wonders. Just at present the political outlook seems gloomy; he feels certain that Turkey will not yield the limits ceded by the Treaty of Berlin. "Patience, oh just Aristides!" is all that the sympathizing stranger can say to him, "far more difficult things have been accomplished even in our day." Whereat with dark eyes brimming and with a nervous twitch he pokes his stick into the sides of the donkey, which has taken advantage of the interesting conversation to come to a full pause.

Nor should we pass by this occasion without noticing another leading trait of the modern Greek. Not only does he look up to the ancient worthies of his nation and seek to inherit their celebrity and culture, but he has also a modern Idea, which constitutes the very marrow of his being. That Idea is the enfranchisement and regeneration of the entire Greek race; in fact, the whole Orient is to receive a new birth through the new Greece. The Greek Revolution failed to emancipate the Greek; only a little over one million out of twelve were then freed. "But," says Aristides, "we won then by force of arms; now we shall conquer by intelligence. We intend to kindle such a light here in the East that the Turk will have to get out of its glare. Thessaly is already ours by the consent of Europe; then Macedonia will follow; Constantinople is the goal and we shall soon be there in our ancient imperial seat. To-day our university educates the brain of the Turkish empire; those barbarians would be helpless without Greek intellect. Yes, the Orient must become Hellenic again, and Constantinople is to be the capital."

Such is the great modern Idea of which our modern Aristides is a most zealous expounder. But it is just this Idea which Western Europe from various causes has refused to accept. England, in particular, has set herself against the hopes of a whole race allied in religion and civilization, in favor of the barbarous Ottoman. Assuredly the Oriental policy of England has been a mistake; it is always a mistake to run counter to the struggles of a great people for enfranchisement and unity. Yet such has been hitherto the attitude of England in the East. If she had put herself at the head of this strong national aspiration instead of stifling it, the vexed Oriental question would now have been solved, or have looked to a happy solution in the near future.

Indeed, upon an inspection of some of these Oriental transactions of the English, one is inclined to ask them strange questions; among others this one obtrudes itself into the soul: Do you then believe that there is a God in the universe? If there be, he is with the people who are with deepest longing and agony struggling for light and freedom, however awkward and absurd these attempts may be. England does not believe in the deity of ignorance and slavery; yet she persists in doing that which she does not allow her God to do. She preaches at home the divinity of liberty and humanity, and will defend the same with the last drop of English blood; but abroad she upholds the Mahommedan Tartar against the Christian Greek. Strange that England has still any faith in a God. Yet she is to-day the most religious country in Europe, it is said; her upper classes are often declared to be the only upper classes who are generally imbued with a strong feeling of religion. The Englishman has certainly a high conception both of deity and humanity; he would scout a God who could create the institution of slavery or make heaven a harem. But looking at the Eastern question and its history can any one doubt that he will retain his fellowman in bondage to strangers in faith and race, that he will give himself privileges which he refuses to his God? The worship of the highest, most universal type ought to produce the highest, most universal conduct; but it must be set down as characteristic of England, and also of New England, indeed of the whole Anglo-Saxon consciousness, to divorce speculation from action, to nurse conviction with effeminate fondness just one day of the week, then carefully to lock it up the remaining six as something too tender and impracticable for daily use in this exceedingly practical world of ours. So the Greek Idea is theoretically very fine, even merits our sympathy, but it is not practical. Ah yes; what we worship as truth in God, we put down as a lie, or at least as a delusion, in Man.

Who, therefore, can blame Aristides if he has no love for England? I believe that he has a right to his indignation; therein many an Englishman, I would fain believe the majority, would join him and me. So we go on discussing in the rain the Great Idea, which is the matter always uppermost in the heart of the Greek, and which, I imagine, he pours out more freely to an American, who can not help being sympathetic. But from the Great Idea he suddenly falls to punching the donkey, which takes many a little liberty during the time we are absorbed in conversation, and will not suffer us to forget its important presence.

This is the picture which I would have you look at with a little interest: two persons in shaggy capotes are walking up the valley of a small stream, amid the gray drizzle; they often slip on the wet stones with their soggy shoes which are continually getting broader and threaten to go to pieces; they slowly wind around in the tortuous mulepath through the many folds of the hills covered everywhere with underbrush and rocks; their two voices can always be heard, in question and response, wandering through the deserted glens which, affrighted at times, send back a fleeting answer; one of the voices is strewing curious fragments of broken Greek through all these solitudes, to the repeated horror of fair nymph Echo. Clouds at intervals descend to the earth and enwrap the two pedestrains in a moist sheet of mist; then they rise again, having discharged their watery burden, and for a moment break into silvery translucent fleeces behind which gleams the Sun, whom they now promise to unveil; but there follows a new gathering of the cloudy squadrons over Marathon, which pass heavily above and throw down a pitiless shower. Aristides turning nervously around and looking up at the skies, sees the fresh storm coming; getting in a hurry he pokes the donkey.

And that donkey, the third of our goodly company, must not be omitted. Patiently it steps along before us, selecting always the securest way through the slippery rocks, while we blindly follow. Not infrequently it will prick up its long ears and look intelligently at some object by the side of the road, then it will calmly lay them back at a change of thought. That play of the donkey's ears — backwards and forwards — what is the meaning of it? That were a new and curious subject of speculation; to me it is one of the great mysteries of creation. Once he turned around his big head and with jeering eye looked at us engaged in animated talk, then mingled a loud bray with the Great Idea; so the two notes went echoing together over the hills.

The donkey is small, not much larger than a Newfoundland dog, but he is every inch — a donkey. He has a sort of dry humor in him which always makes him a good companion. Imperturbable, almost indifferent to blows, in lead-colored coat of hair he plods on, playing backwards and forwards his ears, having some secret inner entertainment all to himself. He is an indispensable beast of burden mid these stony mountain paths; no horse could ever travel over this road with safety. The donkey is not rapid, but he sets those little round hoofs of his down on the earth with a swiftness and dexterity that make his four feet twinkle like so many dancing stars. See how mincingly he treads, picking out the way so daintily, never making a false step — a solid joy to the sympathetic companion behind him. But at times he unaccountably stops right in the road, stops us, stops the conversation; then comes another fateful punch from the hand of Aristides.

On the back of the little animal is the store of Aristides, who has just supplied the women of Marathon with dry goods, in return for which he takes the fruits of the earth; he has now a large quantity of almonds in an enormous package lashed to the crupper of the donkey. Thus the greater portion of internal trade is carried on through these regions. The traveling merchant is one of the main figures in the social organism. He is usually capable and well-informed; he scatters not only goods but ideas, especially the Great Idea. He knows every body, he brings information to these villages in regard to the latest diplomatic relations between Greece and Turkey; he scores early every approach toward Constantinople. New thoughts, new hopes, new political catchwords he sets in circulation among the people, all of which in their own good time will bear fruit; but his chief yet self-imposed duty is to be the unflinching advocate of the Great Idea. Sharp at a bargain this Greek trader is without a doubt; but my Aristides, I do not believe, is dishonest, he is just, I affirm, notwithstanding the bad name which many people give the Greeks. Certainly he is very friendly, and I should call him tender-hearted, were it not for the way in which he pokes his stick into the withers of our third companion, the donkey. This fact I have repeated to you before, I believe; still my repetitions are scarce as one in a hundred to the thrusts of Aristides.

Down comes a heavy shower again; we pass through a wild mountain glen in which is situated an old lonely mill with mossy wheel; we reach a grove of beautiful plane-trees and ford the Marathonian brook, now somewhat swollen with the rains. In this secluded spot a man dressed in white fustanella approaches and talks with us; Aristides tells me that it is a neighboring land-owner. I was surprised to find in him a person of an exquisitely refined address, with an ease and grace worthy of the most cultivated society. The wild scenery around us was in marked contrast to his courtly manners. He inquired the news, was deeply interested in politics, as all Greeks are; on learning my nationality he spoke in friendly terms of America, and at parting he put the two latest newspapers from Athens into my hands. His polished address seemed like a brilliant gem lost amid those solitudes; I would have picked up the gem and brought it along, if I had been able.

Still Aristides and myself converse, walking defiantly through the passing showers, and many are the things which he tells me. His characterization of the various peoples of Greece is good and trustworthy, for it is the result of long intercourse. Implicitly he places the Greek first of all races; he is himself of pure Greek blood and takes pride in his lineage. He says that there are very few genuine Greeks in these parts, that there are more at Oropus, his town, than elsewhere. He considered the Wallachians to be a more capable people than the Albanians, though he thought well of the latter; for Albanians, besides making the best soldiers in the East, had turned out excellent scholars, philologists and theologians.

I liked the talk of Aristides much; there was in it no excess of any kind, it had the Greek moderation as well as the Greek aspiration after an ideal; his condemnatory judgments of men and things would always in the end brighten into hopefulness. Only concerning a very few of the country women in these regions, his report, given in response to a question of mine, was not favorable. But his statement in regard to the morals of the Greek peasantry in general may be taken as true, and coincides with the declaration of many observers, that in this respect they are the most exemplary of all peoples in Europe.

At one place he suddenly stops, shouting a halt to the donkey, which willingly obeys. With great deliberation reaching his hand into his pocket, he takes out a pentari — a coin worth not quite one cent — and deposits it in a small square hole hewn into a stone which stood at the side of the road. I asked him what he did that for? He pointed to a small dilapidated building in the distance and said it was for the repairs of that church. The offerings of the pious wayfarers were placed here; accordingly I went up and laid down my cent too, then continued my journey, feeling much better, I thought. There lie the two cents exposed on the stone alongside of the road, without danger, it seems, of being pilfered. I thought to myself: Where in the neighborhood of my town could two cents lie exposed in that way without being snapped up by one of her bank presidents, perhaps, or at least by some ruthless urchin who would bring them in all speed to the nearest candy shop?

Then Aristides gives the donkey a smart poke, and we are off again, having performed our work of charity. Not without a happy sense of victory, not without an internal feeling of unassailableness by the tempest do we draw our meandering line around the hills, through the vales, over swollen brooks, dashing into walls of clouds and showers. At last the storm gives up the task of subduing us, the squadrons flee, the Sun bursts out of the sky with shining face and laughs in a chorus with us.

In the meantime Aristides becomes also more confiding; he tells me the story of his courtship and marriage; how he fell in love with a pair of eyes jet-black and of infinite sparkle but without any money, though there were wealthy brothers; how he succeeded in getting the wealthy brothers to give a portion to the sister, 3,000 drachmas — say 600 dollars — cash; how he then pounced down and carried off both maiden and money, the lucky man! Thereupon in the pride of success he embarked in an unfortunate speculation, lost all, all his, all hers, and more too, the unlucky man! Now the black eyes, no longer so sparkling as they were, he possesses still, but without the beautiful drachmas; nay, he has in addition two small mouths, making four altogether, which must have bread. At present he is reduced to being a pedlar, to going about the country and selling by the cent's worth, — it is a lot too hard, too humiliating! "Alas! Aristides," cries the condoling companion at his side, "such is the common destiny of us all; thou hast indeed seen better days, so have I, so has the donkey."

But Aristides cannot be melancholy for more than a moment, he always turns the darkest thoughts of the past into bright gleams of hope. He is not weary of life, far from it; nor does he love his wife the less because he has lost her money, as is the case with some men whom I know. The only failing I have found in him is the energy and persistency with which he punches the ribs of our patient third companion, the donkey. The brave little animal still moves its ears backwards and forwards with a silent humor; it still trips along with an inner complacency, although I notice that with heavy burdens and bad roads it is beginning to give out. At last out of so many steps taken to-day it makes one false step — Aristides and I have made a dozen such at least, without any load, and we have slipped and slid quite to the ground on the wet stones; but that one misstep brings it to its knees, then down prostrate under the superincumbent weight. Thereupon follow still sharper punches than ever; I had to cry out: "Be just, oh Aristides, be just even to the donkey; see what a burden of yours it is carrying, think how courageously it has held out to-day, show yourself now worthy of your great namesake; be just."

So with kindly hands we help up our fallen companion; passing a little hill we enter the small hamlet of Capandriti where we hasten to take off all his fardels and give him rest. Then we go into the wineshop and sit down on the bench; we are still wet, but we dry ourselves with abundant draughts of the golden recinato — that wonderful liquid, which wets the dry man and dries the wet man. It is already high noon; we order a dinner of eggs fried in oil, and black bread; no Parisian dinner, according to my taste, ever equaled the luxury of that repast. There are also two merry Greek hunters at the wineshop who at once take a share in the talk and in the viands.

Let us now look at Aristides with our two new associates, squatting at the flue and making a cup of coffee. Each of them has a small tin pot, holding hardly as much as the ordinary teacup; this is filled with water and shoved into the coals by its long handle till the water boils; then a couple of spoonfuls of coffee with some sugar is thrown into it, when it is shoved back into the coals and brought to a boil the second time. Thus they squat there before the fire, preparing their warm beverage and talking politics. All Greek men do likewise, and indeed all Greek men cook, and often cook well; if the wife happens to be in the fields at some task, the man will go to work and get a dinner, and a good one too. Many a Palicari have I seen twirling before the fire a spit laden with a turkey or with bits of meat; he knew what he was about. But the coffee of Aristides is done; it is not discolored with milk, nor is it strained or settled; he pours it off into a cup and sips it with a decided relish. I have already said that a cup of coffee of this kind, prepared by the keeper, is usually sold for one cent in the provinces; but often it is prepared by the drinker himself for the sake of greater economy.

Such is the picture, then, which the traveler will carry away with him from many a hearth in this country: several men are grouped around the fire, cooking their coffee; each has his long-handled cup which he manipulates with a curious dexterity, in the mean time talking in animated gestures of the Treaty of Berlin or discussing the last phase of the Great Idea. I hold that those old fellows, politicians and even philosophers, were of a similar cast and had similar ways. A political ideal is still a part of the intellectual inheritance of the modern Greek; it belongs to him as much as it did to ancient Plato. I should say that these people are still the children, rustic though genuine children, of the father of the Platonic Republic. They have not his notions exactly, but they are like him;

they are forever building the gorgeous commonwealth of new Hellas in the pure ethereal blue of their own heavens. What man will not take pleasure in looking at it, moving there in the skies amid gold-bordered clouds — will not shout applause at the lofty structure afloat, crying out: Bring it down to the earth and set it firmly on eternal rock, if ye can! Nay, what one of us would not give, if we could only catch the rope, a good pull to help fetch it down into solid reality? Poverty may cramp into helpless fetters, writers may scoff with bitter satire, the Great Powers may violently repress, still the Greek is going to Constantinople, if not by land, then through the air.

But alas! now I have to part company with the merchant Aristides, who has to attend to business, selling his wares from door to door and haggling with the women of the village. I would be glad to go with him through the country here, which he knows so well, if I could wait for him; still I have promised to visit him, if convenient, at Oropus, and see the worthy schoolmaster Aristoteles. I have spoken so much about Aristides because I believe him to be a typical man of his class, being a kind of mediatorial character among those towns on his route, and carrying on not only a commercial but also an intellectual exchange. For he brings them not goods alone, but light. He may sometimes be made the instrument of political partisanship, still every throb of his heart beats for his country. After he had put me into the right road, we parted with renewed hopes of seeing each other at Oropus.

So I am alone again — yet, I maintain, in good company; with package slung over my shoulder and heavy staff in hand I pass down the road to Marcopoulo. The town is, according to report, about three hours distant; the Greeks measure distance by hours. The great coat is no longer wet and unwieldy; hunger and thirst have been fully satisfied; the clouds above are breaking into golden shreds which race joyously through the sunbeams and attune the beholder to their sport; with light-hearted buoyancy he looks off before himself up to the green summits over which he is to pass. This traveling in Greece is of itself intoxication, were there no reciuato.

But the sunshine was of short duration. Once more the clouds began to gather in heavy black masses and dash against the tops of the mountains; then the battle in Heaven opened with new energy. One may well imagine that the scene was somewhat similar to that which the old Greek beheld over these ridged summits and wrought into fable; it was one form of the combat between the Giants and the Gods. Zeus, the pure ethereal sky, Diospiter, the father of day, is surrounded by the conflict of dark, many-shaped monsters — of Briareus the hundred-handed, of Typhon, fire-spitting, reaching to the skies; but in the end the father of light sends them down to gloomy Tartarus and asserts anew his place on the sunny throne of Olympus.

Thus one looks at the angry gathering of the tempest with its many shapes and transmutations, and he can not help thinking that he beholds the natural source of the highest principle of Greek Mythology — the conflicts of its supreme God. Off there in the sky, in serene light, Zeus is seated; mostly he dwells in happy repose, but sometimes is involved in dire struggle with the gloomy powers. To-day is one of his gigantic battles; he is the cloud-compeller, rejoicing in the swift lightning, he is the heavy thunderer, as the Iliad often calls him, indicating his realm as well as his origin. Nature may be taken at this hour as the symbol of conflict within itself, as a mirror of all spiritual conflicts. Zeus is fighting the old dark Gods, the mere demons of chaos, and will put them down; then he will bring back the light and become the deity of moral order, law, and institutions, such as he was worshiped in Greece. Thus his conflicts are made the types of the conflicts of man, of struggles external and internal, of revolutions moral and political.

Greek Mythology is an utterance, the supreme poetic utterance of the race, taken from Nature directly and true to her in the highest degree, yet always reflecting therein a spiritual visage. Olympus is made up of Gods, who from physical have become also internal divinities; they have been victorious over the frantic worship of Nature whose deities now lie in Tartarus, though with many rebellious attempts to rise. So Apollo is still the sun, was once the outer sun, till he became the inner and brighter sun, transferring his seat from the East to Delphi, whither I begin now to see this path of ours is tending through many sinuosities.

But we are still here in the mountains amid the undecided battle of Zeus; in other words it is raining, raining with pitiless energy, as if this solitary pedestrian were some hundred-handed Titan to be swept down into Tartarus. The great coat has become heavier than ever; there is no tree for shelter, only a thick growth of low brushwood can be seen; there is not a single farm house for refuge along the road. Clouds collide and roll, like two contending dragons twisted together, right over me, throwing down their contents; sometimes I can see a short distance before me, sometimes a mountain of vapor falls upon me and cuts off all vision. Am I actually then some earth-born Titan, that I arouse such anger in the breast of Zeus? The modest conclusion is, that I am not, though you may think I am mounting up dizzily near to his throne in the clouds.

But what is that sound off to one side, heard very distinctly through the mist? It is a human voice, and, as it seems to me, is an utterance of pain. What can be the matter? I stop and listen, but it ceases; then I pass on through the driving rain. But there! I hear it again, off to the left; it is a child's voice, a young boy's one would conjecture. Very disagreeable it is to go out of the road; yet that voice surely has the tone of distress. So I push through the wet bushes in search of it — a most uncomfortable business in Greece, and savagely discordant with the Greek mood. I shout, shout in high Greek through the storm; but the piercing cry never seems to penetrate the thick walls of vapor shutting me in. Again the voice ceases for a time and I return to the beaten track.

I go straight into a dense cloud which has collapsed over the road; this road is now filled with a little river through which I wade up stream. Rain, Rain; the wet now touches the skin, the great coat has its full capacity of water and overflows everywhere at the edges into small cataracts. I stoop under a bush; but what is the use, the bush is as wet as I am, with pearly cascades spouting from the tip of every leaf. Such is traveling, such the traveler; but I affirm that the Greek mood is not by any means drowned out of him, he still has high company, the very highest — Jupiter Tonans with the red right hand is his next neighbor.

But there is one disturbance, I hear again that wretched voice which distresses me. Still I shall not stop; one may be excused for not being inclined to benevolence with such an overcoat. But the dolorous cry continues, coming out of the mist; it may be some human being who is worse off than even I am. So I start after it once more through the dripping brushwood, not at all in a good humor with the voice, which is spoiling the Greek mood far more than the showers of Jove. But listen! in the opposite direction on the right side of the road can be heard another and similar voice from the vaporous distance; it has the same wail, it may be an answer to the first. Are these people then all in grief, shepherds perchance, wailing over the mountains? It is impossible to help so many of them, therefore the just tourist will lean toward impartiality and help none — so onward through the falling water-walls! But the mystery of those voices coming out of the fog — what can it mean? what can it mean?

Still up the mountain the road passes, higher and higher; now the heavy rain slackens and one comes into the region of pure fog with a continuous light drizzle. One winds around peaks and gets faint views into tremendous chasms beneath, wrapped in magnifying mists; it is the world of dewy vapors and undefined shapes. Peasants I find cutting brushwood up here. How far to Marcopoulo? One hour. On, on, the distance is not long; patience, thou much-enduring, wet-skinned man! Fill thy imagination with antique clear visions and forget this outer foggy world; think of old Ulysses, the long-sufferer, who in the brine of the sea was tossed about by a storm, clinging to a billet of wood for two days, and was rewarded on shore by seeing the fairest of earthly maidens, that sweet Phaeacian girl, Nausicaa. Some such shape may be waiting for thee, when thou comest again into sunlight.

Thus the traveler in Greece passes through fierce storms and dense fogs, unconquerable, unassailable; descending the rock-strewn slope he leaps from stone to stone, with an occasional slip, but always accompanied by a bright image or perchance by a God who will help him if he falls. If he have brought the material along, he can weave many a radiant fabric out of ancient lore, as he tramps away, up hill and down over the wet rough thoroughfare. Now he descends, and the fog lifts; passing by a little church he stands on the ridge and beholds the long sweep of the mountain slanting into the green valley. Lying on the slope just below him is Marcopoulo breaking suddenly into view; its chimneys are sending up thin curls of bluish smoke which spread out at the top and join the clouds. There are bright fires on those hearths; the mere thought sends hope and gladness into the heart of the dripping traveler.

I was not slow in reaching the khan or Greek inn, which was pointed out to me by a rude-looking but friendly Albanian; this, too, is an Albanian town, though the innkeeper is a Greek. I drank a raki with my informant at the usual rate of one cent a glass, and then sat down on a bench in my heavy wet garments. It was a most dismal place for a rainy day — dark, damp, chilly, uncanny. The bench on which I sat was soon covered with little streams of water, whose fountain head was my overcoat, finding their way down the grooves, and filling the worm holes. I can say with truth that I was uncomfortable; in a fit of sinful weakness I was quite ready to curse all traveling, and harbored for an instant the thought of giving up the great tour of Greece afoot and alone. As I look back, I now consider that to have been a decisive moment, for just then the landlord came and asked me: Would you like to have a fire?

He took me to his own blazing hearth around which the

children of the household were playing — bright-eyed, dark-haired little ones, full of impudence, merriment and mockery. It is true that no small portion of the smoke refused to pass out of the room through the chimney; but who can describe the luxury of that fire, the old fire in the hearth, on the evening of a chill rainy day? I sat down before it and dried myself; soon the waters of the wet garments began to rise up around me in great clouds of vapor somewhat like those of the mountains. I sat there and steamed, as if I were some aqueous shape and were boiling in my own kettle; no aroma of incense or of burnt-offering could be more delightful than that steam as it ascended to the nostrils. The old fire-place of boyhood came back, with the merry sports of the long winter evening; but that was without the luxury of this exhalation wrapping me in my own clouds. Now I wish to be only a traveler and to travel on rainy days.

The landlord made the first preparation for supper; he placed an ample pot of beans over the fire. The mother was absent on a visit; the father went out to his wineshop, and a pretty Greek girl entered to tend to the children; jet-black sparkling eyes, fair features, gentle innocence were there, yet with flashes of sadness through her young face that stole down into the emotion of the beholder. She was called Euphrosyne, that is cheerfulness, and moreover, the name of one of the Graces. I could not succeed in getting the young Grace to talk much; she was shy and doubtless understood very little of my high Greek, though I toned it down as well as I could with the popular Romaic.

But those children were not sad — three of them together came capering around the bright hearth. They were soon acquainted, nay, familiar with the stranger and began to play him little pranks. Euphrosyne, herself hardly more than a child, could not restrain them but had to laugh along with them when they tipped him over as he sat on the three-legged stool enveloped in the steam of his garments. Their Greek nature showed itself in their little Aristophanic mockeries; I could say no word, make no movement, without their throwing it back into my face in caricature. Particularly Zacharias, a little fellow of four years, showed his inborn genius in mocking my broken Greek, then all three would repeat what he said in a chorus of infant laughter.

Well, what of it? you ask. Do not all children do the same? It may be so, but I was unwilling to entertain such a thought. You must recollect I was, and you ought to be, in Greece, hence I could see and you must see in these children the infant germs of those supreme merry-makers and mockers of the world — Aristophanes and Lucian. Into such ancient shapes the little ones grow before me while I sit here at the fire, with no pleasant vapor rising now, for the garments are completely dry.

The mother comes home; it is time for supper; I congratulate myself on the prospect of taking a meal with a Greek family. The host was going to give me a place at one side, all to myself, but I asked the favor of eating with the wife and children, and he gave his consent with manifest pleasure. First, a large mat was spread out on the floor upon which we all sat down in a circle; a stool was offered to me as a special honor to the guest, but I refused it and took my place on the mat with the others. The table was brought and placed between us; it was circular, without support, and lay flat on the floor. Thus we were squatted around it; the rest took off their shoes as they sat down, and crossed their legs. I followed their example. Stocking feet, nay stockingless feet appeared there at the table, while we lapped our limbs over like so many tailors. The position was not an easy one for me, the sartorious muscle soon began to twitch and squirm with pain at this unaccustomed duty.

The large crock of bean-soup was placed upon the table, redolent with oil and steam, sending up a fragrance not ungrateful to the hungry traveler. *Kalos oriste* — they all muttered, crossing themselves several times; this was their way of saying grace, as the landlord explained. I repeated the same words and went through the crucial motions too, rather mechanically I think. I did not want to excite any religious questioning again, as I had unfortunately done at Marathon. My special distinction was to have a plate of soup all to myself; the others dipped freely into the common dish. Our bill of fare was as follows: good black bread, very palatable and nutritious, crumbled into the bean-soup; cured fish from Constantinople; goat's cheese; but the supreme delicacy of the meal was a species of clam taken from the neighboring Euripus, which was roasted in the hot ashes of the hearth and flavored with a drop of lemon juice. Finally, let it not be forgotten, for we did not forget it: a huge demijohn of recinato stood at the side of the host, its delightful gurgle would always come to our assistance and wash down the most obstinate mouthful.

Besides myself there was present another guest, a Greek from Thebes, a jolly old fellow, in a rather besmirched fustanella; he took his place on the mat barefooted, having removed his red moccasins at the door, according to custom. He sat next to the hearth, and while doing full justice to his supper, he found time to superintend the roasting of the clams. Varvouillya everybody familiarly called him. I admired and highly praised his expertness in his present occupation, whereat he exerted anew both skill and speed, of which I derived the chief benefit. Then there was the host with the demijohn at his side, a man naturally of a jovial temperament, now becoming more jovial with the minutes. The wife placed herself a little to one side with the children, squatting like the rest of us; she was very quiet, though I insisted on drinking repeatedly to the health of our hostess. She, too, probably did not understand my Greek very well; certainly I did not understand hers. The husband excused her, saying she spoke a peculiar dialect; but he would never fail to answer the toast himself, with a full bumper. He spoke Greek well; he had been a student of one of the Greek gymnasiums, and had read the ancient classics.

So we sat there around the low table, and feasted and chatted with many a merry dash at waspish old Time, proposing healths to one another with lofty compliments, not failing to drink long prosperity to our dear Hellas and our dear America. The host became illuminated, he dropped unaccountably his native Greek tongue and insisted upon talking Italian with me — a most unintelligible broken Italian, to which for the life of me I could get no clew; either he or I or both of us had become dazed. Still Varvouillya kept raking the clams out of the hot ashes and we ate them; while the host on the other side of the table replenished our mugs with recinato from the demijohn; between the twain I sat and receiyed from both directions. Meantime the children had finished their supper; they nodded, rolled over on the floor beside the hearth, and were soon asleep. The host talked louder, faster, in a still more unintelligible Italian; Varvouillya raked out the last of the clams; but there was still recinato in that demijohn.

The wife, who, if I had read her aright, had begun to grow a little sulky at our prolonged and ever-increasing festivity, now interfered; she declared that she wished to retire, and as this was her bed-room as well as parlor and kitchen, we had to vacate. Varvouillya slipped into his moccasins and slid off into the darkness somewhither, like a bat; I was shown to my chamber by the merry host who had grown very affectionate and embraced me with an unexpected kiss, not uncommon in Greece, as we parted for the night.

It requires a little touch of anger against future generations to be a writer, and I felt in altogether too good a humor to take even a note that evening; the wise and foolish things said and done must now be handed over to oblivion. But as I lay in bed and reflected on the battle of the day, I concluded that after many fluctuations, after temporary defeats even, it had ended in a glorious victory. In the forenoon I had been assailed with no little energy, but I was fortunate in having valiant Aristides as a fellow-soldier at my side; in the afternoon the enemy, enveloping me in thick clouds had attacked me alone from all quarters within and without; still I had won the day. On the whole this was my Marathon; I felt that henceforth I would pass through Greece from end to end in a kind of triumphal march. List! the rain is now beating on the roof, still the elements are angry, to-morrow threatens to be again a day of battle; but to-night at least I shall not borrow any trouble.

VI. RAINY DAY AT MARCOPOULO.

As I rose in the morning and looked out of the window, every appearance indicated that I was weather-bound. It had rained all night; though the rain had ceased falling just at that moment, the clouds looked leaden and surcharged, and flew by the window with a sullen threatening. I did not care to venture another day like the preceding; my Greek mood might under too great stress, break down. Nor could I proceed, if I would; the streams had doubtless risen to such a height that they were impassable. The nature of the Greek rainfall had often been told me by way of warning; a heavy shower descends; the brooks, previously a mere bed of dry rocks, become suddenly mountain torrents which cannot be crossed by man or beast. Nor are there any bridges worth mentioning in Greece; indeed any ordinary bridge would be apt to be swept away in the first storm.

It is winter, but winter in this country means the rainy season. In the valleys very little snow falls, and when it does fall, it lasts usually but a portion of a day. Still there is hardly a point in Greece from which you cannot see the snow upon the mountains, and in the course of a few hours you can reach the snow point. It is possible in a single excursion to pass through the four seasons at certain times of the year. I recollect a day's walk which I once took in the Parnassian region; below in the Krissæan plane at the level of the sea there was tropical vegetation in its full luxuriance; at Krissa garden vegetables grew in the open air; at Delphi, still higher in the ascent, these same vegetables would no longer grow, and the olive ceased to flourish, though it quite reached that point; about Arachoba, and a little above it, the growth of the grape had attained its highest limit and the heat of summer is scarcely felt; at the Kalyvia, in a table land on the Parnassus, the hardier grains only would thrive, and people would not remain there during the winter on account of the severity of the cold; still higher were the pine woods, and finally the unbroken surface of the snow. Thus the Greek had the advantage of all climates at his very door, and this variety of nature was stamped upon his varied and versatile character. Somewhat of the like instinct in our own country is seen in the vast summer migrations of the people; but to attain the variety of one Greek day, we have often to travel hundreds and thousands of miles.

On looking around the room, sundry indications of the tastes and customs of the people become manifest. Ancient heirlooms are here — weapons of various kinds, garments decorated in a sort of barbaric splendor with gold tinsel and strongly contrasting colors. It was here, I think, that I saw the likenesses of King Otho and Queen Amelia in rudely colored prints suspended on the wall. You may know that these persons were the former king and queen of Greece who, having been expelled, were succeeded by the present sovereigns, George and Olga. I found still among the Greeks in the provinces a lively feeling of gratitude for their former rulers, and many persons, though having no dislike for the present dynasty, thought that the previous sovereigns had been treated with gross injustice. The change was repeatedly declared to have been a revolution brought about by the politicians and schemers at Athens, backed by the intrigues of certain European powers. Still the Greek people as a whole have sanctioned the result, and it must be confessed that King Otho with his Bavarian tendencies had succeeded in making himself very unacceptable to the more aspiring portion of the Greeks.

There are no utensils for washing in the room, nor any water, but there is plenty outside, for it has rained all night; so there is no use of despairing of an ablution. I go down the stairs into the yard; the little serving-girl, pretty Euphrosyne, appears with a tin cup that has several holes in the bottom, out of which the water issues in convenient jets; she partly pours and partly holds those jets over the hands of the guest. Zacharias is also present and still keeps up his mimicry; whatever I say or do he instinctively imitates with a ludicrous twist of the mouth. The family have already breakfasted, but enough is left for me, and more — for the children come again to the table and with great freedom take hold along with me. I am sure I enjoyed their presence and I shared gladly with them all that was there. At only one thing I rebelled; it was when Zacharias took the knife from my plate and began scraping the mud from his shoes. It was so muddy out of doors, he said. Three small children keep the mother busy without attending to scrupulous niceties of housekeeping. A simple economy reigns throughout the household; a hole in the wall, besides being a window, serves as cupboard, knife box, provision chest, and for miscellaneous articles.

I would like to continue my journey, but the host tells me that it is impossible on account of the freshet, and that in particular, there is a large stream, the Asopus, which can not be forded till the waters have run out. He might be interested in detaining me, though what he said seemed very reasonable; but Varvouillya, the Theban, who also is eager to go forward to Chalcis, confirms emphatically the statements of the host. So both of us resolve to stay till to-morrow, and then make the journey together. A day, therefore, a rainy day at Marcopoulo is our destiny, for a passing shower drives us from the yard, where we are discussing the matter, into the wineshop.

A number of Albanians entered, dressed in their coarse kilts, with bandanna closely wrapped about the head; they look wonderingly, half suspiciously out of the corners of their eyes; yet there they sit and say nothing, content to gaze and puff at their paper cigarettes. The traveler will seek on a rainy day to find out something about their ways, their life, their consciousness. Now one of the main tests of the character and abiding worth of a people is the interest they take in their own origin and that of their race. Do these people know whence they came? I asked them; they knew of Albania, and that their ancestors had emigrated thence into Greece. But when? The most ready man of the company answered, that the emigration took place about the time of the Greek Revolution, but that they or their parents knew nothing of it. But it is usually placed by historians far back in the middle ages, and not fifty years ago. I tell them the fact, whereat they are surprised; but their comprehension of five centuries does not seem to differ much from that of half a century.

A still deeper test of the inherent worth and vitality of a people is, whether they keep alive the memory of their great men, reverencing them along with their deities. This remarkable fact came to light, that the Albanians in Greece still cherish the traditions concerning Scanderbeg, their great national hero, in fact, the only man of universal fame that Albania has produced. His heroic defense of his country and of his faith against the Turks, survives in the memory of his people after more than four centuries. Scanderbeg, however, did not succeed — his country was subjugated, yet his name and deeds endure, even though he was unsuccessful. The hero, the great national man, must always rank next to the Gods of a people; he is veritably the highest embodiment of the divine principle on earth, visibly appearing to the men of his nation and race, and realizing what is deepest within them. Their yoke, too, he must bear with bitter suffering, their struggles he must endure for the sake of all; what they are dimly and incompletely, he must be clearly and perfectly, making himself a mirror, as it were, in which they for the first time may fully behold themselves. It will be a calamitous hour, when they forget him; one may affirm, it will be the hour of their disappearance, for their ideal, their essence is then lost. So it will delight the traveler to find that, in these rude huts, far away from the primitive home of his people, Scanderbeg is still alive in his deeds and example.

After having talked awhile and at frequent intervals

gone to the door to look at the weather, I took out my note-book, to beguile the tedious minutes, and began jotting down some little incidents, for it never passed out of mind that I might desire to tell them to you who are now present. My Greek host, at all times full of curiosity, looked over my shoulder, and, though he could not read the strange characters, he nevertheless knew what I was about. "I see that you are going to write a book on Marcopoulo," says he; "come and take a glass of wine, so that you can write better; I wish you to put down in it all my family — wife, children and myself." Therewith he brought me a glass of his best recinato, which he had hitherto kept back; I promised that I would obey his request — and I have tried to do so, as you can now testify. It was not the only time that such a demand was made upon me. I sat down once by chance before a house which had a small, rude balcony, the pride of the owner; first, two women came out and looked at me with staring wonder; then they called two men from within, when one of them spoke down to me: Put my balcony into your book. Even the peasant has some vague notion about the immense amount of writing to which his country has given rise, and he naturally suspects every person who passes through as intending to be guilty of a book. It is a suspicion only too often well-grounded, alack-a-day! I did not escape it, notwithstanding the look of innocence which I tried to put on. I might as well confess the truth now — I was guilty, murder will out, be it the murder of a book.

But the shower passes over and permits me to leave the wineshop; I go out to see the ruins of a temple supposed to be that of Amphiaraus. Exactly why he should be worshiped in this locality is not easy to tell. Amphiaraus was a hero and a prophet; he combined the courage of the one with the foresight of the other. He stands in legend as the type of a man who foresees the fatal act of his people and tries to prevent it; but, when he cannot prevent it, he goes with them and perishes, the victim of his own prescience on the one hand, of his sense of duty on the other. He was one of the seven chiefs in the expedition against

Thebes, whose unhappy termination he foretold; but he had a power over him stronger than his prophetic power — it was that fatal necklace, which, coupled with his own deepest instinct, we may add, drove him to the war. The chieftains were defeated and mostly perished; Amphiaraus, beloved of Jupiter the Supreme God, with horse and chariot was swallowed up in a sudden opening of the earth, where he swayed long as a prophet, and was consulted by the people. This whole region on the borders between Attica and Bœotia seems to have been one of the chief localities of his worship; off yonder over the hills not far from Tanagra the exact spot, called Harma or the Chariot, was anciently pointed out where he disappeared.

Therefore, if we take Amphiaraus as some form of the Divine which the old Greek dwellers along these slopes adored, we may say that this was the idea in their souls: a heroic individual gifted with foresight, combining in one grand endowment both courage and prevision, who, foreseeing death as the consequence of his deed, nevertheless marched bravely forward and met it. Assuredly a manifestation of the Divine is this: to be able to subordinate death to duty. Every human being, therefore, may with reverence tread over these stones, may have sympathy and admiration for the people who once walked up this inclosure with worship for such a principle in their hearts; nay, he may worship here himself, if worship be to him any thing else besides orthodoxy. Amphiaraus, beloved of Jupiter, was not destroyed, though received into the bosom of the earth by the God; long he existed for the people, showing heroism in his example and uttering wisdom in his oracle; still he lives for the traveler looking only on the rubbish and ruins of his temple. His conflict is one that will exist as long as man exists; it is based on some question of this kind: Is life then the highest, or are there other interests in this world higher than life? Very unwillingly do we pawn the precious jewel of existence; but Amphiaraus did it, did it with calm foresight; hence in the olden time he was both a hero and a prophet, nor can I see why he is not the same still. So the Greek came in his perplexity to this spot in order to get the answer of Amphiaraus concerning some important matter of conduct, of vocation, of patriotism. I cannot think that the old seer gave any other response than this: Look at my deed as thou approachest my shrine; foresee, and then die, if such be thy duty.

From the temple I am driven back to the wineshop by the brewing of a new storm, whose huge brewery, cloud-wrapped in the heavens, rises up yonder over the sea. The day begins to grow monotonous, so do I; my disappointment will be great if I do not succeed in vividly reflecting this monotony in my talk. I hope to be able to make you all yawn, and thus to impart to you the spirit of the occasion. I have nothing to do but to sit around the house moodily and see it rain, or, when the rain slackens a little, to look off eagerly into the clouds for clear weather. The feeling of desolation is increased by these Albanians who straggle into the sombre wineshop, draw down the head into a shaggy capote and say never a word. A Greek lawyer temporarily stopping here drops in, and we all wake up again in a lively discussion about Takos.

It is obvious that the chief incident of modern Greek history held in remembrance in this town is the fate of the captured lords and of their captors, whom our narrative left some time ago on the road to Marathon. Takos, the brigand chieftain, passed through Marcopoulo with his prisoners, and is said to have met with no unfriendly reception from its people. Before me some of them now are, some of the very men who received him, and the affair is discussed with as much palpitating warmth as at the time of its occurrence. The object of the chieftain seems to be clouded in no little mystery; just now the question springs up and is debated with vehemence, whether Takos wanted amnesty, or merely ransom for his prisoners; the two educated persons of our party, the lawyer and the host, take opposite sides. The constitutional question, whether the state could grant amnesty to a criminal before his condemnation, winds subtly through the discussion. It is also intimated that the whole affair was simply a political move, and that Takos was hired by the enemies of the ministry then in power to make a diversion in their favor. So the disputants continue to weave about the event many intricate conjectures till the matter itself becomes lost in its own entanglements.

Far more interesting are the manifold myths which have spun themselves around this occurrence; the old mythologic vein has been made to pulsate with new activity, while popular poetry has seized the subject and wrought the tragic story of Takos into many a strain now sung over these hills. It is indeed a dramatic theme in its development and fatal end, exciting in the highest degree the imagination of the people. Just before me an old but lively peasant can restrain himself no longer, but breaks into the cobwebs of the discussion, and with wild gesticulations goes through all the incidents of the affair, showing what the lordies did and what Takos did in those last dire moments of death. He springs about on the floor of the wineshop, stirring its ancient dust into wreathing clouds, as he represents the various positions of the conflict and turns red in the face with loud talking and violent exertion.

Such is the drama which this rustic actor tried to play, rudely boisterous, though in deep earnestness, and of which there is everywhere the most lively recollection. The boldness of the crime, the swift punishment of most of the perpetrators, and the suffering of innocent people drawn into the fateful net of guilt, have gone deep into the very souls of the peasantry. One always thinks of a classic comparison in Greece; I can not help comparing the present feeling in regard to this event to the feeling which lies back of the Odyssey, and always bursts up into its calm sunny narrative whenever it mentions the crime and punishment of Aegisthus, the murderer of Agamemnon. That wretch who in the face of all Greece had committed the bold and for a time successful act of villany against her leader and most conspicuous man, was finally punished by the son Orestes in a manner at once startling and just. The wrong and its retribution seem to have left upon the old Homeric Greeks the one lasting impression, that there is such a thing as justice in this world, and that the Gods really exist in order to administer it.

Thus the ancient poet sings of the nemesis of the guilty deed; Ulysses himself, the supreme ethical hero of Greece, as his last and greatest act will avenge the wrongs done by those profligate suitors. But we may suppose that the case of Aegisthus both expressed and awoke the consciousness as well as the terror of punishment for the guilty deed, and the old bard palpitates with that conviction whenever he mentions the murderer. And one can not help thinking that such a conviction among the people listening in silent awe to that rapt utterance of the poet helped greatly to raise Greece out of her Trojan period, to change her from being a loose group of bands of marauders into a nation with an organized system of justice. Arm a man with the settled conviction that guilt is followed by the penalty and that the Gods exist to punish the secret or the powerful criminal — such a man is ready to belong to a social organism.

One may well think that the swift vengeance sweeping down upon these brigands of Takos is the event which has quite cleared Greece of brigandage in recent times, and has wonderfully enlightened her peasantry, inspiring them with a just dread of the Gods. The direct blow came from the government of Greece, let the fact be duly noted to its credit; but the indirect power behind the blow came from the public opinion of the world, expressed in journalism. A new and mighty force it is, mightier than Orestes, rather it may be called the new Orestes, the modern avenger, whose hand even the unlettered peasant in his hut far out of the path of civilization, feels in a dark mysterious way, and fears the Gods once more. I thought I saw in these rude faces terror still at the occurrence; they seemed to manifest, at its recital, a feeling of dismay before the secret unseen agency which brings back to man his guilty deed.

The traveler will be delighted to think that the ancient Goddess who once swayed in these parts has risen from the rocks, determined to rule once more her former abodes. Look down toward the sea; below in the valley a few miles away can be seen the site of ancient Rhamnus, where are still the ruins of the splended temple to Rhamnusian Nemesis, she who brings home to the doer his deed, she who restores the disturbed balance between right and wrong. She once enjoyed a special worship in this locality, then came the storms of the world, casting into dust her form and throwing down her structure; but again along these heights she rises from the broken stones of her temple and asserts a new authority over this people. For it is her thought, the thought of Nemesis, that has taken its seat deep in the hearts of the peasantry and rules them once more with becoming rigor. Yet who could blame the simple hind, if he became confused about the moral government of the world, when he saw villany go unpunished, and the honest man who sought to bring the criminal to justice, fall a victim to private revenge? A person might well say in his heart, there is no God; or, if there ever has been, he has fled from the face of the earth. But the Rhamnusian Goddess, Nemesis, has leaped up from her ruins of a thousand years, has taken possession of her primitive seats, and the prayer of the traveler is, Long may she remain and sway with her iron scepter this her ancient territory.

Listen now to a divine legend of this same spot. The old statue of the Goddess of Rhamnus was made out of a block of Parian marble which the Persians, in their haughtiness, had brought to the Marathonian battle-field, for the purpose of erecting a trophy over the vanquished Greeks. Phidias the Athenian, the great revealer of the Gods, took the block and hewed out of it the statue of the Goddess Nemesis, says Pausanias. Thus from the very triumphal stone of the enemy sprang the avenging deity; the artist wrought of the marble a symbol of retribution against the invader who had brought it there to celebrate his insolent wrong. Thus too springs from the unjust action the scourging Nemesis, as the Goddess sprang from that block, and brings to the doer the penalty of his guilty deed.

Such then were the two temples that anciently stood in the neighborhood of Marcopoulo — that of Amphiaraus and that of the Rhamnusian Goddess — the latter of which lay at some distance but may be said to belong to this region. But the most interesting as well as the most beautiful of all the ruins in Greece, nay, I should say the most important remains of antiquity which have come down to our time, lie around me everywhere, and have been lying around me during the whole journey: these are the remains of the old Greek language and of old Greek customs. Here they both exist in living activity and make that ancient world a new one, born every moment into life by speech and action. One will notice old forms of words which have been manifestly preserved by tradition from ancient days, for they are not found in books, yet seem to be in consonance with certain old Greek dialects. I do not feel very sure upon this ground, for my ear is not yet accustomed to niceties of pronunciation; but so much may be affirmed, that this is the true field for the student of Greek philology: let him spend one half of his course among the living dialects of Greece, and the other half among the dead grammarians at the University.

But of the antiquity of many of these customs there can be no doubt. You move in an ancient atmosphere, not by any means of your own creation, though you must bring some image of antiquity with you. Indeed the entire background of classical literature clears up into a mellow sunshine, and the cadaverous classical dictionary leaps forth a living body, with its dead and scattered members now jointing themselves into a vital and beautiful organism. Far more than all the museums of Italy and of other countries, does Greece to-day contain of ancient Hellenic life; elsewhere antiquity is a mummy, here it lives, lives in an ever-flowing fountain of speech and manners. The Greek temple is here, though in ruins, for have we not just seen it? Broken parts of column and entablature lie scattered about or must be dug up from the soil; still from these fragments the temple can be constructed anew in its original vital unity. But to see the dry, anatomized dictionary actually sprouting with fresh buds every day, its old withered limbs covering themselves with green leaves and sproutings, is a joy like that of the new spring-time after a dreary winter.

Yet amid so many delights I must confess to one disappointment: I have not seen Helen nor indeed the possibility of Helen. I do not now expect to find her in this portion of Greece. The Albanian type has had possession of these hills for some centuries, and though the Albanians have adopted and preserved much that was Greek, and may have had a common origin with the Greek in the old Pelasgic stock, they have no Helen. Onward then, still onward we must pass in the search, yet not without hope; for where so much has survived, she too may possibly have survived, in primitive youthful beauty. Also a faint rumor we have heard with new encouragement, that off somewhere in the distant mountains she is concealed in peasant garb, accessible only to the most enthusiastic and determined suitor. Looking in restless expectancy at those mountains with summit and sides wrapped in clouds, yet thinking always of what they conceal, we shall still keep up our light-hearted journey. But it is a rainy day and we are penned in by the storm; it offers therefore a good opportunity for retrospection and renewed purpose; so we resolve with fresh ardor to maintain the quest.

Long we continued to sit around the table sipping the moments away with the golden recinato, while the tempest was whistling and whirling furiously outside. One begins to feel cramped up, the wineshop is already too small for the chafing spirit, Greece itself appears to be getting too small. Suddenly the lawyer began to talk about America: that is a country large enough for anybody to stretch himself out upon. He asked me if I knew some person at Boston; I had to tell him that between my home and Boston lay an extent of territory much greater than that between Greece and Rome, the two main centers of ancient civilization, a distance hardly less than that from Greece to North-Western Europe, the seat of modern civilization. With such slow and painful steps does our world seem to move in that Eastern continent — be it said with all due gratitude and reverence. But on the other hand the distance between St. Louis and Boston, if we reckon by time, by ease of traveling, even by expense, is not as great as that between this little Attic town Marcopoulo and Athens. Nor did I fail to maintain to those two keen-witted Greeks before me the metaphysical subtlety that in America Space is destined to sink away, and be subsumed in Time really, that is, to the very senses of men, as it already had done ideally to the mind of the old Greek philosopher.

Having thus once more felt in that little wineshop the free range and the boundless expanse of the prairies of our western world I could not help enlarging still further, and spoke again of those space-devouring Americans with their inventions — the Telegraph which extends its arms around the earth and drops its message at any point; the Telephone, which carries not simply the written word, but the voice in all its tones through Space; finally the wonderful Phonograph invented this very year, the machine which speaks and proposes to carry the voice not through Space merely, but through Time itself, so that the spoken word, in all its modulation and color, shall become eternal. I added with the most mysterious air at my command: Time, too, like Space is destined there to be no longer an impassable limit within which man is kept in a prison-house, but will sink away for the senses, and be subsumed into a higher entity. Then those Greeks were lost — lost in blank amazement; they seemed touched almost with despair at the wonderful achievements of a superior race. For the lawyer was actually brought to declare: Yes, your people are most like to our ancestors, and to us.

Giving them honest words of assent and comfort, the speaker, true to his nationality, could not so suddenly stop that flight of winged words, for he must now make a speech, and so he continued: The ancient Greeks indeed created the ideal types which we have filled, and are still filling with reality. What are all these mechanical wonders, for instance, but the realization of what that gifted people, your forefathers, suggested in thought and in imagination, in their philosophy and in their poetry?

In fact what are they but the fulfillment of prophetic gleamings found in one Greek man, old Homer? What is the Telegraph communicating its message to the ends of the earth but Hermes, messenger of the Gods, with winged sandals swaying over land and sea, bearing the news from Olympus down to mortals at a thought? What is the Telephone but the far-sounding Jupiter, sitting above the clouds in the pure noiseless ether, uttering his word to the people, not exactly in thunder now, but in a way even more emphatic and far-reaching? And what is the Phonograph but that wonderful voice of the Poet himself, still heard sweetly singing down through the ages in all its luscious color and modulation, and which will go on singing to all eternity? Voice too fixed now strangely in characters which the bard himself could not read, were he at present to come back to earth again.

These forms of the imagination are in our day being realized, made palpable in material shapes; thus, however, they must descend from their height, must drop from poetry into prose. So one may well believe that the World's History is always doing; the forms of the imagination seen by Poet or Prophet are made actual; thus the truest work that our latest civilization has done is to translate Homer into prose; this is indeed the best translation. Nor can we stop yet; plenty of work has the old bard given us to do for indefinite ages to come, if we would completely fill his forms with reality. Not until every individual can be his own Hermes, put on some mysterious talaria or sandal wings, grasp some unknown strange caduceus or serpent wand, and thus equipped strike out boldly through the air to the other side of the earth to visit a neighbor or take a look at the Parthenon before breakfast — not until then can we be said to have done with this question of translating Homer.

Which is the greater, he or we? one will hear it often asked. He doubtless is the creator, he created in beauty the forms which we are seeking to endow with material reality; we are but carrying out the instructions, working after the pattern of the master; we are simply fulfilling his prophecy, or are the offspring of his typical characters.

He is the original, he is the greater. But each one of us sits on a throne, as Jupiter on Olympus, controlling a world; we lord it infinitely like a deity, little restrained by the limits of Space and Time; we do and are quite all that the old Greek divinities did or were. We mortals have indeed become Homer's Gods, and mightier; we are the greater.

But hold! I find that I have completely fallen out of my part; I began by making this speech to the Greeks there in the wineshop, but I have gradually lapsed into addressing it wholly to you here. Such tricks the rainy day plays upon us with its driving tempest of reflections. Still something of the kind was said then; there was the lawyer sitting with the host, both of whom could understand me; there too was Varvouillya, the Theban, with a huge wart on his nose, lying back in a kind of mystified revery, yet never failing to take his portion of recinato. Most of the Albanians went away, preferring the rain outside, of which, to be just to them, they and their garments were in greater need than of my sort of drenching. Still we continued to quaff in gentle measures the golden liquid, more wonderful than the touch of Midas, who could only turn material things into shining metal. At last the sun himself came out, golden too, and shone upon the table before us, promising a glorious morrow.

And now about all this drinking — what does it mean in you? Thus I have been repeatedly asked, particularly by young ladies. Did you really drink all that you say you did — you have more the appearance of an apostle of total abstinence than of a jovial Greek — did you drink all that wine? So they ask me, getting a little solicitous about my personal habits while away from home and its good influences. But on the whole I have to answer: Yes, so it is and not otherwise. You see that Greece is not Greece without its wine, and I for one went to see Greece, and even to be a Greek as far as I could, while I was in that land. Nor would there be any complete Italy without its wine; it so partakes of the life and poetry of these classic lands, that it can not be left away. If any one wishes to enter into the manners and realize the mode of living in

Greece, he can not omit the wine. The poorest peasant has two green spots which he carefully cultivates with his hands and cherishes in his heart: they are his vineyard and his grain field. I have often seen him going to his work to remain the whole day; his dinner is a loaf of bread and a canteen of recinato. These two things, bread and wine, are the two elements of his existence, and the two objects for which the labor of his days is given.

Thus they constitute quite the entire circle of his simple life; they maintain him, he maintains them. But to us they have come to stand in a new and peculiar relation. These two simple staples have been transmitted from the Orient to the Occident in the highest and most venerated of all its religious symbols, in the bread and wine of the Lord's Supper. The Savior took the two chief elements of the material existence before him, when he wished to typify the higher or spiritual existence; they were the symbols most manifest to the poor and unlettered peasant, as they were taken from his most intimate daily experience; they were also the two segments which made up for him the completed circle of life, thus representing the completeness of the higher sphere. But for us the strange fact appears that one of these elements is often considered to ally us not with the spiritual, but with the bestial, and that many persons can, without any apparent inner dissonance, take it one moment as the symbol of God and the next moment reprobate it as the product of the Devil. Such a discord would utterly destroy our Greek mood; we shall try to banish it now and forever.

Also the mighty difference between the two articles should be observed by the thoughtful seeker of nourishment. Bread alone supplies the body, but even the peasant scorns such gross living and adds the wine. Bread furnishes bone and muscle, wine enters the blood and excites the soul, the inner genius and energy of the man. The former enables him to walk, but the latter gives him wings. In other words, bread is prose, but wine is poetry. Nay, it is the only poetical drink conceivable, celebrated by poets in all ages. To sing the praise of any other beverage will not succeed, somehow or other; the song of water is insipid, the song of beer is gross, the song of whisky is frantic. Wine alone can be sung about. Life, the dullest life, has in this Grecian land its prosaic and its poetic ingredient — bread and wine, not all bread and butter. To travel through Greece and leave the poetry out, would be indeed a most melancholy journey; do not ask me to make it, still less to tell of it afterwards. Rather, I should advise, let us add a little of this Greek wine to the bread of our own daily lives.

Moreover it is a principle with the true-hearted traveler, to live as the people live wherever he goes, to throw himself into their life and consciousness, into both their physical and spiritual condition, to be one with them and to exist for the time being sympathetically along with them. To take a lofty stand-point above them, and thence with an air of superiority to look down upon their life and manners, and to criticise what you have not lived, is the way to deceive yourself, — to think you know all about them when you know nothing. One person, at least, whom I am acquainted with, does not propose to travel in that way; he is going to drink recinato and like it, even if he did not like it — which, as I happen to know, is not the case.

Thus it is, too, with the fustanella, the Greek male costume, of which much fun has been made. I do not deny that I at first thought it was the most ridiculous garment I ever beheld on a human body — a man in tights and ruffles, dressed like a ballet-girl, walking the streets in open day. But I confess that the liking for the costume grows upon me as I see it in its true place on these hills; it is just fitted for this climate and for this clear atmosphere. It has, too, a poetic phase, being very different in this regard from the prosaic utilitarian dress of the Franks. That white shape, seen far up the sunny slope, though it be following the laborious plow, has the air of an eternal holiday and seems rather some sculptured relief in marble representing the toiling husbandman than an actual ploughman. To me at least it is a sight most pleasant, surrounding the prosaic occupation of life with an ideal atmosphere of joy and beauty. Still, I am not so far advanced as to drop my present garments and don the fustanella, as Lord Byron is said to have done; you must not expect too much at once; the journey is not half over.

Well, another shower! What a dull rainy day! In order to impart to you a most lively impression of it, you must be made drowsy, which literary quality I do not despair of infusing into my words. If you have not yet yawned, I hope to succeed in making you harmonious with the occasion by the following reflections, which give a more general statement of the question just discussed. This question is, at bottom, concerning the difference between morals and manners. Morals are universal; the whole civilized world has fundamently the same code of morals; concerning the moral violation there is in general the same opinion. But manners are very different with different peoples. Do not judge men by the cut of their dress, by their cookery; do not judge of the world's history by the ways of making a bow. Still further, do not condemn morally a people whose manners are different from your own; who wear the fez and fustanella and you do not; who drink wine and you do not; who even go to a spectacle on Sunday and you do not. Ask rather this other question, if you wish to find out the relative moral bearings: Are these people as great drunkards as I or my people; do they steal as much as I or my people; are they as faithful to domestic life, to patriotic duty as I or my people? Nowhere in the world is it possible to conceive of a rational being who has any doubt concerning the moral character of such actions. But when there is an important difference between peoples, you may generally assume that it lies in the sphere of manners rather than in that of morals. Men do not differ about the nature of murder, they do differ about the propriety of eating with fork or finger. Travelers are too often inclined to play variations on this one jejune theme: the manners of this people are ridiculous, perchance immoral; reason: they are not my manners or those of my people. On the contrary, no manners in the true sense of the word can be immoral — they have no moral character one way or the other; they are all equally good, let everybody take his choice. Make then most sharply the distinction between morals and manners; change the latter with every new people you live among; but be careful about changing the former with the change of climate, since they are a matter of universal validity.

But let the mind turn once more from this dry discussion to the liquid source, the recinato, whose throbbing beads we raise now to our lips before parting, and empty our final glass amid hearty gushes of good feeling. As I spring up from the table and look around, I notice that the sun has again come out and is throwing his declining rays aslant the door sill; it is a joyful invitation into the fresh, clear air out of that cheerless wineshop. Behold, the rain is over, the sun is descending in a blaze over the mountain top; the last clouds, scattered and broken, are fleeing across the sky, riding with breakneck speed, like routed dragoons. It is, however, too late to do any thing except to take a walk to yonder pine woods. I go down the road which leads thither, the grass has a new and deeper tinge of green after the rain, and many a little flower thrusts out its mottled head from among the rocks, filled with some secret instinct of showing its beauty.

The fragrance that rises from the pines meets the approaching guest more than half way, and pleasantly invites him forward to their shelter with repeated waftings of incense. The fresh smell of the showers mingles with the odor of the woods; the sombre forms of the conifers are lighted with the slanting rays which glide among the small, needle-shaped leaves and transform them into millions of mellow gleams ever dancing between green and gold. Suddenly, from a covered copse just at the side of the path, the voice of an unseen person pierces loud and far through the air, now washed clean of every mote; it is quite similar to that voice which we heard through the fog yesterday so mysteriously on the mountains. A few steps reveal the form; it is a shepherd girl; and here is her flock browsing about her through the woods. Her call is for some distant companion, possibly for her lover, whose answer in like tones can be faintly heard from a hill-side far off to the left. That peculiar intonation she makes seems to cut through the air, buoyantly riding over the dales, creeping up the sinuous mountain slopes, and dropping faintly at last behind the farthest summits.

But we shall not yet turn back to the village; the spendthrift, Nature, is this evening indulging in one of her wildest debauches after so long restraint; let us too be filled with a little of her extravagance. Behind these woods is a distant view of a cultivated valley which breaks fitfully through between the trunks of the trees whose branches form close-woven vistas down into the rolling fields of grain. Farther on we come to the road winding over the hill-side; we reach a turn in it, when suddenly there bursts into view the sea, calmly carrying the eye over its level expanse into the Invisible. This is the Euripus, southwards breaking into the open sea, but in front being only a narrow strait dividing the island Euboea from the mainland Attica. The waters now lie almost in repose, with just a slight tremble under the rays of the setting sun, from which a long golden wake passes over the surface of ripples to the eye of the beholder, as if the chariot of Apollo was running across the sea just there out of the sunset, and throwing off from its wheels blazing flakes of sun-fire. Over the waters is spread a very thin transparent robe of haze, tenderly blue, not hiding but rather revealing what it veils. The wake of palpitating flames extends across the channel to the other shore and lights up Eretria, village white and fair, lying on the border of the sea. The town seems just now to have crawled out of the waves, like some white-bodied ocean-nymph and to have lain down in the sun at the edge of the water. There she looks at herself in the glassy depths and smiles, beholding her own face in that calm mirror. In a happy sunlit serenity the silvery line of houses is reposing along the bank; thus one is compelled to endow the mild marble outlines of the spot with some Greek plastic form. A flock of pigeons whirs above the head; high over the water they flap their wings transmuted in that sunny haze to resplendent pinions; then about half way across the channel they sweep about in a long curve and fly up the strait toward Chalkis, disappearing in golden flames.

Thus fairly on the sea rests Eretria yonder, bending like a crescent of white marble; but now glance behind the town to the heights there for the final scene, where this day's drowsy drama is brought to an end in gorgeous spectacular pomp. Running through the island as far as the eye can reach is a line of mountains snow-mantled, along whose ridged summits the last beams of to-day are reposing with a lustre soft and soothing to the sight. There the colossal hoary shapes sit, as it were at some Olympian feast, marble Gods with heads garlanded in sunshine; beyond this first line can be seen other heads looming up at that banqueting table. See how the white drapery of snow glistens through the deep rows of mountainous statuary; notice too the sun's line drawn along the billowy crests, while dusk keeps shading more deeply the slants below; nearer the tops that lustrous line is always climbing; now it quite touches the shoulders of the tallest white-draped guests sitting there in stately order. But in the midst of them stands their king, ancient Basilicon, towering far above all the others in proud majesty, the Jupiter of this divine throng. Beside him, indeed, the rest seem to sink down to the level of the earth; soon their heads are covered with shadows, bowed, as it were, in his presence and slightly muffled; while Apollo, as his grand final act of the day sets on the white brow of the mountain king a golden crown, flashing to this distance with rubies and amethysts amid a fitful sparkle of snow diamonds. That regal pageant will not release the eye till the crown with all its brilliants is lifted from the summit into the sky, and there just above the peak is set in the clouds, which are gilded for a few moments and faintly studded with gems; then the clouds too fall under a deepening shadow which converts them at once to dun dragons of the air. It is a sudden, fearful transformation; startled I turn around to retrace my steps; the pine woods have changed to a dark tangled mass of serpentine monsters; above the tree tops is a faint throbbing twilight which only brings into stronger relief the black funereal conifers pointing in ghostly silence upwards to the Heavens. Do not be scared, but I had to shudder, and I hurried past the woods to the village with something following me close to my heels; through the dark lanes I wound swiftly to my quarters, where I burst open the door in some perturbation, a demon being ready to grasp me just as I sprang across the sill.

But as I enter, behold! there is the blazing fire in the hearth, with the children sporting around it; the table is spread on the floor, Varvouillya is raking the clams from the hot ashes, the host is sitting, cross-legged on the mat, with the demijohn of recinato at his side, I squat down in my place, and the symposium begins anew. But things may be repeated, words ought not to be; good dinners can be repeated often, good descriptions of dinner sate soon — one is enough. So this second festivity, though quite as merry as the first, may be forever chained down in the dark prison of the Silences. But to-morrow is a day of rich promise; I predict that the sun will shine, the birds will sing, the high waters will run out, and the traveler, light-hearted and light-footed, will shoulder his knapsack once more, and will follow the bright image fleeing before him along the banks of beautiful blue Euripus.

VII. FROM MARCOPOULO TO AULIS.

Two nights and one day I had remained with the host of Marcopoulo, when early in the morning of the second day I asked him for his bill. Five francs he replied. Without a grumble I handed him a piece of Greek paper money representing that sum; then taking a final sip of recinato with him I prepared to set out. At his request I promised to give him and his house a good name, which I hope I have not failed to do.

Varvouillya who was also going to Aulis on his way to

Chalkis and Thebes, had already gotten his two donkeys in trim and had started a little before me. Soon we are among the hills green with early spring and fresh with the recent shower; the rising sun is beginning to reach out to us over the mountain tops and fling into our faces his first handful of rays. You would say that Nature just now is rubbing her eyes, about to leap out of bed into the happy daylight. At her during this operation, the traveler will gaze with unabashed joy and behold beauties never revealed to the garish mid-day. So for a moment imagine yourself to be the traveler, as he passes along looking up to the illuminated summits, and peering down into the verdant valleys, while he snuffs the delicate fragrance of the pine on the morning air.

Varvouillya walks also for some distance, but he enjoys the luxury of riding far more, and soon mounts the back of one of his little donkeys. These have but a slight burden, consisting merely of a saddle, two or three blankets and some provision for our luncheon. This Greek saddle is a curiosity. It is a rude scaffolding made of cross pieces and placed on the back of the donkey; it can be straddled by no mortal rider but only by the Gods. Therefore a man when he mounts must sit in it like a chair, with both feet hanging down on one side. I never saw a Greek rider that did not keep his feet swinging to and fro, and at intervals thrust his heels into the withers of the animal, which would respond not by hastening its pace, but by dropping back its ears in defiant humor.

Thus Varvouillya springs upon the donkey and settles down into the saddle as if taking his seat in his customary chair; with shoulders slightly inclined he sits there, in dreamy relaxation of features; his steel-gray hair falls below his close-fitting cap, now somewhat soiled around the edges; feet, dressed in red-leathered, sharp-pointed pumps, are swinging stockingless, to and fro, in alternate oscillation; what is he, brigand or honest man? He professes to be a carrier of merchandise through these parts; evidently he is a very different person from the merchant Aristides; I do not deny being a little dubious about him. Still he is very friendly, he has repeatedly asked me to ride, but at present I much prefer the exhilaration of walking. The gait of the little donkey is slow; I pass on in advance, then wait, sitting down upon some seat of the Nymphs to look at an attractive view, or take a note. Still the rider's feet keep going backwards and forwards, and, whenever the donkey stops for a passing bite at some green bunch of leaves along the roadside, he gives a smart kick with his heels, accompanied by a deep grunt of reproof.

Soon we descend into an extensive plain and cross a small stream whose high waters have pretty well run out; this is an encouraging sign, for we have been in some anxiety about the fording of the Asopus. The fields are musical with larks through whose song we pass till the road comes to the sea, the Euripus. Along the coast just at the edge of the water the road leads us for miles; under the slight breeze the surface is in a gentle tremor, and the ripples beat up the shelving shore incessantly breaking at our feet. The wavelets are good company, yet quite different from the society of the running brook; they have a sort of absorbing fascination, as you sit and gaze at them, for you are caught into their rhythm, and break on the shore along with them. That regularity of the ripple, that ever-recurring beat of the sea becomes one with the throb of your heart, with the flight of your moments which, like these wavelets, roll up from the infinite sea of Time, break to pieces on the shore of the Present, then vanish into Eternity. It is never difficult for the soul to be absorbed into the sea and become harmonious with its waters; the sea is indeed naught but an immense musical instrument, one may imagine it to be a colossal bass-viol which sets the world throbbing to its notes. Thus the minutes of life fall to-day into a measure with the vibrations of fair Euripus, whose billowy mirror reflects the two wayfarers, who are passing on its stony beach; at this moment I behold the form of Varvouillya crumpled in the wavelets with feet still swinging to and fro on his donkey.

It seems but a short blue span to the other side of the strait where the mountains of Eubœa rise up, snow-capped, dazzling in the sun. They extend northward as far as the eye can reach, forming a kind of back-bone to the island. From the summits comes a chill air, when no current of wind interferes from another direction. A thin, narrow cloud lies on the side of the mountain, pulled into transparent fibers, like a flock of wool; above this cloudlet is the snowy line of tops, no longer looking like marble Gods at the banquet as they did yesterday, but rather like the white teeth of the upturned jaw of a monster, ready to snap at the deities of the skies. Far above all the other summits towers the monarch of the mountainous realm — called by my companion Basilicon or the Royal Mount, but more commonly named Delphi — richly ornamented on his sides with those silvery clouds, and wearing a crown made of flashing snow-crystals and sunbeams.

Above our heads the crows are flying; they must not be forgotten, the naughty crows of Greek mockery. Their cry seems somewhat different from what it is at home; more garrulous, chattering, spiteful. In irregular lines they streak the sky beyond the mountains, and pass overhead with so much angry disputation that they must be going to hold a congress or agora somewhere among the hills of Boeotia. The crow may be taken as a comic bird, full of caprice and infinite noisy loquacity — a true type of certain phases of Greek rhetorical volubility.

As we skirt round the shore of the Euripus, a town appears off to the left several miles, lying calmly at a slight elevation along the hill-side. It is Oropus, the home of the merchant Aristides, and of the schoolmaster Aristoteles; I shall not be able to pay them a visit and take you along with me as I had hoped; these worthy names we shall have to dismiss from our Greek journey. In antiquity Oropus was an important post during the border wars between Athens and Thebes; in modern times its main distinction is derived from Takos the brigand chief who stayed there several days with his prisoners. He and his band went to church while in the town on Palm Sunday, and like good Christians devoutly performed the prescribed rites; all of them obtained branches of the palm from the hands of the priest, and, in accordance with a religious custom of the country, switched one another for good luck with the holy sprig. Thus they thought to secure the favor of Heaven for their enterprise; but despair not, ye true believers, for the ancient Goddess Nemesis has again arisen, angry, inexorable, and at this moment is silently casting her net from these hills; the Greek soldiers are approaching in secrecy and have begun to surround the town.

But let us pass by the work of the Goddess for a while, and notice this plain locked in by hills, of oblong shape with the sea stretched in front. It is fertile, stubble fields dot it here and there; it brings back to a certain degree the impression of Marathon, and is large enough to maintain quite a community, if well cultivated. It is moreover separated from its neighboring plains by hill and sea, giving to it a certain physical independence, which anciently was supplemented by a political independence.

This fact brings up the reflection which has often been made in regard to the geography of Greece, that it shows the character of the Greek people as distinctly as their spiritual products. But to the traveler these natural features with their strong suggestions become a living presence which moves at his side with every step, and gives a new utterance at each passage of a range of hills. The whole country is cut up into plains and valleys often capable of high cultivation, separated from each other by chains of mountains which it is not easy to pass. If you could look down into the country from above with a bird's eye, you would behold a territory hollowed out like the honeycomb, with cells full of honey, ready to nourish the offspring of its busy bees. There are no great plains like the valley of the Euphrates or the Mississippi; the Earth is roused from her flat indifference into tender embraces, embosoming these clusters of small depressions; all Greece, you would say, is but a group of rock-protected bird's nests, being in antiquity mostly those of nightingales.

Just in this physical division lies the image of the leading trait of the Greek nation. Each of these separate valleys had its own town, sometimes several of them, whose strongest characteristic was autonomy as they called it, that is, the right of governing themselves according to their own laws and institutions. Still further, each of these communities had its own special forms of worship, its own manners, even its own costume, and it sang its own song. Every village was, therefore, an independent whole and was different from every other village in Greece. Such was the boon of individual self-development, now born into the world; yet this very boon was the source of the disunion among the Greeks, which at last caused their downfall.

If we elevate this trait into an expression for thought, we may call it individuality. Thus, primarily the Greek territory was individualized; then the Greek man sought a bodily individuality by special gymnastic training; in a still higher way he strove for a spiritual individuality through the Fine Arts and Philosophy; but above all his ideal of the State was a political individuality, comprising his own community, with full autonomy.

Here then Greece stands in the strongest contrast to the Orient with its immense plains capable of nourishing millions of toiling bondmen, equal simply in servitude, as we behold in the valley of the Ganges, Indus, Euphrates, Nile. In them is the natural home of despotism, where man is as level, low and uniform as the plain which he tills. These Greek hills enveloping Marathon will not permit subjection; they seek to shake off an Oriental sway by their very nature; nor on the other hand will they suffer a dull dead quality among the people dwelling under their protecting summits. In such a land freedom can be born and cradled.

But the march of empire has passed from the far East through the Greek mountains into the far West, and in this latter territory civilization has again settled down into a plain vaster than any in the Orient — the valley of the Mississippi. That the center of the world's culture is destined to be in that valley at some period, is pretty generally conceded, even in Europe; — but in what form?

The Illinois prairie merely as a thing of nature, means despotism as much as the valley of the Nile; certainly it does not signify freedom, as is sometimes stated, though it may signify equality, the dead equality of its own surface. Therefore for us arises this question: Are the institutions of man so far developed that they can overcome this gigantic nature and convert it into a perpetual realm of freedom? All of us believe that they are and that we already possess these very institutions.

But notice again this Greek landscape and connect it with our own; it is the mediatorial element between the East and the West. The Greek mountains fought at Thermopylae and Plataea quite as much as the Greek men. That vast Oriental plain pressing down over the land like an iron sky was pierced by the mountain tops of Greece in a thousand points and shivered to atoms. Nature was there the ally of man, nursed him, protected him; consequently her visage of freedom was taken up by the Greek into his institutions, and thus has become the possession of the race forever, for institutions are the abiding element of the World's History. Yes, though the assertion seem strange, the image of the Greek landscape has come down to us in America, and is the chief aid in solving our political problem, which is to combine the autonomy of the Greek world with the territory of the Orient.

But the second leading element of the geographical character of Greece must not be omitted; here it is at our feet and is seldom out of our sight — it is the sea. These rocky walls with their tendency to crystallize into a solitary exclusiveness are broken down and dissolved by the sea. Just as you behold mountains everywhere in Greece, so you behold from the hights almost everywhere the sea. What the mountains separate, is joined by the infinite number of straits, gulfs, bays, which bite into the coast on every side. The sea is indeed the world's highway and the world's freedom; no chains can be laid upon it, no castle can command it, no robber can seize it and lay a toll upon exchange though it be as free to the pirate as to anybody else. The old Greek belonged quite as much to the sea as to the land; the physical character of the one gave him intercourse abroad, the physical character of the other gave him independence at home.

Suddenly our reflections are stopped by the banks of a stream, muddy and swollen, which had been hitherto hidden from view by the reeds of the plain. It is now manifest that we did well in lying over yesterday, since the marks of much higher water than the present stage are visible in the tortuous line of sticks and scum along the banks. But there is still a strong current in the channel, and of course there is no bridge. What is to be done? Varvouillya offers one of his donkeys; but I am not willing to trust myself on its little low back, with my feet quite touching the water; moreover the donkey is as likely to be swept off its legs or fall as I am. I prefer to take my bath alone, if such is to be my fate; accordingly I prepare for the only other way — that of fording.

The stream is the famous Asopus, still called by the same name as in antiquity. Many a conflict has taken place along its banks, of which the most celebrated was the battle of Plataea, fought farther up in Boeotia. It is ordinarily a sluggish reedy stream, fed from the springs and snows of Mount Kithaeron, yet liable to rapid rise from showers; armies have been suddenly stopped on its banks by a fall of rain. Attica sought to make this stream its boundary towards Boeotia, hence its chief historical significance.

Dignity is not one of the articles which the traveler must take with him in a trip through Greece, it is altogether the most burdensome article he can carry. In short, I pulled off my shoes, tied them to my knapsack like a true pedestrian, and waded into classic Asopus. Mercy on us, how cold is that water! Rightly so, for it is largely composed of melted snow from Mount Kithaeron. Then too the sharp edge of a pebble presses into the bare flesh of the foot, causing the wader to drop quite to the surface of the stream, in order to get a little relief from that unseen enemy. For crossing we had selected a place rather wide just above a swift narrow current, correctly surmising that it was the shallowest and least rapid point. But in the middle of the stream, the current was still vigorous, and the heels became remarkably light, with a continual tendency to fly up where the head was. But I splashed through without any accident, Varvouillya came out safely, and the donkeys feeling their way with unusual care, threw back their long ears in great astonishment and bravely made the passage.

So we forded classic Asopus, and were exalted to a triumphant vein by its success; it was indeed a memorable feat and in memorable company. Thus, thinks the enthusiastic traveler looking back at the boiling current, must many an ancient hero have crossed this stream. Those Homeric chieftains, on their way from Pelops' isle to the grand muster at Aulis, whither we too are bound, could not avoid passing here; behold them in white folds, splashing through the turbid waters; Agamemnon himself, king of men, coming up from golden Mycenae, is, you can plainly see, one of them.

But it is almost an absolute certainty that Socrates, not a dialectician on the streets of Athens now, but a heavy-armed soldier or Hoplite in the Athenian ranks marched through this plain against the Theban foe, came to this river and had to wade through its muddy current. But the waters, I surmise, did in no way cool his philosophic ardor, though they were of melting snow, nor did they prevent him from applying his all-subduing elenchus or cross-examining thumb-screw to the fellow-soldier at his side, the tanner Hyperbolus, there just in the middle of the chilling stream. But onward the philosopher marches bravely and disputes, till late one afternoon his countrymen are consummately whipped by those whom they call swinish Thebans, on the field of Delium. The philosopher too is defeated in spite of his elenchus; for what good will the dialectical instrument now do, brandished in the faces of angry Thebans ranked twenty-five spears deep? The philosopher had to run, run like the rest of his people and run hard too — yet after showing prodigies of valor, as was always said by his enthusiastic friends narrating the occurrence. Indeed it was the first time that he was ever compelled to turn his back on the face of a foe; these are manifestly none of those foes of the market-place, whom he never failed to make shout in excruciating contradiction by the torture of his thumb-screw.

Thus Socrates the philosopher returns to classic Asopus in a great hurry, much greater than when he crossed it going forward to Delium. Some time in the night he must have arrived here; without hesitation he dashed into the current wrapped in demon-breeding darkness, possibly beholding at his back phantasms of Thebans in angry pursuit; other soldiers that I know of have had a tendency to behold similar phantasms under similar circumstances. At least the probability is that this time he did not stop a moment in the middle of the stream, nor can we imagine him now drawing out that wonderful instrument of his in order to use it upon his neighbor who is evidently in as great a hurry as himself. Still destiny bids that the philosopher be preserved; hereafter we shall hear of him at Athens when this night's hurried tramp is over; not by thrust of Theban spear or by a watery death in the Asopus shall he perish, but by the cup of hemlock — rather the most glorious death after that one other, which has yet been recorded. But what the philosophic consciousness was evolving in the shadowy night when the plunge was made into the chilly waters is something which we would all like to know.

Varvouillya gets ready to go forward while I continue to exult in the victory over the river-god: whereat the yellow-haired divinity seems to grow more angry in his turbulent tossings and writhings at my feet. Two pedestrians, Greeks, come to the opposite bank while we are waiting, and attempt the passage. One of them in white fustanella, insists upon trying where the current is narrow but swift, notwithstanding the warnings of Varvouillya. The water dashes around his naked calves, he begins to back out, but it is too late, his feet are whirled up by the current and he falls with a splash, down he floats on the surface of the stream. With violent gestures he seeks to rescue himself, and is soon washed up against a muddy shrub which he catches hold of and crawls out on the bank. What now shall we say to the shining white fustanella after a bath in turbid Asopus and a couch upon its alluvial banks? He looks like some ancient statue, just dug up from its earthy bed, and now for the first time since many centuries exposed to sunlight, revealing many a stain in the solid marble. The angry river-god has shown his power, but not upon our company; so we still exult with mingled pity for our less lucky fellow mortal.

The unfortunate man had in his hand a bundle which is now gaily dancing down the surface of the stream, till at last it is fished out by his companion. Still he lies there on the bank in white fustanella, not so white now — the joyless Greek, that stained piece of marble, sunning himself — waiting perchance for Apollo to instill into him courage sufficient to attempt the passage a second time. Then both of them, with some trepidation to be sure, ford the river successfully under the direction of Varvouillya, just where we had crossed it. They turn out to be two small traders who are also going to Chalkis for Monday's bazaar.

Now we begin the journey anew, six of us together, four men and two donkeys. These small, patient animals again attract my sympathy and admiration; I have told you a little about them before, but not by any means enough, judging them by their importance. Calmly they pass before us, heavy-eyed, much-enduring, with their long ears now erect, now dropping backwards; they have the appearance of overgrown rabbits, moving in single files through the bushes. Their thin legs twirl so quickly, with such a dainty trip that there is a kind of dance in their tread, two of them now stepping in chorus; still they can never be brought to a trot. The donkey has, in proportion to his body, a large head, which is necessary to contain his enormous gift of obstinacy. But it is the eye which is the most characteristic thing about him, showing power but indifference; out of it he has a look of oriental resignation to the will of fate; let come what comes, is his motto, I am going to remain a — donkey. But that fate is now behind him, ever ready to overtake him, in the shape of a long gad in the hands of Varvouillya who unmercifully belabors the poor beast of destiny. Still the donkey takes it all as a matter of course, squirms a little, possibly steps for a moment with a quicker gait, then settles down into his old tread with a complete resignation to the strokes of fate. Out of his spare flesh a bone protrudes at the haunch, covered with a very thin coat of hair, but made callous by blows from aforetime; upon that protruding bone Varvouillya directs his strokes with a vigor of arm and certainty of aim which at first make me shiver; but I soon came to the conclusion that I was hurt worse than the animal, and so began to stop wasting my emotional nature. Indifference to the blows of destiny is the prime fact of the donkey.

A curious incident now began enacting itself under my eyes: our two new companions also started to drive the donkeys. So those three men passed along the highway, grunting, yelling and beating the two little animals, which courageously performed their part of obstinacy. The strangers were quite as zealous in their new duties as Varvouillya himself who accepted their assistance as a matter of course. This, then, I infer to be one of the customs of the country: when you meet a man on the road you must show your good will by helping him drive his donkeys. Moreover the Greek driver has a peculiar language in his dealings with his charge, which with much philological curiosity the traveler will at once set about learning. It is mainly composed of a great variety of grunts, all of which have been handed down from the ancients, I hold, like every thing which the exhilarated vision beholds in Greece; for instance, to stop is a grunt with the falling inflection; to go is a grunt with the rising inflection; to turn aside is a double grunt with an aspirate. This tongue has a number of delicate shadings, all indicated by the grunt. I might be asked to give you some practical illustration of the language, but I find that I can no longer catch the true Attic accent of those sounds.

Thus we wound along the white edge of the blue silken ribbon of Euripus, flashing in the sunlight and rolling gentle wavelets which break at our feet. Sometimes the waters would move out of sight, when we entered a thicket or passed behind a hill; but soon they would leap into view again with a laugh. But, would you believe it? Such is the power of human example, and the absorbing fascination of this Greek climate — not an hour had passed before I too began driving the donkeys with the others. I even caught myself raising my staff to give the blow of destiny to the perverse little beast which had stopped just in the path before me without any perceptible cause. But Pallas Athena held my arm, and Varvouillya anticipated me with his long gad. Yet in speech I falter not, I practice with diligence the new language, and try to imagine what ancient worthy could have done the same thing in the same place. So all four of us pass along the road, grunting, shouting, and talking to the music of the beautiful blue Euripus which rolls at our feet.

Our company approaches Delisi, ancient Delium, now a small poor hamlet, but once it shone with a temple of Apollo lying at the edge of the sea and viewing white graceful forms of column and frieze in the tranquil waters. To the rear of it is a low succession of hills inclosing a small plain; somewhere upon these hills the battle of Delium must have been fought, now chiefly famous on account of the presence of Socrates. A very unimportant fact at that time, merely one Hoplite in the Athenian ranks, but now the best-known incident of the battle: thus do great men often lend to events their whole distinction. Still there is another and far deeper meaning to the struggle at Delium than the accidental presence of the philosopher; for this combat is typical, and gives an image of all Greece at its date. It is the time of the Peloponnesian War and the Greek world is perishing through internal dissolution; formerly it had united and maintained itself against the external power of Persia, but now it has turned its hand against itself and is in process of being destroyed from within. Such is the great transition of Greek history — just this transition from the plains of Marathon to the hills of Delium;. the sympathetic traveler will leave the former with the triumphal notes of victory still ringing in his ears, but he will pass the latter rent by an inward sorrow and dissonance, premonitions of Hellenic decay and dissolution.

This result sprang from the extreme application of the fundamental Greek principle — the principle of autonomy. With it alone, in its one-sidedness the political unity of the Hellenic race was impossible; a thousand limits were thus created, and were perpetually rasping against one another. Hence these independent communities, left to themselves and without the fear of any external power, began to grind in violent struggle. For wherever there is limitation, there is sure to be conflict; both men and states are impatient under restraints. Now if we, with that bird's eye, look down again from above into the honeycomb of Greece, we shall behold all the little cells in fierce agitation; each is trying to burst its bonds or maintain them against some intruder. Then these small communities group themselves around two leaders, Athens and Sparta, though not without many jealousies, bickerings and acts of violence. Still further this dualism of headship enters every village and splits it into two bitter factions. What now has become of the harmonious Greek world with its nests of nightingales? Terrific discord, with the screams of vultures has succeeded — of which one echo is still resting on these hills of Delium.

Now if we wish to grasp in our thought the deep-seated source of this calamitous outcome of the Hellenic world, we must see what is lacking in the Greek consciousness, especially in the Greek political consciousness. This may be expressed in one word: Recognition. The Greek community would not, or indeed could not, recognize the right of its neighbor to be just as good, nay, to be just the same as its own right. It could not see that if it destroyed the autonomy of the little town next to it, it was destroying the principle of its own autonomy. It was a most jealous lover of its own freedom, but not of its neighbor's freedom; but the truth of logic and history is that the freedom of its neighbor which it trampled underfoot, was at bottom its own freedom. It lacked recognition, yet there were far-off glimmerings of the principle; in fact this principle seemed once on the point of realization in the Achaean League. But Greece was then dying, and it never had the insight practically that right is universal, belongs to all equally, and that the nation which violates it in another is violating it in itself. For it is thus doing a deed which must return to itself, and is preparing itself for retribution through its own act. Nemesis for the individual the Greeks believed in, for we have already seen temples to that Goddess, but they knew no Nemesis for the State.

It is not difficult, with the modern world and our own form of government before our eyes to point out the solution of the Greek political problem. We feel that the Greeks needed the Confederacy with constitution and paramont governmental powers, whose object would be to remove the narrow pinching limits on the one hand, and on the other to preserve the full internal autonomy of the community. Thus the small state would be all Greece, yet it would remain itself. One half, perhaps the nobler half, the Greek seized fully and carried out, namely communal freedom, local self-government, as we call it: But the other half does not belong to his consciousness, had not yet risen in the consciousness of the world; twenty centuries of struggle were to elapse before it could be realized. His political system perished because it was a half, because it was limited to the boundaries of his own little state — for it is the law of existence that only the whole can endure.

The battle of Delium was fought between the Thebans and Athenians, two Greek neighbors who ought to have lived harmoniously together. It may be taken as an image of a hundred combats during that wretched war, and it illustrates what was transpiring on nearly every boundary between the communities of Greece. It is therefore a type reflecting much, if we look into its depths and gather its true meaning; though so distant in time, it still seems to throw these hills into discordant undulations. But it is not the only dissonance heard upon this spot, there is a modern note of horror here which strangely mingles with that ancient clangor of arms.

Varvouillya suddenly halted his mules near a clump of bushes along the road; he took from the saddle a kind of haversack filled with bread and cheese, and prepared lunch, for it was already past noon. Our two new companions were invited to partake with us, and were not behind us in their appreciation of the frugal meal. When it had ended, Varvouillya rose in silence and walked a few yards away, then he turned and called to me: "Here the English lord was killed. Yonder another was found murdered. Over that low hill Takos came from the direction of Oropus with his captives, pursued by the Greek soldiers. When he found that he could not escape with his prisoners, he killed two here and two further up." Saying this, the speaker stood in silence, as if lost for a moment in revery, nor did the two companions manifest a desire to say any thing about the affair on this spot, though they showed that they knew all about it from beginning to end. It may be my own fancy, but I could not help thinking that they were touched with a slight terror.

But such is the final act of the drama; that capture near Pentelicus, which was at first supposed to be a comedy, has turned out a tragedy of the bloodiest kind. When the prisoners had been assassinated in cold blood, the approaching soldiers opened fire upon the brigands; the brother of Takos with seven of the band were slain, and four others were taken prisoners; Takos himself with ten of the band escaped, some of whom were afterwards caught, and executed.

This event has injured Greece more than all her other faults and misdeeds put together; yet it is hard to see how the Greek government can be blamed for the occurrence. Certainly it tried to prevent the crime and punish the criminals; the band did not belong within the borders of Greece, and had been hunted from place to place by Greek soldiers before Takos suddenly appeared at Pentelicus. The chief reproach which can be cast upon it is, that it paid too much attention to English advice. Yet it is chiefly the English press and the English government which have sown this unjust judgment through the world. Greece was called in the newspapers and was treated as a nation of brigands, in spite of the most evident facts to the contrary. Over one hundred peasants and shepherds were arrested for having furnished aid or information to the band; two English barristers were sent from London to watch the proceedings — a piece of bullying the more reprehensible on account of the weakness and embarrassment of poor Greece. Most of the arrested persons were acquitted on account of a total want of evidence against them; a few were sentenced to various degrees of punishment. Such was the action of the Greek government.

It must be granted, on the other hand, that there had been too much toleration of brigandage among a portion of the Greek peasants, and that some of them had a tendency to turn brigand with good opportunity. The effect of Turkish oppression which drove the strong man to outlawry and the weak man to passive submission to wrong, may not have wholly ceased under a free government. But this occurrence has wrought a change. When the peasant saw his neighbor taken from home and brought to trial for having aided a brigand, his ideas of justice and duty underwent a revolution. He felt that a terrible unseen power was on the track of the evil-doer, and as has been already stated, he came to believe again in a Nemesis who pursues the wicked act. Some such feeling, vague and dark, yet real, the traveler will come in contact with among the people. It is healthy — let the Gods be again believed in, though they be not worshiped as of old.

But wherever a wrong has been done, there must follow the penalty; if England has been guilty of injustice, Nemesis will be upon her, for the Goddess is universal in her sway, and is not merely for the Greeks. So it turned out: the worst compromised man, the only man of social standing, and the sole educated man among those arrested for abetting the brigands, was an Englishman, son of the proprietor of an extensive estate in Eubœa. Shall we then say that English gentlemen are supporters of brigands? Not by any means; but let them not make this charge against the Greeks on such grounds; if it be unjust, Nemesis will bring it home to themselves. For the Goddess has arisen once more, and in swift anger is determined to requite the guilty act, by whomsoever it be committed.

Such is Delium with its two jarring notes, an ancient and a modern one, both indicating the deep-seated discordant throes of their respective epochs. But let us flee from these horrible dissonances and follow the donkeys into some harmonious spot; they are now passing over a line of low hills covered with brushwood. Even among the brambles there is the interest of a delightful antiquity, for all of these bushes and plants have been fragrantly preserved in classical poetry. Here is the arbute known to readers of Theocritus and Virgil with its bright red berry resembling the strawberry in look but not in taste; sometimes it is called the strawberry tree. The schinos or wild mastic — not the aromatic mastic of Chios so much used in the East for its fragrance — is here with its ancient name still, just as it was uttered by the Sicilian shepherd; its leaves are employed for tanning, according to my informant, one of the new-comers. Pine grows in abundance, often chipped for its resinous ooze to put into the recinato; a species of scrub-oak is very common — yet there are no tall trees making a forest. One of my companions tells me the names and uses of the various shrubs; to my special delight he points out the wild olive, on which the tame one is grafted to produce the hardy tree. Who can forget that it was one of the trees which furnished cover to Ulysses, asleep, after his shipwreck near the Phæacian isle, and from whose concealment he came forth to greet fair Nausicaa? So every bush, every flower has, besides its native virtues, the delicious fragrance of old Greek poetry which rises up like incense from these green hills.

Since I am trying to take you with me, I must not allow you, even at the risk of repetition, to lose from your view the mountains, besnowed above and green below, that always accompany us just across in Eubœa. There is still that thin flock of translucent cloud, bound immovably to the brow of the range, while above its tattered strip the white summits point upwards, on which the snow is sparkling in the sunbeams; silvery garments with golden lining apparel the heights in regal magnificence—you will say before you can get the sentiments fully under control.

Soon again we come out of the brushwood to the Euripus growing bluer in the deeper haze of the afternoon, yet with the same tremulous play of the wavelets rolling against the beach. The mountains and the waters have gone along with us all day — hundreds of times the traveler looks at them with the same fresh delight and wonders if he cannot in some manner carry them with him forever. Glance at them once more and turn away.

From early morning I have walked, helping to drive the two donkeys — no small labor; Varvouillya now repeats his invitation to ride. This time I accept, for I must confess to growing weary. He gives me the smaller and more tractable of the two donkeys; it has no bridle or halter or headgear of any kind whereby it can be directed, but it patiently follows the other and elder donkey, upon which Varvouillya himself is mounted, swinging his feet. Our two companions have fallen behind and we are again alone. With an easy spring one lights in the saddle, that Greek saddle, very comfortable and convenient, though very awkward. There I sit sidewise, swinging my feet also, often thrusting my heels back into the flanks of the animal and grunting out commands in imitation of Varvouillya; at all of which the donkey would merely lay back his ears and move just as slow as before. But he felt the increased burden, and began to meditate how to get rid of it. Wherever there was a bush or limb along the way, he was certain to rub as close to it as possible. The first two or three times I might have forgiven as accidental, but by the repeated brushings I received when there was no necessity, I was forced to the conclusion that the rascal was trying to scrape me off. He had a great advantage over me, as he was without bridle or halter; the only thing I could do was to lean down from the scaffolding of the saddle and box his long ears in the right direction. Then with what supreme innocence he would lay them back, till in fact I would feel ashamed of myself, as having done him a wrong. But at last he did catch me; he was taking me straight into a thorn-bush, there was no escape, I whirled and sprang off on the other side, with considerable agility, I thought. Then for the first time during the day, I was going to declare, during my whole life, I saw a donkey run. It was a clear confession of guilt on his part.

But Varvouillya was soon after him with the gad of destiny, and his meek eyes at once showed complete resignation to the decree of fate, and to the burden of my body. Now if you can bring before you the two small donkeys, patiently stepping along, the one behind the other, with the two riders listlessly sitting sidewise, and swinging their feet, you will have an image of our cavalcade as late one afternoon amid a golden languor of classic sunbeams it entered the village of Vathy, lying on the harbor of ancient Aulis. Varvouillya halted before a wineshop where we were to remain for the night; the people of the town, mostly Albanian, flocked around us in a white throng of fustanellas; Varvouillya seemed to know everybody.

Although it be just a touch of self-praise, to which you will have to get used at intervals, I am compelled to say that the old fellow appeared to be proud of his companion. He was at first astonished to see me persist in walking — gentlemen in Greece usually ride, he said; but when I forded the Asopus, I had taken a lofty place in his esteem. That a man who talked high Greek and read books should go in such fashion over the country, was something quite unheard of. "Yet," said he, "that is the only way to find out anything about us. Those gentlemen who rush rapidly through the land on horseback, know nothing of our people." I was glad to have such a sensible approval of my way of traveling.

Then Varvouillya exhibited me in that place to the astonished multitude, with extravagant phrases making them believe that I had lately arrived from the moon. We went up the road on a visit through the village, a crowd followed in a long train, little children peeped around the corners of the houses at the stranger in Frankish garments, wives with babes in their arms glanced through the half-opened doors, peasants returning from the fields stopped their beasts of burden in the street, and eagerly inquired: Who is it? What is it? The people were bringing me to the wonder of their village, an old man, formerly a sailor, who spoke Italian well and a little English, but the latter tongue he had about forgotten. I found the Nestor of the hamlet at his hearth sitting in his armchair — a man who had seen all parts of the world, and whose talk was full of experience and a natural wisdom. He possessed also a quiet humor which would suddenly dash through the wrinkles of his face, lighting up its aged furrows with a glow like that of the phosphorescent sea in the wake of his ship. After many an adventure he has returned to his native town and is here passing a sunny old age — sunny with good reason, for at his side is now sitting a young Greek wife with a babe in her arms. No, he is not old — there is no old age in Iphigenia's Aulis. But I must be off; after drinking of his hospitable wine and at request exchanging names, I find my way back to the wineshop without Varvouillya, who has gone to take care of his donkeys. There also generous citizens insist upon my taking with them a draught of recinato; I return the friendly bumper, then slip out the back-door and wander off alone in the dusk to the sea side which is not far away. There I sit down at the edge of the water.

Here, then, is the bay of Aulis where the Greek fleet assembled for the expedition to Troy. The Euripus forms at this point quite a large quadrangular basin, protected by hills; in the center of the basin rises an island, rounded off to the full firm swell of a virginal breast, on the top of which one places, in defiance of the antiquarians, the temple of the chaste huntress Artemis and the sacrifice of the young virgin Iphigenia. The sparkling water at one time plays over a sandy beach, at another time it hides itself under projecting rocks which have been eaten away underneath by the ceaseless nibbling of the waves. One can still see in the dusk the ancient heroes bringing up their dark ships alongside of this protending rock, and then leaping on shore, in order to go to the tent of the chieftain for important deliberation. Achilles, the type of eternal youth, who prefers dying young with enduring glory to passing an inglorious life in his own country, has left his aged father Peleus in his Phthian home on the banks of the Spercheios and has arrived, not unwilling to meet the hour when he must die, but thus live forever; Ulysses, the man of intelligence, hence the man who has to endure, gifted with infinite subtlety and just for that reason meshed in infinite struggle, has left behind a young wife and child in sunny Ithaca, and has come to give his wisdom to the expedition; Nestor, the white-haired eloquent sage of the Greeks, from whose tongue words dropped sweeter than honey, who had lived three generations of men, and is therefore old enough to stay at home, is also present, with his two sons, having come all the way from sandy Pylos to join the great Hellenic enterprise. Youth and age, bravery and wisdom are all represented — and now flit in white robes through the palpitating twilight.

And what is this trouble about? Helen the most beautiful woman of Greece has been carried away to Troy; but the East shall not have her — such is the universal shout of Hellas, of its old and its young, of its wisdom and its valor. Now the chieftains are assembled, preparing to attempt the heroic work of recovery; they have quit their country, have left behind in many cases their own wives and little ones — a chaste Penelope and an infant Telemachus — in other words have given up State and Family, for the sake of runaway Helen, of dubious fame but of surpassing beauty. Still it is a national undertaking, altogether the most national undertaking of the Greeks, for they were more united in the expedition to Troy than they were in driving back the Persian; they were more ready to do without freedom than without beauty.

But as one looks at these shapes tripping through the twilight, there seems to be sometimes a little hesitation, a little doubting as to the success of the enterprise. One is emboldened to address them in words of prophetic confidence: Courage, oh ye long-haired Achaeans, I predict that ye will not only restore Helen, but that ye will take Troy itself and raze it to the ground. Helen will be brought back to Greece, there to remain yours forever, but only after ten weary years of struggle. And thou, Ulysses, dearest of all my friends here, thou too wilt return, though thou hast before thee a greater task than even the restoration of Helen. Ten years first must thou battle before Troy for her sake, then ten years more hast thou to wander through things visible and invisible till thou reach sunny Ithaca and chaste Penelope.

But the brusque shade turned and asked me: What, oh child of the setting sun, art thou doing here, among us hoary shapes of eld, in our struggle with the sons of the Dawn? I answered: I too am in pursuit of Helen, I have come to Aulis, I also wish to go with you to Troy.

A wild goose snattered overhead, the ghosts of the old chieftains at once vanished, slowly I returned to the wineshop, wondering how a ridiculous goose could put to flight all the heroes of Troy.

VIII. AULIS AND CHALKIS.

When I had come back from the bay, it was dark and the wineshop had closed, accordingly I went into the adjoining house where I was to remain for the night. There was a bright fire blazing in the hearth; around it the company were squatted on rugs; the flashes from the flames lit up all the faces which were gazing intently on the fire. Outside of that illuminated circle a small lamp struggled with the darkness; the naked rafters could be dimly seen overhead hung with various articles of the household. We had one-half of the house, which consisted of a single oblong room; the other half was taken up with the stable; the difference between our part and the donkey's part of the house was not marked by any partition, but by a floor slightly raised from the ground. Sometimes in Greek dwellings you will not find this distinction of a floor retained; man has not yet weaned himself from the bosom of his primeval mother. In the stable were a donkey and a lamb; each of them in its own peculiar note informed us at intervals during the entire night of its presence.

Also the company around the fire is worthy of notice. There we sit looking at the blaze and watching the supper which is cooking before us; hunger is throned in every eye, and observes the various stages of the culinary process with no little impatience. I am squatted in front of the hearth, deeply absorbed in the turkey now being whirled on the spit and oozing all over with fragrant juices; Varvouillya is next on my right, he is telling some of his stories of travel for our amusement; next to him comes Yanni, our simple Albanian host, with his hands locked around his knees and rather stupidly rocking himself backwards and forwards on his haunches. Yanni's mind is evidently divided between the stranger, the like of whom he has never seen in his house before, and the turkey, with the preponderance of interest in favor of the latter.

But on my left sit two new characters, women, two other guests besides Varvouillya and myself. They are Wallachian shepherdesses who have come down from the mountains with their products, and are going to the bazaar at Chalkis early to-morrow morning. There is a wild look about them, they are genuine nomads, children of Nature, living in the open air among the hills, like birds amid branches. Their dress is rude, of very simple construction; from below a short kirtle their naked feet peep out, resting on the hearthstones, and evidently not accustomed to tender usage; they had shoes, but these had been taken off at the door according to custom. The youngest of the two was a girl of about eighteen, who sat next to me; she could not well be called beautiful, but I admired her unstinted physical growth, the fullness and natural luxuriance of her body. Dark tresses fell down her cheeks in the wild negligence of nature; from beneath them, as out of some dim grot gleamed two bright warm eyes. I began to talk with her as she spoke Greek; I told her that I wanted to see and to live with the shepherds in their tents of brushwood, then I asked her if she would not take me with her to the Wallachian village in the mountains. With a shower of unusually vivid sparkles from her eyes she replied that she would. But the next day she said that she had to go to Chalkis, and could not well look after me there; still she would return in the afternoon and would then gladly conduct me to her home. I am compelled to say that I backed out, though I wanted very much to go to her village, and I debated a good while with myself about the matter. But I concluded that I had better stay with Varvouillya who was going forward to Thebes the following day. I now regret that I did not accept her invitation, for I had never afterwards another opportunity of the kind, though I sought one repeatedly; also I might have remained in that Wallachian village and become a shepherd.

Her associate, a woman in middle life, is of a very different type; she has a strangely fine face with subtly woven lines, though it be somewhat wrinkled and haggard. Slight curls hang down over her features which seem to be marked more by mental than by physical endurance. I can not help thinking that she has suffered, the spirit within appears to be in dumb protest with this pastoral life of hers. She must be some waif of civilization, a lost child of Europe whom destiny has cast among these shepherds. But how has she come hither? There is ancestral dignity still remaining in those fine lines; some fall speaks unconsciously from her sorrowful look. A whole romance I seem to read, plainly writ in her face, but when I questioned her about her origin, she says that she is merely a shepherdess.

Next to her in the circle is Yanni's wife who is occupied in turning an iron spit over the coals. She is dressed in the white Albanian costume, and seems very shy and taciturn; she never shares in the laugh, and often tries to hide her chin and forehead more deeply in her headkerchief. Every few moments she fetches a deep sigh, this is repeated so often that I inquire the cause. I was told that there had recently occurred a death in the family — this was the form of mourning. In all parts of Greece the same custom can be noticed; the women, not the men, utter the lamentations, which are kept up beside the hearth long afterwards, as if to invoke the missing member to take his place at the domestic gathering. It is essentially the ancient custom; at the house of the deceased and in the funeral procession were heard the wailings of females, who represent more intimately and intensely than the man, the domestic ties. Thus, as in life itself, the saddest note of Nature would spontaneously well up and mingle with our animated words, tingeing and often extinguishing them; good Varvouillya tries to give consolation to the poor mother sitting at the hearth, while we look on in sympathetic silence, but the consolation only sharpens the pang and the tears begin to fall.

That spit which is now taken in hand by Yanni, must also have its jot of attention. It is an iron rod which pierces a turkey; this is turned continually before the fire till the fowl is thoroughly roasted. All other meats are cooked pretty much in the same way; they are cut up into small pieces which are pierced by the spit and held over the fire. Thus the Homeric cookery, as seen everywhere in the Iliad and Odyssey, is still prevalent in Greece:

> "his companions stood
> Around him and prepared the feast, and some
> Roasted the flesh at fires, and some transfixed
> The parts with spits."

So the merry Greeks feasted anciently at Aulis; so the traveler is going to feast to-night, for the turkey is done.

The simmering bird is removed from the spit by the skillful hands of Yanni and placed upon the table which is lying flat on the floor like the innkeeper's at Marcopoulo. Around it the three men squat down cross-legged, with eager glances; the three women keep at a distance and pick their bone in their own corner. Women here have not yet risen to the exalted privilege of eating their dinner with their majestic lords. There was beside the fowl, good black bread, a little dry, but floated, as usual, by the pearl-dropping recinato. The host is, as already said, a simple Albanian, without education and without natural gifts, yet he has some natural capacity for turkey and wine. He is kind and open-hearted, but he seems to have passed his whole life in this little village, without any knowledge of the world outside of it. A vague curiosity he shows about lands and seas and peoples of which the traveler talks, but his intellect is hardly capable of more than a stupid wonder. He is quite a contrast to that quick-witted and well-educated Greek, the jolly landlord of Marcopoulo, whom we must not always expect to meet at our inn. He speaks a broken Romaic, I speak a broken Greek, between us the pure transparent tongue of Hellas is badly shivered, as if a costly mirror were shattered to fragments. Still in each fragment you can see yourself; so we manage to understand one another very well.

Doubtless Yanni may be taken as a pretty fair sample of the common Albanian population of Greece. It is still a problem what these people are going to make of themselves; will they finally coalesce with the other elements and aid in forming one homogeneous Hellenic nation, or will they continue to remain a distinct race upon Greek soil? At present the Albanians preserve most stubbornly the ancestral language and customs. The wife before me cannot speak even common Greek or Romaic, though she understands it pretty well; to preserve their language the men often do not permit the women to learn other than the maternal tongue. Their agriculture, their methods of labor, their implements are of the most primitive kind; they allow no improvements on the traditional manner of doing things. This Albanian element seems a most stubborn, stolid, impervious element in the way of the progress of Greece; its conservatism would be excellent, were it not in danger of becoming absolutely crystallized; it can not be kneaded or moulded to any new shape. Still the Albanians are a strong, courageous, uncorrupted race; without their bravery and perseverance there would have been no Greek independence.

Perhaps in the course of time they may add their somewhat heavy ballast to the somewhat light-headed and unsteady Greek character, for in this respect the two peoples are quite opposite. Thus there may arise another great Hellenic nation, combining the versatility of the one with the conservatism of the other element. At present, however, the streams will not mingle. This lack of homogeneity in the population of modern Greece is the most striking fact of its social condition, and excites the observer to various reflections. It certainly indicates weakness, national weakness, for the spirit of nationality is not strong enough to overcome these natural distinctions of race, and to fuse them into unity. Every strong nation must digest the foreign elements within itself and absorb them into its own character, language and institutions by the intensity of its national life. But these three races — Greek, Albanian, Wallachian — have existed here for centuries alongside of one another without being smelted by the fire of patriotism into the oneness of spirit which may be called nationality. Greece is still an agglomerate, not an organic Whole; the want of the central fire which burns up all narrow limitations is still felt; the ancient tendency to separation, which is so strongly marked in the physical features of the country, is now manifested in the resistance to a fusion of races, though in antiquity the resistance was to a political unity of peoples of the same race. Such a condition comes of weakness and can only perpetuate weakness.

Already I had been ruminating on the problem of accommodating this respectable body of people in one room for the night. Yanni began solving the difficulty by spreading out a blanket on the floor for me and then giving me another blanket for cover. Thus I was disposed of; the shepherdesses lay down on a rug in front of the fire, pretty much as they were; it was probably the best lodging they had had in a long time. Tresses became more dishevelled as their heads drooped in slumber; then too they must have forgotten that they were under roof, for they snored away as if they were on their native mountains with only the skies overhead. The family also retire alongside of the hearth; thus we all lie there, scattered around the blaze of the oak branches, head to feet and feet to head, in the sweet innocence of Paradise.

But notice Yanni, thou unsatisfied wanderer up and down the earth! At the other end of the house where the stable is, hangs a small lamp suspended from the ceiling; with a faint light it burns before a rude picture of the

Virgin; on retiring Yanni turns to that light, crosses himself many times, makes profound bows to the image and repeats his prayers. Not before that act is done, is he willing to consign himself to the strange unconscious world which lies between to-day and to-morrow. This question of Deity then has entered the heart of the unlettered man; there is a power above him which he recognizes, and with which he must put himself into harmony, before he can find repose for the night. The traveler observes the fact not without reflection, not without emotion. Mark it well: his own sweet will is not for Yanni the supreme thing; he must at least placate that image yonder, and the power which looks through it into his soul. Recognition of some higher being who governs the universe gleams through the darkness into this hut; it is a gleam, only a gleam like that flickering lamp illuminating dimly the face of the Virgin. But by it you can behold some image of the Divine, rude though it be; whenever you wake in the night, you will see the lamp still burning faintly high up amid the rafters, hopefully trying to show to you also some countenance of love and protection.

Previously at supper, I had noticed 'a peculiar religious trait of Yanni's, or perhaps only a freak; whenever he emptied a glass of recinato, he invariably used this expression in doubtful Greek: *apo ton theon* — to God; he drank his toast to God. If I proposed the health of his family, of his wife, of his country, of himself, he would never fail to drink, but his only response was: *apo ton theon* — to God. Did he imagine that divinity too was pleased with the golden recinato, like ancient Bacchus? Certainly he did not think that the joyous beverage could be of Satan, wherein I religiously believe with him. But the traveler as he looks up will behold a true illumination in that small burning lamp, and will feel a protecting hand reach out from the dim picture; for by the light there the Virgin can see, according to Yanni's faith, and avert any act of villany, and even punish the evil-doer. Such will be the general feeling of the lone stranger, as he drops off into slumber, in spite of the ugly drawback that the brigands went to church at Oropus and devoutly prayed to the Virgin.

Unimportant details I promised to tell you; therefore I may say that my dreams were pleasant, though my couch was hard, harder than any I recollect of having since the days of my campaigning. But when I became sore on one side, nothing prevented me from turning over and lying on my other side, except the danger of stirring up the people at my feet. Various sounds floated through my slumbers that night, some of which I brought back with me from Lethe: the donkey in the stable kept champing his straw, the lamb bleated, the dogs barked, the baby cried; Vavouillya, asleep within reaching distance of me, grunted at his beast of destiny, and then punched me in the ribs. All this I could endure and slumber on in happy Greek mood; but when the young shepherdess, in some dream of pastoral felicity turned over and rolled her stalwart body upon my feet, sleep fled from my eyelids. Meantime the elder shepherdess rose and woke her companion; they talked and chaffered with Yanni about the bill for their lodging; then tying their heavy bundles on their back, they set out for Chalkis afoot, before the rosy-fingered Aurora had strewn a single coral in the Orient. What man in these degenerate days could lift the burden with which I saw my young shepherdess gaily trip along when she opened the door to the fitful glimmer of the moon! Good-by, mountainous nymph, an aching ankle keeps thy mighty image vividly before me, yet darting amid delightful visions of what a life would be in thy pastoral home.

In the morning there is a large company passing from the village to Chalkis in a boat; I go with them. The little vessel went across the ancient bay of Aulis, right through the anchoring places of the Greek fleet, which must have rocked buoyantly on these wavelets. Opening into the large bay is the small bay of Aulis; both of them were required, doubtless, for the old fleet; one imagines those thousand ships still lying on the sea with their drooping white sails in the sun. But it is the island in the middle of the bay which fixes most strongly the

AULIS AND CHALKIS.

attention; round and full it rises out of the water slightly flattened on the top, and seems to dance in the ripples like a ball. As it is the center of the harbor, so around it play all memories of the ancient story — of the ships, of the heroes, of the virgin's sacrifice. Along the shore are beautiful hilltops rising up into sunshine; on them we place some shrine or temple, white with columns and frieze, gleaming afar over the waters. Upon one of these summits is situated the ancient citadel of Aulis, whose remains can still be seen; huge walls with gates are there, speaking of the olden time.

The little boat is full of people; there are several other boats going in the same direction; each has its oarsman with its crew on the benches; thus a new Agamemnonian fleet cuts through the waters of Aulis. Many flashes of old Greek customs the traveler will imagine that he sees in the company. There is the Greek merriment aboard, which at times seems to verge toward childishness, as shown in little tricks and jests; two men of middle age roll over the benches and tickle each other to the amusement of the whole fleet. Many hints of old Greek dress will be noticed in these garments; they are mostly white fustanellas, not spotless now, but suggesting that they may have been anciently so. There is a leathern pouch around the waist containing a long knife and other needful untensils; from it the wearer draws forth flint and punk to strike a light for any purpose which he may have in mind, since it would be a gross anachronism to illumine the bay of Aulis with a modern match. A whole Greek household lies in that pouch; out of its unseen depths the man at my side takes a heavy needle and thread, and sews up a rip in my shoe, for his own mere delectation. Then there is the language; still the Greek is spoken here, and it is probable that the ancient and the modern sailor, could they now address each other in these waters, would be mutually intelligible. Still the most marvelous fact of human speech: the Homeric heroes spake as is spoken to-day in the port of Aulis.

During this little voyage my chief associate I find in the schoolmaster of Vathy (or Aulis), who is crossing over to

Chalkis for some school books, as he says. He was a captain in the Cretan insurrection, was compelled to flee from his native island and leave his family to the tender mercies of the Turk; now he has to be a schoolmaster in a foreign land. It is not long before he begins to complain; manifestly he has lost his Greek mood teaching school at Aulis. Indeed fortune has buffeted him till•he has become like a wind-beaten oak, all gnarled and cross-grained; but to-day the rest of the merry company prevent him from letting out fully his splenetic humor. He invites me to visit his school, which I promise to do when we return from Chalkis where we have now arrived.

The town of Chalkis presented on that morning, which was market-day, a very mixed appearance. The Orient seems to be more strongly impressed upon this place than upon any other in Greece; yet it has also many a fierce reminder of the Occident; clearly it has been a point of conflict and of fluctuating possession in the old centuries. Its importance — for it commands the Euripus at the narrowest crossing — has always made it an object with conquerors. The traces of its various rulers and its checkered destiny are stamped everywhere upon its face, and at once possess the attention and the feelings of the beholder. Here is a Gothic church with its pointed windows, dating from the Venetian occupation during the Middle Ages. It seems like a lost ghost, you salute it and ask it: How hast thou wandered hither from thy home in the dark foggy North? The lion of St. Mark is still seen over the gate of the castle; he yet has the hoary look of a crusader. Signs of Turkish occupation are noticed in the old mosques and towers, in the falling fortifications, in the careless construction of the walls. Wretched patchwork over great remains shows the Turk in Greece. A few Mohammedans are said to linger still in Chalkis, the only place of the Prophet's worship in the kingdom is left here. A few marbles built into the walls of the churches give a slight sprinkle of antiquity; but of the distinctive new Hellas the traveler seeks the signs in vain. But it will come, be not impatient.

The bazaar or market is on Mondays; good fortune has landed me just at the right moment. The streets and particularly the public square are lined with small booths, every thing which the Orient offers is for sale, mingled in admirable disorder with Western merchandise. Peddlers are here from all parts of Greece, hawking their wares; I see my man who fell into turbid Asopus, trying to sell a kind of carding comb; still the marks of the muddy waters fleck the white folds of his fustanella, as he dashes, all oblivious, through the surging crowd. Some American cottons and American cutlery can be noticed, but the English manufacturer possesses the market; for his success he has my best wishes at least, since he does not clamor for protection at home, while carrying his wares around the world. The most obstinate chafferers are the women who are selling, for no women appear as buyers; I am told that Greek women of respectability never go to market. What a bustling, bargaining, yet merry-making crowd! Dried figs I bought, good, yet enormously cheap; for five cents a peasant woman loaded me down, so that I had to leave part of my measure behind for want of transportation. I should have bought only a cent's worth according to the rules of careful economy. My Wallachian shepherdess, too, I saw there sitting among her curds and lambs, with wild luxuriant form now more fully revealed in the clear daylight; she greets me with another shower of sparkles and invites me anew to her mountain home. As I walked through one of the back streets, some Greek boys observing my foreign dress began to run after and mock the stranger; they were joined by others wherever we passed. I darted rapidly through an alley, but the crowd increased till a small mob was in pursuit. I hurried back to the bazaar and lost myself from my tormentors in the throng. The boys did not mean any thing except a little sport; but it was one of two acts of rudeness which I remember to have experienced in my journey through rural Greece. Postal matters seemed rather lax at Chalkis; two visits to the Post Office were not able to procure me an interview with the Postmaster or the sight of a postage stamp.

The Greek shops open with their whole fronts into the street, they always seem to be half outside in the free air. The shoemaker sits before his door and pegs away, the blacksmith's shop is next to the shoemaker's, his bellows can be blown by a person standing on the pavement. The artisans generally are working in the open air, or just across the threshold of the entrance. Public eating places are frequent; the kitchen is where the front window is in our houses; as you pass along the street, you can see the pot boiling and smell the oleaginous fragrance of its contents. If you wish, the keeper will hand you a spoon and a plate of lentils or beans with stewed mutton, and you can eat your dinner under the free blue sky of Hellas.

Thus the shops range close together down the street, like a series of pigeon holes, before which the active chattering folk is swarming. It is the gift of the climate: man cannot endure to be housed up, though it be mid winter. The air invites, confinement within walls is painful, the glorious world is outside and the golden gifts of Helius. Yet just as the shops are open, free, unconfined, so the dwelling houses are close, walled-in, forbidding. There the women are, the family; the world must not be allowed to enter that sanctuary, nor must it come out into the world. I walked toward the suburbs through the more private streets, in the hope of catching a glimpse of some beautiful Greek shape. But there was not one to be seen, not a woman of the better class appeared anywhere. Away then; — no chance is there of finding Helen here in this Oriental seclusion; though Aulis lie just yonder across the strait, resting in tranquil sunshine, yet eternally inviting to a new expedition to Troy, there is now not a sign of a Homeric hero who has come hither in pursuit of his beautiful queen, not a sign of even a wretched Thersites. The day of the Trojan enterprise is indeed past forever; Helen must be recovered in some other way.

In my disappointment I went down to the bridge over the Euripus and looked at the flow of its waters. The first bridge is said to have been built by the Thebans during the Peloponnesian war; the building of it was one of the severest blows that Athens received, and according to Thucydides caused more terror than the defeat of the Sicilian expedition — doubtless one of the two exaggerations to be found in that coldest-blooded of historians. But look under the bridge at this strong current; it seems like a narrow stream dashing down a rocky bottom. Look at it longer; it is not as swift as it was, indeed it changes under your eye from a rapid torrent to a mild unruffled movement of slow waters. If you look at it the third time long enough, you will find that the current has wholly ceased, there is a complete calm under the bridge; nay, it begins slowly to move the other way, and soon increases to the swift dashing stream which you saw first, but in the opposite direction. This change takes place within a few minutes, and sometimes there are several such changes in twenty-four hours. On the whole this is the most capricious thing known of the sea. The cause is commonly said to be some mixed action of tides and winds along with the configuration of the land above and below. But I hold it to be an inherent principle of Greek water that it be able to run in one direction, then to turn around and run back again; true to the Greek character it sometimes has the capacity of being the opposite of itself. Enemies call this trait by the ugly name of lying or treachery; but let us call it versatility, the ability to turn about.

From this narrowest point of the Euripus we see plainly what the island Euboea is: simply a fragment torn off from the mainland and thrown into the sea. The mighty giant who performed the feat was a veritable existence to the ancient eye looking at yonder ragged mountain and beholding this rift filled with water; nor will the modern observer fail to have some faith in that deed of wonder. The old myths are often the truest expression of the Greek landscape to this day; far truer to me than the imageless impersonal geological description. That angry Titan who tore up a mountain and hurled it at Jupiter, with the forests still on it and with the streams still running down its sides, can yet be seen with a good vision. Euboea is an island, but it becomes mainland by a bridge. Such is the physical aspect of Greece; land and water lie in brotherly embrace, ready to furnish mutual assistance; but they can be made to hold aloof from each other with sullen defiance. The continent, too, is filled with islands, quite like the sea, for what else are these plains and valleys held asunder by the mountains, requiring that climbing ship, the donkey to pass them?

In the afternoon the same vessel with the same company returns to Vathy. As I sat on the shore previous to departing, I was surprised to hear myself addressed in good fluent English by a man in the baggy blue breeches of the islanders. I greeted gladly my native speech in that strange spot, where I least thought of hearing it; the unexpected meeting of lovers after long separation, could not have been more tender; under such circumstances one is astonished to find what deep affection he has for his mother tongue. The man had been many years a sailor in the English merchant marine where he had learned the language. But shove off, let us leave living Chalkis and once more rock over the ripples of the Euripus to the more real forms of those ancient ghosts at Aulis.

For after all, the supreme interest here is the deserted harbor, the invisible ships, the vanished temples. Yet Nature also is in harmony with the spell, if she does not produce it; the blue waters beneath us gush around the keel in quiet joy; the gentle curvature of the hills throws its soft lines against the sky; these hills too are waves in that fixed rocky sea above, now also faintly blue with haze; over their tops Apollo with the coyness of a new love tenderly feels with his golden fingers. It is classic repose in classic outline; the soul into which these summits have been born can never tolerate extravagance, violence, horror. In that line of tranquil undulation, there is movement, much movement, but no throes, no wild fury. There is struggle, — for note how yonder mountain strives to reach above its neighbors; still there is the final reconciliation, the final solution of the conflict in a grand harmony. Passion too is here, the heights roll and heave over some mighty throbbing heart, but there is no giving way, no despair; each throb reveals the motion of a Grace and its very calmness signifies its energy. Blood-red intensity you will say, yet somehow united with a sunny tranquillity, making a new sweet but deep-moving music over these heights.

You, the spectator, are drawn into the soul of this landscape, though the crowd in the boat laugh at your absence of mind; emotions awake deeply within you, though they cannot boil over into frenzy, passions even rise but are gifted with a strange self-control. You are rent with some unseen conflict, some unconscious struggle, as if the old powers still lurked in the place and wrought upon you with demonic sympathy. What is the matter with you? What influence is this which hurls you into the hopes, the fears — into all the tossings of a conflict which does not exist for the sober senses — is it memory, is it imagination merely, or the nature around you? You weep or are ready to weep amid the wild gayety of the company in your boat; you struggle within yourself, you resolve, you make the sacrifice, you repent. Finally you ask yourself: Whom shall I place in this landscape to give it expression? Whom shall I place here to give myself expression? For the typical person must be found around whom these dim emotions cluster, and in whom they have utterance; thus they are thrown out of you and give you relief from their throng. Already, I imagine, you have had glimpses of a form flitting through your soul amid the clouds of feeling; that form begins to walk out of darkness into the gleaming radiance of sunshine; it is a young virgin dressed in spotless white; there she stands before you in clearest plastic outline. Who is she? And who is that man standing behind her, in brazen helm and mailed coat with a spear in his hands. He seems a Jove-born king, of great authority in his look and pride in his mien; yet there is deep tenderness, nay, sadness in his eye. It is Iphigenia with her father Agamemnon; they have just landed on yonder round island in the bay, upon whose summit the temple stands; he drops behind her secretly to throw away a tear.

Bump — we too are landed; the boat strikes the shore

heavily, having crossed again the harbor of Aulis. I am thrown forward by the jolt into the lap of the Cretan schoolmaster, the crabbed Didaskali, who asks me to accompany him directly to his school. We soon enter the building, which is substantial, but has no floor; twenty-five little urchins walk about in the dust with this clear advantage, which the expert will not fail to appreciate: it makes their steps wholly noiseless. Every one of them is stockingless still in February; they wear low sharp-pointed pumps and high trowsers, the naked flesh intervening you may imagine, if you wish. As soon as the Didaskali enters, his impatience begins to manifest itself; he finds fault with all that he sees and with whatever has been done during his absence; nearly every boy into whose copy-book he looks, receives a thump. The son of the Didaskali, a youth of about fifteen, helps him teach, and presides during his absence; that son had his cap knocked off his head across the room by his irate father. The term *zoon*, animal, was the favorite word of the Didaskali, though he employed other heavy artillery of that sort which I did not fully understand, except its thunder. Taking me along, with switch in hand, he goes around the room and inspects the hands of the little fellows; he strikes their fingers light or hard with his switch in proportion to the dirt on them. Cleanliness received that day an immense advancement in Aulis. But judging by the condition of those fingers generally, I could not believe that such a tour had been the teacher's habit every day; the reflection would force itself upon the pedagogic mind that he did all this for the special honor of visitors — as some of his fellow-craftsmen do in other lands upon occasion.

Yet the boys are learning, the school is by no means bad. They write well, spell readily from dictation, and are drilled thoroughly in the rudiments of arithmetic and geography. Certainly the country schools which I attended in youth were not better, some in our land are far worse to-day. The seats and desks are of the improved kind, there is a blackboard and it is used. The main object of primary education is manifestly attained here; the

AULIS AND CHALKIS.

common branches, those great instrumentalities of all culture, are placed in the possession of every pupil. If any of these boys has the divine spark within him, he has now the means in his hand to kindle it into a flame. Also there was order, though it was too much the discipline of terror. Very interesting it was to hear the old verbs conjugated with the instinct of a spoken tongue — verbs which were droned over by young Thucydides and Xenophon. Nothing can please the lover of Greek literature and of that ancient Greek world more than to see these old forms and expressions welling up again into the spontaneity of living speech. Therefore the Greek school is the most interesting of all schools and one of the most interesting things in Greece. Do not pass it by in your trip.

But the Didaskali is a grumbler; knocked over and belabored by ill-fortune, he has become all bruised and crumpled up in spirit; I cannot think of straightening him out now; it seriously clouds my Greek mood even to be with him. First, he has the eternal grievance of all teachers that I ever saw, male or female: he receives too little salary. This is sixty drachmas a month, he informs me; in our money less than twelve dollars. Yet I have to tell him that poverty-stricken Greece pays relatively better salaries than rich America to her instructors, which is verily not much consolation. Then too the lack of promotion is another complaint, for he feels himself capable of teaching in the Hellenic School, the next higher grade; in fact he knows himself to be far more deserving than a certain Demosthenes who has been put up by favoritism.

Here then is another case of unappreciated genius, which we never fail to meet, whithersoever we may turn upon our broad earth; to greatness that is unknown the world is indeed cold and indifferent. A sort of disease one may call it, of which hardly any human being, however humble, is free; at some moment, whatever his stoicism, he will be heard to cry out in pain: Alas, I am an unrecognized mortal in this life! The malady has seized our schoolmaster in its most violent and eruptive form, breaking out continually into speech, whose burden is, My genius is not appreciated at Aulis. So he heralds the fact to me, and I herald it to you who listen and are touched upon a chord more or less responsive. Such is, at bottom, the trouble with the Didaskali's discordant temper; for what harmony can come from a soul that so profoundly believes in its own genius, yet has to live in a world that so profoundly disbelieves in the same, or is totally ignorant of it? Shrillest discord must result when such a soul and such a world come in contact with each other, as they have to do; yet it is a very human note, universally heard among men. The traveler may laugh a little at the Didaskali, but has to reply sympathetically: Yours is just my case, too, in my country; I also am not appreciated there; but our talents are invincible, our merits are bound to shine through all clouds of envy and favoritism into full recognition, if we can only in the meantime keep in a good humor.

His abode was in a room to the rear of the schoolhouse, where he boarded himself with his boy. He complained of his wretched quarters, and his room did look as if no woman's hand had been there for many a day. Unwashed plates and spoons, table and bed were promiscuously scattered about the room, which state of things seems to be his own fault. A pot of beans was boiling over the fire for his meal; this with the recinato is enough for human want. Miserable existence, he cried. I answered: no, my friend, I deem your lot an enviable one, I would like to exchange with you. To be schoolmaster in Aulis is to be prince of schoolmasters; heroes are your next neighbors, poets are your dearest friends; monarchs are your associates, if there ever were monarchs on this earth. Homer, Pindar, Aeschylus are here with an infinite train of successors who have made this spot the setting for their rarest jewels. And those old heroes who still haunt this place — whose tramp can still be heard on the night-air and whose oars still rustle over yon bay in the evening wind — are they no company for you? Give me your school, this room where we now are, your pot of beans and demijohn of recinato, with those rare old books of

Troy — and I should be willing to stay here forever. I should like, however, before I begin, to have these dishes washed and the bed cleaned up — I did not speak aloud this last sentence, but I could not help thinking it.

I now escape from my colleague who has told me so much more than I wanted to hear of, supposing by my look that I knew all about his sort of grievances, and I make my way across the fields to the hills overlooking the bay. That will be a relief indeed, for there far other company awaits the sojourner at Aulis. The common people when I meet them on the road, stop and curiously inquire: Where are you going? What business have you here? Not in an unfriendly spirit, but in simple rustic curiosity they catch me by the arm and hold me, as if I or they belonged to the brigands. The word which one hears holds buried within it a whole history of society — *ti douleia*, what occupation is yours — literally what slave-labor is yours, for in antiquity the slave chiefly labored; but now that word has come to mean simply work, thus resembling our word service. As the slave has risen into the free laborer in the course of centuries, so has that word been ennobled along with him, till now there is no object corresponding to its former sense, and it indicates one weighty point of superiority which modern has over ancient Greece. *Ti douleia* still heard on these hills gives a peep back through two thousand years when slave met slave on this spot and asked: what slave-labor is yours?

Before a house or rather in the door of a house in one place a man sits thrumming a stringed instrument whose notes vibrate softly on the sunbeams in some secret harmony, you must believe, with the mellow golden afternoon. It may be the old lyre in one of its forms, it has the sweet low thrill of the Italian mandoline when there is a perfect lull in the air. Into its strain there fall at intervals the stray notes of a song, as if the idle player was merely preluding at random to his own vacant fancies. In front of his eye as it glances out of the door lies the harbor of Aulis whose distant waters seem to be gently quivering to the touch of the instrument. Will any one blame the traveler as too fantastic, if he again thinks of

Homer's men — of Achilles who was found before his tent playing his harp to his own dear soul, when the embassy of Greek chieftains came to pacify his anger and to urge his return to the war? But this present hero is not Achilles, nor does he seem to have any destructive wrath, nor has he lost his Briseis, who just now stands before his tent wrestling violently with a sullied fustanella.

Therefore we may pass on. But at the view of the bay and of the hills the secret combat rises again in the breast, the two antique forms come up with startling distinctness, filled with their intense conflict. Do what you will, every other deed, every other shape is swallowed up in the struggle between father and daughter. She, the young, the innocent, the spotless, must be immolated to a supposed necessity of State. That the winds may blow favorably, and the armament sail successfully to the Trojan shore, her sacrifice is demanded, for to the Greek, to her own father far more important it seemed that Helen should return than that Iphigenia should live. It is an old but undying theme, which both ancient and modern poets have treated with a tragic depth and energy; woman, guiltless and removed from political strife, is nevertheless snatched from the Family and made to suffer or even to perish that ends of State may be attained; whether she be the king's own daughter Iphigenia, offered for the sake of the great national enterprise, or the modern princess, Blanche, led to a political marriage bringing peace to the nation perhaps, but to herself only wretchedness and slow death.

Furthermore, that these early Greeks should sacrifice virgin purity to beauty distained is a prophecy, a double prophecy: it foretells the supreme glory of their career, and at the same time indicates the moral disease which must finally eat away their character and energy. They will bring back Helen to Greece and realize beauty beyond all other peoples, but the ethical violation hinted in the death of Iphigenia will remain and become the seed of inner corruption. For mark! she and what she represents is gone, destroyed; her fate will wake the avenging Nemesis that will bring back her loss to the people who have immolated her, and hence possess her no longer. Thus they reveal themselves and their destiny in their legend.

It is true that the ancient legend rescues Iphigenia from the sacrificial altar by the intervention of the Goddess Artemis. But she is taken to a barbarous land, to Tauris, where she is preserved as a priestess to the divinity who saved her; there too she becomes the bearer of all that Greece represents. Again look at the prophetic image in the legend, for it is the Barbarians, that is, those who are not Greeks, the modern world if you please, who have taken up and saved Iphigenia, cherishing her with a deathless affection, while she on the other hand as priestess of the temple in foreign lands, has brought to them the humanizing influences of Greek culture. Chiefly from such a point of view is the famous *Iphigenia* of Goethe written, the finest of all the dramatic elaborations of this legend. In it we see the modern Barbarian, now the Poet filled with the inspiration of the Grecian priestess, and paying back to her a tribute greater and more beautiful than anything which she herself has received or transmitted.

But the old Greek legend likewise brings her back from Tauris, after many years of banishment and priestly service, to Greece, restores her from the hands of the Barbarians to her ancient home. Such is indeed that prophetic myth which our own time has seen fulfilled, but which the dawn of Goethe's poem has not yet beheld. For it is the strong arm of those whom Greece called Barbarians, but to whom she imparted her culture, which has broken her chains and restored her to freedom and nationality. Nay, they have brought back her own civilization to herself, increased with tenfold spoils, it is true, but still bearing her impress. So we may now say with the old legend that Iphigenia has returned to Greece.

The account of the sacrifice of Iphigenia is not the creation of Homer; the entire story at Aulis he passes over in silence. On the contrary it is a development of later Greek consciousness, of the tragic and not of the epic spirit, though it doubtless had its germ in the

Homeric Age. This intense conflict in which father sacrifices daughter belongs to the domain of tragedy. Two struggling principles, each with its own right, assail each other in the very bosom of the Family, and just at that point where its tenderest emotions are knit together. The time of the tragic poets was indeed a tragic time, whereof they are the true outgrowth, a time in which Greece was immolating her own daughter, and was growing conscious of the fact, which consciousness found its intense expression in the drama.

Yet, on the other hand, we must not misunderstand that father, Agamemnon. He was leader of the Greek hosts, the representative of the Greek State; moreover he possessed the heroic character, which sacrifices all feelings to the public end, and courageously endures. The pang in his breast for the death of his child was as great as that of any parent. We must not suppose that he was devoid of tenderness and pity; on the contrary they surged up and dashed around his purpose like the waves of the sea in a tempest. Still that purpose stood, had to stand, firm as a rock mid the terrific upheaval of emotions; for he must be the hero, placed there at the head of the expedition, he must subordinate to the great national end all his feelings; the most piercing cries of his own soul in anguish cannot make him waver for a moment. Once more take a glance with me over the waters; can you not, on yon round island aslant the evening sunbeams, behold the father, pale, trembling, weeping, yet resolute — now leading his daughter, robed in white folds, up the knoll to the altar? There is the temple of Artemis, within whose marble embrace the two forms slowly disappear; the eyes of the Greek hosts who look on from this shore with us, and from the ships lying over the bay, are not dry — nor are mine.

Then a voice comes to me and asks: would you sacrifice your daughter to the State? No, I would not, I answer, not directly at least. I do not pretend to be a hero, do not wish to be one. This is sentimental, it is true; but I am sentimental upon this subject. I do not wish to pay such a large price for heroism, I prefer to be ignoble and keep my Iphigenia. Still Agamemnon paid it, had to pay it, all great world-historical characters pay that or a greater price for their destiny. This is just the tragedy of the hero — the conflict within tears him to pieces; still he, subjecting his emotions to his principle, heroically makes the sacrifice. But we have no such sacrifice to make in this expedition, praise be to Artemis and the rest of the Gods; no world-sustaining heroism is now required; all the omens are propitious, all the winds are favorable; besides, we are going to take a new route in the pursuit of the fair runaway.

Thus the Agamemnon of the Iliad is not wholly the Agamemnon of Aulis, though the two fuse together in the imagination; the latter the tragedians have modeled, making him the bearer of a terrific internal struggle, in addition to his being in the external struggle with Troy, which now falls into the background. This transition from the outer to the inner conflict indicates a deepening of life and of consciousness; spiritual suffering has seized hold of man, and that simple, happy epical world of Homer has departed forever. Such is the soul of the legend which can be felt even through the superficial half-mocking treatment of Euripides. Still the scenery of Aulis throws the beholder into that ancient tragic struggle, he lives it over again within himself as he saunters around the hills, looks up at the skies, and floats over the waters.

Whether these characters were ever living persons or not, whether the Trojan war be historical or not, can make little difference. That conflict has furnished the most abiding types for the race, types of heroism, endurance, wisdom. And what more can History do than furnish its great characters — those eternal symbols by which whole ages think, live and die? Here at Aulis once more rises the thought of the struggle between the East and the West; all the Greek armament was animated by this principle; the Iliad is but the first heroic utterance of the conflict. The day lowers, but the traveler is filled with the spirit of the air — it is the same air breathed by those ancient heroes and is still laden with all the energy of the old enterprise. Nay, the conflict between East and West is here before him to-day, smothered though quivering, as he looks out toward Troy.

My friends, you will recollect that our last turning-point, whence we began a new direction in our journey, was at Marathon. The battle there was historical — the greatest battle in History. On its plain the East and West grappled; it was the East which then attacked, but was victoriously met and repulsed. We have marched forward to Aulis, it is true, but in reality we have gone backward into the twilight of fable. Now the Greeks are the aggressive side, and assail their enemies on Asiatic soil, yet it is the same question, the same principle at issue. But to pass from Marathon to Aulis means to remount from clear history into the misty mythical origin; still this myth expresses better than history the dim primitive instinct, the unconscious germ of the Hellenic world. This goal, then, we have reached, yet not the further road to Troy shall we go, but turn from Aulis and move forward to a still deeper phase of Greek spirit, — to the seat of oracular wisdom and of reconciliation. Through Thebes, full of profounder tragic destinies than even Aulis, we shall pass toward the place of harmony, toward the God whom Hellas chiefly adored in the greatest and intensest period of her life, and whom she besought to harmonize her inner struggles. In the track of Orestes driven by Furies, we shall approach the temple of Apollo the light-darter, who could bring atonement to the guilty soul and thus solve the ancient tragedy. Here then we stand at the very opening of our Western world. Having courageously marched thus far, and having cast many delighted glances into that dawn across the sea, we may catch breath again for a few minutes before we turn up the road toward Delphi, the next stadium of Greek civilization.

IX. FROM AULIS TO THEBES.

Early in the morning Varvouillya stood before the wine-shop with his two donkeys; he called me out, who was there celebrating a farewell to Aulis in company with three or four citizens. I grasped my staff and knapsack and hurried into the street, Varvouillya grunted at the beasts of destiny, and our procession began to move up through the main thoroughfare of Aulis towards Thebes. The Cretan schoolmaster with friendly smiles came out of his house and saluted me; in the sunshine of this Greek morning he looks as if he had resolved during the night never to get into a bad humor again, being now in the first full glow of his new resolution. Also the Nestor of the hamlet appeared, standing before his gate and leaning on his staff, with enthusiastic gleams ploughing his wrinkled features as I shook his hand. Happy old man, with a background to his age fresh as the blooming meadows; for behold that young Greek wife of his now peering out of the door behind him, with a babe in her arms. One may well liken him to the aged olive-tree of Aulis, not far from which he is standing — wrinkled, bent, silver-haired, but ever sending forth fresh blossoms.

The village was astir for the duties of the day, white fustanellas were hurrying in every direction toward the fields. Many women were already at the various pools and fountains engaged in heavy labor, others were passing thither with rude troughs and batlets on their shoulders. Soon the last house is behind us, and we see the husbandman at his work; he is trimming his vineyard or plowing with a yoke of oxen, seldom with horses. The plow which he employs has a very primitive look, not very different from the Homeric plow. Yet I ought in justice to add that along my route I have also seen modern plows. The land which he turns over seems rich where it is arable, but it is often rocky. Certainly a much greater portion of it could be brought under cultivation; some blastment rests upon the soil, lying here rudely tilled or often wholly neglected. The earth, the great original implement of man, is not half utilized by those who are wielding it here at present.

The morning changes to heaviness, the sky lowers and begins to threaten, except from the East where through a rifted cloud Helius persists at short intervals in strewing his golden arrows over the Euboic hills. What are you thinking of as you gaze at the heavens? On such a morning as this the ancient sacrifice might have been made; through the darkened canopy above, the Goddess broke in effulgence and rescued the virgin from the altar. On the Euripus are now standing white sails, in listless calm, seeming to rise straight out of the water, for in that distance no hull can be distinguished. Two or three such little boats are at this moment to be seen, flecking the blue surface; each sail is an expanded swan's wing hovering over the sea; they multiply at once to a thousand sails floating around the full swelling island capped by the white temple. Scarce a breath of wind can be felt, certainly there are now no unfavorable breezes for Troy, the Goddess has been manifestly appeased this morning.

The locality grows upon the traveler, and he leaves it unwillingly. Slowly he walks up the slightly ascending plain which lies to the rear of Aulis; often he turns around and looks at the sea, fair Euripus, whose waters are still quivering in the distance with some hidden strong emotion; he is indeed parting from that which he loves. He is filled with the spirit of the air which is charged with the ancient enterprise. Doubtless memory aids him in calling up that world long since passed away; but there must be something else, I believe; there must be some hidden sympathy of nature, for nature, too, preserves dim memories of the great deeds that have been enacted before her, and retains the faint impress of heroic forms that have once been in her presence. So he would fain think; at any rate, there is the one emotion, the one central figure here. Ah Iphigenia, what a symbol hast thou become for men! All thy struggles, all the struggles of thy wretched parents rise in my breast as I thread around through the hills. I have to wrestle with thy conflicts, they seethe within me as if they were my own; I am indeed become one with thee. Now I turn across the last comb of the hill, Aulis passes out of sight, still thy struggles are raging within me nor can I rid myself of thy heart-piercing destiny. Why is it, I ask myself. Because thou art truly a sacred symbol of mankind, not a mere thing of reality — thou art a Universal, embracing all men in thy sad destiny, and for them thou dost suffer.

Yet it is but a story, there is no reality in all these events, they never took place. This does not alter the case, in fact it increases their significance. Very profound and far-reaching is the saying of the old philosopher, that fable is truer than history. The legends of the race are still worth more than its history, its poets are to be placed a great way before its historians. The pure fact is often an insignificant thing compared to the pure fancy. For the fable of a people can embrace its whole truth — all that it spiritually possesses, institutions, religion, art, character. No mere record of what happened here and there, no account of political and social events can show its entire life, its whole truth. But the genuine myth will manifest its vital principle and put the same into an eternal type outside of Space and Time; while history is of all things in Space and Time, broken off at each end, and often cracked badly in the middle. Yet do not underrate history — only this torso is ours to-day, and we should preserve it with sacred care as our chief boon; for we moderns can no longer make myths, we can make only history. But if there be a few who may still be able to construct a mythical world, we may well give them the honors due to the Poet and the Prophet.

Still certain historical questions will rise at Aulis, and demand some answer. It is the play of erudition to give as many responses as possible, since all of them are equally without value. One such question comes up before me just now: why was Aulis selected as the place of assembling the forces of Greece? Or, why did the

Poet select this spot? Either of these inquiries must remain a question of mere historic probability, and hence any answer to it is intrinsically worthless. Aulis is as good a geographical center as any other protected harbor in Greece; but for no small portion of the armament it was the less convenient place. Let us then conjecture political reasons: the restoration of Helen was the cause of Southern Greece, of Menelaus and Agamemnon; it was, therefore, necessary to take every means of interesting and arousing Northern Greece, of giving to that part of the country the easiest opportunity of assembling. Ulysses did not want to come, according to the legend; his little island lay far off to one side. But Bœotia, Thessaly, Phthia, and Northern Greece generally would center here. So we may go on spinning conjectures indefinitely; they are the merest figments of probability; the answer to such questions, however plausible, must be in the nature of the case, without import.

Historic probabilities let us have as little to do with as possible; they are the poorest glass beads that we can pick up on our way; very sparingly shall they be strung on the variegated strand which is now being made out of the incidents of our Greek journey. For instance, what concerns it thee whether Achilles was ever in flesh and blood, whether he ever was a spatial reality or not? Two things can at present be affirmed of him with great certainty: first, that his flesh and blood are now earth-mould, if he ever possessed them; secondly, that he still exists as spirit and will exist perdurably. The last fact is the interesting and worthy one for us in many ways — it even hints what there is immortal here on earth. But the great question of erudition whether this soul of the hero ever had any body, may be dismissed without loss. And that still greater question of poverty-stricken erudition whether Homer be really Homer or somebody else of the same name, as the perplexed student once put it most accurately, ought to be cast away as a worthless counterfeit of Greek gold. Suppose that he is, suppose that he is not, suppose any thing — what difference does it make? Will that give us a new Odyssey, or will it interpret for us the old one? Yet there is a tuneful spirit called Homer singing through the ages; even now a voice comes riding on the air, saying: Why hunt after my body which has perished, why seek for my existence in Space and Time which has vanished? Listen to my voice — that is my immortal part, that is what I have left unto you as my sole gift. By that alone may I be remembered!

I have employed the word symbol quite frequently, but I must give you a warning in regard to its use. The symbolism of the Greeks in their great creative period was not conscious, was not design. They did not say: come, let us make a symbol for all the world and for all time. Then they had not done it, they would have lost the very germ of their Art — spontaneity. Unwittingly in all the little particulars of their life and their activity they manifested the Generic, the Universal — they could not help being artists. For Art must always have this universal side, must be a symbol — yet on the other hand it cannot be divorced from the living spontaneous actuality. To succeeding times the unconscious insight of the Poet may become a conscious reflection; but then its true poetical nature has departed. Later in their history the Greeks betook themselves to conscious symbolizing; little heed do we pay to that part of their work now. We may know more about the Poet's process than he does himself; we stand and look on while the demon struggles within him, imparting inspiration or fury perchance; but his and not ours is the poetic creative act, ours is rather the act of destruction. The symbol, recollect then, whenever the term is employed, lays stress upon this universal and eternal element in all artistic creation, yet does not imply conscious purpose on part of the artist.

But Aulis has now passed out of view, and must be dropped; we have entered a small valley through which we are winding solitary; only flocks of birds rise from the fields, whirl in the air for a moment, then flutter into the low bushes. There are no trees, the soil is untilled, yet seems capable of some cultivation. The valley is delightful, the breathing of its atmosphere is like a draught of mild wine; it is watered by a brook running through the middle, along whose border passes the road. Up this road or rather bridle-path Varvouillya is driving his donkeys, which move slowly through the landscape with their look of Oriental resignation.

I have now been with Varvouillya nearly five days, and have conceived a strong liking for the man. He is a character — hardy and rugged, yet somewhat mysterious, and I hold him to be honest. For forty years he has driven his donkeys over these hills in the way of transportation and small trading. At Aulis he acquired in some transaction an old flint-lock which he now carries slung over his shoulders. He knows every point of the country, and is acquainted with every human being we meet. Though without education he has picked up in this mode of life a great deal of curious information, half mythical, half actual; thereto he adds experience with men and a rude subtlety. Moreover he is the possessor of a strong rough will, with a very decided impulse of generosity and of hospitable feeling. He is evidently recognized as a sort of leader among these people; he is of them, yet with a little stronger purpose, which they feel and call him playfully by the name of Capitanos. Humor and mockery he possesses in a true Greek vein; behind the wine-table he sits deep-voiced, with a phthisicky laugh which always ends in a red-faced fit of coughing after he brings out the point to one of his best stories. This cough is always heard in chorus with the laughter of the merry company.

Thus I have seen him during these days, and a strong attachment has grown up between us; to his appearance, even to his garments, I am now fully reconciled, though at first both were objects of distrust. Unshaven for some weeks, his beard comes out bristling over his face in frosty stubble; his hair too is grizzled by age, but is still full of spirit; a small stained cap fitting close to his head but unable to restrain bunches of hair from gushing out in front of his forehead is not out of harmony with the man and his general costume. His body is slim, wiry, and supple; the stubbled face, when he speaks, is lit with a smile rudely generous; a large wart lies just on the tip of his nose, and flattens out, spreading all over the same when he laughs.

But the mental trait which chiefly distinguishes him is the mystery in which he vails himself to the world and the world to himself. He has his own view of the way in which things are done in this universe of ours; a supernatural power peculiar to himself reigns in the invisible realm. He is what many deep and uninformed natures are — a mystic, perhaps superstitious; in his struggles of life events have taken place which he cannot account for by ordinary experience, and so he has a special solution of his own. Driving his mules for forty years over the lone hills he has had time to think in his uncouth way; but he cannot lift the cloud from the world, nor from himself, and he has landed where nearly all ignorant but inquiring men arrive in the end. Appearances just in this locality have obliged him to resort to a mystical machinery; if I understand him aright there is in him a dash of the old Greek belief in Pan, nymphs and satyrs, yet not now dancing in ancient sunlight, but enveloped dimly in clouds. Indeed who can live in intimacy with this Nature without feeling her old influence at work upon his soul? Still she subtly creates her ancient forms for the true-hearted worshiper leisurely resigning himself to her shaping hand; even the prosaic traveler she will transform, to the wonder of everybody, if he but submit in good faith to her gentle guidance.

Varvouillya is a curious compound of the ancient and modern, he is mixed like the language he speaks, like Greece of to-day. He was born in Janina under Turkish rule; the secretiveness begotten of Turkish oppression still lurks in his character. In many ways he is the contrast to the traveling merchant Aristides previously mentioned — far more reserved, less intelligent, with much less education, yet with a stronger character. I doubt whether he can read the newspaper, which with its contents seems to him to lie in the world of mystery. But both of them are men of influence, both are true Greeks, both believe in the great Idea, though Varvouillya sees it rather dimly; both are mediators for the communities which they visit.

Off to our left at some distance lay the ancient town of Tanagra, through whose neighborhood we cannot pass without a delightful thrill of memory. A little community it was with its own distinctive character, as we can plainly see from ancient books; an ideal sense of the Beautiful and of the Divine prevailed there in pleasing contrast to other towns. The fairest youth was selected to carry the sacred lamb at the festival of Hermes; the shrines and temples were built by them away from the profane part of the town, away from business places and dwelling houses. An ancient observer has celebrated the women of Tanagra, giving them the palm over all Greek women for graceful form and harmonious movement.

It seems to have nourished a peculiar phase of Art too, springing from its special character, and uttering the same in beauty. Recently this Art has been resurrected from its tombs, and the Tanagra figurines in our day have carried the name over the world, coupled with a sweet grace and delicate form. Only some six or seven years ago did this great resurrection of the old Bœotian town take place, giving us many a peep at its life and manners, even at its fashions and frivolities. Eight thousand tombs are reported to have given up their shapes, which, like restless ghosts, have wandered into every corner of the globe. At present, however, Tanagra is quiet again, and the cornfields are growing over its sepulchres.

But that which gives to the town its chief title to remembrance, is the poetess whom it produced, beautiful Corinna, she who is said to have won prizes over Pindar and even to have been the teacher of the Theban bard. Her fame was the town's fairest jewel, her image was seen in its most prominent places, she was altogether its greatest name during many centuries of its existence — she, a woman and a poetess, some 500 years before Christ. Long and nobly was she remembered, and if she was able to surpass the greatest lyric poet of all time, what skill may we not suppose to have been hers? But an ancient authority slyly hints that it was her beauty more than her poetry which moved the judges of the contest, for she was also the most beautiful woman of her period. An old traveler more than six hundred years after her death still beheld her monuments in her native town; in the gymnasium was her picture bound with a triumphal wreath in honor of her victory over Pindar. Thus the little community loyally kept before themselves their greatest character — a poetess; wherever they are, her image must fall into their eyes. One of those Tanagra figurines I take to be Corinna, with lines from her picture possibly; nor can anybody help thinking of her, when he notes the type common to all these images, as if the town in its character and in its works moulded itself instinctively after its supreme personage. She was its ideal, she will, therefore, be the inner creative principle of all that its people are or do.

But we ask for her words and her music, for the utterance of hers which may have come down to us. Alas! it is all broken and disjointed, very difficult to piece together now. Time has shivered her lyre into fragments, of which many are lost, others remain incoherent; a few indistinct sounds of her voice you may with effort catch out of the distance. Still she is the prophecy of the poetess, whom we all have to recognize in our day, somewhat as those old citizens of Tanagra did. A broken murmur of song only is left of her strain; still we may think of her in her own image, "singing sweet love notes to the white-robed dames of Tanagra, and greatly delighted is my city at the clear-twittering voice."

Such was our ancient Tanagra, with its temples and famous statues; above all, with its poetess, beautiful Corinna, the divine utterance, both in form and in speech, of Tanagra. But, threading up the valley in company with our reflections, we have suddenly arrived at quite a different sort of habitation, belonging to the present, and with another kind of woman for its central figure. This is the Wallachian village situated near some springs which give rise to the small stream along which we have been passing. Some twenty or thirty families form the community which is always ready to take wing for other parts. The dwellings are of primitive architecture, indeed the original pattern of the house can be studied here. Four forked posts are driven into the ground, and cross-pieces are placed from fork to fork; upon these cross-pieces sticks are laid, and the whole is covered with twigs over which is a thatching of straw or leaves. A court or inclosure made of stone or brushwood, is built to each house; this inclosure is large enough to shut in the flock of the owner. The Wallachians, as has been already said, are shepherds; at present the men are absent from the village, guarding the herds in the mountains. Ferocious dogs rush out at us, but a mere motion from Varvouillya, as if he were reaching for a stone, is sufficient to keep them at a distance.

Here again appears an ever-recurring scene in the Greek landscape: the women of the village washing at the fountain. Their costume verges toward the undraped; there is such a display of nudities and negligences that the traveler is forcibly reminded of the antique, particularly here in Greece. These forms are the sculpturesque decoration of every town and fountain. But the Wallachian women are not of classic mould; it is easy to observe in these people a new type, bodies are thick and broad, in contrast to the tall thin-waisted Albanian, or to the symmetrical Greek; limbs, which are freely exposed, are large and powerful, but somewhat stumpy; the half-opened bosom reveals the mighty mothers of the strong-armed people. A little study, which the honest traveler will not fail to give to this matter, reveals the development through labor, and not through training; it is an irregular growth according to necessity, not the free, harmonious unfolding of all the members according to some ideal divine pattern. The garments of the Wallachian women are particolored, which is a new contrast on this soil; no longer we see the white robes of the Greek, but a feeling for color is noticed — color without form, such as is often observed among the more northern peasantry of Europe. The dresses are made of colored patches and of striped goods; to the eye, now accustomed only to the white raiment of the country, this new confusion of tints gives an unpleasant jar.

The washers rub away without paying much attention to the curious gaze of the passer; but among them the traveler will particularly notice a young woman with long heavy braided hair dropping down her back; she is not beautiful exactly, but in the exuberant may-day of youth, rejoicing in the free working of an enormous and perfectly healthy organism. Broadness is her characteristic — broad-faced, broad-backed, prodigiously broad-bottomed, still one cannot say that she is unwieldy. She lays the garment which she is washing upon a stone, after lifting it from the boiling cauldron, then she pounds it with an immense bat or maul. What a terrific swing in those naked arms, whose thews double up into huge knots as she smites it with her merciless weapon! And those garments, look at them, if you would see from what stains purity may come; they require just such a bat swung by just such arms, for it is nothing short of an heroic enterprise to make them clean — and here is the heroine. Thick-bodied, invincible, she swings the bat with shuddering might; the traveler will rejoice that he has no conflict with these arms of the maiden of only sixteen summers. But who would not take pleasure in beholding the perfect health and the perfect working of that organism! The child of Nature she is truly, living a life like the birds of the field, without pain, without struggle. She turns her broad face up to me, with a look of shy wonder, while I stand there; but her glance drops with a bashful smile when she observes that the stranger is noticing her and her alone; she seems to understand very well that she has attracted his attention, and, I believe, rejoices in the thought. Throwing her braid back, yet never raising her eyes, she swings again her bat, bringing it down with an unearthly thump, much heavier than before, as if to inspire with new awe the beholder. But what a luxuriant sport of her members! Exertion and strength are but ease; every limb rollicks with delight in its own motion. She is not Helen, she does not possess grace, or form; but with some curse that eye must be smitten which can find no pleasure in the perfect health and massive exuberance of her physical development.

The village is now left behind, and therewith this bit of a journey is accomplished. It has the characteristic Greek scenery: a pleasant valley through which runs a brook, with hills on each side; on some small eminence the trace of a ruin is often noticed; the patient donkey plods through the sunny noiseless landscape, only the Greek driver breaks the silence at intervals with his customary grunt of command; into the whole view is blent a mild shining repose, broken at times to-day by fleeting patches of clouds. It is indeed a pleasant vale filled with many a legend and many a heroic form; for this was the route from Thebes to the sea, from the West to Aulis. So the traveler has no difficulty in filling the solitary dale with ancient shapes among which he moves with a strange reality, and to which he may even speak; nay, in his most exalted moment he may see a faun skipping in sunshine over the hill-side.

By this time, the traveler, looking back at that classic valley, will have run against an embankment, up the sides of which he springs with curiosity; behold, the scene changes. The Great Road, the *Megalos Dromos*, is now under his feet, he stoops and looks up and down it wondering whence it came. It is the carriage road built by the Government between Chalkis and Thebes, and extends to Lebedeia and Lamia. With it the modern, in fact the western world, breaks into view suddenly; Macadam, of euphonious name, is now the hero, for the road is macadamized — and in that word what a diabolic mixture of Greek and barbaric speech! Rudely the word jerks us out of antiquity and plunges us into the seething present; yet in the olden time the engineer was not without fame, but was held to be of divine origin, for in the ancient poem we read of the road-building sons of Hephaestus, who constructed the way to Delphic Apollo, whither we too are going. Offspring of a God then we may hail the hero Macadam, at least in Greece; even the modern Great Road shall not lead us out of our antique realm, but rather conduct us back into it by a new route. We are still in the Greek world, let us then pass on.

But here a real sorrow overtakes me: I have to part from my friend Varvouillya who has been for so long a time my faithful companion. Everything which man may expect from his fellowman in the way of disinterested kindness he has shown me. Yet he is a person whom the ordinary traveler seeing upon the highway would tremble at for fear lest he might be a brigand. I myself regarded him with distrust at first, as you will recollect; in spite of his favors I watched him closely all the way from Marcopoulo to Chalkis; but my suspicion was unjust, I did him a wrong which I now am trying to atone for. Under that fustanella, soiled though it be, there beats a warm, hospitable, honest heart. But we must not separate without a little celebration; a wineshop is at the crossing, though the keeper is in the fields at work; we call him in and have a final symposium. Putting me into the Great Road, and pointing to the west, he said: There, follow this highway and in three hours you will be in Thebes. Farewell, good Varvouillya, hardly shall I meet thee again in this journey, but I have hopes that on sunny Olympus we shall yet banquet together in presence of the Gods.

Once more alone after so many days, I step off rapidly toward the Theban plain through a sun-filled but bracing atmosphere. The Great Road with its modern face is not unpleasing; the work on it is excellent. It is built upon a raised bed with strong embankments supported by stone through low places; the outer dressing of broken rubble is pressed hard into the dirt. Along the road at intervals are piles of rocks for the purpose of repair, and I have not observed a spot in it which is out of order. Upon one of these piles after a brisk walk the traveler will sit down to rest, will take out his map to identify the various localities which fall into his vision. For the question is always before him: how did this little tract of land succeed in producing such a race of men, how did it succeed in elevating itself into the beautiful symbol for the whole human family? One fact grinds itself into the American brain here: a big country was not the cause.

Still along the spurs of the mountains the villages are lying peacefully and beautifully in the sun, somewhat as they must have done of old; one cannot help recalling the ancient in the present, and think of the stirring communities which once lay upon these slopes. Each was roused by the story of Helen, felt the mighty national impulse, and sent its contingent to the Trojan war under its strong man; the names of towns and leaders can still be read in the famous muster-roll in the Iliad. What a development of individuality in these small places! Each had its autonomous life, its special worship with temple to the God; each had its hero and its local legend connecting it with divinity. Mycalessus could not have been far from this crossing; it is the spot where the cow bellowed which was conducting Cadmus to Thebes with that wonderful alphabet of his, still the chief instrumentality of knowledge. So says the fable, and the name of the place, which is derived from the bellow of a cow, is cited in proof. Another legend was anciently told here which I like and would fain believe in its true sense: Demeter, Goddess of the harvest, was the presiding deity of Mycalessus; at the feet of the statue of the Goddess the people would place offerings of flowers of fruits which ripened in autumn, but in her presence they would remain in bloom the whole year round; such was the creative power of her immediate glance that the flowers never withered. A little further on was Harma where the chariot of Amphiaraus, Hero and Seer, was swallowed up in the earth by the special favor of Zeus: thence he gave responses far over this territory. Yonder above on Mount Hypatus just before us stood a temple to Zeus Hypatus, Zeus the Highest, nearest there to his own ethereal clearness; shining with column and entablature it crowned the summit with its joyous wreath of marble. Pausanias the traveler, a century and a half subsequent to the Christian Era, speaks of the ruins of the towns here; then already decay had set in, the old spirit had fled. But the Homeric Hymn to Apollo is still fresh with the young life of the localities along this road.

A mounted soldier comes along, for the route is carefully guarded. Let not the traveler leave any article upon the stone-pile where he has been sitting; the cavalryman will pick it up and carry it off to the nearest station, where it will remain till the owner call for it. An accidental wineshop where the thirsty son of Ares reined in his steed for a glass of recinato saved me a trip back to Chalkis for my note-book, which I had left for a few minutes on one of these piles. The traveler will also take the opportunity to swallow his lunch of black bread and cheese, as he sits there in happy mood looking up at the hills on either side of the way. Native pedestrians he will meet who will stop and question him; carriages will pass with tourists from Athens who have ventured to take a ride as far as Thebes, and who look out of the window of the vehicle at him with some anxiety, lest he be a brigand; the four horse mail coach will go by, the driver asking the lone pedestrian if he wishes to ride. No, he prefers to walk, though the sun is getting a little hot, for it it already somewhat past noon.

There is no hurry then, let us glance around at our leisure. Off to the right is a high range of mountains with its white tops in a long vanishing row, ranked close like the teeth of a shark's jaw; it is Kithaeron. Behind us are the frosty summits of Euboea; especially the hoary giant Basilicon towers aloft, still seeming to be near at hand, with top glistening in the rays of the sun. But before the traveler rises in the distance a new mountain, lofty, snow-capped, which he will watch curiously; notice the thick white cloud which is settling upon the peak — so thick that it looks like a new snow-capped summit piled on the mountain till it rise up and mingle with the Heavens. Some invisible Titan is there, we may imagine, heaping Ossa on Pelion in order that he may scale Olympus, the home of the Gods. Thither we are going, we shall see.

Passing up the Great Road a short distance we reach a low ridge through which the highway runs; from its comb we look forth in front and behold a new landscape, indeed a new country. The Bœotian plain breaks into view at once, hedged in on all sides by mountains; this slight ridge is the watershed. As we pass foward, we notice that form so often seen in Greece — an amphitheater made by nature; the hills retire, then sweep back towards the road in the shape of a half moon, while the road draws a straight line from tip to tip of the arc. So amphitheater succeeds to amphitheater; hills rising above hills make the seats and landing-places; a ghostly multitude of faces fill them from the plain to the clouds. They are looking at the solitary wayfarer who is walking leisurely before them, while he occasionally turns his face toward the still murmur of the unseen throngs on the hillsides.

But what a change! It is a new land, a new world. The soil becomes rich and deep; it varies in color from a light red to a dark red, with a loamy fat-looking lustre. You would say, the very ground was greasy, charged with animal matter. This impression is intensified by the enormous flocks of crows and buzzards which hover over the plain as far as the eye can reach, or drop in long streaks down to the earth. They seem to be able to gorge directly of the soil which lies here like an immense carcass spread over the low tract of the country. The feeling is that the whole land, rank in its own decay, is about to spring back into vegetable and animal life. And such is the case; vegetables and animals are everywhere leaping, as it were, into being over the wide level expanse. Tall grasses now fill the lush luxuriant meadows alternating with fields of grain; cotton, too, is one of the products of this rich plain. Numberless herds of cattle, sheep, and horses spot the distance with many colors; flocks of goats repose on the more remote slopes in sunny patches. The air is filled with an incessant tinkling of bells, far and near, faint and loud, of little sheep-bells and of big cow-bells — all in a sweet chime over the meadows and hills; thus the landscape in addition to its color is overflowing with a mellow idyllic music; even the sunbeams fall around you in subtle harmony with the tintinnabulation of the bells.

Through such strains the traveler passes along the

highway; the image of Iphigenia which has accompanied him from Aulis and filled his eyes with unaccustomed tears, now bids him farewell, she vanishes over the mountains to her home. For she is an Attic figure, the creation of Attic tragedy, she stands for some of the most intense struggles of human spirit. But here in this plain man would seem to have no struggle, no yearning which whelms him into conflict; he will become as fat as the soil and heavy as this dark atmosphere which fills the valley from the Copaic swamp. Yet let us not be too fast with our conclusions; there is stiff contradiction here too, between the bare hill and the rich plain; these will grapple in strife, if nought else.

It is manifest that this land will produce a different class of beings from Attica which we have just left. There the soil is light and thin, the air is clear and genial, the climate dry and exhilarating; the people will have a tendency to become winged, to soar and to sing. But here Nature is fat and heavy, her children will be likely to receive the inheritance. The old reproach "Bœotian swine" now becomes the pithy statement for the clime and the man. Still human beings will not sink into enervation upon this spot, for the climate is far more severe than that of Attica for instance, nor is the plain so large that an enormous mass of humanity can settle here and press itself down by its own weight, as in the great river valleys of the East. This rich earth will have to be stoutly defended against poor and hungry neighbors dwelling on yonder rocky hills; thus there will have to be strength, order, military organization, if the inhabitants keep their lands and their freedom. Men upon this soil will do two things at least: gormandize and fight; and such is their historical character. Yet in the background hover deep struggles of the spiritual kind; fearful tragedies will break up into Theban fable, as if intimating something which lies first and deepest in the instinct of the people.

Thus in Greece Nature herself takes care to individualize her territory and with it her creatures. She cuts it up and separates its parts by chains of mountains; then by means of sea, swamp and range of snowy peaks she contrives to give to each portion a distinct character. This Bœotia, one often repeats to himself, is a different world from Attica, though distant but a few hours' walk; yet there is withal a certain Greek unity in this very differentiation. Copais lake that stretches yonder, furnishes its broad surface for moisture, and the climate becomes damp and heavy; the whole plain too is a swampy sediment of primeval ages, shooting into rank vegetation. But forget not the other side to the prosaic one: this land produced more and a higher mythical lore than any other Hellenic locality, with the possible exception of Argos; it produced on the whole the most ideal man in Greek history — Epaminondas; it produced the lightest-winged, highest-soaring lyric poet of either ancient or modern times — Pindar. Of them indeed we must hear again.

The sun is hot, though it be winter; the pedestrian trudging along the hard-rolled highway will become thirsty. Unfinished wells here and there at the side of the road indicate that others before him have felt the same need of a fresh draught, which, he hopes, will be ready for those who are to come after him; but the most philanthropic hope will not give him a drink of water. The amphitheaters furnish good company, for their stony seats are filled to the very skies with a multitude of spirits, looking at Time's spectacle. A high ridge springs up suddenly in front and compels the road to turn aside — a jagged volcanic product breaking upward in a thousand quivering struggles, and each quiver chilled forever into stone. The eager traveler will leave the highway and attempt to explore, but he has to leap from jag to jag, and his peaceful walk is thrown into convulsions like the ridge, altogether incompatible with classic repose. He soon abandons the frenzied rocks and returns to the road with joyful glances, for, if I mistake not, he begins to see something of Thebes in the distance lying on a hill. But further yet, far beyond Thebes, is that lofty snow-capped mountain which has remained in our vision ever since we crossed the Bœotian watershed; still the solid white cloud rests on the summit, reaching up into the heavens; no eye can tell where mountain ends and cloud begins, so much alike do they seem. Truly the earth seems to be rising there, flying upward at the stars with white wings — what can be the name of the mount? I suspect it, still I dare not tell it now.

But this thirst is a little troublesome and begins to touch the Greek mood. Good luck! — here is a laborer, and he has a skin filled with fresh water which he freely offers to the wayfarer. A great, red-faced, fat man, quite distinct from the common run of people in Greece, he seems to partake of the nature of the soil which he is tilling; sweaty and puffing, with enormous bulk he wields the grubbing hoe; a very type of Bœotia, you will think, being reminded again of the ancient proverb above cited, though the thought be in the present case ungenerous. But let us not delay, with Thebes getting nearer.

At the side of the road is an artificial mound which has been recently excavated; excellent masonry is brought to view, with stone carefully cut; some tomb or trophy is the ready conjecture, and anciently it must have spoken of the Great Deed or of the Great Man to the traveler as he approached the city, filling his heart with the desire of imitation, or perchance with worship. Thus along with the view of Thebes he would get the view of one of its Heroes. Not far from it is a very different object though intended for worship also — a Christian shrine; in a stone frame is set a rude picture of the Virgin and Child, before which the Greek of to-day crosses himself and repeats a prayer. I too stop and look at it thoughtfully; it is well enough just upon this spot to remind the weary pedestrian that there is a providence over him, that he must also have faith — for is not his whole journey based upon the belief that in the next village provision has been made for him, of which he now knows nothing? Otherwise I would not go to Thebes yonder, Thebes would be death — nothingness; as it is, not only will my body find food and shelter there, but I feel certain of receiving some spiritual nourishment.

But it is strange how unnatural that Virgin appears upon Greek soil; she seems not yet at home after this long, long millennial residence. Somehow or other she still looks like a foreigner; nay, she has almost a destructive appearance here, kindly and good though she be elsewhere; the Greek when he begins to worship her, sinks to little or nothing in comparison to what he once was with other divinities in his heart; if she be not some avenging deity, destroying her own worshipers, at least she has been unable to lift them up into their ancient worth. The mule-driver just in advance of us who leaps down from his seat and goes through his devotions before her image, is no unfair sample of her products; he represents that to which she has reduced the Greek from the ancient breed of men who were once born upon this soil. Or turn about the statement, if you please, and say: the Greek having lost his freedom, his faith, and himself, received a new divinity and sank into this new worship. Both propositions are, however, in their essence the same.

Here comes another specimen of a different kind; I take him to be a Bœotian country gentleman. Mounted on a fine steed which steps proudly along the highway he approaches, in big cavalier boots, with bright scarlet fez lying slouched upon the top of his head, while a long very white overcoat shaggy with large woolly flocks gives him the appearance of a white bear—fat, haughty, carnivorous; barbaric ornaments of various kinds are scattered over his horse and his person. So too the old Theban was reproached with haughtiness as well as with gluttony; one will fancy he sees some of these traits still cleaving to the soil.

After some minutes another figure appears in the road, taking a walk out of Thebes which is now not far off. It is a Papas or priest strolling at his leisure outside of the town gates; his long black gown seems to move through the clear air almost without showing any bend in his knees as he steps; a man of quiet contemplation, one would think judging by his face. I address him, and he responds in a friendly sweet voice; he points out to me the various places seen in the landscape and tells their names: in this direction is Kokla, ancient Plataea, there is Orchomenus, now Scripu. But what mountain is that yonder, with the clouds and sunbeams piled upon its summit to the very skies? Parnassus, he replied, and under it is Delphi. He continued his walk, while I stepped quickly forward looking at Parnassus. No wonder that the mountain with its broad-expanded, gold-bordered cloud-wings seeks to lift itself into ethereal spaces, being upheld by a Delphic foundation — Poesy sustained by Prophecy. It is now clear as daylight that the destination of this journey is not Thebes; yonder is the beacon held aloft in the heavens.

But we must not fly off yet, we are not yet even in Thebes, though the suburbs begin to appear. We shall enter by the Proetid Gate, from the East; can we call up the scene as it looked to the eye of the ancient traveler approaching the city in this direction? Along the street over which we are now passing were situated in antiquity the tombs and monuments of Heroes and Great Men. Down the road they stretched for two miles; the stranger was reminded, as he approached the city, of its illustrious characters, both historical and legendary. He could see in the statue, in the inscription, in the monument what men Thebes had produced, and whom she still held in remembrance. Here was her fable, her history, her own deepest character, spread out before the eyes of the stranger, who could read them on entering her walls. The best introduction to her life lay inscribed here; still fragments of it we may read to-day, using the vision of the ancient tourist.

For in the sun of the quiet afternoon the marble monuments begin to rise and glisten; we may pass through them built on either hand, and scan them thoughtfully. First was the tomb of the seer, old Tiresias, more than fifteen stades from the city. The great prophet must stand at the very opening, significantly hinting what is to be; all that comes after is really his prophecy. For he knew and foretold what lay in the germ of Thebes and of her Heroes; advance now and see it unfolded in the monuments which follow, and in the city itself. But we have already left the place of Tiresias rapidly behind, and we come to another monument inscribed *Tomb of Hector*. What does this mean? By the oracle the children of Cadmus are commanded to reverence the Asiatic hero after transferring his bones from Asia. No wonder that Thebes did not furnish any contingent for the Trojan war. It is an indication of the foreign element which lies both in Theban legend and in Theban history; she has Asiatic preferences which bring her into fierce conflict with the other Greeks; she is born to be a city of struggle. On the whole this is the most significant fact pertaining to Thebes: she worshiped the Hero of Asia, the enemy of the Greek Hero Achilles; manifestly she is in shrill dissonance with the rest of the Greek world.

Here too is another and even deeper sign of that dissonance: *Tomb of Melanippus*. This is the name of a Theban Hero who fell during the siege of his city by the Argives, after he had slain the great Argive chieftain Tydeus, whose monument of rude stones is also here near by. Thus the two enemies still glare on each other from their tombs, as they did in life, representing the Theban conflict with Greece; the two cities with their Heroes stand for opposite tendencies of the Greek world, and Argos as the leading Hellenic power of that age seeks to bring harmony out of this Theban discord with Hellenism, which she succeeds in at last by wiping Thebes out of existence. But it is, after all, the strife of two Greek states, the strife of brothers — and here they are, Eteocles and Polynices, the two brothers who perish, each by the other's hand. Thus the Argives were destroyed once, and Thebes was destroyed once in that bitter conflict. The brothers have a common altar here upon which offerings are laid; but behold the fire of the sacrifice, it separates into two hostile tongues of flame which will not mingle. Brothers they are and must remain together, though without hope of reconciliation, enemies still in the grave. Thus Theban struggle is pushed to its last intensity in the direst domestic tragedy; from the first Asiatic dissonance, through Greek civil war it has passed to fratricide. Then still further, to unwitting parricide, for we have now reached the fountain of Oedipus, parent of those two brothers; in its waters he washed off the bloodstains of his own father after murdering him; still the stream runs red, to the sympathetic eye. But we have already crossed the Ismenian stream, now quite dry at this point, and we have arrived at the Proetid Gate. Such are the monuments which the traveler anciently beheld here in reality, but now we must behold them in image, unfolding gradually a deep tragic scission to the very heart of the city, and ending in bloody catastrophe. This is our introduction to Thebes as we pass up the Chalkidian road — a true introduction to her legend, to her history, to her character, written with her own hand and placed here before the eyes of all who are able to read her monuments. It is an honest writing, I should say, instinctively revealing to the traveler what she is within, what she must be in the future, for these are the records of her innermost being. Unconscious is the expression of her life here, and therefore sincere; like a prologue to some fearful tragedy it has been uttered in our presence, and with premonitions upon us we enter the gate of the city.

X. THEBES AND PLATÆA.

Slowly the pedestrian winds up the hill into Thebes. After he has passed through a small modern suburb and entered the town on the declivity, he soon reaches the central place of business, which is indicated by wagons loaded with cotton, by a stage-coach and by numerous wineshops. It is not yet evening, there is time for a preliminary saunter through the town. Its whole activity is confined to one broad street, along which the shops and stores are ranged side by side; most of the houses have but one story with low roofs projecting in front over the unpaved sidewalk. The cobbler sits in the open air, with old shoes lying around him in winrows; the blacksmith, the tinner, the gunsmith are hammering away in an anvil chorus of rattling iron; village industries appear to be thriving. The dwellings may be pronounced on the whole substantial; a few may even lay claim to some elegance, if the standard be not placed too high.

Still the town makes the impression of undue eating and drinking, which was the reproach cast upon it in antiquity. The fertile plain gathers and concentrates itself upon this hill where it finds its last expression in the character of man. It produces not the refined epicureanism of the voluptuary but the gross pleasures of the gormandizer. The wineshops are all open and ablaze with activity; in a public garden one can see a throng of people sitting and sipping their recinato with loud buzz of talk and hot political discussion, for the election of Demarch or Mayor is approaching. On the street there is in general a well-fed appearance of humanity, verging toward obesity in those who have battened on this moor. Kitchens abound just on the sidewalk; cookery instead of taking place in some obscure corner to the rear of the house, hiding itself out of sight for shame, shows itself, brazen-faced, to the very eyes of the customer, and the aroma of his dinner first ascends to his nostrils. Pots are arranged, bubbling and steaming, under charcoal fires in the front window of the public eating-houses; stewed meat and vegetables are handed out to the passer on the sidewalk, or he may take a seat within at a rude table. These customs are not peculiar to Thebes, we saw them at Chalkis and shall see them everywhere on Greek soil; but they seem intensified here. Perhaps I observe only the old in the new; still that is just the object of my trip and yours. In accordance with our duty as honest travelers let us fall in with the customs of the place and order a stew of lamb and potatoes.

A short walk let us then take up the street to the walls, whence we can overlook the country. The wonderful situation is at once revealed; this is just the spot for the city. The hill rises up from the plain, and is surrounded by a deep natural trench on all sides except where at one narrow interval it slopes off gradually into the valley, as if to stretch out there a friendly hand. Imagine a huge saucer with a line of hills for its rim; such is the total landscape before us. Then imagine a protuberance in the bottom of the saucer somewhat to one side; upon this protuberance almost as high as the surrounding rim of hills Thebes is built. It is an acropolis raised by Nature, and fitted for commanding the plain far and wide; the people who dwell here must be the rulers of those who dwell below them and around them, if they be true to their situation. The headship of Thebes is written upon this natural elevation, one can still read the decree ineffaceable by time. Therefore this is the holy hill, the Cadmeia, the special gift of the God who is here worshiped by his people in his own temple built upon its summit. For did not ancient Cadmus, coming from abroad, follow the indication of the Delphic oracle and settle here where the sacred cow lay down? It is indeed a devoted spot, the strength and protection of the people, who with sacrifice will long appreciate the gift. Into the plain it slopes by one narrow passage, easy to descend, hard to ascend against resistance. Such is the donation of divinity, one can still connect his presence with the hill.

Another blessing has the God granted to this favored situation: on each side of the hill run two streams of water from large pure fountains. So our city will be called by the poets two-rivered; Dirke and Ismenus are the names. Just now we are standing on the site of the old temple to the Ismenian Apollo, titled from the stream flowing at his feet; deservedly he will be regarded as the chief deity of the city on account of his two presents, the hill and the streams; they indeed make up its special characteristic. These noble benefactions came from the God to his people; if not from him, whence did they come? So thinks the pious Theban; so we may think with him, forgetting our geology, which, after all, only removes the difficulty one or two steps further back.

But the long shadows over the Dirkean runnels admonish us that we are not in that antique world where the sun is always shining; turn about then, and go back to modern Thebes. I have noticed one man persistently following me through the streets, and disturbing my reveries. Twice already I have shaken him off, but the third time

I send him away with reproaches, even with a firmer grasp of my staff. He now leaves me to myself; but night has already drawn a sombre curtain over the plain, and distant Parnassus, otherwise so white and shining, has been darkened into a creole beauty. Alas! I must now take leave of the ancient company and seek shelter and food, for I am not yet ready to dissolve wholly my connection with the present. I go to a kind of hostelry and look in; there is the landlord, the very man whom I had so unceremoniously driven off. I feel ashamed to ask him now for what he previously had been trying to thrust upon me; a little touch of Nemesis it is for my gruffness. But I shall not stay there, I walk up and down seeking another inn; this is the only one in town, I am told everywhere. So I have to return, putting on my most friendly look, and not forgetting to rattle some silver drachmas conveniently in my hand. My amiability was irresistible, or perchance my drachmas, falling into his Greek eye. I apologized gently; I told him that I thought he was so and so, whereas he was not, but so and so — that is, a gentleman; let the end be told at once, supper and lodging. But such is the first penalty which Nemesis lays upon the traveler for being ill-tempered in Greece; beware of the second, it may be more severe.

Thereupon I retire in good humor, nor did I forget to look back at this curious trip, as I lay upon my couch; more than a week, nine days to-morrow morning, have I been on the way from Athens. A fragment of life not uneventful to me, full of real sights and classic visions, making many shapes hitherto dim and dreamy actual as life, yet opening many other glimpses into things uncertain; but whatever else may be said of it, a happy fragment it has been, and thus a clear gain wrenched from the clutches of old Time. Yet the reverse side of the picture must be given: I did not think, and I can now scarcely believe that such a short period would produce ten long talks like these to which you have been listening; yes, ten, more than one for each day. It is startling, I am frightened at my own possibilities. What if every day of my life should result in a chapter such as this!

What a Niagara of speech would pour out of me! Nay, further, what if every person would produce an amount equal to mine every day, as is his perfect right! Think of every human being turned to a dark cataract of printed books with endless deafening roar! Such is to be, I predict, the second deluge overwhelming the world for its sins; many are now the signs thereof and this is one. My guilty participation I cannot deny to you, but I may allege a single extenuating circumstance; not with these nine days only have I seen, but with all my days lying back of them and preparing for them; so too it is not the nine days alone which are speaking now, but my whole life finding utterance in them at this moment.

But another more harmonious note will soon possess the drowsy ear in passing to dreamland; faint snatches of music will already have hummed through the head like a distant strain, and then have died away at any attempt to catch them distinctly. Aeolian fragments you will think them coming down from ancient Pindar who once sang here; still they seem to be wandering through the air on which they were once hymned. Fair choruses begin to sport round the sacred hill of Thebes, to whose rhythm all her legend and history fall into soft attunement. To some melodious line and more melodious image of the bard you will pass into slumber, when you will listen all night to the songs of the festival and behold the graceful youths stepping lightly in the dance. Early by a dim echo you will be roused — by a dim echo of voices which are singing of the morning sun as it rises over the Dirkeian streams. Get up quickly; that too we must witness in all its effulgence casting its rays upon the bosom of the musical Nymph. Therefore this morning let us hasten to the Northern side of the city where it is married to the plain, and there descend. We shall pass a high tower supposed to be Byzantine, we shall go by the public threshing floor, and at the foot of the hill reach fair-flowing Dirke, holy water.

But as we move through this locality led by our ancient guide Pausanias, another form springs up, a woman, with heroic features, but with a fiercely discordant note in her soul. Here is then the *Syrma* or Place of the Dragging, for it was here that Antigone dragged her dead brother to the funeral pile in defiance of the command of the King. It is wonderful how much more real the story of Antigone is than any historical event which has happened upon this spot, and how much more vivid the heroic woman stands out than any historic personage. Her conflict is of to-day and will remain forever an expression for man of what is eternal within him; thus must true poetry be always above history tied down to Time.

This, then, was in part the scene of that famous Oedipus legend — Oedipus who slew his father and married his mother, unwittingly. Such was his profound ignorance that he knew not father or mother; yet just he was the surpassing wise man of the Thebans, the man who had guessed the Sphinx riddle, and to whom the mystery of Egypt and of the Orient was no longer a mystery. But another and deeper riddle comes up to him for solution, far deeper than the Egyptian one, and threatening to destroy not only him but the whole Greek world. It is one phase of the infinite riddle between the subjective and the objective, as the philosophers speak; the bottomless chasm between what is the *I am* and what the *world* is yawns for Oedipus, and he falls in, not to be rescued by any hand of that age. Man violates the sacred prescriptions of his own time and indeed of his own nature, yet he does so unknowingly; alas, what is to be done with him, what is he to do with himself? It is veritably a riddle, or better, it is a conflict between the profoundest spiritual principles, between the inner and outer Reason, between the law of the man and the law of the institution. In that disruption the human being is torn to pieces, becomes in the deepest sense a tragic character. Oedipus does the wrong, unwittingly it is true; nevertheless the wrong exists in the world, the great violation remains the same, he must be punished — must punish himself. Yet he was innocent as the inner man, he had no intent corresponding to the deed. But he, the wise man, the guesser of riddles, ought not to be entrapped in a riddle. Yet he was entrapped and could not help himself — and so on to infinity must the wrenching contradiction be continued at Thebes; thus the poor old man, with soul torn to very tatters, has to flee, he leaves his own city and passes down the road toward Athens, led by his daughter, having plucked out his physical eye when he could not see with his spiritual eye. Abandoning Thebes full of unreconcilable struggle he will find at Athens atonement for his guilt and a solution for his new riddle — whereof nothing at present.

Thus has the Athenian poet shown the Theban Oedipus, and has touched a theme which must come home to us all. This existence of ours lies between two riddles, the one of which we may guess, the other not. Every human being now treading the earth, however great, however little he may be, hovers between the known and the unknown like Oedipus. With that unknown he grapples for dear life, conquers much of it perhaps; but wrestling still with it, he is at last hurled into his grave. With the Greek poet some of us may assert that reconciliation is to be found here before death, but the most of our race seem to expect it only after death in a soul-renovating paradise.

A daughter, a truly spiritual daughter of Oedipus is Antigone who also must be located upon this spot where we are standing. One problem she too has solved — it is the duty of performing the last funeral rites for her outcast brother. Frantic she comes, with maniacal hair streaming in the wind, frenzied with resolution; upon this spot she drags the corpse of her brother, called ever afterwards the Syrma, or the Place of the Dragging. Then upon the funeral pile she places her dead brother, and performs the sacred ceremony; a sisterly deed full of the deepest devotion and fidelity, and to the heroine the whole world shouts approbation. This problem then she has solved to her and our satisfaction; but let us see — what is this other mighty contention springing into view suddenly? A new conflict arises, in the very act of duty she has violated duty and is destroyed; a power rushes in and sweeps her off, it is the authority which she has assailed. So the one riddle she solves, the other solves her, not without tears and perhaps execrations from us; still the power makes away with her, and most effectually too. Thus the daughter of Oedipus has her soluble and insoluble riddle; she who can master one problem to the admiration of all ages, is ground to death by the second problem.

Such is the Theban image in legend, full of riddling discord; nor must we forget the two sieges of Thebes in legendary times; in reality, however, two phases of one siege, which ends in the capture of the city. Let us glance at the Theban image also therein reflected, and try to reach its true purport. It has already been stated that Thebes and the Cadmeia sprang from a foreign element, and that they seem never to have lost a foreign sympathy. This hostile influence in the heart of Greece must be overcome in order to unify the Hellenic people within; thus they will be ready for the great external conflict with Troy, which, it is clear, is soon to be. The siege of Thebes, then, is an inner adumbration of the siege of Troy, or perchance a preparation for the same, since Troy lay outside of Greece which has first to purge itself of its own Asiatic element before going to Asia itself. Some such hint lies in the legend for the true believer, and such is the relation between the two famous sieges, the Theban and the Trojan, the internal one and the external one; both, too, were essentially conflicts with the Orient. Also the Argives who were among the chief leaders in the Trojan Expedition were those who subjected the foreign influence at Thebes; or, to state the matter otherwise, they put down the contradiction, the sharp dissonance with the Greek world in the latter city. This dissonance during the siege of Thebes culminates in the combat between Eteocles and Polynices, brother against brother, both fateful sons of Oedipus, victor and victim of the riddle. But in their case the riddle annihilates itself, the conflict ends in the mutual destruction of the colliding sides. Thus Greece frees itself for a time of this riddling discordant Thebes, and is united for the great foreign expedition, in the catalogue of whose participants the Theban name does not and ought not to appear.

Everywhere in the legendary epoch of Thebes the foreign element comes to the surface; it is her great unsolved contradiction which brings her into conflict with Greece, with herself, which conflict is imaged so vividly in her tragic characters. The Hellenic people cannot endure with such deep dissonance in their very heart, it must be got rid of even by violence. Justly then the name of Thebes is not set down in the Iliad, being stricken by the bard from the grand muster-roll of the Greeks against Troy, which was the pride of so many small Hellenic communities. The great mythical expedition against the Asiatic is no part of her glory; she herself was the Asiatic in Greece who had first to be put down; still she remained Trojan in sympathy, for did we not see the tomb of Hector outside of the Proetid gate among her heroes?

Such is the legend, which some may be inclined to pass over as a thing unreal. But in that second great muster-roll against the Asiatic — the muster-roll called before the battle of Plataea just over the comb of yonder hill Teumessus, where was Thebes? Alas, more than missing; worse than stricken from the list of patriotic combatants is her name; the historian now comes forward and points her out standing enranked with the Asiatic against the Greek, and fighting desperately for the domination of the Orient. Again she plays the foreigner on Greek soil, and shows herself in history as well as in legend to be a traitor to Greek civilization. So true is the legendary as well as the historical character of the city; both are alike, being two different reflections of one and the same object. She lives over in history what she had sung of in legend; she can only make real what poesy had presented as ideal. History then can simply act the fable over again, with much additional noise and confusion perhaps; it is the second yet more turbid fountain, having its source in the first clear one; yet both will mirror the same face.

Thus we pass through the Syrma, seeking to make its dust give up the ancient shapes that lie here, and to animate them anew with their innermost spirit. It is a spot of tragic conflict, of terrific dissonance, which to this day jars fiercely yet sympathetically in the breast. But of a sudden the sounds change, we come to the banks of the Dirkean stream, over which hover untold melodies, swelling up to the heavens. Whence can arise such a sudden transformation of echoes? All the daughters of Mnemosyne are now singing in unison their strains over Dirke, rearing a wall of music against the strifeful spot of the Dragging. Through that melodious wall over the brook let us leap at once, we have entered another world, the tragic discord of the Syrma has been cut off and left far behind; and man has become a most harmonious being, who dwells forever amid the tuneful spheres; we have entered the house of Pindar.

Upon this spot it stood according to our ancient guide; here the poet when he rose at morn saw the first beams of Helius play over the Dirkean waters. The material house has indeed disappeared, but that other house built by Pindar stands visible, nay audible to-day and forever. For it is a musical house still, though partly in ruins; the most happy musical temple ever erected out of the lofty hymn. Into it we may enter and tarry long, catching its harmonies broken at times, but still possessed of the sweetest and sublimest cadences.

Many were the miraculous things told of him in antiquity, indicating that he was truly a child of the Gods. On that hot day while he was going to Thespia, he seems to have received his first revelation; he fell asleep along the road and the bees lit upon his lips, depositing there waxen cells for honey; when he woke, he began to sing; such, says the ancient narrator, was the beginning of his making hymns. Then the appearance of Persephone, Goddess of the Lower Regions, to the Poet in a dream, complaining that to her alone of the divinities he had never written a hymn, was justified by his character; dark Tartarean realms he avoids, but delights to dwell on the upper earth in Greek sunshine. Therefore he was the special favorite of Apollo, God of Light, whose games he has celebrated in such rapturous splendor; the priestess at Delphi announced to all Greece to give to Pindar a share of the first-fruits equal to that of the God. Then too the proclamation was long afterward heard at the Delphic shrine: "Let the poet Pindar come into his supper with the God." Indeed he is the product and culmination of Delphi, thither we shall have to follow him in order to reach the deepest and richest vein of his character. In the dell of the Oracle, at the fount of Castalia, under the tops of Parnassus, we shall have to place him, where prophecy and poesy rocked the hills with musical wisdom, whereof he is the highest expression. Pindar, on the whole, may be taken as the best Delphic utterance remaining for us to-day.

Still he belongs here too, and in him all Thebes turns to harmony — that discordant Thebes so full elsewhere of tragic destinies; nay, that sensual Thebes, receiving its nickname from swinish indulgence, becomes through him the most ethereal of poetic existences. It is one of the marvels of this land that it could bring him forth, him the most ideal of men. From this fat soil he sprang, this heavy air he breathed, upon this gross vegetation he fed, yet he has the freest rein and the widest bound of all poets, often a little too sudden in his earth-defying leaps. To-day we confess him unrivalled in the lyric; he has the exaltation, the sweep of imagination and the greatness of thought which belong to all supreme poetic utterance.

But the quality in which he surpasses every poet whom I have read after, is what may be called his harmony. Not that light superficial thing called by the critics harmonious versification is meant now: this true harmony flows from the deepest of matters, it is the harmony of the All, of the Universe uttering itself in the measured syllables of the bard. At his best moment each word is set in vibration which sings long afterward in the ear or rather in the soul, indeed one will never get rid of that music truly heard; but such a word is only a note of the song which in its completeness will make your whole being throb and thrill in attunement with its strains. Yet not you alone, but nature outside of you vibrates to the chords of the lyre which the poet touches; both the inner and outer world are absorbed into the stride and swell of his harmonics. All Time, too, is therein made musical, as to-day sunny Thebes seems to be gently moving to pulsations of those ancient hymns.

Such is the Pindaric music, unattainable by any external combination of sounds and syllables, or by any arrangement of the scanning machine; what modern would get it, if only thus it could be reached? It goes far deeper, as it must in all true poetry; the rhythm must lie ultimately in the thought wedding itself to speech; the words are but the outward drapery dropping into symphonic folds from the rapturous pulsations within; the fountain of Pindar's harmony is in the soul, and there only can it be truly heard. It is a great mistake to think that the music of poetry comes from the jingle of sounds, short and long, accented and unaccented, from the employment of open vowels, from the abolition of certain consonants in certain situations. Much talk of this kind has been heard of late; but such doctrines can do hardly more than construct a well-regulated poetical machine which will grind at any time with any person turning the crank; thus we may attain a light-flowing Italian melody at the very best, but not all-pervading, all-subduing organ harmonies. First there must be the thought great and worthy, then it must pulse with an inner ecstasy which bursts forth into utterance.

No counting of syllables, then, is going to reveal to you the deepest secret of poetic harmonies. It is true that in verse measure is necessary; but this is the mechanical part, it is the outer to which there must be an inner that creates it and puts it musically on like a rich glowing vestment. Poetry cannot do without that fixed recurrence of accents called meter; even the sea, most melodious of Nature's instruments, has a measured rhythm, a regular beat in its rise and fall, as if the waves were keeping time after some invisible master. Yet hardly are we to think of the meter the while, but to hear the music; it is the harmonious thought of Pindar which makes every word drop tuneful from his lips; too often his strains get lost in that labyrinth of metrical schemes, which produce so much discord, at least among grammarians. I cannot help thinking that Pindar's verse, and all true verse, makes its own scheme as it goes along, to a degree; it throbs great waves of harmony through any soul musically attuned, without scansion; for I must refuse to believe that the dry prosodical man who scans Pindar is the sole person who has become heir to his melodious wealth. An inborn poetic sense may perhaps be better tested by Pindar's verse than by that of any other poet; if no music be heard there, whatever the outer ear may be, the poetic soul is of dubious existence.

This harmony, then, combined with his exaltation is Pindar's highest poetical characteristic. Next to him perhaps Dante should be placed, who likewise possesses the power of setting all in vibration to the strains of his poetry; even the dry abstractions of scholastic theology move in his *Paradiso* with a strange enraptured rhythm. Here also lies the chief miraculous gift of our Milton, though he is behind the two who have been mentioned. These are pre-eminently the poets of harmony, to my mind; others greater than they have existed because of the possession of a still greater quality, in conjunction with this one.

Pindar is the most rapt expression of the Greek world, the Delphic utterance of it we may say. His sympathy with Hellenic life is complete; he is in the main content to live as his forefathers lived; we do not find in him the profound questionings of the Attic poets, he is too harmonious. He does not assail the established, he is at one with the religion and the morality of his age — a conservative poet we may consider him. Yet he will not accept all the myths which have been handed down, nor does he fail to castigate certain evils of his city and time. But he is not a satirist, not a revolutionist; he is in harmony with the world and the world with him; so that he becomes the throbbing utterance of the games, of the festivals, of the songs in that joyous Greek life around him.

But it is time to leave the unseen musical house of the poet, and take a morning walk with him up the Dirkean stream which winds around the hill on which the city is built and babbles transparent at his very door-sill. The slanting rays are glancing over it somewhat as he beheld them; yet in his lines even the sunbeams are gifted with new splendor. One looks up at the old walls still girdling the brow of the hill with their remains, those are the stones that danced into their place yonder to the tune of Amphion's lyre, according to the fable; still there is a rude harmony in that massive Cyclopean work of the olden time. A pile of stones which has been pushed from the wall, one will think, shows the trace of Alexander who destroyed the city anciently; there they have lain ever since. Gigantic masonry was that of early Greece, laying foundations to last forever, and jointing the huge boulders to the sound of music, it is said. But look at the modern hut upon the wall, and, as it were, growing out of it; the little stones seem about to fall asunder, held together by no strong cement nor by gravity, nor by any harmony; one small window looks down upon Dirke, out of which a rag is hanging. Such are indeed often the ancient and the modern in contrast, forming the two interchanging threads of our Hellenic journey.

Here the stream divides into two channels, an artificial and a natural one, running almost side by side. Further on, little arches and aqueducts appear, many now old and neglected; there is a sort of play with the waters whose current is just large enough to allow itself to be pleasantly handled and toyed with. On the roots of an old elm the pedestrian will sit down for a while; not far off is a rustic bridge spanning the brook, composed mainly of ancient materials, if not ancient itself, for the eye is often greeted with a finely cut piece of stone or even of marble. Underfoot traces of foundations come to view, hardly determinable now; shrines and temples we place here, for we know that this little valley was full of them in antiquity. At one point, from the marks yet visible, and still more from the situation, I imagine some fane to have been built over the stream, for here Dirke ripples along most happy and full. Some caves too we shall notice, once inhabited by the nymphs; the niches to hold the image can still be seen. Thus Dirke sweeps around the base of Thebes from the semi-lunar ridge toward the North; for the circular Cadmeian hill reposes in the arms of another hill, crescent-shaped, like the old moon resting in the new; between these two hills Dirke keeps up her babble. Happy stream! try to look at it with ancient eyes as a thing divine, bestowing good gifts, purifying the land and the people; still more regard it with the eye of the old poet as a thing of beauty, in whose waters are often seen shapes hinting of what is fairest and best in that antique world.

Still modern matters must not drop out of view, so much duty we owe to our own time that we should at least live in it. White fustanellas are before our path, following the plow in the narrow valley between the city and the crescent; you will see the plow turn up the relics of a whole world passed away; the soil is filled with bricks, tiles, mortar, bits of marble and potsherds. Only in the invisible realm can it be constructed again, and this is also one of the duties of the traveler in Greece. New voices now float in the air; they come from gossiping washerwomen who are still heard along Dirke, invoking the nymph of the stream to aid them in the great work of purification; their tongues at least falter never — be it prayer, or some bit of village scandal. A school-boy passes with books under his arm; I stop him and inquire much; he reads me a passage from the *Education of Cyrus* in old Greek, there under the elm. Go on to school, thou art indeed the star of hope for Thebes, for Greece, rising over Dirke and illuminating her waters.

So we may follow Dirke up to one of her sources; half a mile or so from the city the stream forks, and we shall wander along the branch to the left with its high banks above us. Soon we approach the gushing source — a veritable shrine of the Naiads, tricked out by themselves for their own chosen seats. A light waterfall leaps over, the wall of the rock underneath is wet and mossy, with veins of water everywhere pulsing through the green matted moss; the rills gathering into one stream meet behind a small island on which is quite a large willow with drooping branches. Just the combination of rock, water and sedge; in a lone spot; filled with old memories — it was certainly a shrine. Laugh at your extravagant traveler; but he would be worth nothing, I maintain, if he could not overflow with the gush of this spring, in deep joy, saying to himself: "Yes,. I have found it, this is the home of the nymphs of the stream, here they dance on the sedge, yonder they bathe, always from this source they wander down to the city joyously leaping over the pebbles, making sweet music to the sport of the waters.

A walk up Dirke will eminently repay us, though we have to add much to its present appearance in order to recall its ancient glory. Plane-trees were here and pleasant promenades, with many a white statue and column glimmering through the leaves. But mainly Pindar was here, and daily took his walk up and down this brook; still it is musical with his voice and attunes us to his strain. Who cannot behold him, sauntering along, turning up his face gleaming with exaltation as he looks at the sunbeams falling over the Dirkean stream, the holy water? In him indeed the nymph has first found utterance; and still it is not she so much as he that holds us on this spot in a miraculous spell. Such is Nature; we hear her mostly through the Poet, to whose vision she truly reveals herself. Without him Dirke is only a brook, nothing more, just like thousands of other brooks; but now it is a symbol, beautiful, perchance sacred — he has made it. Take a drink, wash your face in the Pindaric waters, then spring up the bank.

So long has endured our peaceful, idyllic mood attuned to Pindaric strains — but hark! a trumpet blowing the blast of war comes echoing over yonder ridge. Thither accordingly we must go, hastening up the slant of the hill to see what is taking place beyond. Passing over its crest we note a wide valley moving into view, upon which many herds are grazing; through that valley winds a stream, not large, but called here a river. It is the Asopus, which once before we have come upon further down. Peasants are here trimming their vineyards. What is the name of yonder village, lying at the foot of the mountain across the valley? It is called Kokla, ancient Plataea.

Here, then, we look upon the battle-field where the great struggle of Greece with the Orient, called the Persian War, was brought to an end. What Marathon had prophesied was now made actual, the full meaning of that victory was confirmed upon these meadows. Greece is henceforth to be left to develop within, and soon the external war will be transformed to an internal one; the Persian she will find in her own people. Lofty Kithaeron yonder looks down upon Plataea from his snowy summits — will he ever behold another such a struggle at his feet? Hardly within any imaginary cycle of years; the battle-line of the World's History has moved far forward. Over the meadow, then, toward ancient Plataea we must pass; perchance the place will yet give back some echoes of the old conflict. Wet spots and streams again obstruct the way, but they are easily forded; thus for hours we ramble through the valley listening to the ancient clash of arms and the tramp of the war-steeds, mingled now with the very pacific refrain of pastoral bells.

But the chief interest circles around those battlements yonder, still visible though in decay. On the whole the ancient village that lay there may be said to have possessed the most intense individuality of any Hellenic community large or small; its people were the most Greek of the Greeks. We have already heard of them, when they sent their whole population to Marathon, 1,000 strong, to drive out the Persian, the only town outside of Attica which did so; that was, however, but one characteristic deed. They appear in the first great muster-roll of the Greeks against the Asiatic, the Homeric catalogue; with their modest armament of nine ships they open their career and remain true to its principle to the last. For it they suffered untold afflictions, yet we read of no bending, no compromise. Destroyed and restored at least three times in the course of Greek history, the community preserves the same inflexible character, the same fidelity and patriotism. Through the legendary and historic epochs it exhibits the one fundamental trait; in the mythical conflict on the plains of Troy, the little town on the slope of the Kithaeron is not absent, nor in the supreme conflict of history, fought at its very gates. That town is Plataea upon whose site we, with a slight effort of imagination, may consider ourselves now to be standing.

Scarcely five miles distant in a straight line from Thebes, it is in every respect the opposite of that city. The fact has already been mentioned that there was always a foreign element at Thebes, hostile, or at least, unsympathetic with the Hellenic world. Not without good reason did the ancient traveler consider the Plataeans to be sprung from their own soil, in contrast to the strangers, who settled on the Cadmeia across yonder ridge on the other side of Teumessus. Hence the bitter enmity between Thebes and Plataea; the resolute little town never would submit to that foreign influence like other Bœotian towns. It is the one great Panhellenic spot in Bœotia, though other Bœotian towns are not devoid of patriotism, particularly Thespia. Nay, this may be said of Plataea, that of all the villages famed for heroism, it occupies rather the highest place in the World's History. No other small community that I know of, can show the same unswerving devotion to the supreme interests of its nation, and of its race, amid such continued and terrific outpouring of calamities. Through all the great Greek historians its story moves, fortunate at times, oftener unfortunate — but always glorious and honorable. Destiny justly placed the final victory over the Orient under its very walls, and called that victory by the Plataean name; and on that famous day the meed of being the bravest of the brave was given by the voice of the assembled Greeks to the Plataeans. In their territories the monuments of the victory were erected and stood for centuries; new temples to the Gods were built from the spoils of the vanquished; Zeus the Liberator, the God of this Plataean battle, and of the whole Persian War, was henceforth to be the special divinity of this spot, and games in honor of the event were celebrated by all Greece under the presidency of the Plataeans. Then the cloud gathers and bursts in the Peloponesian War; now it is brother against brother; brave little Plataea is encompassed with fire and sword; but I cannot give you history here, read the account of its siege and destruction in the adamantine yet deeply pathetic words of Thucydides.

Yet one more peculiarity must be mentioned in regard to this town: it produced no mighty towering individuality, no Great Man, in whom it seemed to sink away; scarcely has the name of a single leader been preserved. Far different was it elsewhere in Greece; the Hellenic world developed the individual above all other times or nations; its great characters are still our exemplars, our heroes. Not so Platæa; its people seem to have acted collectively and of their own spontaneous impulse; in the great battles we always read of them as a whole — the Platæans were there. No Great Man then can be named; the result was that the town seems to have been freer from dissension, from the partisan conflicts of powerful leaders than the other communities of Greece, it acted as a unit under its deep Hellenic impulse. It did not rear men stronger than itself, men too great for the State, but each member of it seems to have fitted harmoniously into the whole. As intense as its enmity to Thebes the stranger, was its friendship for Athens the defender and bearer of Greek civilization; and this friendship, so true, yet so humble, is one of the tenderest throbs out of the heart of Greek history.

Thus the Asiatic is defeated and expelled at Platæa; all Greece is now in happy jubilee and harmony with one chief exception. It is that old discordant Thebes with its foreign note on Greek soil; during the great Platæan day, its people fought desperately in the ranks of the Asiatic. The dissonance must be got rid of — so thinks the victorious Greek army still encamped along the Asopus; forward then to the discordant city. Again an army of heroic shapes appear before the seven gates of Thebes, capture it and purify it of *Medism*, of Asiatic tendencies. So we recollect that the Argive band in the legendary age took it and attuned it to a Hellenic note, for a time at least. History and legend give the same utterance concerning Thebes; they give the same utterance also concerning Platæa; the two Bœotian communities, about four miles apart, represent the mightiest opposing principles of the World's History.

In such manner Greece is again made harmonious by casting the discord out of Thebes. But who does it? Pausanias, the great leader of the allied Greeks at Platæa. By his victory over the Persian and by his eradication of Theban Medism, he has thrown himself to the front of the Greek world, and become the bearer of Greek civilization. But his success has made him too great for his time and for his country; he, after putting down the Asiatic and the Theban, falls at last himself into their guilt, becomes inharmonious with the Greek world, and *medizes*. Thus he, too, like those old legendary Theban heroes makes out of a life a tragedy. But not he alone; another Greek looms up during these Persian wars greater than even he, in native genius the mightiest individuality that Greece ever produced — Themistocles, the Athenian, hero of Salamis. What becomes of him? Alas! he meets with the same fate; he flees to Asiatic soil, he seeks the favor of the Persian monarch, under whose sway it is said that he died the death of nature, still he died with the purpose which made him deeply tragic: the purpose of undoing all his great work for Greece and for civilization.

Such is the end of the two most distinguished, and we may say, mightiest characters of this mighty epoch; after performing the greatest and noblest deeds for their country and race, they become harsh, all jangled and out of tune, winding up in shrillest discord. They give an insight into the deepest phase of Greek spirit; the heroic character was developed to such an extent that it became too great for its country. This tendency belongs to Greece; to all Greece; in the present case it is a Spartan as well as an Athenian whose greatness becomes discordant with their little states. Never has any society developed the individual so perfectly and harmoniously as the Grecian; still the end was a dissonance; as the result of his training and life he became mightier than his country, mightier than institutions and dropped back into despotic Orientalism, which can endure only the one individual. This danger the Greek communities themselves felt, and it was a problem with them what to do with their mighty characters, too mighty for them. The ostracism was merely a peaceful means whereby a Greek city sought to get rid of one of its Great Men when it was too small to contain so many of them, with their ambition, strength of will and intellectual resources. Nearly all famous Greek characters have the one epitaph: too great for their country.

The historian Thucydides who belonged to the same epoch and whose style shows the same towering individuality, has told the story of these two typical men, Pausanias and Themistocles, with an awe-inspiring directness, as if he himself were dazed at the consequences which he beheld in their fate, however much he tries to suppress himself. Well may that narrative inspire terror in the nation which has within it such a terrific contradiction. It reveals to the Greek world that of which it is to die; for in these men it can behold its own limitation, can look down from the very pinnacle whence it will be dashed to pieces. That story has still a throb of dismay breaking up through the stern self-control of the historian, and moves the reader with a kindred awe. Well it may, both for us and for the old Greeks, since it shows the outcome of their most illustrious characters, and of their world. It is a prophecy indeed — because the profoundest fact of the nation and age.

These great characters, then, are the handwriting in which we may read the destiny of Greece, their end prefigures her end. The disease of which the Great Man dies is the disease of his country, sooner or later his fate will be her fate. For she has brought him forth, and imparted to him the intensest phase of her own nature at his birth; concentrated into one burning point of individuality he has all that she has — both her strength and her weakness. The mother's mole flames red from his forehead, had we the eye to see it there; upon his acts is always stamped in letters of fire her character, indeed her destiny. So this happy harmonious Greece will become all discord, nay, is destined to relapse into the very principle which she has so gloriously met and put down. After the greatest deeds and mightiest harmonies, she will fall into contradiction with herself, like Themistocles, like Pausanias. These two are her prophetic sons, in their actions foretelling her end; she will, after conquering the Orient, drop back into Orientalism, and be absorbed into an Eastern empire; she brings forth Alexander, conquerer of Asia, mightiest of all her sons, mighty enough now to destroy her, and fulfill the prophecy of Themistocles.

Such is the account of the Greek Historian; but the same story had been told long before him quite as impressively and in far more brilliant colors by the Greek Poet. Legend too has revealed the Greek character in its deepest phase and made its innermost spiritual scission the theme of its greatest masterpiece. In the first book of the Iliad is narrated the famous quarrel between Agamemnon and Achilles. Who is Achilles? The surpassing Hero, the great Individual who spurns authority and moodily retires from the conflict, letting the enemy conquer. There also the Heroic Individual is too great for obedience to the established institutions; there also untold calamities fall upon the Greek host and many souls are sent to Hades; and the Poet must sing, as his truest poetical theme, not the taking of Troy or the submission of the Orient, but the wrath of Achilles, the Heroic Individual. Homer and Thucydides, singer of legend and writer of history, so diverse in form, give the same fundamental utterance concerning their own nation's character.

But there is one heroic individual of Greek history who does not produce this discord, and strange to say he is of discordant Thebes. Look off yonder from this Platæan height where we now stand, to the left some five or six miles; there is the field of Leuctra. Let all else sink out of sight, as it well may, but notice that man marshaling his Theban wedge of soldiery and smiting the hitherto invincible Spartan column with utter discomfiture — it is Epaminondas, the most ideal man in Greek history, evidently the completest most universal Grecian man. Though endowed with the highest gifts of thought and action, though harassed by envy and persecution, he will never become discordant with his city. We may pronounce his fundamental trait like that of Pindar, to be harmony — harmony developed into thought, deepened into character, and finally realized into action. The greatest qualities he possessed, yet not in conflict with one another nor with the world, but trained to a perfect symmetry, or even musical concord.

Throughout his education we find that he lays stress upon harmonious development of both body and mind. His early gymnastic training sought physical power combined with ease of motion; then he exercised himself in the chorus with dancing, which gave rhythm and grace to his movements. Music he learned with great assiduity, — the flute, the lyre, the song — thus attuning his emotional nature to the agreement of sweet sounds. But the highest branch of his education was the study of philosophy, the supreme science, which orders and attunes the whole universe for its true disciple. Also the philosophy which Epaminondas studied should be noted; it was that of Pythagoras, whose principle was based upon number, like the science of harmony itself, and whose supreme utterance is heard in the music of the spheres. Such was his education, in violent contrast to the ordinary Theban athlete, overfed and ignorant, the gross product of Bœotian vegetation; but he is the completely harmonious man, gifted with utterance too, for in eloquence he rivals the great Athenian orators, winning laurels even from silver-tongued Callistratus.

With such a happy training let us proceed to the final test, the action of the man. Here we shall all confess, that the deeds of the patriot Epaminondas are the supreme harmony of Greece in the realm of noble conduct. He never became too great for his country, and turned unharmonious, like those other mighty characters. He brings organization into the Theban polity, and organization of the highest order is harmony. Nay, his whole purpose extends beyond his own city's narrow limitations, and seeks manifestly to bring some kind of harmony into discordant Greece. The chief glory of Thebes is that she produced Epaminondas; without him she is nothing, worse than nothing, as regards action. Pelopidas shines too, but by his light, as his friend; this friendship, this perfect accord with another soul, must be noted as one of the harmonies of his life, and is one of the sweetest notes of the period. Epaminondas is all Thebes, all Theban history of honor; when he is taken away, there is left mainly her discord, and her sudden supremacy sinks with him into the grave.

Such is the Theban man of action. But as we come back toward the city, thinking of him, Dirke is again babbling over the pebbles at our side. Pindar too arises, not the man of action, but the singer of harmonious action. The two, Pindar and Epaminondas, truly belong together; each is perfect in his sphere, in happy concord; each is supremely harmonious with the other. In them the world of action and the world of musical expression are two great symphonies in complete unison. Like Pindar's broken lyre, the life of Epaminondas has reached us only in fragments of the grand Whole — fragments handed down mainly by an unfriendly historian, Xenophon; still, even under the touch of an enemy, that harmonious life reveals all its notes. In him there is no excess of hatred against his foes, no cruelty, no jealousy of rivals, no wild ambition, no avarice, — all is in happy rhythm and proportion. But mark the most harmonious strain of his character: he can obey as well as command, fulfill the humblest duties, as well as the highest. Never forget that typical anecdote how he, serving as common soldier, is called forth from the ranks to save a Theban army from destruction, and does save it; thus he sweeps from the lowest place to the highest authority, without extravagance or infatuation, without dissonance of any kind. So we must place him above all, above Pausanias and Themistocles, who became discordant; — Epaminondas is the completest, most universal Grecian man.

Thus we ascend again into Thebes, the Ismenian stream runs through the valley in many a conduit, and recalls tuneful shreds of hymns vanishing melodiously into forgetfulness. It too vibrates gently to the music of ancient Pindaric measures, lying embedded there like a jewel; but the harmonies of the poet now pass over into deed, and his exalted rhythm realizes itself in the actions and character of a man. Pindar is fulfilled in Epaminondas. From the twain old discordant Thebes is throbbing with new melodies; those tragic dissonances, which we heard at the beginning of the day, are swallowed up in the happy strain of the evening. Let us enter the walls, those walls whose stones moved into their places to the sound of Amphion's lyre, marching forth from their quarries; still they palpitate in the twilight to the ancient music. The temple of Ismenian Apollo rises anew on the sacred height now in our presence; it shows the white columns in soft movement around the holy shrine out of which well forth the strains of the God of music. Such a result has come out of dissonant Thebes, the fierce dualism has vanished; now you may understand why Cadmus, the fatal stranger, was wedded to Harmonia, the daughter of Zeus.

XI. FROM THEBES TO LEBEDEIA.

We must get up early, if we wish to make the present trip in one day, at our customary gait. For we cannot think of hurrying through this classic landscape, as if we had on our hands a piece of pressing business. Much is there on our way to be looked at with leisure; therefore about an hour before sunrise we slide out of the door of the wineshop into the street still dark, and grope along down the Theban hill into the *Megalos Dromos*, or Great Road which leads to Lebedeia. We pass by Dirke, not now radiant with the sun glancing over her waters, but wrapped in a Stygian cloak; well it is thus, for she must not detain us to-day. Cotton wagons are already moving with slow rumble over the highway; the burdened donkey trudges on through the dark, all invisible except the ears which still move backwark and forward; dogs rush out at you, but you must keep in hand the protecting stone which they have the power of seeing by night as well as by day.

But the Dawn has now come, suddenly, silently — still here she is, softly throwing her cream-colored mantle over the mountains. Aurora is indeed a light stepper; nobody ever beheld her face, only her shadowy white folds trailing behind can be seen after she has already darted by you. During some wink of the eye she came and went; I wake up of a sudden to observe her already flown far to the West. But she has left her blessing; at her touch all forms begin to free themselves of darkness and grow distinct. The wagons roll by now visible; ask the drivers how far to Lebedeia. The first one will say, ten hours; the second, nine; the third, noticing the sharp gait of the pedestrian in the morning freshness, will answer: Thus you will make it in eight hours. All of them pronounce the name of the town *Lebedeiá* throwing the accent forward to the last syllable, in Romaic fashion.

The twilight of the morning seems to hover longest around yonder hill off to the right; you can notice it wrapped in a fine-woven shroud of haze, while the plain about it reposes in clearest sunlight. You are continually coming nearer to it, still the dim film of Dawn refuses to reveal distinctly the summit. That is the mountain of the Sphinx, she who gave the riddle which was solved by Oedipus, being still to-day somewhat wrapped in haze. After its solution, says the legend, she cast herself down from her eminence and perished; when her secret had been guessed, she could no longer exist. But approach the mountain and look up with sharpened vision; you will still see the face of a woman there in the rock gazing intently upon the waters of lake Copais. Then she has not cast herself down but remains high up there, with her old riddle for you and me as well as for Oedipus — which riddle we too must solve at the peril of our existence. With rude stone features she gazes into the mirror of the reedy Copaic waters, trying to behold some image of herself therein, one thinks. That seems to have been the old problem: to see her own visage, to find out what she is herself. Very difficult indeed it is, O Sphinx, for thee to behold thy face in the unsteady and often slimy surface of Copaic slough; still on sunny, windless days thou mayest witness some dim image, which, however, vanishes with the first strong breath of air among the reeds. Gaze on — thousands of years, I prophesy, must sweep over thee before thou canst fully behold thyself reflected in the transparent crystal at thy feet. Another Oedipus, many others must pass and give some answer to thy question ere thy foundations of rock will tremble, and thou wilt precipitate thyself from thy altitude to the common level of the earth. — We must move on, and leave the Sphinx still gazing down into the waters with the thin veil of haze slightly drawn over the stony face; there you too may behold it in your journey.

But on the left we glance over the ridge with a different kind of feeling. For behind there we recollect that ancient Thespia lay, from whose ruins still comes a fresh breath of Panhellenic patriotism. With Plataea it refused to give earth and water, the symbol of submission, to the Persian; its name appears in the two great muster-rolls, the legendary and historical, of Greece against the Asiatic. Nor must we fail to do our share in correcting the injustice of fame; 700 of its citizens, though dismissed, refused to leave Leonidas at Thermopylae, and perished with him there; yet those Thespians, with equal heroism and greater devotion, seem always to be forgotten in the glory of their fellow combatants, the 300 Spartans. But we shall not forget them, the brave men, as we look upon their land; nor shall we pass over those 1,800 survivors of the little town who came to the Greek camp to fight at Plataea, though their homes had been plundered and burnt by the enemy, and though they in consequence of their losses were too poor to purchase equipments; still they came with undiminished fortitude to take part in the battle, without armor, determined to be present at any rate. Such was one vein of the golden character anciently to be found in Thespia.

But not because of its glory in war would I go there, if I were the ancient traveler, but to behold the masterpiece of Praxiteles, the statue of the God Eros set up and worshiped in Thespia. Thither in antiquity many pilgrims flocked to see the Divinity of Love in his supreme manifestation; thither many of us would go now to catch a glimpse of his true features, or perchance to conciliate him in some desperate venture. Nor should we forget upon this spot the stratagem of Thespian Phryne beloved of Praxiteles, who offered her the choice of his statues. But she wanted the best, and he refused to tell her which he thought was the best, till one day she started the shout that his house was on fire and his works perishing; then he uttered an anxious cry for his Eros, whereupon Phryne chose that. Here she dedicated the beautiful image, in this her native town, after a life devoted to the God, deeming, in a way strange to our modern consciousness, that even her vocation was not without some gleams of divine influence and participation.

To-day we are hardly allowed to speak of this power as a God, as the ancients did; it is, however, a power still felt, divinely felt. Man's being is twisted together out of many strands, some dark, some bright; but the brightest strand is that contributed by Eros. In fact life is insipid, utterly prosaic, if it be not flavored in some way by his fond presence; from him still springs the youth, the poetry of existence. Unaccountably he winds through and colors all our actions as well as sayings; nought is sweeter even in our worn days than a true utterance of him either in word or deed. It is no wonder then, that in the olden time admiring crowds came to Thespia, just to behold Eros in his highest revelation; thither we too would go with joy to see such a conception looking out from the marble.

Nor should we fail to hunt up in the Thespian territory that spring which punished the fair youth Narcissus, who despised the might of Eros; looking into the clear waters he saw his own face, and fell so deeply in love with it that he wasted away to death. Such was the just penalty inflicted by Eros upon the youth who contemned the divine gift, for he who cannot love, is smitten with a desperate self-love, in which he pines away to some miserable end.

Such, at least, would seem to be the warning of the God, transmitted in his legend; such too is that wonderful spring mirroring some inner as well as outer visage of the person who gazes into its depths. To it you and I would now go, were we certain of finding it, and look upon its glassy waters, without danger from the image therein reflected, I am sure.

Thespia was indeed with justice a favorite resort of Love's pilgrim anciently; three statues of marble stood there — we may think of them as standing side by side — which must have been the whole revelation of this theme. There was first the goddess-mother, Aphrodite herself, queen of Love and Beauty among the Immortals; then came her son, Eros, not a babe but a youth in whom the mother shows all her might, and communicates it to men; finally there was the mortal form Phryne, in whom the divine fire was most perfectly manifested — she who was loved by the artist himself, and through whom he was led up into the ideal world of his Art. Such was the trilogy of Love composed by Praxiteles and possessed by the Thespians, for which he above all sculptors was best gifted, since the point wherein his style culminates is to express the honeyed languor, the dulcet pains which come from Love's early wound. Strange old town to have such a worship filling the hearts of its people, and harmoniously regulating their lives! Yet no enervation seems to have resulted, as one might think, but the most intense energy in warlike deeds could be aroused there upon occasion. Once more call up those three sculptured shapes, all seeking to reveal Love to men and to attune their lives to its sweet concord. Nor was this worship a foreign one, introduced from abroad, but it came down from time immemorial; for the oldest statue of Eros there was simply a white stone, hardly more than a primitive fetich. The special character of Thespia must have been chiefly moulded as well as expressed by this deity.

But there was another worship in this town which ought to be mentioned. We shall not wonder when we learn that the Muses were specially honored at Thespia, for the Sisters Nine always follow in the train of Eros and never cease to sing the strain dictated by him. Love indeed is the chief inspirer of poetry and the chief theme thereof; it first makes existence musical and then demands some musical utterance of existence; in one or other of its manifold forms it gives the glow, the rapture, as well as the tuneful movement of the great works of literature. If we get into the heart of them, we shall find this emotional thrill of Love; with it human speech will throb in unison, being thrown thereby into the rhythmical cadence of song. So we may rejoice in the ways of the old Thespians who did not stop with the worship of Eros, but added the Muses to express him worthily, and to reveal truly his musical nature. Take him away, little work would be left for the Nine Sisters, in fact one Sister could easily do all of it.

Moreover there was at Thespia a great festival sacred to the Muses, celebrated with due splendor and with a mighty outpouring of song. For it seems to have mainly consisted of a musical contest in which all the poets of Greece might take part in competing for the prize. Thus the singer came and sang in praise of the Muses, in praise of his own Art, which gives the tuneful utterance, whereby all Thespia must have been filled in those days. Therefore the Thespians were the guardians of the shrine of the Muses on Mount Helicon, to which we have now come; here is the mountain on our left. So we wonder at the life of man in ancient Thespia filled with the worship of Eros and the Muses; a delicious existence, one imagines it to have been, overflowing with Love and Music. More than a thousand years the town lasted, we know, adoring its melodious deities, and sending up delightful strains which still to-day seem to be lingering around Helicon.

Thus one seeks to make the old Thespian character rise from its ruins, and take on some definite shape; for even ancient writers have assured us that every town in Greece had a character of its own, distinguishing it pointedly from all of its neighbors. The leading bad trait of each important Bœotian town is given by an old traveler, Dikæarchus; each had its controlling vice as well as distinct virtue. As we look around ourselves and observe the distant landscape with its ranges of hills running crosswise and lengthwise, we remark again how under our very eye this plain of Bœotia divides itself into several lesser plains, each of which is centered in its own community. A self-contained life is possible here; autonomy is printed on the face of Greece everywhere, spelled out in rude strong letters by the mountains and valleys. Whenever we cross a ridge, we may always say: this is a distinct part of Bœotia with its own character, with its own towns boiling over in fierce energy anciently; each is seeking primarily to be itself and nought else. Yet there was too a Bœotian league, we know; there was a common Bœotian principle in them all, which had to be adumbrated, though dimly, in some institution.

Villages appear to the right and left; some of them seem to be lying far out amid the reeds of the swamp, others are placidly perched upon the hill-sides; their different characters one may to a degree imagine from the situation. We pass by ancient Onchestus, and do not forget its distinctive mark, which was the temple and grove of earth-shaking Neptune, celebrated in many a Greek book from the Iliad down. But a touch of anxiety begins to trouble the mood within as the overcast sky darkens the landscape without; clouds are resting upon the mountains and sullenly look down at the pedestrian, threatening him with a dash of rain. Zeus, the cloud-compeller is up there, brewing another storm; but I pray him to hold up the showers in those deep fleecy folds of his celestial drapery till I reach Lebedeia. That one rainy trip you may recollect; it was enough for me, and for you too.

One name lingers in the mind upon this road, that of Hesiod the Poet, and you often ask yourself: what produced him here? His birthplace lies up the hill to the left, ancient Ascra, still inhabited but producing no Hesiods. I met a peasant boy at the side of the road ploughing: "Point out Zagora to me" — such is the modern name for Ascra, manifestly corrupted from the ancient one. His reply was, What are you going to do at Zagora? Are you a didaskali, a schoolmaster? Such was his view of the stranger asking for the birthplace of Hesiod.

But we have already arrived at grassy Haliartus, not now so grassy, probably as it was in Homer's time, but watered still with abundant streams running through its meadows; one of these streams we shall cross and enter the wineshop where there is a chance for a luncheon with recinato. One half of our journey to-day is done, yet it is forenoon still; more leisurely we can make the rest of the trip. We may note, too, that the sun has come out amid the clouds, Zeus has heard our petition and will not be angry to-day. Pleasant are the meads and rills of Haliartus flowing full of ancient legend; fresh too is the breath of Greek patriotism which wafts over its pastures; that ancient half-burnt temple set on fire by Persian invaders, stood here, which the citizens would not rebuild, but left standing over 600 years at least, a continual reminder of the eternal struggle of Greece against the Orient.

Emerging from behind a low hill we again come to lake Copais, or swamp, as it ought to be called, full of reeds and grass; far off toward Orchomenus the narrow stream of the river Kephissus, marked by the absence of marshy vegetation, flows sluggishly through the standing waters. Around the edge of the morass we now skirt for miles on the semilunar bend; sometimes the shallow water sweeps up and touches the bed of the highway at our feet. In antiquity we must suppose a different aspect, for this whole swamp was drained, and thousands of acres of the best land in Greece was redeemed for cultivation. Still the old catabothra or underground drains can be seen, tunneled through the rock in part, but now choked up; even this rubbish from her great ancient works modern Greece has not yet been able to remove. These drains seem to have been made in a fabulous era, though not by any means fabulous things; for yonder they exist, an astonishing feat of engineering to-day. But these reeds we shall not wholly condemn, for of them was made the ancient flute which gave the rhythmical beat to the choruses of Pindar. Thus even in reedy Copais there is music, provided the man may be found who can extract it.

Here then we have passed a new ridge and behold a new plain; therewith rises a new question which is, however, but the old one; who shall control the plain? In like manner we crossed the Theban ridge from Attica, and the Platæan ridge from Thebes; now we enter the Copaic plain, with the same fierce question, anciently to be settled by desperate warfare. Thus our Greece is individualized; this plain too will give, with its adjacent swamp, a different character to its dwellers. Look across the water, yonder is Orchomenus, the abode of the Graces; still its white dwellings seem to rest gracefully on the hill-side above the surface of the lake. Once she was mistress of this valley, a wise one, if we may judge by her works; but at her ascendancy every town squirmed, fell into resistance, loving its own autonomy at least, though not so intensely that of its neighbors. Such was the education of Greece — each man must be a hero, and each town the mother of heroes. Every person was of importance in such a community, he was never lost in an untold Oriental multitude. To such a consciousness does his training lead — to make him a complete individual.

Often one hears a sigh for the political unity of the Greek cities that the fair Hellenic flower be preserved. No, that could not be; if she had had within her the germ of unity, far different would she have been — indeed she would not have been Greece at all. The conditions of her beauty are the sources of her decay; the flower would not bloom, if it did not wither. Achilles, the heroic type, of surpassing form, fleetness, and strength, is fated to die early; so does Alexander the historical Greek hero. A strong central government for Greece! not at all. Her glory is that she gave a free and full development to the individual, untrammeled by the fewest external restraints. Never has man upon the whole attained to such a musical existence, and made of himself such a harmonious physical and spiritual being — one who in himself combined all without dissonance, reflected, we may say, the Universe. Exemplars they must furnish to the race eternally, for they were whole men. Now man has become special and a specialist, an infinitesimal part of the colossal organism around him. Yet we must not forget the exception even in Greece, namely, those mighty individuals who at last became discordant with their country.

But there is no discord now; in tuneful company the traveler marches along at the foot of the mountain, for it is Helicon. It is a mountain delightful as of old; to-day it has the same friendly appearance which was anciently praised so much. Its soil was the most productive of any mountain in Greece, we read: wild fruits grew there in abundance, and to all its products it gave the sweetest flavor; herbs and roots which were elsewhere injurious to man, lost upon Helicon their native poison; even noxious serpents became harmless upon its meadows. One can well believe that it has some such power to-day; it draws all care, all biting anxiety from the heart, as one looks up at its happy summits sporting through sunshine and clouds. The touch of the Muses it has still, though their voices have fled from its dells. Nature is essentially the same to-day on Helicon as of old; that wonderful drug Nepenthe, which was the gift of Helen, she administers through the breathing of the air. Thus we wind round the Heliconian crescent having Copais at our feet, with breezes slightly rustling amid its reeds and rushes.

Nature, the gazing traveler often repeats to himself, remains the same to-day on Helicon that she was of old; but where are those other objects of beauty which once skirted the lake? For many temples were built here looking off over the waters; and the ancient pedestrian always had one and perchance several of them in his view, cheering him forward to their inclosure with a mild joy. Statues, too, there were, wrought by famous masters; for did not those old Greeks need in daily life, amid their toil, art as much as bread? Particularly Athena seems to have been honored here; the Goddess is reported to have appeared at one of her temples with Medusa head, and turned the priestess to stone who beheld the awful visage. There the stone woman stood and had an altar; daily an attendant put fire on her altar and cried out:

"Iodamia lives and asks for fire." O Iodamia, why did the Goddess turn thee to stone? Yet thy stony statue was thought to live, and being of cold material, to cry out for fire, wherewith to warm itself. A wonderful statue indeed, not easy to be hewn out of speechless marble, yet possible for some old Greek artist, who could make stone speak.

Nor must we omit the fountains which gushed from the sides of Helicon; we are continually passing their waters and shall always stop to listen for a moment to their music. These Heliconian fountains have had a strangely tuneful destiny; they have become the types of poetic utterance for all time seemingly, still they are welling forth melodiously from the depths of the mountain. So the streams of poesy rise from their deep sources, like Aganippe from Helicon, which made musical whoever drank of its waters; like Hippocrene, bubbling up here to-day from the track imprinted by the hoof of the flying horse, Pegasus, and overflowing the woody dells with clear melody, as the steed mounts heavenward; like Tilphousa, sweet warbler, near whose stream Apollo thought of establishing his temple instead of taking Delphic Castalia. All these fountains are still on Helicon and we may reach down and drink of their waters; but the fanes built over them have disappeared, the nymphs have fled. Nature is still here, but she no longer calls forth the deification of herself into art. The images of marble are gone never to be restored by mortal hand; but that other image of Helicon, its spiritual image with all its fountains leaping forth to the sunlight, endures and will endure; human speech has chiseled out new statues of its deities made of the substance of man's very soul.

But along yon Heliconian heights was witnessed in antiquity a worship which characterizes Greece better than any thing else; there was the sanctuary of the Muses, the givers of harmonious utterance of every kind, the inspirers also of harmonious lives. The musical gift which is heard not only in human speech, but subtly orders and attunes Nature, was there the special object of adoration; the whole mountain was a sacred place; a large grove was filled with shrines and statues, through which one passed and beheld the revelation of this fairest side of existence. There was first the holy fount Aganippe at the entrance, whose lustral waters purified of discord the worshiper as he passed in; then were the images of the Nine Muses wrought by famous artists, filling the beholder with infinite harmonies which were to transform him into a musical being in thought, word, action. Nor was the nurse of the Muses, Eupheme the Sweet Voice, absent from the group, though they were daughters of Zeus the Highest and of Memory who brings to the present the great deed of the olden time. Not merely by poets were they addressed in prayer, as in our day, but also by the common people, by the humblest man, since he sought to make himself a tuneful note, though small, in the harmony of the Universe.

Next were the images of famous bards, those who had been breathed upon by the Muses, and whom they had gifted with musical utterance; these bards were indeed the first teachers of the race, taming wild men to the sounds of concord by voice and instrument. Linus was there, whose name goes far back into fable, and is coupled with the earliest form of song; he is said to have been slain by Apollo when he had reached so great excellence as to equal a God in his strain. Thamyris, the blind bard, stood there touching his shattered lyre, the result of defeat in a contest with the Muses; Arion was present, still perched upon that dolphin which he had charmed by song to bear him safely through the waves of the sea to land; finally Orpheus was there, the greatest of all these fabulous bards, surrounded by brazen and sculptured animals under the spell of his strain amid the listening woods; thus Nature is subdued by the poet's voice, and becomes musical, when she finds expression in him. Nor should we forget the tomb of Orpheus, upon which the Thracian nightingales built their nests and hatched their brood, for thus the young birds sang more sweetly. Similar was the case of the Thracian shepherd who at mid-day fell asleep on the grave of Orpheus and at once began to sing in so loud and sweet a strain that all the shepherds and plowmen from neighboring districts flocked to listen to the song. Of that shepherd we may think as the first pastoral poet, the first Theocritus. Thus in many a luscious bit of legend has that harmonious world come down to us, setting us too in a soft vibration to its notes. Helicon represents it still; along her summits all nature is attuned to a hymn and subdued by some melodious spell; trees, animals, man fall into the sweet measured rhythm sent from the Muses.

But no certain word of these ancient Heliconian bards has come down to us; only concerning their power and excellence do we hear a few fitful strains of fable, which we may well believe in the true sense. Now we come, however, to the central image in this sanctuary, altogether the most significant figure here — it is the poet Hesiod. His voice has reached us quite full and resonant; still we may hear it echoing through the dells of Helicon. Look upon that face of his which has possibly preserved some of the features of his statue standing here of old; Helicon culminates in him. One looks up at the summits and asks: How did ye produce a poet? In what way did ye mould his character? Thus the traveler winds around the mountains, praying Mnemosyne to call back for him some strains of the old bard, and to attune him to their keynote.

Here, then, he arose and sang his song — a song of significance to-day. A hard, unbending, somewhat crabbed genius; still a genius, gifted with Heliconian dower. That old poem of his, called *Works and Days*, is a genuine Bœotian product; anciently on Helicon it was shown, written upon a leaden tablet. Many a harmonious pulsation it has, though at times rude enough; still better, it has a philosophy of life and its own view of the government of the world; thus it must have gone deep into the hearts and actions of men. It strikes at first an exceedingly discordant note, for it seems to imply that the Gods who are to be worshiped have become the enemies of their worshipers. A woeful view of the world is that, quite enough to fill anybody with harsh jangle and biting acidulous utterance. The story of Prometheus, the friend of man, who has covertly to steal fire from Zeus; the myth of Pandora, the beautiful woman, sent as an evil upon man, express the hostility of the Supreme Ruler; the poet might as well cry out: the Gods are our enemies. A melancholy spectacle indeed is man when he has fallen out with his Gods.

It is clear that the old poet is grappling with a tough problem, tough still for us to-day: the problem of the origin of evil. Who made evil? Who permits it? Zeus certainly, if he be the Supreme God; a thought distracting, of diabolical dissonance in the soul. To account for its beginning Hesiod has given two legends, that of Prometheus, and that of the Five Ages; both, however, go toward the Bad, and end in the Bad; the poet has suffered evil, much evil; he asks how it came to be and finds that it is by the will of the Gods. Then he is unhappy; all men are unhappy in like condition of mind; the unhappy consciousness it may be called. Not a poetical mood is this, one thinks, not a harmonious strain; still, if the poet have in him the gift of healing this deep disruption of soul, he can change it to one of the grandest themes of song.

A second dissonance heard in Hesiod, in strange contrast to other utterances of Greek fable, is his dislike and contempt for women, revealed in his legend of Pandora and in several bitter outbursts. He connects her indeed with the origin of all evil in the world, making her somewhat similar to Eve in another more authoritative book. Yet she cannot apparently be got rid of, so the old surly poet makes some scanty provision for her in the Family. Strange that he too should carry back our original sin to the sexual dualism, which he would like to abolish, but does not see his way clearly thereto. No beautiful Helen floats before his imagination the worthy cause of Trojan wars, but homely Meg is his, she who can spin and grub. Far different is Homer who has placed in his ideal household that supreme type of womanhood Penelope, and limned many an outline of fair maidens alongside of his heroes.

However not woman alone, but man too comes in for

a share of his objurgation — nay, his own brother named Perses. The latter has spent his part of the paternal inheritance in riotous living, and is now seeking to get by foul dealing that of the poet; he has even corrupted the judges to decide in favor of his unjust claim; it is a most unbrotherly act. So the poet addresses advice and rebuke to the erring brother — good advice, sharp rebuke; this is the frame-work in which the whole poem is set. Also the town Ascra, where he lives having for neighbors those unrighteous judges, is smartly goaded with some passing strokes: "Wretched town, near Helicon, bad in winter, miserable in summer, never genial." His age, too, is the iron age, glorious ages have preceded it, but this unhappy age is left for him, and bitterly he laments his lot: "Would that I had not mingled with this race of men, but had been born before or died afterward. It is indeed the iron race, and never will they cease from toil and wretchedness." Thus our Ascræan pipe gets scrannel, grating its squeaky tune, and all Helicon hisses in shrill discord.

The sullen old grumbler, after venting his spleen, will change his note, and pass on to tell of agriculture; what else can a man do but forget himself by labor in such a bad world? A soured, gnarled, unbending nature; who could help being thus when all the Gods have become his enemies? It is not a cheerful state; woe be to the man who has fallen out with his Gods, believing in their power but distrusting their goodness. Such a person must be wretched unless he in some wise run away from himself; so the crabbed but defiant Hesiod will turn and swink in the field to escape from his unamiable theology. Therewith we are on the way to get rid of the world of hateful Gods and of moral disorder, and that Hope which was left in the cask of Pandora as the last solace for poor mortal men, begins to fill the breast with her mild illumination.

It would therefore, be a great mistake to suppose that the poet gives no solution for the present order of things. He does, and in this lies the value of his poem for men. The Gods have hidden the means of living, therefore the human being who eats must work. Such is his destiny written upon every spot of earth — work, work. For, says the poet, if a man in one day could get enough for a whole year, then would the rudder be laid aside, and the labors of oxen and mules would cease from the land. Therefore work, work; every human being must have something to do; if he has no work, then he has no business to be, soon will not be, by decree of the Gods. In former ages men lived a golden life, without toil and care; the earth brought forth her fruits spontaneously, and he partook of them; there was no wrong, nothing to do wrong for; but in this age the jealous Gods have laid upon mortals the hard necessity — work, work. Nor is the compensation of work absent; we through work defeat the spite of the Gods who sent upon us evil; we bridge the terrible chasm between ourselves and the world, and even get the better of the divine decree. The Gods themselves are conquered by work; their hostility turns into a blessing by work. The necessity, nay the absolute worth of work marks the deep strong touch of the poet, who therein changes from a discordant grumbler to a true singer, and rescues men from a world of ethical confusion, elevating them into a tuneful sphere. Hence he sings of Works and their Times, first as his own solution of the great problem of evil, secondly as advice to the erring brother.

And that brother who seeks to get on in life without work; nay worse, who seeks to possess others' work by fraud and by bribing judges — what shall be done with him? Shall we work and let him riot? No; and here this poem of Hesiod introduces the second principle which supplements work and overcomes the wrong of the world. It is the conception of Justice — Dike. A deep unshaken faith in Justice is the highest attribute of the poem; though the Gods fail, still there is Justice. Here she comes, a virgin born of Jupiter, illustrious, worshipful among the Gods of Olympus; she, clad in the viewless air, comes bringing ill to wrong-doing men who have driven her away and have made an unrighteous decision; irresistible is her course. But whoso doth not transgress Justice, for these the city blooms and the people are prosperous; peace reigns among them, nor is there famine or calamity, but happy festivals. The earth bears for them much substance; on the mountain stands the oak with acorns amid its branches and bees in its trunk. Thus the poet describes the glories of Justice, with the deepest insight into its character. For he plainly sees Justice to be that which keeps the world from falling into chaos, and he has stated in the most direct manner its fundamental principle: the return of the deed upon the doer. Listen to him: Man working evil to another is working evil to himself, and evil counsel is worse to him that hath devised it.

In such wise with rude yet mighty words he announces the supreme law of the ethical world and smites with it in Titanic energy. Well might that brother quake with secret terror after hearing such an exposition, for the intense faith is here expressed that the wicked act will be brought back to the doer, if need be by thrice ten thousand demons, guardians of mortal men, avengers of wrong, hovering in misty darkness everywhere over the earth. Oh, Perses, reform thy ways; if thou wouldst live as a true man in this world, work, work; then be just, recognize the work of thy brother as fully as thine own. By such conduct we shall circumvent the spiteful Gods; toil, which they sent upon us as a curse, will change through Justice to a blessing which orders and upholds the Universe.

Thus the Ascræan pipe undergoes a change and now begins to discourse harmoniously: the discordant notes are all swallowed up in sweet melodious utterance; the very strength of the former dissonance adds to the depth and intensity of the new harmony. Helicon grows musical again, the Sisters Nine return to their abode, and we see why they handed to the poet the laurel branch, holding which he sang his strains. Still the fierce dissonance can be heard whistling through his song, like a northern blast through sunshine. But you come to love the rugged nature with its adamantine integrity which not even the spite of the Gods could shake, and whose harsh features often kindle into a soft glow of poesy whenever he speaks of Helicon and its Muses.

Such is the purport of the poem, though its parts be

often distorted and jumbled together at hazard. You obtain a strong image of the Bœotian farmer and his life; a character is here, rude, honest, yet thoughtful, and of granitic toughness. Amid his rustic precepts are many poetical gems shining with their earliest unworn lustre. He tells you that you must never cross a stream without praying — a truly Greek instinct; nor must you defile the spring or running brook — 'tis an unholy thing. Beware, too, of Fama or Report, she is a goddess, easy to excite, hard to calm — Goddess is the report which many mouths utter. Most genuine, too, is the connection of the poem with nature; it hangs from her as fruit from the branches of the tree; the verses seem to be a product of the seasons, or a pendent of the stars, like the words of which they sing. There is no artificial time measurer, but nature herself calls the husbandman, when the cuckoo sings in the oak foliage, when the snail climbs shunning the Pleiades, when the cry of the crane is heard overhead, when the young fig-leaf is as large as the crow's foot; the stellar sky in the night speaks down to him, from strong Orion, from Arcturus leaving the sacred stream of Ocean. The ox-track full of rain is the measure of the rain-fall, and early precursor of science. Bathe your hand in crossing a brook, otherwise you are hated of the Gods. Primitive spontaneous utterances of poesy are in this book, revealing nature as she was looked upon by the new fresh eye of the young world; yet amid the green branches are dry twigs enough, abstract doctrines, proverbs, maxims of prudence, pointed sharply to penetrate the thick skull of the peasant, especially the Bœotian peasant. Many of the poet's views incline to the form of proverbs, some bluntly inculcating the homely virtues, others rising into a sort of esoteric vein; particularly we catch breath at that quite transcendental one: "Fools, they know not how much more is the half than the whole," and we ponder whether we may not be of the persons addressed. But it is high time to say good-bye to the old bard; hereafter we have hopes of meeting him often and of hearing his lines, steeped in the memories of Helicon; his book is indeed henceforth a new book.

As you saunter along, looking up to the glorious heights of Helicon, the old woman will meet you, rude-visaged, with skin wrinkled and burnt by the sun of the plain, but hardy, long-striding for a woman. Of course you will address her; broken fragments of Greek fall from her mouth, not easy to piece together; some dialect you imagine, with ancient turns perhaps. Many an old word she employs, though wholly uneducated; still there is a delight in listening to her, for what was before inanimate, suddenly becomes living speech. She drives a donkey — so did her mother 2,000 years ago. She takes a by-path down into the reeds of Copais; I pass on, still glancing up at the summits of sunny Helicon, and wondering: Can this be you? How is it that just you have come down through Time in an eternal glory, and have traveled over the world, across the ocean, and are still winged and in flight? Other hills too have had fair dells and sunny heights — why just you? Some great man made you, you never made yourselves; some bard it was, the man who alone can attach pinions to the hills, and send them on their flight through Time.

But whatever we may think about the old woman's origin, we may affirm that the genuine descendant of the old crow is here, sweeping over the ridges in enormous flocks and lighting upon the fat meadows. And here too we pass ancient Coroneia or Crow's Town, famous for the battles which took place in its vicinity; still the air seems laden with curses upon two men — Lysander and Sulla. Both of them meet a most deserved fate from the Gods for their evil doings in this plain, whose jarring note we shall at once dismiss. Further up is the fountain Libethrias, a true nymph, lying deep in the earth, now turned to solid rock; from her stony breasts gush forth two fountains, whose water the ancient informant declares to be like milk. Yonder too is a pretty village so cosily perched on a picturesque platform in the mountain that one cannot help imagining that it must produce a poet. About half way up the mountain it lies; the peaks above seem to look down upon it with protection and love; its name I cannot tell you, but simply let it pass before you as a pleasing Heliconian image.

The declivity of Helicon at this season of the year is in possession of the Wallachian shepherds — a foreign race on Greek soil. Several times to-day I have passed through their flocks, browsing on either side of the roads or reposing on the hill-side in the sun. New-born kids you will notice lying against a bramble, while the young mother, frightened at your approach, runs off a few steps and then turns and looks at you with shy maternal anxiety. Every ewe or goat has a little one, sometimes two, running along at her side and bleating, fine-voiced; thereto she answers by a bleat of far deeper tones; thus thousands and thousands of notes are resounding to-day over the mountains; such is now the music of Helicon.

In the midst of his herd, upon a rock, stands the shepherd, shaggy-mantled as one of his own sheep, with his long crooked staff in hand, gazing down at the passing stranger. He will call his goats and sheep by name, as if they were human beings, in inquiry, in caresses, in reproof, like old Polypheme; often a shrill whistle is the note of warning for them to keep away from the tilled field, which whistle can frequently be heard coming from the sunny slopes when no whistler can be seen, for he is screened by the rocks and brambles of the mountain. Some of these Wallachian shepherds cannot talk Greek, some can; of one of the latter I ask: 'Where do you live? — Twenty-five days' journey from here, on the Pindus. — Will you take me with you when you return home! — Yes, but we shall not start for some months yet. — That was the end of the plan. But what a life! To spend it among sheep, by yourself, in the open air, on the mountains, calling your flock by name as familiar friends! I cannot sleep in a house, said one of them, I get sick; women and children live in houses, not men. — Such was the pastoral view of human existence.

But not shepherds alone are found upon Helicon, there are also shepherdesses; and it was there I learned a new admiration for the latter. The heroine was a Wallachian woman. She was sitting amid her flock on a stone; in her lap lay a bundle which she seemed to arrange with unusual care and tenderness. As I approached I was astonished to hear a faint cry proceed from the bundle; at my request she threw open the folds of an old shawl covering it, and there lay a new-born infant. New-born indeed, for its eyes were not yet open; it lay there still red with the friction of parturition, and appeared to be enjoying the luxury of its first scream in the free light of heaven. She arose from her seat and threw a stone at a ewe which was trespassing on the grainfield. "What," I cried, "are you already up and out?" To my amazement I learned that she had been overtaken by her labor in the field some hours before; but stopping a few moments and wrapping the little new-comer in her garment, she went on about her business; amid her flock, she too had given birth to her kid. Great was the sympathy of the traveler at first, but she needed no sympathy — for was she not there in perfect health and without pain? Still I could not help filliping a silver drachma as a beginning in life to the youngster, now growing louder with the minutes. Such was our real Helliconian shepherdess.

All day Parnassus has been looming up in front of me, growing nearer; yet sometimes I have quite lost sight of it in the envelopment of clouds. One may well wonder what is there, what it has in store for the traveler. Repeatedly it came forth, having top and sides strown with sunshine; but rain is still threatened, and Parnassus for the most part hides itself in cloudy drapery. Not yet has it revealed itself to the approaching guest, but he looks forward with longing glances, and in golden sheen at times beholds his goal. Mighty, but very vague and uncertain is the expectancy hovering around its summits, yet even upon the clouds there the day's radiance has a tendency to disport itself. Will the Muses strip off that vapor and come forth into clear Greek outline? Wait; we shall see.

But we have already reached a spur of a mountain running out into Copais; it is the extreme tip of the arc upon which we have been moving now for several hours; let us turn around and look back at it. In a long amphitheatrical curve it sweeps around from the opposite tip for many miles; Thebes is out of sight, but villages fleck the distant hill-sides; cotton carts can be seen far across the lake slowly rounding the curve. And that immense curve walled in by the mountains is one of Nature's own, carefully drawn by her with a huge pair of compasses from a center taken somewhere far out in the swamp. Behold her, the first geometrician, now in the very act.

But up and forward! Turning the spur and following the road a short distance, we come to Lebedeia, lying between Helicon and Parnassus. What a musical spot ought it not to be, situated between two such abodes of the Muses, who may sing to each other from top to top! Glancing between the twain, one seeks to solve this question: Why of all the world did their worship locate just here? The two ranges confront each other like rivals; rivals indeed they were; the people in antiquity, one feels sure, held in the valley between a tournament of the Muses, trying to settle the dispute as to where was their true seat. Such, it would almost seem, was then the vital question through these hills and valleys — a question which must be settled by trial and decision. But what people at present deems such a dispute of any significance? The other great question has now arisen: Who shall trade with the Ashantees, who shall sell a penknife to the South Sea Islander? For such and similar questions much blood has been spilled, while both Helicon and Parnassus with their sweet rivalry have been quite deserted; in mute protest they still stand here, wondering to-day at the new ways of the world.

As we approach Lebedeia and glance at its situation, we ask, what is its character? What are the secret suggestions of Nature upon this spot? For we may be sure that the Old Greek felt them and wrought them into some form of utterance, legendary, oracular, divine. Most intimately he felt what surrounded him and then bodied it forth into the myth; this myth, too, bore the impress of his spiritual existence. There the Greek mythical world beautifully hovers, between Nature and Spirit, spanning both like a rainbow, yet reflecting both in one fair image. Whoever says that Greek Mythology is of merely physical import, mistakes; whoever says that it is of merely spiritual import, mistakes. In like manner the Oracle sprang up, even the God had the same origin. On every spot of Greek ground rose that mythical rainbow from Nature there into the heaven of Spirit above it; so we look now before us with expectancy and ask: What shall we find at Lebedeia?

Entering the outskirts of the town, we note first that it sits at the mouth of a defile; it seems to have been born of that mountain just behind it, which is Helicon or a continuation of Helicon. Springing out of the rocky depths, the town lies there, now in the sunlight, but once hid in the dark stony womb of the mountain; still back of the houses you will catch a glimpse of the obscure gorge which opens into the town and seems to have just spit it out. Lebedeia thus appears at first view to be a product of the cleft, yet lying outside of its jaws; she must be a child of this mountainous Nature, resting at present in the bright gleams of Helius, but still partaking or hinting of her gloomy origin. Some slight touch thereof will be felt by the sympathetic traveler as he enters the town.

But listen! a noise is continuously humming through the streets, but it is not of men; some sound of Nature you will at once discern it to be. It is the song of a brook coming out of the cleft there and dancing in many a rivulet through Lebedeia. It too is born of the gorge, from that same dark mouth it spouts forth, like the town which it fills with its murmurs. Springs too gush up from sunless depths of rock and laugh in the sunbeams; their pellucid flow and babble seem to have that primeval joy of first beholding light. Thus a perpetual undertone of musical waters attunes Lebedeia, mingling with the words of her people. Something therein is hinted; brook and town are in a secret harmony, both suggest the outgiving of Nature, yet bear a spiritual impress. Assuredly some character is here which we must further seek for; legend must have given a voice to the spot, the God himself must have found a holy utterance for the place, which the sensitive Greek heard and in some form expressed. It is no wonder that an Oracle anciently stood here, the Oracle of Trophonius, whose cave is still in yonder mountain. We too shall consult that Oracle, and see whether it may utter any word for us, since it can never be, to the true believer, wholly dumb.

XII. STOP AT LEBEDEIA.

It was getting late in the afternoon when I reached the khan, to which a mule-driver of a very friendly and talkative turn conducted me. The house is unpretentious, the chief decoration being a porch to the second story; in the rear is a large yard, filled at this moment with carts and donkeys, among which wind tight-trowsered red-moccasined men in fustanellas, rudely hurling fair fragments of old classic speech at their dumb beasts and at one another. The traveler will speedily engage a room for the night, and will ask to see it; on being led thither, he will find it absolutely empty — bare walls, bare floors, chairless, bedless. But let him not get out of humor; whenever he wishes to retire, the youth in attendance will bring an armful of mats and blankets which will be spread upon the floor, and he will be spared the labor of climbing into his bed.

There is still time for a short stroll through the town; that undertone of rushing waters is always heard and excites curiosity concerning what it may be saying. Upon a bridge I stop and look down at the current; I feel a twitch at my coat and turn around; before me stands an officer of the Greek army. He had observed my foreign dress and manner, and had concluded to enquire where I was lodged; when I informed him, he pressingly invited me to share his quarters with him, but I thought I must try the khan for one night at least. It was only one of several offers of hospitality extended to me in Lebedeia, though I was an utter stranger and without letters of any kind. With a very pleasant impression of the town, I go back to my room, and lie down to rest with that curious sound of rushing waters leading me along sunny banks into happy regions of slumber.

Such was dreamland; but in our real world there had been pitchy darkness filled with driving rain-storms during the entire night. In the morning the weather looked unsettled; the streams had overflowed their banks, the roads were muddy, for the Great Road had now been left, and only mule-paths led forward to Parnassus. So we shall lie over a day at Lebedeia, not without some hope of entertainment.

When you wake you will again hear the sound of rushing waters, now much louder than on the previous evening; the stream, which flows through the middle of the town, is full. After an early lunch you will hasten to this stream and begin to follow it up to its source, for surely it has some very near relation to the place. Thus you will be led to the mountains back of the town, toward the gorge. At many points can be noticed springs, small caves, precipices beetling over the dash of the furious torrent. The mountain shoots up into a number of peaks which look like the pipes of an immense organ, upon which, you may think, Heliconian music might still be played. Nor will you pass unnoticed some plane-trees which hang around and over the stream in a sort of fond caress. Arched bridges, too, you will observe, spanning the stream in romantic spots through the town, joining together in happy embrace what had been separated.

Large fountains gush up at the foot of the hill near the mouth of the gorge, and flow in swift clear streams, walled off into artificial channels which wind round among the houses. Here must have been those two famous springs, Memory and Oblivion, of which the ancient traveler drank when he consulted the Oracle; we, too, shall taste of them now, and seek to get its response. Notice the wild current boiling out of the gorge; it is Herkyna, the dashing Nymph who still makes music through the town; anciently she had a temple here and was worshiped by the people; her voice it is which we hear humming the undertone of

Lebedeia. A legend was told of the origin of this stream: Proserpine was playing with a goose in the grove of Trophonius not far off, when the goose escaped and hid under a rock; Proserpine ran after it and removed the rock, when behold! uprose the stream and flew down the channel on its white wings, continuing its flight ever afterwards and being called Herkyna; in the temple on the bank was the statue of Herkyna holding in her hands the goose, which was ready to fly, we may suppose.

Up this stream into the gorge whence it issues we shall continue our walk, in search of the goose, perchance; on either side lofty walls of stone rise toward heaven and form a darkened passage which gives a feeling of initiation into some sacred mystery. Cavities you will observe, natural and artificial; places are cut into the rock above, in which you will locate ancient shrines. Here, too, is a pedestal built against the steep cliff just at the edge of the torrent; above it are half a dozen small cavities, hollowed out for images, you will conjecture. Immense boulders which have fallen from the top lie in the middle of the stream, around which the waters roar and surge down the chasm. Thus you will pick your way through the gorge, at times with difficulty avoiding the splashing swift current, which roars around you, filling the hollow passage with its echoes. At one point you will try to climb up the sides to the top, but you will be cut off by an overhanging rock. Descend again into the gorge and listen to the genius of the place, for the God will not yet suffer you to come up into sunlight; you must first catch its dim whisper.

What, then, does it all say? Can any one blame the ancient dweller if he came into these secret hollows and asked them to speak? It would seem that they have some utterance for man, though vague and mysterious. Still the people of to-day place in these shrines images of the Virgin and Child, and name them after the Saints, as if there were yet some divine influence in the spot. The whole expression of the locality was anciently collected into one voice — the voice of Trophonius, the Prophet, who was the most ancient dweller amid these rocks.

Upon the hill overhanging the town was his sanctuary, whence he uttered his oracles; long they maintained their credit, it is said till every other Bœotian oracle had ceased.

The rite is given by our ancient guide Pausanias who consulted the Oracle in person. Preparation was insisted upon — purification and sacrifice, with bathing 'in Herkyna. After much cleansing, by night the consultor descended into the cave of Trophonius, which had a large subterranean chamber, when he had drunk of the two springs — of Oblivion, that he might forget his worldly life, and of Memory, that he might remember what the Prophet told him. Into the cave was an opening wherein he put his feet; suddenly he was drawn into a still deeper cave in which he saw things otherwise invisible. When he came out, he was placed on the throne of Memory, and his vision recorded. Yet the process was without danger for the pure in heart; only one death from the consultation is recorded, that of the soldier of Demetrius, who descended into the cave with the hope of getting money there. But the indignant Prophet cast his dead body out of the earth, not even by the ordinary passage.

Such was the Oracle of Trophonius, whose proceedings seem not without a touch of priestcraft, but on the whole they seek, at times with the strictness of an allegory, to figure the descent of a man into himself, into his own soul. To purify that by many days' discipline till it becomes transparent and reflects clearly somewhat of the Divine, has been always one of the rites of religion. So old Trophonius commanded, and was a true prophet for his people; so Nature commands here to-day in this gorge, very dimly to be sure, still it is a command. Her obscure voice was gathered into the Oracle, which has now grown almost speechless in a much clearer light.

Upon this spot, then, arises the necessity of the religion of Nature, who was consulted in her Oracle, for here she has revealed herself in a wonderful way. If now we can only gather her voice, that voice may mean something — that voice is, I hold, Trophonius. Such is our oracular country, with scenery somewhat resembling

Delphi, particularly this gorge. But Delphi is far more colossal, and has many things wanting at Lebedeia — whereof we may hereafter have somewhat to tell. Lebedeia with its Trophonius forms the transition out of Bœotia with its Helicon and Muses on the mountain tops, to Delphi which has both Oracle and Muses in the abode of divine Apollo. Trophonius is only an Oracle, not a God; Nature here takes a more earnest, darker phase than at Delphi, for Delphic Apollo is the Light-God, and becomes the union of poesy and prophecy in their supreme manifestation. Trophonius is still the dark symbolism in which the unclear struggling soul finds expression, and which has not yet been fully unfolded into sunlight.

Thus we have here some faint anticipation of Delphi. An Oriental symbolism of obscure characters and rites belongs to Greece also, is in fact its primordial unripe stage of development. But the Greek mind will unfold out of this dim condition; Greek Art will abandon vague forms and leap forth into the clearest outline. In the meantime the traveler also will have come out of the dark gorge and reached the transparent fountain of Memory, who will treasure what the Oracle has told him here. With the utterance of Trophonius deeply impressed upon his heart, he will descend into the town and mingle among its people.

There as you cast glances into the passing faces, you will consider another transition to be manifestly taking place — the transition to a new type of people. I think that every attentive observer would notice the change; finer, more regular features begin to appear; besides, there seems to be something of a mental wakening up — more quickness of apprehension, more vivacity. You will imagine, as you scan the faces and the manners, that here is a truer Hellenic type, that some drops of old blood have percolated through so many generations. Women, too, begin to appear, though shy still; their faces are getting to be more free from Oriental wrappage; one I have seen, which I shall remember — dark, fine-featured, with lively looks. Children, too, show improvement in beauty; sometimes they have blue eyes and the appearance of blondes. The traveler will saunter through the lanes and alleys to catch some glances; he comes to the conclusion that now there is hope of Helen. That which he has hitherto almost despaired of seems to be growing possible; here is the dividing line perchance, with a mixed race. But off in the mountains yonder she must be hidden, probably undeveloped, in the garb of a peasant maiden, still the germ of the Argive queen.

Also one will not fail to notice, if he be faithful to his main task, many instances of the Old in the New; those two youths passing down the street, locked in each other's arms, call up the ancient conception of friendship and even of love between the same sex. Young fellows embrace each other and kiss with a sort of rapture — a little touch of Platonic Eros, innocent enough, I imagine. They will sing a song together with much exaltation — a possible consequence of an overdraught of recinato, which mellows the heart wonderfully in this Greek climate. Friendship let it be called, with a strange interplay, perchance, of sexual feeling, somewhat remote from the Western consciousness.

I turn into a wineshop; here enters a woman with perfect Greek outlines in her face, but with a bold stare in it which will not turn aside at the glance of a stranger. She is the first Greek female that I have seen in such a place; she mingles freely among the boys, smoking her paper cigarette; she talks with volubility and badgers them jestingly, in words which I do not understand, and it is probably just as well that I do not. But her remarks excite their laughter; I ask my neighbor: What, is that the custom here for women to come to the wineshops? — Oh, no; she is the only one in town that does so; it is Maria, do you not know Maria? — I cannot say that I do; but it is Maria, is it? — Very manifestly it is Maria — Maria Magdalena, but as yet without the repentance. With sorrow one turns away, seeing this phase of the antique still in the modern, yet casting glances at those perfect lines in her face which was anciently a Phidian model.

In the afternoon the rain begins again, and the sauntering comes to an end. I take refuge in the lonesome khan, go up to my naked room and look out of the window, seeing it rain, with a slight shiver. To-morrow threatens to be an ill day again; the thought is distracting. The place is gloomy, the hours grow unendurably tedious, the two or three books have been read to death. Now the traveler begins to repent again; the God of Light has fled with the sunshine, the classical mood departs when you see nought but clouds and rain through the window of a Greek khan. It is the reverse side of the picture, more ugly because you have been spoiled by the previous glorious days; your wings refuse to fold themselves in rest. But so it was once before on a rainy day at Marcopoulo; then followed a happy journey—so it may be again to-morrow. Hope then; yonder is Parnassus, visible often through the clouds; one day's journey will bring thee thither. Put the sun-god within thee; have him rise there in all his majesty, scattering his beams; then thou wilt be independent of him in the outer world, and canst let it rain in peace.

Yet one will be glad when the shower ceases for a time, and will seize the opportunity to hurry into the street. The roar of the waters is now louder than ever; the gentle nymph Herkyna is changed to a wrathful torrent. But she is always a delight, for she always shows in some way her love for her own dear town of Lebedeia. For the town is truly married to the stream; its waters are borne everywhere through many a conduit and rivulet, which turn an indefinite number of mills. They pour over dams, forming cascades of various sizes, the sounds of which are always heard through the town. This is the well-known undertone of Lebedeia, the voice which is always speaking, not unpleasantly; it is the most important member of the community, the one who has most to say with genuine Greek garrulity and sprightliness. So Herkyna with her many runnels spreads out in manifold ways, now darting under bridges, then drawn into millwheels, often washing the stone wall of some house that has a portico extending over the stream. Therefore we may call Herkyna a blessing, a divine thing for Lebédeia; to her the ancients might well erect a temple. What can be compared with her beneficence! The entire prosperity of the town is connected with her movement, her many winding channels are its arteries, through which pulses its life-blood; — purifier, too, she is, bearing away disease and discomfort; truly we may call her useful in the best sense of the word.

But that for which she chiefly deserves divine honors is that she is beautiful, with her clear full gush from the caverns of darkness rippling into daylight and rejoicing therein. One will notice from the khan a sort of horseshoe falls which dashes over and pours down like a little Niagara, then the watery arm twines in a loving, mysterious manner around among the houses. Never did I see a town so intimate with a stream; Verona with its Adige leaves some such impression, but not so strong and unreserved; it is a marriage, not of convenience, one will affirm, but of love, in such mutual joyous embrace do they lie. Not too large is the stream, not an uncontrollable giant, in many places it can be easily stepped over on the friendly rocks which it offers in the middle of the current. But, to-day, till the flood runs out, which it will in a few hours, the Nymph is somewhat untameable, even wrathful.

Yet another shower, extinguishing the kindled hope! Assuredly the Naiads possess the town; even the sky has become a fountain this afternoon, spouting down innumerable jets of water; the happy Gods above seem to have been changed into water-nymphs. Behold the descending streams of rain; Lebedeia with all her runnels has gone up into the clouds, filling the air with perennial springs which now fall down into her earthy lap. The unwilling brooks refuse to be separated from their dear town, but are dropping back entire into her embrace from the skies, quite as they once rose out of the earth to greet her.

Thus we may connect Lebedeia with her stream and springs, with her gorge and mountains; we think of her as born of this Nature, and reflecting its visage in herself to a degree; this rise out of the physical world must have been also the spiritual principle in her worship. So the Nymphs were born, so even the Gods were born, like Herkyna, like Trophonius, like Lebedeia herself. Where is the Poet that he may express this fact? For it must have been sung, being a true theme of song, of deep musical significance; certainly it must have attuned some Greek voice. Out of Heliconian mist a face begins to peer, a familiar face; it is that same Hesiod whom we have already met with upon Helicon. But now he has a new book which bears this title: *Birth of the Gods;* a very different book, you will observe, from the last one which we spoke of, yet with many sisterly traces of relationship. Some old Bœotians denied its authenticity; we shall not do so, but place it somewhere here, as having its origin upon the Heliconian range. Without violence we may think of it in connection with Lebedeia, with its dark beginning in Chaos and bright outcome in the reign of Zeus.

The Poet has called his work a Theogony, in which he propounds a problem of sacred import: The Birth of the Gods. Think of him dealing with such a theme; he and through him his nation have then arrived at that stage of spiritual inquiry, in which they ask and seek to answer this question: How did the Gods above us come to be? It is the search for origin, origin in time; where will it end, having all duration back of it? At bottom it is one with our modern question: What is the origin of Man? Thus we at present state it, having no longer any Gods to account for. But ancient Hesiod, not yet having lost his faith, puts the inquiry in this shape: What is the origin of the Gods! Which being found, it is easy to discover whence man came.

This is indeed one of the strangest phantasms that worries the human intellect, this question of the Beginning; it asks for the origin in Time of that which lies out of Time — Time itself being one of the products of Creation. It is a ghost with a mirror eternally producing its own shadows, yet each shadow holds the same reproducing mirror infinitely multiplicative. Most obstinately the phantasm lurks in the human mind, haunting the thoughts of the little child; for at Sunday-school it will ask its discomfited teacher: If God made me, tell me who made God?

The Poet as the Teacher of his age sets about answering the question, and thereby converting empty phantasms into images of truth, even though they be dim and remote. We see, however, that this scheme embraces a grand transition from the old to the new Gods; just that is its essence. Thus it is plain that he believes in development, there is progress even among the Gods, in them the Greek may worship advancement, and theology with him becomes a progressive science. Not at all is there here the lapse from the perfect to the less perfect, a fall from the Divine to the Bad; the beginning is with the rude and formless among Gods, thence they rise into a higher order.

But what does this transition from the old to the new Gods signify? Fundamentally the greatest of all transitions, the one in which the culture of the race moves — it is the transition from Nature to Spirit. Such is indeed the true birth of the Gods — to be born out of Nature into Spirit. The Theogony begins with Chaos and rises to Zeus, passing from dark disorder to sunlit order, from the rude primeval forces of Nature to a spiritual authority. Zeus is the central principle of the world; before him was chaotic struggle of turbulent Powers, after him the beautiful Gods appear, his sons and daughters; with them, too, Greece is born, and from them takes her character. The Heroes also are born, coming forth like sculptured forms into a serene light, and the dark poem clears up into sunshine playing amid statues. This is the new-born Hellas.

The transition from the old to the new Gods is then the important thing in the poem. But it takes place through terrific conflicts; Zeus has first to put down his father, Cronus, whose leading trait is the unfatherly habit of swallowing his own offspring. Therein Time is hinted, which consumes its own progeny; but it has begotten a son greater than itself, greater than Time. This merely

destructive might of Time must be brought to an end by
a universal or spiritual power; so Zeus arises and accomplishes the first great act of culture. Nay, he makes his
father vomit up the swallowed offspring to light again —
a strange yet true image of the manner in which Spirit
treats the temporal; what has disappeared in the ages,
suddenly springs up from its resting-place. So we are
now making Time give up its ancient cities, long since
swallowed and even forgotten; vanished Troy, lost
Pompeii have been vomited from the capacious maw of
Cronus. Indeed every spiritual son of Time must do as
Zeus did, must make the pitiless parent reveal the
swallowed world of the past. Such is truly the greatest
conflict of Zeus, greater than the one with the Titans,
rude primeval forces of Nature which must also be put
down, subjugated to the reign of the new Gods, ere a well-ordered existence be possible for Man.

But will there not be a new development of Spirit outstripping even this last — will there not arise still again
new Gods, newer than Zeus, with whom he will collide?
It would seem necessary by the theory of development
which the Poet holds. Yes, here he appears, Prometheus,
the Titan heaven-defying, with his protest against Zeus.
On the whole this myth of Prometheus may be called the
myth of all civilization. A figure of stupendous proportions; he is the thinking Titan who thinks in advance of
Zeus himself, and has to suffer for it, for his forethought.
So do all thinking Titans; they must conflict with Zeus,
with the established Gods, working for the benefit of the
human race; yet bitter is the draught they drink. It has
justly made the strongest impression upon men, this myth
of Prometheus, for it is their myth in the deepest sense.
Poets have seized it and wrought it over in the spirit of
their own time from Aeschylus to Goethe. It is only too
vast, the mind may well be paralyzed at trying to fill the
myth with its full import; it would seem to be able to
hold the whole human race and have plenty of room left
for somebody else.

The myth of Pandora occurs again in this book and
connects it intimately with the *Works and Days* already

mentioned. Here, too, man is punished by having the woman sent upon him. She is the attractive being, decked out by all the Goddesses; irresistible is her power, for man, her victim, has in him that intense love of beauty, cause of all his ills. Yes, man must love her, that is, he is not adequate in himself, is not self-producing; his own individuality suffices not, he will perish unless he has that other individuality called woman. Such is his limitation, a hard lot truly, a curse of the Gods in the language of the poet, yet not without its compensation. Pandora is manifestly the Hesiodic copy of Helen whose beauty caused the Trojan War and its grievous calamities; now she is the disaster of the whole human race. Prometheus, however, did not win in his conflict with Zeus, and man is still to this day afflicted from that scourge of his evils, Pandora.

But another Prometheus rises dimly in the background, the true one now, Zeus's own son by Metis, who, it is prophesied, will overthrow his father and establish the newest Gods. So the Nemesis continues, father is punished by son, receives in turn just what he has done to his own father. A fresh problem is this for Zeus, and solved by him in a novel way; the new germ he swallows with its mother, makes it his own, then reproduces it as Pallas, Goddess of Wisdom. Thus he masters the new principle by taking it into himself: in such manner it is not another's and an enemy's, but his own. By this act he becomes the true Zeus, and his rule must remain perpetual, for he has taken up his last foe into himself. Such is the image of all true authority; that threatening Prometheus with his new principle must somehow or other be swallowed, else he will swallow Zeus in his turn. Thus, too, the long line of dark retributions between father and son among the Gods is brought to an end; Zeus has absorbed their principle, and the circle terminates in him. Thereafter he begets the bright Gods — the Graces, the Muses, the Hours, Diana, Apollo; the beautiful Greek world seems to spring at once into sunlight. The heroes, too, are born, even the heroes of Homer — Achilles and Ulysses; the Hesiodic

Theogony, accordingly ends with bringing forth the Homeric poems.

Such is, then, the course of the work; it unfolds the transition from the old to the new Gods, the rise from Nature into Spirit. It is on the whole a dark chaotic production, though it terminates, like night, with a sunrise, and has lights gleaming through it at intervals, like stars. The story of Uranus is an enormous extravaganza, with a certain dim symbolism underneath, quite foreign to the Greek mind of the Homeric stamp. It is the rudest, most fantastic piece of Humor extant, for I cannot help thinking it humorous to a degree. The battle of Zeus with the Titans is pushed to the very verge of the Burlesque, and the whole work has a tendency to pitch over into the Burlesque, in attempting to portray as persons the colossal powers of Nature. Still we feel it to be an honest attempt to construe the world; its dark utterance has a certain consistency with the dark matters whereof it sings; and the bright forms of the new Gods exhibit a significant contrast to the obscure convulsions of the primeval Gods.

Sometimes it is plainly allegorical, and runs along with a transparent meaning; then of a sudden it dives into unseen regions where no eye can follow. The total poem is not an allegory, one big key will not unlock the whole at once; it requires many different little keys, and at times no key at all, but something quite distinct from an allegorical key to reveal the hidden purport. Nor can it be tortured by etymology or other learned thumb-screws into a self-consistent allegory. A phantasmagory one would better call it, with myth, parable, hymn, even gleams of history intermingled. Yet meaning will be found in it as a Whole; that meaning is the origin of the Gods, the rise from the Natural to the Spiritual, more particularly, the birth of the Greek World. To the old Greek, therefore, it was a true book; we may still look at it with his eyes.

Modern critics have mercilessly cut to pieces the Hesiodic poems, applying the analytic knife at every joint; an unpleasant and in the main an unprofitable business, unless the work be put together again. Far more satisfactory is it to contemplate these poems as Wholes; in fact, this is the true way; we must behold them springing from one thought, or at least from one general consciousness belonging to the age in which they were written, and of which they are the expression. But after cutting up the old Poet, the critics, like the daughters of Pelias, have been totally unable to restore him to life, let alone to rejuvenate him. We, however, in our Greek journey wish to see him alive and throbbing with musical utterance; therefore we must look up to the heights and listen to his "voice divine, singing a beautiful song of both the future and the past, while he feeds his lambs under sacred Helicon."

But we must turn away from ancient Hesiod and take a glance at this modern weather, also a dark theme of contemplation. At six o'clock in the evening it is still raining; but between two successive showers, veritable sheets of water hanging down from the clouds, I succeed in slipping out of the khan in search of a little diversion. The fierce roar of the stream floats through the darkness; Herkyna seems to have become more wrathful than ever at the muddy torrent poured into her bosom. I dropped into an eating-house; there a Greek gentleman came up and began to talk with me in such a friendly manner that all moodiness of the day took wings and flew off into the darkness. After some pleasant conversation he insisted upon my going home with him and staying there for the night. His invitation was joyfully accepted.

The wife and children received the stranger in hearty friendliness; it was a Greek family of the better class. One of the daughters was lying on a couch near the fire — a young lady rather beautiful, but in still more beautiful neglect; she had flowered into womanhood, but her body still showed the weariness of the effort; she seemed to droop in maidenly languor on the couch, where the fresh outlines of her form were revealed in a modest though bewitching fullness. She arose at our entrance with evident effort; but after a few moments she wilted back, as it were, into her former posture. The mother is an exceedingly bright and energetic woman, with a hospitable grace which at once puts the guest at ease; no such woman have I yet seen in rural Greece. A roasted pig's head serves as the chief article of the evening repast; lively talk rises all around the table; the merry children could not restrain their laughter at the odd accent and ways of the stranger. Of course I could not help letting out what was in me, for I asked after the beauties of Lebedeia, in a sort of furtive inquiry; then I wanted to know about those of Arachoba, of whom I had heard along the route. The mother gently inclined to the opinion that the young ladies of Lebedeia were the handsomer.

At the hour for retiring. I was conducted to a bed, the first real bed that I had seen since the second morning of my trip; I hailed it as an old friend met after long separation. Also here is an actual bedstead, now become quite a curiosity; I grasp the posts to see if they be not some phantom floating through my Greek dreams. I drop into slumber to the music of Herkyna, which surges heavily through the lighter notes of the falling showers, not far distant from the bedroom window.

In the morning preserved citron with a glass of water is offered me, instead of the cup of coffee, which the rest of the family drink, but I do not. As I had often inquired after the beautiful faces of Arachoba, and seemed interested in those of Lebedeia, the young lady appeared this morning in full toilet, which, vanity persisted in whispering, was just for my benefit. Bright colors danced through her dress, which had also a long trail; then, too, the Parisian coiffure was not wanting. She certainly succeeded in surprising me with her array, which was set off by red cheeks, dark eyes and fairly proportioned features. She conducted me to the loom which was standing in a small chamber with a half-woven garment; at my request she played upon the instrument with much skill, I thought. The music of the shuttle and beam made me think of the piano; I tried to describe the instrument upon which our American young ladies played; but she had never seen anything of the sort, and she affirmed that there was no such instrument in Lebedeia. "Boorish place," she cried. Nor was there any teacher of song or music in the town. After she had shown her accomplishments at the loom, she took me to a large trunk which contained all the stores of her past labor — quite a display of multitudinous finery, which, to be honest about the matter, I very imperfectly understood. Still I paid her some awkward compliments, which she modestly received, and I promised her in return, when I reached home, some specimen of my handiwork in a different line.

Then there was the little girl, eight or nine years old, who from innocent blue eyes gazed at the stranger; pretty little thing, to me the chief delight of the household. Reclining at her mother's knees she looks in childish wonder, with two braids down her back. How could I help thinking of one of the same age, now separated from me by the continent and ocean! She goes to school, she says, and is ready to spell out for me her reading exercise, somewhat like the last lesson I heard before leaving home. Sweet little Corallion with her two braids! This morning, as I came out of my sleeping room she ran up and put into my hands two flowers which she had just plucked for me; with full eyes I leaned over and gave her my best reward — a kiss. Ah, little Corallion, you do not know how home-sick you made me that whole day!

But it is not possible to leave Lebedeia in this weather, for there is still the threatening rain as well as the swollen streams. Upon the hearty invitation of the host and hostess, I promised to remain with them another day. There is nothing to do but to go down town in search of some amusement. Here is a spacious coffee-house, which no citizen seems able to pass without entering; a peep into it reveals a large assemblage of men sitting at tables and wreathing their heads in tobacco smoke. Let us enter, too, for nobody is excluded; here the people, high and low, are amusing themselves. Drinks of various kinds besides coffee can be obtained; cards, backgammon, dominoes add a pleasant condiment to the heavy hours of a rainy day. There is heard the buzz of many voices speaking at once, not always harmonious; for have we not to discuss, with Greek vivacity and volubility, that immense theme, the treaty of Berlin, and the annexation of Thessaly and Epirus? Thus the disputation grows hot while the coffee gets cold; mouths even foam while the beverage long since has lost its last bubble. Town politics is not wanting, for an important election is approaching; several candidates wind around through the tables with their happiest smiles for the dear people.

No distinction of rank is observed in the coffee-house, nor indeed in Greece: the peasant and the laborer sit beside the officer and the merchant; as for aristocracy, there is none. The red fez is almost universal, European costume is the exception. There is a tradition here that Lord Byron walked the streets of Lebedeia in fez and fustanella. The buzz continues loud and long from full tables; but the emphatic undertone of the town can also be heard — the rushing and dashing of waters, for Herkyna plunges furiously alongside the coffee-house, washing its very walls; over the stream a portico extends on which one will sit and watch the whirling current fall and rise with the passing showers. So the nymph mingles her angry voice with the Greeks, as if adding volume and determination, then madly dashes away under a bridge and hides from the eye, still tossing her waters.

The traveler will seek to form an acquaintance with the man at his elbow; it is not difficult, for all are ready to talk, sometimes in a variety of tongues. The head waiter is said to speak six or seven languages, and is the marvel of the town. An officer of the Greek Army sought to practice with me his little English, now somewhat rusty. He is an old hunter of brigands on the Turkish border, and hopes soon to cross the frontier in search of a Turkish army. The Surgeon also joins our company, a man of the strongest aspiration and enthusiasm; he is still young and would go to Paris with me in order to perfect himself in his profession, were there not work for him at home in the near future. Says he: Greece is the only civilizer in the East; we cannot take our Greek provinces by arms, we are too small; but we are going to conquer them by light, by education at our university of Athens, by our schools, by our literature. Then there will arise a spiritual union which must in the end bring about a political union. Such is the destiny of Greece once again in history: to civilize the Orient.

Still Time has no wings for flight on a rainy day in a country town; he rolls over you heavily, crushing you into the earth, or smiting you with his hour-glass. The coffee-house thins out at intervals; I fall asleep in my chair, looking at Herkyna, as she sings her loud lullaby. A drowsy time; but Parnassus looms up yonder, now without a cloud; the summit has been cleared by the rain. In the late afternoon the elemental war seems over, and the skies beam with peace.

The housewife, too, I meet in a saunter; it is Persiphoneia — Proserpine. Indeed! Your husband has to thank the Gods for that divine name; it must require much good conduct in you to overcome its suggestion. Wife of the Infernal Regions, here of the household; so the old Greek Goddess has impressed herself upon the modern woman. It was at Lebedeia that I first heard the name Elpinike, though known in antiquity as the name of the sister of Kimon; often afterwards I heard it in the Delphic olives. Plutarch, too, still lives here, not far from his ancient abode; I saw him in the coffee-house of Lebedeia, darting among the tables in fez and fustanella.

In accordance with my promise I went to the house of my hostess early in the evening, and remained with the family. Nothing was spared which might conduce to the guest's entertainment and comfort; certainly it is the most generous hospitality that I have ever met with anywhere. The daughters are still in gala-dress; whether in honor of me or of some saint whose festival is to-day I dare not inquire. But a merry time we had sitting in the room around the fire with occasional sips of recinato. They jested me about my Albanitza or Albanian woman whom I said I was going to take with me to America; the witty hostess asked me in banter how many pounds she could carry — these Albanian women being famous for their strength. Here I observed some indications of discord between the Greek and Albanian races. These people rather despised the Albanians as uncultivated and barbarous; the contempt is generally returned by the latter who consider the Greeks as effeminate and tricky. But the difference is great in one respect: the sunny atmosphere of this Greek family is a strong contrast to the gloom of the Albanian hovel, where there is often no light except what comes through the door. Here all is bright, cheery, truly Greek.

Some relatives dropping in, there were persons enough to have a little Greek dance or chorus. The circle is formed, the dancers wind about to their own song or rather sing-song; the people seated around the room join in the chant. Then there is at times a verse with its answer from two different sets of dancers. Not much can be gotten out of it; but I am promised beautiful choruses, that is dances, when I come to Parnassus.

The dance ceases, and we turn to more sober things. A Greek girl asks me about the marriage portion given to young ladies in my country. This is a very important matter here, this matter of *proika* as they term it. The young lady is always attached to a dower by which she takes her rank in the scale of being. To my surprise I heard a stout protest against this immemorial Greek usage; a lively girl insisted very strongly upon love without a marriage portion — to which proposition one could only give his heartiest assent. Of course I did not dare ask her whether she were one of the dowerless ones, but she divined my smile, and replied that she had a *proika*, I need not laugh.

But still more emphatic was their condemnation of the present position of Greek women; particularly the mother — a keen, lively, energetic person — thought that there should be some change. Not that they were violent supporters of women's rights — they did not know what that meant; but there was a feeling of the need for the industrial emancipation of women. I gave a little account of the station of the American sister; that is what we want to some extent, she said. Certain employments now closed to females should be thrown open to them; the seclusion of the Orient should come to an end.

Also desire for instruction I found there; all had some

education and hád read a little. The daughter wanted to study French; an old text-book of that tongue was brought out and shown me; it was indeed an ancient book both in type and in method. There was no teacher in town, and my proposition to stay and become her instructor she evidently regarded as a jest. Such aspiration will be found in that friendly, sunny Greek household, the joy of the traveler.

In the morning the anxious sojourner will first, when he rises, shove the curtain aside and look out of the window to see what Zeus commands him from the skies. Not a cloud is there, the rains are over, the order to-day is manifestly to march, the Sun himself is in the heavens lighting the way. I have to part, there is no use of hesitation, though the hostess gives a pressing invitation to stay. I break the pang of separation by saying that I may return — well, I may. Good-bye; a kiss to little Corallion who brings some more flowers; she with her sweet face and two braids down the back, stirs the waters deep within, all unconscious of her power; I kiss in hers a little face 5,000 miles away. Good-bye; a final glance into the group of dark eyes hanging around the door, and I am off. Passing down the street I look back once more; a handkerchief waves out of the window, to which a like response is given; then a corner is turned and that family has become a pleasant dream.

My friends, let us stop for a moment, ere we separate, and look back at our whole journey in its different stages. We have traveled along a geographical line, filled with the fairest and most varied views of Nature, delightful to our vision; but we have also, I hope, traveled along a spiritual line into which the old Greek elevated Nature and of which he made her bear the impress. Him we have sought to follow, first through Marathon with its historical Deed, then back through Aulis with its mythical Deed; in both we have beheld one struggle, that with the Orient, and have seen Greece come forth therefrom new-born, ever rising into something truer and more worthy spiritually. Already to Helicon we have come —

the third act of our little drama; here, among other wonders, we have beheld the birth of the Gods themselves, those who victoriously controlled that conflict; here we have seen the old Gods arise and be put down, like the East, like Nature, too; now the new Gods are sunnily seated upon their mountain throne and sway thence the new world. This is the new Hellas, illuminated by a new sun shining out of the victory of Marathon, out of the capture of Troy, out of the subjection of Cronus to Zeus; quite the same thing they all are in Spirit. Such, too, is the key-note of happy Helicon, heard in the voice of her Poet, ancient Hesiod, heard also in her Oracle, old Trophonius. Still this is but the exultant beginning of the day, it is the glorious sunrise of Hellas; somewhat, we may imagine is yet to follow.

Part Second.

XIII. FROM LEBEDEIA TO CHÆRONEIA.

The prolonged stay in Lebedeia has come to an end, and the traveler is now stepping lightly over the highway with a new view in his eye and a new hope in his heart. The stress of weather which forced such a lengthy delay was a blessing doubtless, but one of those blessings which are not appreciated at the time; they must be past before they can be rightly valued. Irksome hours those were often, with Parnassus in view, but unattainable. But now we have started again upon our light-hearted quest; a happy journey we pray it to be still, radiant with joyous visions, yet filled with an earnest purpose; assuredly that image, so long pursued, is still fleeing before us, not yet overtaken. Down the Great Road we pass in solitary joy; the music of Herkyna, the wild babbler, faintly sounds out of the distance, as if to entice the wayfarer back; the fair nymph excites, it must be confessed, a momentary regret at parting, but her charms must not detain us longer. The clouds have fled, the sun is keeping a festival over the hills, the air is full of wine, and man has nought to do but to be hilarious along with the Gods.

We shall now have to leave the Great Road, which has been so long in our company, and has so kindly laid itself down under our feet, as if it made itself just as we needed it; but here it gives a gentle turn, as if unwilling to quit our society, and crawls around a hill, where it disappears in a direction whither we can not follow. We run down its embankment and enter a thicket of low brushwood, through which winds the mule-path conducting us toward the plain of Kephissus. It is the old kind of narrow bush-wreathed way which led us such a devious course in the early part of our journey. Clamber over the stones, push through the branches — their hostility is but feigned, they will retire before you with a laugh, if you keep up your Greek mood.

Emerging from a little glen, the traveler will overtake a couple of Greek soldiers, for these roads are always kept patrolled. Quite different was the old Greek soldier who marched up this valley to famous battle-fields. The modern uniform is very like that of the American soldier; here are the blue cap, blouse and trousers, with musket and knapsack; nor can one omit to notice the broad-bottomed shoe, a very familiar object in other times. Those muskets winding around through the bushes with the blue garments vanishing among the leaves, seem a shred of our own Civil War dropped suddenly into this Hellenic landscape.

But the old is still in the new even here, and that too in the most emphatic manner. This Greek soldier is indeed a descendant of the ancient one, did we truly trace the genealogy. If he had appeared on the field of Chæroneia with his loud-resounding death-dealing musketry fire, he would have been considered a demon armed with Jove's thunderbolts; some demon has stolen the weapons of Zeus from the forge of the Cyclops, the frightened Hoplites would say, and at once take to flight. The old mythus, the spiritual image of what is to be, has now become reality, and no longer hovers a poetic dream over the Greek fields and mountains; here it is an actual thing right at the foot of Parnassus. We moderns have indeed stolen the weapons of Zeus, and have become even mightier than the God; thus man ever must do, must realize the divine upon earth, bringing it down from the skies; he has in the truest sense naught else to do. The old Greek soldier had in his worship, when he prayed to Zeus the Highest on that fatal day of Chæroneia, the prophecy of this modern Greek soldier carrying gun and cartridge box. Thus the sacred arms drop from heaven and remain thenceforth terrestrial, according to holy legend itself; what is adored by one age as godlike is revealed to another age as human. In such way has our modern life realized Homer's divinities, being true divinities once because they had just this germ of reality in them. So our Greek soldier, an humble private in the ranks, trudges along in blue uniform, with rattling cartridges in his box, all unconscious that he is armed with Jove's thunderbolts, mightiest weapons of the old Gods.

But as you halt for a moment between two bushes, look up to the horizon; there you can not help seeing another transmutation even more wonderful. On this side lies Helicon, yonder towers Parnassus; both are seats of the Muses, it was said of old. There the two mountains actually rest, filling so much space in the vision, yet under our very eye they seem to change into something beyond themselves, into something better, more beautiful than themselves, dissolving out of nature musically into an image. Thus they continue to do at every glance; what does it mean? repeatedly asks the astonished beholder. That must be the touch of the Muse, touching her own mountains and transforming them from rude rocks into her seats forever. Yet what does that mean? he will again ask, and you too will ask probably, being as much mystified as he.

But a few miles apart the two summits lie, easily visible, nay audible to each other, one will think. They seem to be engaged in a sort of *carmen amœbæum*, or rival song, like the two shepherds of Theocritus who stand opposite and sing; thus echoes rise out of the two ranges and mingle over the valley. The umpire, too, is worthy of mention; nothing more or less than the world which has been listening to these mountains ever since the first song which they sang to each other. When was that? Very difficult to tell; but we still catch the echoes going back some eight or ten centuries before the Christian Era. A conflict it was clearly, a conflict for the seat of the Muses; here it arose among the people on the opposite sides of this valley; a deep, intense struggle we may well imagine it, for the possession of the true shrine of the sacred Sisters. Yet it was just the problem which these people had to settle for themselves and for all mankind; it was just their stage of development which commanded them to seat the Muses upon these summits where the latter have remained to this day. I venture to think that in that ancient rivalry, the woodland slopes resounded with never-ceasing strains, and this valley was filled with a continuous music of pipe and song; for it was the life-work of the people to do this and nothing else, to give a seat to the Muses upon our earth; and well have they done their work if we may judge of it by its durability.

But which of the two mountains won in the contest? The judgment has been rendered, and we all know it; like the umpire in the idyl already mentioned, the world has concluded to call both mountains the seats of the Muses; both have won the prize. Ancient Hesiod sang upon Helicon, as we have before noted; what Parnassus has in store for us in our journey, we shall wait for with no small degree of expectancy.

It is, indeed, one of the greatest wonders, this transmutation. How have ye, O hills, become eternal, not as granite, but as an image, which floats through and wings the beautiful utterance of all lands? You seem not yourselves, but are at once transfigured into spiritual things; rock you are, I see and feel; the dull swain and his herds trample you daily with ignoble feet, yet you are not as other hills; who gave to you pinions to traverse the whole earth, and fly down all time — just to you and to nought beside? It is the work of the Muse, weaving thereof her garment of beauty; she transmutes the rugged bare cliff into her radiant vesture, and the very stones turn to words which are everlasting.

Such is, indeed, all Greece, and not merely this spot;

such is, too, the traveler, a little exalted, I think, as if he also were trying to elevate himself to yonder peak of the Muses, and to transform his own stony speech into their breathings. But if you are fair to him, you will say that therein he is only trying to do his duty in this land. Nature here is no longer an outer world merely, but suffers a rich sky-change into a Beyond, though remaining always herself. For when I say Helicon, do I mean yon towering rock only? Impossible; I cannot utter the word, I cannot even see the thing, without feeling at the same time a transfiguration of the vision, a vanishing of the natural into the spiritual. It is the exaltation of Nature into the mythus on the spot; before you everywhere the old mythology springs up in native spontaneity; and you yourself become a mythus — must become one, if you truly travel in Greece.

Mythus — I say not myth; let us attempt to restore the word to its original birthright, by restoring its original form. Myth means falsehood; mythus means truth, or the utterance of it through the image. Originally it meant the Word, sacred, mysterious Word in which was imaged the world of spirit by the Poet or Maker. Its lost soul let us restore, which we ought to do, with Parnassus in sight.

Whither now? Yonder is the veritable Parnassus with his immense head of snow, not a cloud at present rests upon the summit; the glistening crystals shoot their radiance into the eye, fiercely yet with some deep fascination. Thither we must go; the direction which the people give, is to pass by a narrow path over the intervening hill into the valley of the Kephissus — Bœotian, not Attic Kephissus. There is Chæroneia, which is worthy of a view, particularly its Lion of stone. Thence we can still, to-day, reach Daulis at the foot of the Parnassian range. My kind host of Lebedeia has placed in my hands letters of introduction to his friends along the road, the first that I have had. Such letters are usually procured at Athens, often from the government; I started without them. The result is, that I have been allowed to wander at my own sweet will undisturbed by the attention of any official. I turn about often and look at Lebedeia; pleasant town, lying at the foot of Helicon, whose tops are sprinkled with snow — town full of delightful memories. It passes out of sight; the traveler finds himself in the Kephissian vale, a new little Greek world.

Far across its level expanse filled with a sunny repose lie villages on hilly slants, memorable in antiquity; through the plain straggles Kephissus, winding like a glistening snake among his reeds. It is Sunday morning — in the literal sense a day of the Sun, who seems to be strewing his tranquil light in his sweetest mood. But this plain has been a terrific battle-field for Greek, Roman, Barbarian; one thinks still of the tumult of war, of desperate conflict, in contrast to the present repose. But we shall not go across it, though we may make many a little excursion out into it, among its flocks and its cultivated fields; — yet, on the whole, it seems rather uncultivated. Keep along close to the foot of this low range of hills lying between Helicon and Parnassus, else we may miss our destination. Warriors surge through the sunlight darkening it, as by a faint shadow cast from their ghosts; but there is one image that will not out of the mind — a peaceful, sunlit image; it is that of Plutarch, a native here, whose memory still lurks in the sunniest spots, and fills them with a new splendor.

' Skirting the low hills in sunshine, one gets attuned to the happy nature, which seems to be making up for having been darkened so long by the clouds. The sun comes out as if he were atoning by his shining deeds for some misdemeanor, and were determined never to be guilty of hiding his face again. Glance up the sunny slopes, look across the level valley, behold the snowy peaks — there is variety enough to occupy you with its music. For some days the traveler seemed lost in the storm, now he has found himself again. It is like an ancient dramatic festival which from dark tragic deeds, fitful strokes of fate, bursts into sudden joy and comic hilarity. What is the man thinking of while he is passing along? It can hardly be called thought, it is rather enjoyment — the happy balance between his senses and soul, in which both make one melody and are not seeking to cast each other out, as if one or both were devils. Many images indeed dart through the mind; it would be a motley picture, could it be painted — rather a whole pallet full of paints dashed on the canvas in some instinctive harmony. No definite picture there is, but enjoyment, a delightful mood, filled up with the sun, field, mountain — mood of Greek strains to be enjoyed, possibly to be communicated, not to be portrayed.

While going along the bushy path, I fell into a curious conversation with one of the soldiers, a man of some education and who had his own ideas about this world, one of which has taken complete possession of him. It is that civilization is not a good, but an evil to man, and that it would be far better if the human race remained in primitive ignorance and innocence. The tree of knowledge has yielded him only bitter fruit so far as he has tasted of it, and he maintains that the nations which have existed in the past, particularly old Hellas, perished by refinement of intelligence. Nor is he slow in predicting the same grand cataclysm for the present order of things; the world is too wise to exist. Truly here is a man who has fallen out with the new Gods and wishes to return to the old ones — to the reign of Cronus, and that primordial state of felicity which knows nothing, nothing even of itself. "Yes," says he, "Hellas must sink again, there is too much education already here, it must sink again." So he spake with foreboding, and with extraordinary terror at his country's intellectual illumination. I looked up, behold we were in the plain of Chæroneia, an ominous name which still startles the sympathetic traveler, the most ominous name in Grecian History.

Thus one in mood now clouded, saunters along for a couple of hours over the plain till he pass around the bend of a hill when he beholds the houses of a small village. This he will recognize to be Capurna, ancient Chæroneia. He will move to the side of the road where a tumulus which has been excavated arrests his attention; going within the inclosure, he will behold the *Chæroneian Lion*, prostrate on the earth, and broken to fragments. We are then on the battle-field of Chæroneia, where the Greek world received its death-blow at the hands of Philip; we stand upon the very tomb of the Greeks who gave their lives for their faith in Hellenic worth; indeed here is the very monument of the Theban Sacred Band, who are said to have fallen to the last man upon this spot and are buried beneath us.

Fate then has come at last; Fate so long prophesied in the books of Greece, so long imaged in her poetry, so long threatening from the Orient, but always valiantly repelled, has indeed arrived. Here it is, behold its dark approach to this plain from the North like a whirlwind — Philip with his phalanx coming down from Macedon. Greece can not resist him, she becomes a tragedy, such as was often adumbrated by her poets, now a real tragedy. Deepest grain in Greek character is that Fate, going back in manifold forms to the mythic times; Achilles we recollect lamenting his destiny and prophesying his own death; he touched the profoundest note of his people and hinted their destiny in that of himself, their ideal hero; but Fate here becomes reality. Henceforth Fate is supreme, must be placed even above Zeus now, if not before; for the Gods of Greece are subjugated, and from this time on may as well shut up Olympus. For what is a conquered God?

From the battle of Chæroneia, which was fought in the year 338 B. C. between Philip and the Greeks, dates the loss of Greek freedom, as the books say. True; yet we may be assured that something else had been lost before, that this grand defeat was but the outer blow which merely put an end to that which was already dead within. Such are usually the great battles of History — the finishing stroke to a body whose spirit has really departed. Let the corpse no longer cumber my earth, says the world-judge, and thereupon he sends some executioner, often a horde of barbarians with fire and sword, to bring the ghastly spectacle to a termination. Greek freedom perished on this fatal field of Chæroneia, but all which made Greece worthy of freedom had already perished, otherwise the finality could not have been here.

That autonomy for which Greece had fought and suffered so much, now comes to an end, having fulfilled its mission. The most beautiful political flower of the World's History: such is the common shout of admiration among men. But it is now smitten by an outsider, the Macedonian Philip, who has inherited Greek intelligence and Greek organization and transferred it to Macedon, a foreign and hostile land. Moreover he is the One Man, not the Few nor the Many; an absolute ruler has arisen, determiner of Grecian destinies; two qualities he has which are the death of the old Greek political spirit, he is a foreigner and an irresponsible monarch. So the star which we saw rise at Marathon sets at Chæroneia.

We ask on this battle-field, where is the mighty individual to meet Philip? who commanded here, whose brain controlled? Alas! there is no Great Man any more. Greece has ceased to produce mighty individuals, those great men of action who were once only too abundant — so many of them indeed that Athens had to get rid of some of hers by ostracism. But that was just the glory of Greece, her function in the World's History: to rear mighty individualities. Now she has become barren of them; she no longer produces that which she was called to produce; it is indeed high time that her career should close. Having ceased to bear great men, let her cease to be: such is the oracle distinctly pronounced upon this battle-field. Thebans were here, the Sacred Band of Theban youth perished to a man, and lie buried under yonder Lion of Stone; but they were here without an Epaminondas, and their desperate valor availed nought. Athenians were here, but with whom? Not with a Miltiades — woe be to them; but with Demosthènes, a great talker — indeed rather the greatest talker of all time — such greatness only can Athens now produce. If Philip could be talked down, clearly Demosthenes was the man, the very best man that ever was born to do the work. He tried to do it for fourteen years with thunderous philippics, so called from this very Philip: speeches which have been the wonder of the world. But the outcome of his magnificent oratory was Chæroneia; words, the words of even a Demosthenes, are no match for deeds, the deeds of even a Philip. Yet do not underrate the value of talk, great speech is still greatness when in its true field, though it cannot take the place of great action. I would not disparage talk, if it be not too much and too diluted; we all talk, I cannot hide the fact that I am talking now; so I would not have you underrate the value of talk, particularly of these talks upon Hellas.

Meantime, the modern Greek soldier has passed on out of sight, still uttering his doleful prophecies, believing that there is too much education and not enough ignorance in Greece. Civilization brings on always a battle of Chæroneia, he thinks; thus the new Hellas is soon destined to end in a mighty overturn like the old one; the essence of true wisdom lies in the lack of knowledge: such is his faith. But from a far different cause ancient Greece fell; and modern Greece disjointed, and scattered as it is, excites in our hearts a hope of far different results. Turn about now and look at the Chæroneian Lion.

Here, then, it lies on the very spot where the ancient traveler saw it and wondered at its power; it still typified with fierce energy the spirit of the men that lay beneath. Then for a thousand years it disappeared under the soil, covered up by the gentle action of the rains and frost, or it may be, buried by some tender hand, as if for a remote future time which would unearth it and possibly make it live again. No modern traveler before the present century or the Greek Revolution speaks of it, — merely the tumulus lay there undisturbed. The manner in which it came to light in recent times is curious: a fragment of its marble body protruded suddenly from the ground during the late war for Hellenic freedom; an excavation was made, and a Greek chieftain is said to have broken it to pieces in the hope of finding concealed treasure in its cavity.

Thus the Lion still remains lying on his back, in fragments; head, breast and mane are yet entire, of enormous bulk; the head seems four feet through as I stand alongside of it and measure its size by my own height. Its surface yet shows signs of ancient storms during these hundreds of years that it stood guard over the tomb, grinning and growling even in death. What a symbol of that ancient day of Chæroneia! what a symbol still. Truly it is an utterance of Grecian despair at that time; a work of art; nor is it without significance to-day, as it lies in pieces upon the ground. The dying Lion prefigured the dying Greek world then; now even the symbol is broken to fragments, — thus it has become the symbol of a symbol, for the work of that old Greek world is at present but fragments — fragments of the Lion.

The effect is certainly strong in these massive features, particularly about the jaws: bitter agony there is combined with stubborn ferocity. Then, too, its present attitude makes it all the more striking; it looks as if by some violent thrust it had reeled over on its back and is now dying. Here is a monument that works like a prophecy of the fate of ancient Greece; looking back more than 2,000 years we wonder at the power with which the sculptor has told his story, and embodied the belief of his time: it says that the Greek Lion is dying, dying on this field of Chæroneia. It stood above the ancient tomb, erect, still defiant, for over 500 years after the battle, when it was seen by an ancient traveler; now it lies prostrate in fragments, being smitten by a new blow just as it came to light in a new world.

No patriotic inscription was engraved upon it in antiquity we are told; nor was there need of any. Even in the presence of the Macedonian victor all is told by the Lion. Look at the eye, though much worn by the weather, it is still weeping, it still has a cry of anguish, if we note carefully the expression; mingled with its pain is the growl of wrath -against the barbarian conqueror. Writers have asked to have the pieces removed to Athens and set up in a Museum, after being put together again; such a procedure might tend to the preservation of the precious work, but I doubt whether it could produce half the impression that it does here on the spot where the Lion was pierced, under this strong sun now beating down on the foot of the hills. Rolled over on its back, in a death struggle, smitten to fragments which still growl — that is its power.

Recent chippings from the body I notice; alas! it will not lie here much longer; the rude peasant boy and the barbarous tourist will yet continue to lacerate the Lion as he lies in agony; soon therefore his members will be dispersed to remotest quarters of the globe. Here is an immense foot with its four claws, lying several yards from the body; sympathetically one will pick it up and seek to restore it to its place as nearly as possible. A broken hind leg lies yonder, struggling to be restored it seems still; but it is too heavy to be lifted by one pair of arms however eager. A dozen large fragments can be counted, as they lie scattered about the stony carcass — what is it but dismembered Greece, which no foreigner, whatever be his love, can unite by outside piecing?

The mound has been rudely excavated, and in the excavation lies the fragmentary body. Strange, that when the Greek Lion comes to light again in modern times, it should be merely a heap of pieces. Yet such is the case universally in regard to Greece. Greek history, Greek poetry, Greek art, the Greek world in all our modern excavations, reveal only the beautiful fragments. And the new resurrection of Greece to nationality — what has it revealed as yet but fragments of the old Greek Lion? Still they are genuine Greek fragments, with their aid we can often reconstruct the Greek Lion; for even from this claw we may obtain some image of what he was when alive in all his strength and undaunted energy.

While I sit there looking at the fragments, a man comes along, a Chæroneian, and begins to talk to me. With curiosity he asks me why I am gazing so intently on the Lion, what I am doing here, whence I come? His last question only I answer, when he bursts out suddenly: Why do not you Americans come and help us fight the Turks who refuse to render us our own — our Thessaly, our Islands, our Epirus, our Constantinople? I proceed to give a little idea of the difficulty of such an attempt, but it hardly satisfies him; he utters a growl leaning on the Lion's head, a deep, fierce growl against the Turk, and speaks with despair of the scattered fragments of the Hellenic nation.

Such is the modern lament heard at this moment in the town of Chæroneia in strange unison with the ancient lament heard in the voice of the Lion. Here at this passage through the valley the barbarians of the North entered, the final desperate conflict was fought unsuccessfully — the Lion still growling in the throes of death; and when Barbarism came in, Greece was at an end, was shivered to fragments, and has thus remained even in its modern resurrection; for hardly one-fifth of the Greeks belong to free Greece. So this man before me is a fragment of the old Greek, he wears fragments of the ancient costume; but above all, he speaks the old tongue, broken to pieces like this Lion, yet in its expressiveness still recalling ancient utterances. The rent trunk of the tree is still green and sends forth new buds — there is indeed hope, and his very speech shows it now. So I say to him: "Patience, oh friend; I prophesy that you will yet put together the broken Lion; it lies here still, sending forth its fierce growls, looking up into the clear blue heaven at the promise of retribution and restoration, praying as if for help from the Highest. Where is Philip now? Where will be the Turk? See, these fragments yet live, and call aloud for help; they have obtained even partial resurrection; put them now together. Lofty Parnassus yonder across the valley looks down upon you eternally with sympathetic joy — and what it smiles upon will live forever."

The man was probably not used to that sort of address, still he must have understood me, for he asked in astonishment: "What, do you know that? I believe so, too, for it is said here that the Great Saint will soon come from the City (Constantinople) after having driven out the Turk; he will pass through our village, Capurna, and after service in the church, he will put together the Lion, and baptize him, when there will be a long time of peace and plenty, and no work on holidays." In some such way the legend ran, as he told it, unless he manufactured the story on the spot for the credulous stranger. At least it expresses the modern Hellenic faith in national restoration, and the fervent prayer of the traveler is: May the Chæroneian Lion again have all its scattered members brought together, and breathe with the same vital all-conquering energy as of old.

But while we are looking at the fragments of the Lion, a joyful sound begins to rise up from the village, borne on the sunbeams which seem to mingle with it caressingly. It is a musical sound, though rude; somewhat like the tones of the bagpipe, steadied with regular taps on a drum. It is a strange music; sometimes too are heard the notes of a song. What is the meaning of it? My informant tells me that there is to be a wedding to-day at Chæroneia — a very important event there, and that these sounds are the merry prelude of the nuptials. Thither accordingly we must go, with some haste, for all of it must be seen. Still that ancient question asked in the Odyssey by Ulysses: Is it a wedding? may be asked this very day at Chæroneia by the casual wayfarer as he hears the joyful notes of song and music in the village.

Following the direction of the sound, one will not be slow in arriving at a small plot of grass before the church where the dancers, youths and maidens, are winding through the figures of the chorus to the notes of the music. They are mostly dressed in white — both sexes, and furnish a delightful view suddenly to the traveler; the clear-outlined sculpturesque shapes of old come to him with the force of a living reality. Is it possible that Chæroneia still offers such a sight — something similar to which ancient Plutarch himself must have looked upon at some festival? But pass them by for the present; let us climb over the fence and go to the front of the church where the priest in the open air is going through with a peculiar ceremony, in the presence of men, women and children, idly looking on. In that crowd you will see at once all eyes turned upon yourself, as if wondering whence this sudden appearance of a man in Frankish dress, with staff and knapsack.

But be not abashed, go near to the happy couple that you may see and share a little of their joy. Both bride and bridegroom preserve the most determined cast-down look, as if they were present at their own funeral. The bride will not laugh, though I catch her eye once and try to coax a happy smile from her — she looks down ever afterward defiantly on the ground. She is deep-brown in complexion, with profile rather tortuous — evidently a simple country girl, from whom one ought not to expect too much resemblance to ancient Helen. She has a manifold, indescribable head-dress; an immense number of silver coins, said to be her complete dower, are strung in strands about her neck; her gown is short and many-colored; she has striped stockings and low morocco shoes with elegant ribbons tied in them. The bridegroom stands patient, very sober, in an elaborately wrought cap and fustanella. The priest in black stiff cap and dark stole, both of which have evidently been at many a wedding, performs the ceremony with much chanting through the nose and mysterious manipulation; I noticed that he broke off right in the middle of his service to scold with the utmost ferocity a little urchin who was bringing a wax taper and let it fall. At last the pair are crowned, march around an altar which seems to be ancient, the relatives and other friends dropping numerous copper coins into a cup of holy water; I go up and drop one in too as my share of the entertainment. The priest offers the couple some bread, which falls out of his hand on the ground; he picks it up and rubs off the dirt, and gives it to them to eat. How much of this is essential for securing the marital knot, and how much unessential, I do not undertake to say, I give it all.

But at last the ceremony is over, the couple begin to march off toward their home, followed by the dancers and the music and the miscellaneous throng. I too fall in line and march along; a friendly Chæroneian takes his place at my side and keeps me company. "Have you such things in your country?" was his first question. "Yes, people get married there too, but we have no such music, nor have we your white folds." Meantime we kept moving to the sound of the caramousa and drum; the long statuesque procession crossed over a classic stream which runs through the middle of the town; I begin now to feel my Frankish garments to be a discord amid these white-robed shapes.

We reach the house on the banks of the stream; the bride and bridegroom stop before it and are greeted with a hymeneal song from within — a song not easy for me to understand, but rudely celebrating domestic bliss and wedded harmony, as near as I could gather from bystanders. Then came a responsive strain by the friends outside, when the couple disappeared behind the door; these are admitted with deep obeisance on part of the bride, while the groom strides in proudly erect. Thus they celebrated in simple idyllic art their entrance into a new life — that of the Family in which man and woman try to realize their love, the twain now living together as one person in a mysterious higher unity. Truly the first and most universal theme of all Art is this, for the humblest as well as the highest, since that secret bond must insist upon some utterance, nay, a beautiful utterance if possible; so the bridal song is still heard among the peasants of Chæroneia, and the village gives itself up wholly to the festival.

Then follows an indiscriminate pelting of candies from the house, out of the windows, around the corners, from the roof even they shower, to the great amusement of the children who scramble for the delicacies, and of some who are older. Let the stranger beware, since his foreign dress marks him out for a special benison; let him shade his face with his hands against two or three persistent maidens who bombard him from a little knoll above. But this ceases like a passing summer shower; then the sun comes forth, namely, the golden recinato, which flows out of the house in radiant streams, and of which the entire multitude partake, including the traveler, who will empty not less than one glass to the health of the happy pair. In such way will you or any stranger be treated if you appear on a wedding day before Lent in the little town of Chæroneia.

Again follows the chant; it would seem as if song were here inborn and had to find expression, gushing up like yonder source from the hill-side; the exalted mood of the singers makes the strain throb in true response to the inner ecstasy. A rude, primitive, poetical world, the basis of all genuine poetry is here, yet without its development. These songs recall Pindar with his marriage odes and epithalamiums; they were a reality upon this spot long before him even, and they still exist. But anciently he raised the germ to be flower, to be fruit. This rude material the poet coming along with sacred fire purifies into shining metal. Great need is there of him with his true eye and sense of beauty; one can imagine what the genius of Chæroneia might still do with these uncouth yet genuine melodies, were he to appear and breathe upon them the breath of divine beauty. This poetical world could be embodied yet in rhythmical harmony; but one of its own sons must be reared to feel that harmony in it and endow the same with a voice.

The youths now adjourn to the village green and begin the dance, still called in Greece the chorus; they are soon followed by the maidens, who gracefully join in the circle. The rest of the day is to be spent in festivities; the whole village is in festal attire; white garments are flitting by everywhere through the sunshine; it is in the true sense an idyllic life, not the false pretended one of so much pastoral verse. Old people one meets who seem to have become young again; mothers appear to have been transformed into their daughters and join in the chorus with youthful glee; in fact the whole town appears to have been married to-day in its one wedding.

But we can, not go to the choral place, we must reach Daulis to-day in good season. So let us turn back and re-cross the stream; but from its further bank we shall look around at the dancers on the distant greensward. Can I convey to you a faint picture of them as they wind about in light-stepping turns and simple, graceful movements? A circle is formed, headed by the chief dancer, who hops and skips, often leaping into the air and giving a whirl which fills out the white folds of his fustanella.

The rest of the dancers move more simply, going backward, forward, and keeping time to the music; then they run around in a circle, all joining hands except the first and last. Next come the maidens, forming a row together in white dress, most of them having in addition a many-colored apron and sacque; these last garments furnish the color. Nor are the children excluded from the circle, though they soon drop out. Notice too the movement of the maidens, for now they are dancing by themselves: it seems quite the same as we may see on ancient monuments — long dress, slow step, clear, plastic outlines in this transparent air. There is no wild effort, no frantic tossing of the limbs — but staid, stately, simple motion, free of all pretense and extravagance. Grace is here, an inborn delight in movement for its own sake, with true Greek moderation. The girl who dances at the head holds in her hand merely a wreath, with which she marks the time and the changes of direction for the circle. The youths are dressed entirely in white, which color strongly predominates with the maidens also; thus they move easily without struggle, with their soft, white outlines set off against the green hillside: on the whole it is the prettiest sight I have seen in Greece.

But that music — what shall a person say to it? Certainly it is a strange compound — a drum and a caramousa — a snarling instrument, somewhat resembling in form and in sound the hautboy or the flageolet. Not to our taste, say we of the Western world. Then the music has no tune, but merely rhythm — such is its character. Surely this music is not to be considered as an independent art, which can be enjoyed by itself — it is to give to the dancers the rhythmical movement rather and to keep the time; it hints by its notes the step to be taken, which is rendered more emphatic by the beat of the drum. Rude enough, it may justly be called; the body, however, must move to its sway and keep in rhythm — so much now we can make out of it, and perhaps more hereafter.

The old always transfuses itself on this soil into the new; the hymeneal sports of ancient Greece wind into these dances, into the dress and customs, above all into the song; one feels that he is looking at some antique festival. As one watches the chorus, it will seem to grow more beautiful, ancient things become clear, antiquity seems ready to burst into a living, spontaneous reality, the Graces show themselves, even the Muses will be imagined still to hover around this spot right under their ancient seats, Helicon and Parnassus. On a hill above the town can yet be seen the Acropolis of Chæroneia, with its Cyclopean remains of wall; I cannot doubt that it looked down upon quite a similar chorus 1,800 years ago in the time of Plutarch, nay, 2,800 years ago in the time of Homer. The Greek political world perished in the battle upon these very meadows, but that older Greek world endures along with those adamantine walls of the Acropolis.

In fact the primitive elements out of which Greek Art and Literature arose, are here to-day; but their result is vastly different from the ancient one. The culture of modern Greece does not spring from its own native seed-corn, but from the importations out of the Occident; it seeks to follow European models instead of cherishing an inner self-development from its own germ. What would not a man of the highest native culture without foreign influence make out of these festivals? Think of a Pindar arranging the dance and composing the song and drilling the youths to grace of form and motion, as he anciently did; think of these customs, not as they are now, banished to the rude peasantry, but loved, studied, beautified by the highest classes, by the people of leisure and culture! Here are the germs of ancient Greek poesy and art, one will continually repeat to himself, but the crop, the fruit is wanting. This perdurably vital seed could, it seems, sprout and flower only once.

I do not think that the women of Chæroneia are beautiful, in spite of the exalted mood which the traveler may indulge in. Nor will one admire the men very much; he will, however, find exceeding delight in viewing the people as a whole, for they are the bearers of an antique life still, which means to some of us quite as much as any

thing which has yet been. But in the women he will
nevertheless notice many a fragment of Greek beauty.
Nor must you think that this persistent search after
female beauty in Greece is a mere erotic sport, of doubtful propriety in a grown man; it belongs to the serious
duty of the traveler who may be seeking some origin of
that wonderful Greek ideal which will apparently dominate the Art of the world forever. It is an expression
of the Divine, as well as Religion; it gives its consolation
by its utterance to many a poor mortal otherwise not
to be reached. Art, too, is essentially feminine, finds its
highest embodiment of beauty in woman; while Religion
find its completest embodiment in a God who is supreme,
rather than in a Goddess. Therefore one may reasonably look into all these female faces and mark them
sharply, often exclaiming to himself: Behold, there is a
Phidian or a Praxitilean feature.

Unwillingly one turns away from the view; it has indeed been a revelation — a glance into antique life, into
that oldest poetical world lying back of ancient song
and forming its spiritual ground-work. It is not pure,
now, one feels but too well; Time has thrown into the
stream of custom many a huge boulder and clump of
mud; it is corrupted with foreign ingredients, like the
Greek language of to-day; still the soul of it is antique,
its fragments can be put together; and its old power can
be seen to be gleaming through. It is the Chæroncian
Lion over again, pieces lie scattered around, it is worn
by the storms of ages, corroded by the weather, hacked
and maltreated by the foreigner — still it is a Lion, a
Greek Lion: who can doubt it? Nor can one help crying
out again: Put it together once more, and make this
life live anew in song, in art, in literature; but above all
make the Greek Lion leap down from the tomb upon his
foes.

Again one will stop before the church and glance at it;
the Papas is still there, and observing the stranger invites him to enter; in fact the stranger has received almost as much attention as the bride to-day — the people
always beginning their questions with this one, whether

there be such things in his country, for they cannot believe that so many wonderful things exist anywhere but at Chæroneia. There is no end to the curious inquiries of the people — for has not a man come from infinite space unheralded, speaking in a strange accent, with pack and staff in hand, in unusual garments, dropped out of the skies into a small rural town on a bright Sunday morning during a wedding festival? On coming to think about the matter, it seems a strange thing to myself.

The Papas a second time invites me into the quaint low church, which has a strong smell of age about it, and proceeds to show me the antiquities preserved in its walls. There is an inscription, said to be concerning the worship of Serapis, the Egyptian divinity; thus Chæroneia went back to the Orient even in ancient times for her worship. Architectural ornaments, you will notice, in which the clear Greek form is disfigured by barbaric crudities; Byzantine fancies have been chiseled in an ancient pillar; truly Chæroneia shows how muddied the old clear stream has become in places. Even the religious ceremony to-day seemed a dark Byzantine symbolism engrafted on the bright ancient Greek life. These customs, too, have their root in the old time, with some rude barbarous impress on the outside. Thus, in this church we may read a very plain page of History.

But the Papas, reserving his greatest surprise to the last, conducted me to a marble chair, and said with a look of complete satisfaction: "This is the chair of Plutarch, who was once a magistrate of Chæroneia; in it he sat when presiding at the festivals, and at the theater, whose ruins you can still see yonder on the hill-side." Thus spake the Priest, coupling the chair with the greatest name which Chæroneia produced, and which causes it to be mentioned still throughout the civilized world.

Already the question had frequently suggested itself ere we came in sight of the town, Why should a Plutarch arise at Chæroneia? He is the man of reflection, the man who looks back on the past in calm meditation; I think he belongs here where the greatness of Hellas came to an end, and was henceforth to be one of the chief themes of contemplation. He is the retrospective Greek imbued with a mild philosophy; he looks back at the great characters of his country with a sunny serenity, and writes about them a great book. Yet it is too a popular book, the delight of the whole world, read in all tongues, for Plutarch seems to possess this peculiarity, that he suffers little by translation. The element common to humanity is his to reveal, chiefly to utter for the humble. A world-man; not for the few, but for the mass he wrote with some strange fascination. His book may often be seen alongside the Bible in the cottage of the husbandman who, driven in from the fields by the shower, takes it down and reads of its great examples. Here, at Chœroneia, Plutarch lived and wrote his *Parallel Lives;* in this country place and the places around, what a library for the composition of such a work! Could we but make the earth give up those old books from their ashes mingled with this soil: — that is the next process we may expect science to discover.

Plutarch is a moralist, history with him is a study in morality; he has made of it that happy admixture of moral reflection and biographical narrative, which instructs and elevates while it keeps the attention. Such is his great lesson to the people, who rise through him to being universal in their conduct, adjusting their lives to fixed maxims and not yielding to momentary caprices. Subdue the passions, throw away ambition, avarice, injustice, make existence equable and harmonious; in such manner he preaches with a sweet purity, and with great effect upon the multitude. No one can estimate the value his book has had for the people since it was written; it is not too high for them, yet above them, drawing them always upward, by filling their minds with moral principles accompanied by grand examples. Perhaps it is the most moral of books in the best sense of the word; what morality can do for man becomes therein apparent; it makes him an harmonious being, and gives him a self-centered inner life which is proof against both bad and good fortune.

Still he does not stop with mere moral abstractions: he

gives us the great examples of the past; thus his pages live with individuals. A dry record of virtues and vices would not amount to much, but here they are wrought together into vital unity in character. He still walks among these valleys and hills, and the traveler will often meet him reflecting on the mighty individualities of the past, coupling those of Greece and Rome, the twin factors of the world's history in his time. The old philosopher will ascend yonder summit on a sunny afternoon and look at the curious natural walls of stone which lie there like a citadel; in the opposite direction he will take a long walk through the grassy valley to reedy Kephissus. Of what is he thinking? Of Alexander, of Cæsar, of Sulla who fought a battle on this very spot; look into his book, we can tell just what his thoughts often were as he took his afternoon stroll through these even-topped fields of grain or up the hill-side.

Great is the variety of Nature around this valley, but everywhere musical; Helicon and Parnassus lie on either hand, let him take his choice. The snowy height of Parnassus is just across this little valley; if he wish to spend a day in the cool, fresh breath of Muses, thither he can easily pass. He lives not in a great city now — yet he has lived at Rome; there politics, war, society are troublesome, there is the present. Quiet contemplation rests on these hills to-day, and they produced him anciently; along the road in which we are now walking he must have often passed, at the foot of Petrachos hill, tranquilly looking up toward its sunny tops with a serene exaltation. Lines of mountains run on both sides of the valley and seem to separate you to-day from the world, shutting you up within yourself, in sweet, calm contemplation. Thus the old man from this quiet nook could survey the past period of turmoil and write the biographies of its heroes.

But this walk would not have been altogether solitary in the olden time; people met him on the road with a jar of wine or a skin full of oil, going to the village, as they meet me now; the peasant he would find turning over the sod with a plow which has remained almost unchanged; the driver would sit on the back of his plodding donkey and salute in language like that of to-day. But here comes the finest sight of all; youths winding up the road to Chæroneia, in their gala attire, maidens with gleeful look following after in groups with anticipation of the chorus, all in holiday dress. Such Plutarch would meet, such I meet now going along the way toward Daulis and viewing the old in the new.

This then is the man who proposed to unfold the history of Greece and Rome in a grand line of individuals; these were for him the essential thing of the ancient world. Not an account of the State will he give; the State dissolves into its Great Men, whom he portrays as it were for themselves; history breaks up into biography. I hold this conception to be in a high degree the truest one of ancient history, more especially of Greek history; it is a series of grand heroic individualities, a gallery of ideal sculpturesque shapes. A Greek of the later time the writer must be, a time of regretful looking back and contemplation, rather than of action; the Greek State is lost, but there remains in the past these towering forms. Greece has been conquered by Rome, it is true, but can she not parallel the greatest Roman men? Indeed she can: so a Greek is going to write the history of Greece in the biographies of her great men and set them alongside of the mightiest Romans; this comparison will to a degree take away the pang of servitude.

Indeed such supreme characters are always the center of interest; in them the nation, especially the Greek nation, hints its innermost essence; Greece is but the story of its heroic individuals, whether they be fabulous or real. Who figures in Greek poetry, who in Greek history? Let us look at Plutarch, who opens with Theseus, a hero, a mythical character, to give the key-note to his book. These mighty souls of heroes the State does not absorb, rather they absorb the State; as has been already remarked, their communities find it difficult to subsume them — they become too great for their country. In them is concentrated all Hellenic greatness, let their lives be written and set in a gallery, like Gods in the Greek Pantheon.

Such was the glorious conception of Plutarch to do honor to his nation, to tell the story of the great Greek Individualities — he himself being one of them just in such a conception. His, however, was the later form of greatness, not that of action, but of appreciating action. Greece had perished, that is, had become a fraction in a Macedonian Empire, then a still smaller fraction in the universal Roman Empire. Where now is the autonomous Greek village, the wonder of Time, developing with such prolific energy its great individuals? Sunk, lost to view, absorbed into the new current of the World's History, and therewith have been absorbed its great individuals who were bred of the conflicts of disunited autonomy. Here at Chæroneia that power of Greek individuality came to an end; here Plutarch arises and summons once more those mighty individuals before himself, when they no longer can act but have become a dim shadow of reflection, yet still speaking like the ghost of Achilles out of Hades. Even Plutarch himself writing his book lives in that world of reflection like his own great characters; therein, also, he belongs to them, being able to call up the shades of the illustrious past, and making himself as if it were one of them, and moving in a subtle harmony with them.

Plutarch, therefore, sauntering around these hills in the first century after Christ, has nought to do but to look back at the great ones of the aforetime; thus he still feels the mightiest fact of his nation and hastens to utter the same. Hence he has written a world-book about his Hellas, in spite of what erudition has said or may say against it — a true book of the people. For my part I like it — like even what are called its weaknesses; its gossipy frankness, its love of anecdotes, its belief in prodigies, even its little tattle, all find favor with me, for they grow out of the work and give it a distinct, perennial flavor. Still the old man can be seen, I repeat, wandering along this road, reflecting upon those mighty individuals which reach up through history like so many grand statues. From this point of view, Plutarch is an artist of genuine Greek mould — perhaps the very greatest Greek artist — putting these plastic forms on a new pedestal, hewing them out of material far more enduring than marble. Very different is the circumstance of life with us moderns — now the individual is absorbed into institutions instead of absorbing them; heroes of colossal individuality can hardly be produced. At present, man is a fraction, he must specialize himself in our social organism and contentedly act a very small part — too late by some thousands of years to be a hero. Let him go back then to old Plutarch and read there and so be one ideally; thus he will be healed, that is, made whole by viewing total men once more and not fragments of men. Such is the way the old Chæroneian will helpfully reach out to us still. Yet do not make the mistake of thinking that our modern life is a lapse from that ancient one; the latter had its worth, which we can appropriate; it produced heroes, but we can produce greater than heroes.

If I were to whisper one slight critical word concerning the good old man, it would be this: very little knowledge he exhibits of the profounder conflicts of history, of those deep struggles of principles above States, far above individuals for the most part, principles not historical, but world-historical. Some such insight ought to gleam through certain of his leading characters, though but faintly, as Themistocles or Cæsar; thus he might give the whole truth, yet not soar too high above the heads of the people for whom he writes. For Plutarch indeed this is a moral world merely, somewhat too fixed and abstract; as opposed to this point of view every other has to yield. Hence he sometimes gets his great characters entangled in his moral cobwebs, from which he can not free them, though their glory is to have brushed all such hindrances manfully away on the right occasion. Still for his people he has said the true word, mankind must be moral if nought else; only by morality can the multitude participate in that universal life, without which a human being can scarcely be called human.

A sin less excusable is, that he was sometimes careless

about his facts, was not rigidly critical according to our modern historical standard. No, he did not fully appreciate the value of the fact, I think; he did not recognize that what is, has the supremest right to be told just as it is; aught else is a wrong done to the reality and to history as the record of the reality. Rigidly critical he is not then, still he is far better than a critical writer merely; what modern biographer has equaled him? The man Plutarch we must have, though he be not a critic; his soul is in his book, and we commune with it there — that transparent, antique soul, heroic of its kind too, in writing the lives of heroes.

Let us then behold once more the serene old man summoning before his tribunal the great ones of the Past who move through the mellow sunshine of his book, and are often seen in it to their very souls. Philosophy he calls his sunshine; we thus note what he means by Philosophy — an unruffled movement of thought and a calm elevation of feeling, united into a happy, undisturbed harmony of character. In him ancient Philosophy has borne, one feels forced to think, its sweetest, if not its most perfect fruit. Philosophy with him is not the keen-edged dialectic of human spirit, not the mighty struggle of Titanic souls to grasp the Universe, to think the thought of God himself: all this lies far beyond the range of Plutarch; his is the honey of the world, not its wormwood; a sweet serenity of soul looking out upon the troubled waters of the ocean and telling them how to be quiet by means of amiable reflections. Deep, tempest-tossed natures will hardly be satisfied in this manner; but his words are anchors for the people, and therein he is great, great in the very best sense of the word, giving hope and harmonious life to the Many.

In fact it is not Philosophy at all, if we speak strictly, this tendency in Plutarch; it is rather Religiosity — a deep, pervading sense of religion. Reverence for the Divine, a strong religious feeling in sacred things is his profoundest trait; nor must we forget that he was officially a Priest of Apollo at Delphi, which lies not more than a good day's walk from his home here. We feel in his book that he was a Priest of the truest kind, Priest of the God of Light. I do not think that the old religion fully satisfied him, though he conformed to it; he had risen to a universal religion which attunes the soul to the one Creator, and does not distract it with horrible discordant notes of creed and sect; a pure, humane Religiosity it is, giving to the possessor goodness, and being an endless source of moral elevation to the multitude who read him. In this soft light of his own spirit all his characters pass before us and are illuminated; we see them in harmony or in struggle with this light, and there is left with us some abiding impression of music or of discord coming from their lives. So the traveler on this Sunday afternoon walking through the Chæroneian vale will have a heart full of veneration for the old heathen, will feel some worship akin to his, and will speak aloud to the passing shadow: Yes, Plutarch, to-day I feel thy worth more than ever before, and I see now that among thy many good qualities, the best one is thy Religiosity.

XIV. FROM CHÆRONEIA TO ARACHOBA.

As the pedestrian passes out of Chæroneia, he will take no small delight in the fountain which comes gurgling down the hill-side in a multitude of rillets like a bevy of babbling girls, and runs and hides in the grass of the plain. Nor will he at the view of it fail to remember the injunction of old Hesiod, never to cross a stream without looking upon it and praying. The ancient theater will also be noticed above on the slope — a necessary place of worship for every Greek town, which by festivals and by representations made even its Gods merry. Our view of the theater is somewhat different; at least the divine element of it can now be seen only in Greece.

But let there be no more delay; let us enter the road to Parnassus, the literal one I mean, not the figurative one; otherwise you might hesitate to follow. This road passes at the foot of a low range of hills on the one hand, on the other lie the pleasant fields of the vale of Kephissus, which carry the eye across to a parallel range of hills on whose sides are reposing several villages in sunshine; simply as a white spot you see each of them in the distance; no stir, no life, a sunny rest on the slopes. People in festive dress meet the traveler, it is a holiday, every face has some dash of mischief or of merriment. But the poor shepherdess yonder cannot leave her sheep to take part in the chorus at the village; still she has put on a clean gown of flawless white, and leans against a rock, weaving a garland of leaves and flowers; for whom, let the experienced observer imagine. Not for me, as I learned from the best authority, namely, the maiden herself.

Thus after a two hours' walk full of solid realities and insubstantial dreams, mingled in admirable disorder, the traveler arrives at ancient Panopeus, now called Agios Blasios. Here too are the youths gathered in the dancing-places and winding through the chorus; festivity has been wild all day and can not stop; already the Sun, declining more than half way toward the summits in the West, seems to show signs of becoming wearied with so much sport; still the dance and song run on out of sheer inability to come to a pause. Nor can one look into this bottomless fountain of mirth without seeing therein a grin on his own face. He will remember too old Homer, who called this very Panopeus *kallichorus*, town of beautiful choruses. In such manner the ancient Homeric habit is kept up to the present time: — what the old bard himself may have beheld on a holiday as he entered this village, with staff and wallet on his way to Delphi, is still seen by the modern wayfarer going upon the same journey. Thus the latter will pleasantly couple his own name with that of Homer as his illustrious predecessor, not in Epic poetry, but in seeing the chorus at Panopeus.

Nor will the dutiful traveler fail to look here for some of those clay fragments, large enough to require a wagon for their transportation, the remnants of that clay out of which Prometheus made the human race, and which had the smell, to the nose of an ancient tourist, of human flesh, still in the second century of the Christian Era. This is the veritable locality of that wonderful event, and the old Artist has left a few pieces lying around which belonged to his pottery, the great pottery of mankind at Panopeus. I went along the chasm and singled out a small piece of earth, angular, twisted and full of the hardest pebbles, from which I supposed I might have been formed originally; with curiosity, yet, I hope, with becoming piety, I picked up my ancestor and put him into my pocket.

At once the youths stop the dance and gather round the stranger who has so suddenly dropped into their midst that he might be taken for a phantom fallen from another planet. A glass of wine will be offered him, and he will not refuse it; then follow many questions concerning his personality. Notice that the wine is first given, then come the interrogatories — another Homeric custom; perhaps, however, now merely an accident. A lady towards middle age, with excusable curiosity revealed in certain inquiries concerning his domestic life, invites him to stay that night in Agios Blasios at her house; but look at the Sun yonder, balancing himself over the mountain; there is still time ere the luminary slips under the white cover of Parnassus to reach Daulis, which lies just across the valley, rising from the tops of the grass and stretching itself out full length on the hill-side. With that prospect before his eyes rising to the summit of glistening Parnassus the traveler will turn away from Panopeus, though youths and maidens are still springing in the chorus, and he will strike out into the meadow, through which he will leisurely wander without an adventure till he reach the foot of the ascent.

Again we are in the track of mighty events of the World's History: it was at Panopeus that Xerxes divided his army after crossing over from Thermopylae. The one division marched to the West against Delphi, the other eastward against Athens. Did the Oriental despot know what he was doing? I think that he did; skillfully he directed his blow against the two great centers of Greek civilization. The one was the Oracle, the instinctive expression of wisdom, upon which all Greece rested, as a child upon the mother's breast; this he would assail and destroy, for does it not embody the hostility of the Greek world to the Orient? Nor was the fact forgotten that great treasures were there to be plundered. Still mightier was the blow directed against Athens, the brain of Greece, in which was to be found, not the oracular but the highest self-conscious manifestation of Hellenic spirit. Could he but smite Athens to earth, and roll Delphi from its eminence, conquest would be indeed easy; nought else would be left but the soulless Greek body.

From this Panopeus he smote in the two directions, and failed utterly in both. Yet mark the difference in the kinds of defeat. The Delphic repulse of the Persian was a miracle, it came from the hands of the God direct, who, declaring in oracle, that he would take care of his own, girded himself in his sacred armor and went forth; crags from the summit of Parnassus fell upon the approaching foe. Such was the deed of the God at Delphi, clearly miraculous. But how at Athens? To it also an oracle had been given, ambiguous, soul-perplexing, speaking of wooden walls; what does it mean? It is enough to know that Athens possessed the intelligence to interpret it aright; that is then the main thing, the interpretation, and not the oracle. So the Athenians went aboard their wooden walls, product of their own brains, and controlled by their own skill, and smote the foe; it is victory not only over the Orient, but over the Oracle too; henceforth Athens is to be the seat of Intelligence, and not Delphi.

So the Persian assailed the two centers of Greek spirit, the unconscious, instinctive one, that of the Oracle, and the self-conscious, self-determining one, that of Intelligence. Around these spiritual centers Greek history moves; in the Persian War they are in harmony, but in the Peloponnesian War they become hostile to each other, and the Greek world is rent to death with their strifeful contradiction. It adumbrates the deepest dualism of the

Hellenic mind; indeed of all mind; it is the eternal battle between the old Faith and the new Reason. That road too we shall have to travel; to both these centers, Delphi and Athens, we must journey, yet with far different purpose from that of Xerxes, if we wish to gain the victory. Already we are within a day's walk of the Delphic Oracle, whence we may hope to make in time the transition to Athenian Intelligence. But let us look up, we are not yet at Delphi by any means; here before us is Daulis, whose outskirts we are now touching with fresh joy, for we have reached our day's destination.

Daulis is a pleasant village lying at this moment along the slope in the last handful of sunbeams which Helius is throwing over the top of Parnassus ere he drop quietly behind it. This is a Greek village with more abundant signs of prosperity than usual; houses seem to be newer and in better order, streets are somewhat improved, cotton mills can be noticed. On the whole one feels that there must be a little young life and enterprise in the town; it sends a small fresh breath of the modern world as the traveler touches the foot of Parnassus.

A winding alley leads to the house of the Demarch, or Mayor, of this rural district, to whom I bear a letter of introduction. His dwelling is a substantial structure, in the lower story of which is the stable, while in the upper is the abode of the family. As I ascend the little knoll upon which the house is built, the dogs issue forth with their salutation, fiercely snapping their teeth around a circle of which I am the center and of which the radius is my walking-stick. Soon a large buxom girl appeared on the knoll with a stone in her hand, which she hurled at the dogs with great force and with such excellent aim that they were sent off yelping. A remarkably stout, full figure was hers; health sat in her cheeks, strength was couched in her arms, and in her body so massive and well-developed Nature seemed to be taking an unstinted Greek holiday. But what I most admired was the growth of her hair, which hung in a long broad braid far down her back, switching from side to side in youthful, frolicksome sportiveness whenever she moved, and dropping in a coil into her lap as she sat down. Everywhere now such braids are observable; it seems to be the universal custom here with young and old to wear them; even gray hair one may notice plaited in this way. Thread, too, is used when the natural growth is not sufficient; so much falsity, at least, has penetrated to the base of Parnassus.

Up a flight of stairs on the outside of the house the maiden conducts me to the second story, where the mother receives me. I offer her my letter of introduction, she makes a sign of friendly refusal, which only meant that she could not read the document. Her husband, the Demarch, was not in just then, and she bade me wait till he returned. One after another the daughters entered, first, second, third; to these must be added a young daughter-in-law, quite the handsomest of the lot, who was also an inmate of the house; each of them walked up to the stranger and gave a hearty shake of the hand, with friendly greeting of words. After the customary sweetmeat with a glass of water, we all sit down together around the fire on mats and rugs; a chair is brought for me, which I refuse; I insist upon squatting together with them at the hearth. They remove their *papoutzi* or moccasin-like shoes when they enter the room, which action of theirs reveals stockingless feet, natural as life. I also pull off my shoes, crouch down on a rug and cross my legs, determined to be one of the household, though midst the bantering and tittering of those maidens.

Yet in one respect I have to confess to my weakness. I am as yet not able to work myself fully up to the Greek stand-point; though the whole household is sitting barefooted around me, I can not bring together resolution enough to cast off the last cover of respect for the pedal extremities. Still I like the custom; it is both pleasant and instructive to behold a human being stripped of conventionalities for once — to see what sort of a thing he is anyhow underneath all that society and custom have swaddled him with. Very strange do I seem to myself wrestling now with such a problem, and defeated ingloriously in the struggle. For I, the cowardly child of custom, can not summon courage sufficient to throw off my stockings and be like the others, here in Greece where shining examples are before me, anciently bare-footed Socrates and Phocion, in modern times young ladies sitting in a row around the hearth of the Demarch. Such degeneracy lurks in the might of fashion, laying supreme stress on the unimportant things of life; for wherein is the individual with draped feet so much better than he with feet undraped? Still I was ashamed in defiance of reason and example, and was utterly unable to tear off from me that merely conventional rag.

But I refused the chair which they offered, and cowered down on the rugs there — give me credit for that; then I entered into a lively chat with the girls. They did not understand my Greek very well, it was book-Greek, they said. None of them can read or write, there is no school for girls in the place, they talk the pure Parnassian dialect, undiluted with Attic felicities. *Then exero grammata*, I don't know letters — said the youngest with a face darting sparkles of laughter and mockery that came directly from the Mount of the Muses now just over our heads. But there is present a young son, twelve or thirteen years old, who goes to the boys' school in the town; he acts as translator of all the big unintelligible words which I employ in talking to his sisters. An unusually intelligent boy he shows himself to be, the type of what one conceives the bright Greek boy to have been anciently, full of quickness, versatility and youthful acquirements. The American schoolmaster examines him with much interest, and acknowledges not to have seen many youths equal to him in attainments and rapid perception; more plain than ever does it become that we are crossing the boundaries of a new people, altogether distinct from the stolid Albanian race on the line of our march hitherto. The boy shows not unwillingly what he is; he reads, writes and recites for me many a passage from the old classics, particularly from Xenophon, repeating choice morsels from memory.

But the girls there — we can not pass them by for the sake of ancient erudition or of small interesting boys —

the mischievous, merciless girls, whispering and sniggering among themselves — the frolicsome, heavy-bosomed girls sit there solidly, full of mockery and rude humor, unfolding an exuberant natural plenitude of figure with corresponding animal spirits. Curious questions they asked me about my country and my affairs — among others, whether I had a wife at home? They beg me to say something in my native speech, which I do; they seek to repeat the same with many a twist of the mouth and blunder, ending always in a round of laughter. On request I told them my name; the youngest sought to master it in vain, and then declared that she would not own such a name — never. Thus was my fate sealed. In the meantime they do not forget to keep stirring the pot of beans which is cooking over the fire; first the one and then the other takes the ladle and stirs; I too take hold and stir when my turn comes. I spoke of the wedding at Chaeroneia, when the oldest daughter invited me to her wedding, which was to take place in a few days. In the course of my visit I was introduced to the bridegroom, who thrust at me with no little difficulty the following sentence in Latin: *Delenda est Carthago.* Why just that, I beg? He had heard that I was a Didaskali; he, too, had been at school and had studied the rudiments of Latin.

Such a merry time the traveler will have at Daulis under Parnassus, beneath the hospitable roof of the Demarch. But the old mother who sits near the jamb in moody quiet seeks at times to restrain the mirthful daughters. I noticed that she frequently fetched a deep sigh with a peculiar melancholy intonation. The daughter-in-law, too, uttered twice or thrice the same doleful modulation, though she shared in our jollity during the intervals. But when merry-making Marigo, the youngest and lightest-hearted of us all, gave that profound sigh of wretchedness between two fits of merriment I could not help asking her what she meant — are you then so unhappy, Marigo? Tell me, what is the cause? — I expected a story of the old sort, but there came a sudden change. It seems that the family was in mourning, and this was its expression. A grown son had died some months previously, a noble palicari, as they said praisingly. It is the duty of the women sitting around the domestic hearth to moan, seeing the place of the absent one; thus they utter the long deep sigh, when the departed comes up in memory and must be greeted by the living. As soon as the salutation is ended they begin to talk again, attend to the duties of the household and laugh if there be occasion, which there is this evening. Such seems to be a part of the ceremonial of mourning, as we once before noticed at Aulis; it belongs to the duty of the women chiefly, as in the old Homeric times the captive maidens of Achilles wept openly for Patroclus, but in secret each for her own sorrows.

Finally the master of the household arrives — the father — and salutes his unexpected guest with great politeness. He is indeed the master, for now the laughter ceases, the women retreat from the hearth and take their places to one side, even in corners; silent respect if not awe becomes suddenly the new domestic virtue, unsuspected before; no babble now, or if the girls do speak to one another, it is in a low serious whisper. Such is our Demarch, evidently a strict man, not to be trifled with, though very affable to strangers; I hand him my letter of introduction, which he reads and then he gives me a second hearty welcome. The elder son, too, has come home. All the family is together, the table is spread — the low table, such as we saw at Marcopoulo and elsewhere. We sit around it on our haunches, cross-legged, in excellent humor; but again the sartorius begins to wriggle for pain, refusing to be wrenched about and sat upon in that style any longer.

On the table there is nothing unusual except the famous Parnassian cheese, said to be the best in Greece; in it, however, I could taste none of the milk of the Muses, but good, homely, prosaic, rather sourish curds of some Polyphemus. Let the matter be left to good judges and to cheese eaters; far other diet we know Parnassus has produced, and it is to be hoped will yet produce.

The women, I notice, do not eat with us, but sit off in

their corners, quietly twirling their distaffs. I miss them, regret their absence in secret, and finally break over all restraints of propriety and ask why they are not permitted to share the meal with us. *Mas stenochorei* — they are a bore, said the strict Demarch, used to rigidly enforcing authority and precedence in his household. But I am sorry for the change; there they sit shyly off to one side in the fitful dimness of the fireplace; the tireless merriment and honeyed exuberance of youth have lapsed into sedateness and silence. Yes, he has doubtless trouble enough to restrain those wild, rollicking girls, and keep them in the strait coat of rigid conventionality, — for are they not young, while he is old and Demarch, too?

Conversation lasts till a late hour; father and son are full of curiosity about distant lands and strange customs; particularly eager are they to hear about America and its political workings, since both are active politicians, and are now engaged in an election for the Demarchate, the father being a candidate for another term of that office. Unconsciously — for I cannot now recollect any intention, though the scene before me was suggestive — I came to speak of the superior position of woman in America, how that she too has the opportunity of an independent as well as an honest life there; how that certain occupations are becoming almost monopolized by her through her special fitness; in general, how that she is regarded there as a free human being, and not an unfortunate accident among men, which must be supplied with a dower in order to be gotten rid of by marriage, and which is to be tolerated for the purpose of bringing forth the males for the perpetuation and delight of mankind. A free, complete personality she is getting to be there, possessing a soul in her own right; thus she has become rather the most astonishing of all America's astonishing institutions.

The good Demarch assented or seemed to assent, being a progressive man, he says; though he did not think that Greece was prepared for all that just yet. But I was amused at myself, and began to wonder where I would bring up in the end. I who at home never could endure the strong-minded sister battling for suffrage with red-hot philippics against the tyrant man, seem to have actually become a kind of Apostle of Woman's Rights here in Greece. Is this the Greek climate again, or the first effect of Parnassus? So much, however, remains true: the necessity of female education will be insisted upon by every warm friend of the country. In this very house, the girls, though possessed of the quickest capacity and brightest intellects, are socially paralyzed because they, letterless, can only speak the rustic dialect of their village, even if it be a Parnassian dialect.

Thus the Muse of Learning neglects her own sex at Daulis, right at the foot of her own mountain. What can she be expected to do elsewhere in Greece? Quite the same thing manifestly; no schools for girls are found in the smaller inland towns. Boys alone are thought worthy of education; thus the country devotes half of its brain to ignorance. Certainly that state of things cannot come to good, unless we believe with the soldier whom we met not long ago, that knowledge is the Satan, the fell destroyer of mankind. Many foreign writers you will read with this continued refrain: Greece is over-educated. But she is not half educated when a half of her people remain without schooling, not to speak of male illiteracy, which in some localities is not trifling.

But the hours demand repose; the traveler, wearied with the journey of the day and the excitement of long-continued sight-seeing, wishes for his cot. Frequent yawns have already broken in between his words in spite of himself; clearly the end of to-day has come. A mattress is spread upon the floor in an adjoining room, and in one second he is with the dreams. But let these remain unheralded to the world — indeed they have all passed into hopeless oblivion. Still that sweet rest repaid the day's fatigue; the night seemed compressed to a moment's point; for when a gleam of light fell into my eye announcing the fleet presence of Aurora with her command to rise, I at first answered the silent messenger that I had just lain down — then noticing her still over me with ever deepening glances, I sprang up in great amazement at her rapid return, and gave her my benediction.

I passed back to the former room where is the family hearth; the daughters headed by the mother were already up, sitting in a row and twirling the distaff, quite in the old Homeric fashion, one will fondly imagine. Not a word do they utter now; the father is still present, asleep on his mat alongside of the fireplace. They are spinning the cotton which is raised in the valley; the Demarch has told me that he is the owner of cotton mills driven by water power. Many a curious fabric is made in the household by these busy fingers of women — rugs, carpets, coverlets of divers colors, dyed with the skill of a Maeonian or Carian woman. A whole stack of such fabrics lies in the adjoining room, piled to the ceiling, beautifully showing the manifold cunning of the weaver and dyer. Throughout the Parnassian region these articles are made to great perfection, and the enthusiastic tourist will behold in their skill another trait transmitted from Homeric times. Labor-saving machines are beginning to penetrate hither, but they have not yet obliterated the curious cunning of the hand, which has continued to endure through Turkish oppression, and through the more dangerous machinery which is the product of civilization.

You will respect the silence of the family and the slumber of the Demarch; go out then to the veranda and take a look before sunrise down the valley of the Kephissus to Copaic lake. It is a long level stretch of country, now in a green tremulous undulation of grass and grain; it is said to have been very fertile in antiquity and bordered with rich and populous cities. All over it fierce battles have been fought for the mastery of empires, vast armies in the struggles between the East and the West have met here to settle that Oriental question still unsettled. Now the vale lies altogether out of the way of traffic and war — a quiet, retired vale, remote from the world's highway. Thus it rests now in peace and calm cheerfulness.

The Sun, though not fully uprisen yet, spreads out a golden fan in the Eastern sky, from behind the peak of a distant mountain; gradually he raises himself up, peering over the summit with glowing face as if to salute you; then he begins flinging his treasures all glittering, like a sower sowing sparkling grain over the whole width of the valley. Helicon on the right is intoning a subtle, voiceless music, a silent laugh it seems in the sunbeams; may we not wonder whether it be the Muses waking up to the harmonious bright lyre of Apollo, and chanting in unison? Meantime the Sun's eye has begun to look into yours straight and rather sharp; the steady glance of the God is making you blink, when the friendly host calls and conducts you to the coffee-house for a glass of sunlit recinato, adding new beams to the morning.

He has business, political business; that candidacy of his will not let him rest; man is a political animal, saith Aristotle; already several animals of that species are assembled in the coffee-house, ready to open the gabble of discussion. I surmise that he wishes to get rid of his guest, I know that his guest wishes to get rid of him under such circumstances; moreover, fine hillsides are yonder with running streams, the ruins of an ancient acropolis can be seen on an opposite hilltop; Parnassus beckons up to its snow-line bound around the brow of the mountain like the white fillet of a priestess. After promising to return for dinner, I start briskly for the heights, above the town.

It is truly a happy Greek morning, more deeply attuned to secret melodious Nature than elsewhere, one thinks now; for it is the chief merit, I hold, of the traveler, that out of common things he can make wonders,—that in washerwomen washing at the stream, he can see nymphs of the brook, that to prosaic reality he can give the fresh flush of an image, but above all, that in Greece he can everywhere behold the antique world springing into new life again. At home he would not give a look to what now sets every nerve to tingling with delight; it is the land which thus inspires the Greek mood, bursting up at times into rapture in spite of all the restraints which propriety lays upon him. Let him look at the sources that spring forth in many places on the side of the mountain up which we are now going, then dash down the slope through the town to the valley; they are long-tressed water-nymphs running off with silvery hair streaming behind till they disappear in the embrace of some river-god in the distance.

Thus we pass up the mountain above Daulis and look down: who can wonder if the grateful inhabitant once paid worship to the Naiad who dwells in, or rather is the stream, now babbling above ground, now running in subterraneous conduit till her waters gush forth in a fountain on the market-place? Still let us go upward, often turning around and glancing over village and valley; the scene cannot be imparted to you, but every glance sent out upon its little errand, wanders like a bee over the sunny fields and hillsides and brings back much honey from the flowers there. Now we have come to that snow-line so long visible from below; first are the scattered flakes with undersides slowly melting, drooping away in the battle with the sunbeams, but higher up the surface of the ground is covered white and crisp. On the edge above is the heavy cornice of snow jutting out like purest marble; but far beyond in the distance, reaching up to the clouds, is the dazzling peak of Liacuri, highest of the Parnassian range. Not to-day, not to-day, ye beckoning summits; but if Time holds out with us, we shall reach you yet.

Along another eminence lies a monastery, but thither we shall not ascend, we are not seeking monasteries in Greece, in spite of all their charity and hospitality. This one is called *Jerusalem*, but Jerusalem in Hellenic life is a dissonance, and it becomes a rude jolt on Parnassus. The building is beautifully situated, overlooking mountain and woody glen; but the traveler from the Occident need not go there, for he has the old and the new Jerusalem at home, mostly harmonious, but sometimes jarring with notes of social and religious discord. So he will pass down the slope, across the ravine, and up to the acropolis of ancient Daulis, rude crown of stone set on the brow of the hill, celebrated in legend and history.

One of those transformations so well known in Greek Mythology occurred upon this spot — the legend taking its rise from the peculiar mournful strain of the nightingale, called the Daulian bird by the cold-blooded raptureless Thucydides, citing the title from the Poets. In antiquity it was a famous bird story, rather the most famous one of the kind, unfolding deepest horrors of human destiny, blood-curdling with savage guilt and more savage retribution. In the nightingale's song, Philomela laments her ravishment forever; still the groves of Daulis are said to gush waves of her plaintive notes on the air of the warm spring nights. Even this horrible story one may prefer to think of at Daulis to thinking of the discordant monastery — for we must have Greek discords now, if any.

Here the old town lay, resting upon this steep-walled summit for the sake of security, while the modern town has forsaken the ancient site, and lies below on the first gentle slope from the plain, happily without danger from hostile neighbor or wandering freebooter. The stone walls have fallen to ruin, they protect nothing now, the external violence against which they rose as a barrier is no longer feared. But a new power has taken their place, for modern Daulis is not without protection, though it has abandoned, like a new-fledged bird, its ancient nest of granite. The stone wall has been changed to a spiritual wall, far stronger, more inaccessible; the village can now pass down from its mountain fastness to the hillside and the plain, and there rest in security. What are, then, these new walls of Daulis? Institutions we may call them, most impregnable of all terrestrial fortifications, invisible to the naked eye, it is true, but making the modern town far stronger, safer and freer than the old one, wrapping it in a coat of adamant, which can only be broken when all Greece is broken. Anciently it was not thus; each town for the most part had to defend itself separately, and to be ready at any moment to meet the hostile incursion single-handed. Such is the one side, not the bright one, of autonomy, the side of scission, separation, discord. Hence Daulis had to build stone walls for protection, the spiritual walls were not yet built, though prophesied in those of stone; these ruins lying here deserted, are a dead body, quite decayed, out of which the spirit has fled and assumed a purer, more universal form; that new form of stone walls, girding you and me and Daulis is the modern institutional world.

Nor can the observer looking off from such a height fail to think of the education which it gives to the eye and soul. What variety in this little view; a clearly defined world to be taken in at a glance! It is a work of Art, this landscape, in its well-rounded completeness. A curious gradation of seasons with all their products, as he looks from above down into the plain, will be noticed; winter melts in the lap of spring, spring rushes into the embraces of summer down the side of the mountain. But it is time to leave the old walls with hoary antiquity and hasten to something modern, namely the dinner.

I found the house of the Demarch deserted by the women, who were all in the fields or occupied out of doors; only the eldest son was at home and he was getting the dinner. This is not the first time that I have noticed the Greek men performing the duties of cook; in fact the high-spirited palicari seems to be as able to prepare his meals as the women of the household. And an excellent dinner he spread before us, far enough from being a Parisian dinner, but much more palatable to the traveler in Greece. The skill with which he managed the meat, cutting it into small pieces, spitting it, roasting it before the fire, and finally setting it before the guest, showed that his present was no unfamiliar task.

Homeric is all of this, too, for the fact is worthy of mention only as a little jewel still brightly shining in the actual world, and adding in the soul of the traveler new fresh gleams to the world-subduing radiance of the old poems. Achilles, the surpassing Greek Hero, performed such work when the embassy came to his tent; fat chines he carved in portions and transfixed the parts with spits, while Patroclus, the heroic cook, raked the glowing coals, apart and over them roasted the flesh, strewing the sacred salt. For the Greek Hero is a self-sufficient man, he is able to do everything within the circle of his material existence, he is the subject of no wants which he can not satisfy himself. If he wishes cooked meat, he can cook it, no need can subjugate him any more than Hector can, otherwise he would not be the Hero, would not be Achilles. Great and glorious is the victory over wants; I clap my hands for joy when I witness it. For what is man in the social organism now, when it takes the labor of some thousands of men to make the button on his coat? Hardly more than the pin's point which, perchance, he spends his life in sharpening. Heroic self-sufficient life is at present impossible; still a fresh breath of it wafts to you at times in the Greek breezes even to-day.

There were two or three political friends of the Demarch who had come from the village to take dinner with him; to these, of course, the stranger was introduced. Much good-will they expressed, which was polite, and, as I believe, sincere, though many a book has warned us against the deceitful, flattering Greeks. Then the Demarch repeated what had been said last evening about the position of woman in America, and the necessity of her education. I was glad to see that this fact had struck deep into the mind of the Demarch. But now he meets with violent contradiction; one of the guests in fustanella and red fez with golden tassel was outraged by the very thought of the thing. Yes — says he with an ironical twist of the nose,— education for women — *pepaideumenai eis pornari*, educated for prostitutes. Still that old Athenian conception endures then; still the woman of culture is deemed a hetaera, an Aspasia. Such at least was the view of our golden-tasseled guest: education destroys female virtue, ignorance is the mighty prop of chastity. Then he began a tirade against the whole civilization of the Occident, which, from the East, appeared to him simply an enormous bordel.

The thing nettled me a little at first; again I strangely fell into being the apostle of woman in Greece. Moreover our own countrywoman was involved; and what one of us is not concerned in her honor, and has not felt proud of her when we have seen her in Europe, after eliminating the upstarts, the title-worshipers, the husband-seekers — a goodly but ungodly number, it must be granted? I began in my excitement to splutter Greek, and must have said somewhat as follows: Do you imagine that education is thrown away upon women? I tell you, you are never going to regenerate Greece and the East till woman helps you; you will eternally fall behind. Her culture is transmitted to her sons; they ought to start in the world with a double inheritance, that of the father and of the mother; but a child-bearing animal you make her now, while you ought to raise her into a brain-bearing being. Can you not see that you must forever lag behind those peoples who educate their women? You excuse the backwardness of Greece, you profess anxiety for her progress — double, then, at once the forces of your children by educating the females. But the mother not only transmits herself, she also gives her nurture to the young and her character to society. Make her once more the central figure of your striving, as the ideal Arete in the Odyssey, your first and greatest book of education. But there is a higher view — the view of humanity, and not of Greece merely. The recognition of every human being, man or woman, as a self-unfolding, self-governing person, is the basis of the modern world. Woe be to the nation which denies or neglects that; the penalty of the world's history is written in judgment against it. A soul to be developed into freedom a woman has too; that freedom she can attain only by education; then she belongs to the modern world and contributes her share to its existence. Why should woman become a servile instrument and remain unfree? You make her a very prostitute by such a use, if not of her virtue, yet of her soul, of her destiny itself.

Golden recinato continued to flow during our talk, mellowing the ruffled emotions and changing its own transparent amber in the glass to flashes of red sunset in our cheeks and foreheads. We all sprang up from the table with the most intense brotherly affection, when I declared that I must set out; the fellows embraced and kissed — a horrible torture to me, to be kissed by a man, by a bearded lip with bristles thrust into the nostrils and tickling them to tears. Still I, holding my breath, partially submitted to this Greek custom.

We separated in the most friendly mood, and I certainly was much pleased with my hospitable entertainment at the house of the Daulian Demarch. I shall give him my vote at all events against any opposing candidate. On the door-sill, as I passed out, stood the daughter-in-law, the sweet-faced, with a subdued melancholy tinge softly blending through her bright features — a strain like that of the Daulian bird, Philomela. Her husband, a fine youthful figure, stood beside her; she had the face which I wanted to kiss, and perchance emboldened by King Recinato I determined to try, in the presence of her lord of course. I plead an American custom with a strange lapse of memory, saying that the guest at his departure is accustomed to kiss the hostess; but I failed; she turned aside, declaring with a laugh in which the husband joined: *kake sunetheia* — bad custom. I darted through the door pursued by the merriment of the company, and walked rapidly up the path toward Parnassus. Soon the way leads over the comb of hills towards Arachoba Kalligynaika, whose fame for beautiful women has often been heralded along our route. Daulis is now out of sight.

It is already afternoon, many a brook fed by the melting snows comes running down the slopes in wild cascades, on every side mountains raise themselves up mightily toward the skies, chiefest among which is hoary Liacuri. The eye struggles up the shaggy sides of the giant to the top, with a sense of terrific labor. The narrow glen grows perceptibly darker as one descends, feeling as if he were in the initiatory passage to some great mystery. But here is a youth in the road, driving two donkeys laden with merchandise, and going to Delphi, he says. Now he informs me that we have reached the Schiste, or Split Way, which is formed by three roads coming together through three mountainous defiles.

This spot was renowned in ancient legend; here Oedipus slew his father Laios unwittingly, as the latter met him upon the narrow road; a pile of stones was anciently pointed out as the tomb of the fate-stricken parent. What is the import of that fearful deed? Beware of violence to the unknown stranger whom thou meetest in this narrow passage — he may be thy father, and is certain to be thy brother. Such was the utterance of the ancient pile of stones heaped over Laios at the junction of the Triple Way — a warning of Brotherhood to the wayfarer, and to the pilgrims who flocked by this road to the Delphic shrine: we may think of it as the first warning of the God.

Thus the ancient legend was one of dire significance; but there is also in this locality a modern legend, even more terrible — it is the story of rapine and wild ferocity. A band of brigands made their home here at the crossing, robbed and murdered travelers, and drew upon the neighboring peasants for food and support. Then the soldiers surprised them and all were cut off. Driven by Turkish oppression to mountain fastnesses men became robbers, and plundered the commerce of their tyrants, till the fate of their victims became their own. So the youth tells me with an evident mythical tendency, interrupting his tale with frequent ejaculations at the donkeys. It is the substance of many a Klephtic song, in fact the chief theme of modern Greek poetry. The Turkish rule swept away wealth, culture, civil instincts which had been left from antiquity; there remained the undying love of independence in all its ferocious rudeness, such as the primitive Greek possessed at the dawn of history.

At any rate the two legends — the ancient and the modern — meet at the Split Way, both of bloody encounter and tragic destiny, both characteristic of their respective times. The one speaks of domestic fate, the other of social disruption; the one reveals an inner conflict which is a problem of soul, the unconscious guilt of Oedipus — the other exhibits a dire external power falling upon man and driving him into the guilt of the brigand, into hostility to society. The one with its deep spiritual import can give us a work of art, many works of art will flow from it, and thus there bursts up here at the Split Way that red fountain of Theban tragedy; the other is, and must remain, a story of wild savagery, of men like the beasts of the mountain, destroying cruelly, cruelly being destroyed — yet with plaintive, tragic notes running through it of Nature's own utterance. We pass by the place, the youth at my side cannot help feeling a sort of terror at the tale which he is telling. Possibly he has a little of the brigand in him, of secret sympathy with that kind of modern Greek heroes, and so is in reality recounting his own tragedy. Now we ascend again, up the glen with mountains towering heavily on either hand, through wild, gigantic darkened scenery, quite enough to inspire awe in the Delphic pilgrim in connection with those blood-stained stories acting themselves in the imagination.

I leave my companion and go out of the way to inspect a little eminence, upon the crown of which, in former ages, stood a walled town; still the entire circuit of the wall, made of immense rough-hewn stone-blocks, lies here in its old position. Now the spot is utterly desolate, not even the name can be accurately ascertained — probably it is the Homeric Kyparissos, mentioned in the Catalogue. Here it stood, overlooking the small valley, cultivating the little stony patch of soil yonder — not an easy existence; but it was, one may well affirm, an independent individual, of granite texture, left all to itself here in the mountains to fight its own battle with earth and man. These rocks still speak of its vigor, of its self-reliance, of its determination to defend itself; nay this little rocky nest felt the universal Hellenic throb in the great struggle with the Orient and sent its contingent to Troy; we can still read its name in the old muster-roll, that immortal embalment of its one deed.

But it is growing late; I had hoped to see Arachoba on turning around this intervening clump of boulders; but no! another wide semi-lunar sweep of hills greets the eye, a new rock-built theater in the mountains; through it some peasants are passing. "Where is Arachoba?" "Beyond and much higher up; you will have to climb," and they pointed over the hill-tops. A woman appears and a young maiden; they belong to the peasantry and are returning from labor in the fields — straight, perfect figures, with the mountain complexion, a delicate red in their cheeks. The erect, stately gait as they move in profile against the hill-side in their white garment, with a line of crimson through it, lifts the wearied traveler on fresh pinions, and he forgets the way yet untrod. Note again that costume, with its twin colors moving along in the distance; it is the most striking visual thing on Parnassus to-day. A red apron extends almost from neck to feet, with a broad red girdle around the waist; under it is the short white dress or smock (camisia), giving the snowy background, dashed through as it were with crimson jets. Red and white are the simple strong colors, placed together in a true harmony, first in their dress, then blended in their cheeks, as you will not fail to notice on drawing closer. So instinct directs their decoration upon the mountains.

It is not difficult to see that the new type of people of which we have already noted faint intimations, has now culminated in a distinct stock; the physical beauty of these peasants, their liveliness, even their costume, bespeak a new race. They are rustics; little culture can be noticed, but nature reveals in them some happy mood, some ideal suggestion which one would fain inquire into more deeply. But it is dusk and the traveler is weary; more concerning these matters he will doubtless say hereafter.

A crowd of boorish youths join us going toward the town; from them I received the only treatment like rudeness that I experienced during my stay in this region — not injury, but coarse rusticity. It was already quite late when I entered Arachoba, whose houses seemed to be rocking in dim wavelets, as they lay strown over the ridges of the mountain side, with many labyrinthine paths, now dark and doubly devious, winding about among the dwellings. A friendly hand conducted me to the abode of Iatri Alexandros, to whom my Lebedeian friend had given me a letter of introduction.

Thus the modern pilgrim, on his way to the shrine of the God, has arrived at what may be called an outpost of Delphi, distant now hardly more than an hour's sharp walk; he is alone, not another pilgrim has been seen to-day on the sacred road, whose blocks of paving stone still come to light in certain spots — that road which in antiquity was filled with lines of pilgrims winding through these valleys and over these undulating hill-sides with worship in their hearts. All day the long streak of white tunics has accompanied him, though it be invisible, or a ghostly procession; but each one of those ghosts, it may be noticed, has often raised his eyes up to the snow-crowned peak of Parnassus in some secret glee, has thrust his staff against the stones for support, and quickening his pace, has looked forward in eager expectancy of the moment when the white columns of the temple would joyfully move into his vision. But thither not to-night.

And now, indulgent fellow-traveler, who has so patiently clung to my voice thus far, may I address thee one apologetic word, needful at present, for our mutual understanding, henceforth not to be mentioned more. Often have I spoken to thee of myself in this journey, with due humility I hope, yet doubtless not without due appreciation. But I feel, and I would have thee feel that what I, as simply this particular person, may do, is nothing; I am nobody as long as I am myself merely and nobody else. But if I may be able to be what thou truly art or oughtest to be, then I begin to be of interest to thee; and if I am what all are or ought to be, or can do what all do or ought to do, then I begin to be of significance to many others beside thee; for thus I am not the first person alone, not the second one, but I rise into being a Universal Person, which is my true destiny as well as thine, the true destiny of all rational creatures. So this journey, too, — I would not have it mine alone; may it be thine also! I have made it for thee, whether thou wilt accept it as such or not.

XV. THE NEW LIFE OF OLD PARNASSUS.

The first and simplest natural fact concerning Arachoba, and the one which impresses itself most strongly upon the mind of the traveler who has had to climb so long and laboriously, is that the town lies near the top of Parnassus. A very insignificant observation indeed, and in the eye of science almost valueless; but this natural fact, by some melodious transmutation, now glides over into its spiritual counterpart, and becomes suddenly endowed with a living soul; thus it is a genuine mythus, attuning the man and singing its own transformation within him; and he beholds, as he looks up with fresh vision, not merely the mountain yonder and nothing else, but the peak of the Muses, which pierces that hard outer crust of dead rock and rises beyond into the spiritual heaven. Such, as near as we can tell it now, is the keynote of the new mood inspired by the town.

A certain fame has attached to Arachoba all along our route hitherto; this fame has made it from the first a central point in our journey. It is conceded by the Greeks themselves to possess the finest examples of female beauty to be found in Greece; such a rumor we heard at Athens before starting; such a statement we have read in grave books which laid no claim to admiration for Helen. The town seems to deserve the resonant Homeric epithet *kalligunaika*, famed for beautiful women; let it have the title, with the full effect of the hexametral ending: *Arachoba kalligunaika*. The thought and its echoes put joy into the bosom of the traveler as he lies down to rest this first evening in the place, recollecting his ardent pursuit of the image which now burns his very heart within. Certainly the glimpse of Helen was the storm-defying impulse of you and me hitherto; all we have looked at with Greek playfulness, shaded here and there with fateful earnestness; the fair image we have pursued with the joy and hope of a lover, yet with his pain, too; truly there has been a shadow of pain in our joy at times, a longing sweet but not untroubled. So much for confession which always relieves the heart; but we can now go to sleep in greater secret delight than has yet been felt, and dream more bravely.

My good friend of Lebedeia had put into my hand a letter, the worth of which I shall never forget — it was a letter introducing me to Dr. Alexandros Androgiannes, of Arachoba. I went directly to his house and was most hospitably received; there during my stay, I became acquainted with the character and aspiration of the educated Greeks who dwell in the provinces. Of this class of people the traveler will entertain a high opinion; moreover he will form many friendly attachments which he cannot bear to part with forever, but will promise to return at some future time to renew them.

The lady of the house, to my astonishment, speaks English, together with several other languages of modern Europe. She was educated at Mrs. Hill's school in Athens; Mrs. Hill is an American and pioneer of female education in Greece. I took pride in this new evidence of the fact that our countrywoman has scattered the seeds of culture everywhere among the women of Greece. This Greek lady is justly regarded as the most cultivated woman in the whole country around, and is considered, as I afterward found out, to be a kind of ideal for the entire Parnassian region. The house is indeed a brilliant point of light near the summit of Parnassus, and shining over all its plains and valleys.

Arachoba is a thriving place of some four thousand inhabitants, according to the estimate of one of its citizens; its chief physical peculiarity is the fact that it lies further up the mountain than any other regularly inhabited town. So high is it situated that in the summer it is always cool; in the winter the climate cannot be called severe, though snow frequently falls and stays some time. It is located along a rather steep slope of the mountains, having in it many rugged knobs of rock and natural dells; indeed it appears from the distance to be sliding down the rough sides of an immense heaven-kissing wave, which has been started from the top of Parnassus. Below it runs the little stream called Pleistus, wreathed in a far-extended green band of olive orchards.

Opposite the town the view is cut off by another range of mountains called the Kirphis, with bare precipice falling straight to the Pleistus; between the two ranges, Parnassus and Kirphis, is the famous Delphic vale. Only on the one side, on the Parnassian slope, are there any olive orchards or vineyards. But in this narrow valley there is a variety of nature almost unlimited; no physical aspect has been omitted from the scene; the four seasons lie alongside of one another upon the mountain slants.

You will be astonished to find that there is not a wagon road in the large town of Arachoba, nor any use for one. The Great Highway, which we left some time ago, does not come further in this direction than Lebedeia. Mule-paths and lanes run through the town in many tortuous lines; not a carriage, wagon or cart is to be seen; transportation of every kind is on beasts of burden. Many citizens are now seeking to have some wheeled communication with the rest of the world, such at least as they had in the very dawn of antiquity; witness the chariot of Laios, and the processions to and from Delphi.

The houses are built chiefly of stone which can often be quarried from the spot where the building is erected. There are several stores, coffee-houses, wine-shops in the town; trade is active, though of the small kind, being carried on chiefly by means of copper coins which are handed to the customer for change in heavy packages of one drachma. A dollar thus becomes a serious inconvenience to free locomotion, and several dollars make too much money-to be carried about. For larger sums, Greek paper money comes to the relief of the traveler who has to transport all his stores afoot.

There is one leading street lying between two prominent wineshops; it is in the agora or assembling place of the town, where they talk over political matters intermingled with gossip of all kinds. Arachoba is also engaged in the election of a Demarch; the political pot is violently seething and frothing, indeed it threatens to boil over on the side of Parnassus, so much Greek fire has been placed under it. What is all this confusion about? the traveler will ask. Obscure local issues — but they will not detain him now, he need not travel to Greece to be informed of the nature of such matters.

It is the height of the olive season; nearly all the inhabitants, male and female, old and young, are below the town in the orchards picking the crop. Donkeys laden with bags of olives can always be seen toiling up the rocky paths of the village, attended by a child or a woman. They carry their burden to the mill where the oil is pressed out, or to huge barrels for preservation in salt. Some of the men have already begun to prune their vineyards; the wine of Arachoba is excellent and in much demand. A frugal, industrious, simple-hearted people, living in sunny idyllic quietude on the Parnassian slope; but they become strangely capable of political excitement on Sundays and in the evening when they return from the Olives.

Look at the mule which is yonder picking its way over a stony lane, with gear elaborately adorned in every part. You will think of those Homeric trappings for horses; it suggests that delight in tricking out animals which is manifested in more than one passage by the old bard. The mule before you has a head-band decorated with shells, and a breech-band covered with beads; metallic ornaments glitter from every part of its harness, and it moves along with a sort of low jingle. Behind it strides a palicari with haughty mien, like some ancient Jove-born king, though he be now a mule-driver. The animal is laden with some of Arachoba's best recinato for a distant town, Lamia, it is said on inquiry; and this gaudy gear seems to be in honor of the noble burden. Such is the Homeric mule, still visible in Parnassian Arachoba.

Over only one roof in the entire town can I see steam puffing out — it is a very unusual sight in this part of Greece; steam is still a modern stranger on the slope of Parnassus. I enter the place to greet my old acquaintance; I find an olive mill crushing the fruit and pressing out the oil. But a still more unexpected acquaintance I met there: it was our native tongue spoken by an Enlish woman. What are you doing here? She had married a Greek who had resided in England; now he has returned to his native town to introduce steam together with his English wife. But the steam and the wife were indeed strangers and solitary on Parnassus. She is not acquainted with the Greek language, is cut off from all society, and in fact cannot affiliate with Greek customs. Not a favorable cast of destiny, one would think; here she abides in a strange world, as if some power had picked her up from merry England and set her down on a new planet. A female Robinson Crusoe she may be called, torn from social existence and remanded back to a mere individual life with one family at most. It is not a desirable state; for what is man without the world around him? which world he must take up into himself, if he really exist as a rational being. A person must participate in his own nation, age, race; must absorb institutions and be their life-giving principle. But stript of all these things, what a poor forked animal he becomes — quite like the naked Lear. Robinson Crusoe on the island is the man without his world, without any filling to existence.

But it was pleasant to hear the mother tongue again, off here on another planet, gushing forth in spontaneous utterance; pleasant too it was to respond once more in untrammeled speech, in words which travel to the soul direct and not by way of the head. Nor can I refuse to record another pleasure: it was the compliment which she felt herself obliged to pay me: "You speak English rather well for an American." This with a truly English mixture of simplicity, prejudice and condescension. Sympathy, however, could not be withheld; uncomplainingly she spoke of her lot, still she showed that she was Robinson Crusoe, divorced from country, social life, and, it was easy to see, from fashion. Steam and English, twin world conquerors, thus I met upon Parnassus on their victorious way round the globe; they had indeed strayed far to one side.

Also in that same mill I found, more strangely yet, an American acquaintance — whom do you think? None other than our friend from Pennsylvania — Petroleum, in full blaze in Arachoba. This liquid has traversed the ocean and is now illuminating all Europe, possibly will set it on fire. Well soaked with Democratic America's Petroleum, Europe will burn, if it be not burning already in places, from that cause. Wonderful liquid, a Lucifer or light-bearer, yet a demon too, like the old Son of the Morning! Far more wonderful is its stream than the fabled fount of Arethusa, having crossed the ocean backwards and risen to the surface in old Greece, once the source itself, here on the very slope of Parnassus. This same oil-mill, where they make oil from the old-world olives is illuminated with the new-world flame; for the sake of economy, they say, and better light. The peddler, too, can be seen with cup and tin can going through the alleys of every Greek village, crying out in a long drawl: "Petrayli, Petrayli!" It is our American Petroleum penetrating with his torch the darkest and most hidden corners of Europe, bearing cheap light and civilization. Another view connected therewith: See that woman carrying water from the spring in an empty oil can; never has she known such a convenience as a bucket before. Thus cordially and somewhat patriotically, perhaps, will one greet his countryman blazing up brightly in the same mill with steam and English.

The schoolmaster from abroad will soon stray into a school-house to catch some glimpses of that other kind of light raying out thence and illuminating the village. In this substantial building is the school of Kontos, my sympathetic fellow-craftsman in Arachoba, and in every way a worthy man. It is the primary school; about one hundred and fifty Greek boys are here working away at the rudiments of the Eternal Language, quite the same as spoken in these mountains three thousand years ago. Indeed some dialectical turns have already caught my ear which can be found only in Homer; thus phases of the old primitive dialect, one begins to imagine, have been preserved here from the earliest ages. But these Greek boys, mark them: some are full blonds with blue eyes, others have dark-brown though fresh features with black hair, the most tending to the lighter complexion. Thus the yellow-haired urchin, *zanthos Menelaos*, is still here, radiant, to the surprise of the traveler, who finds such emphatic confirmation of the old poet. The little fellows are ranged in a long row against the wall; I take out pencil and note-book and try to note down for once statistics of the light and dark complexions. But it is to no purpose, these delicate shadings refuse to be expressed in figures; Nature scorns numbers, and I quit, throwing down my mathematical tables on the floor of the Parnassian school-house.

Beside this primary school there was one for more advanced pupils, called the Hellenic school, taught by my friend Loukas, student of the University of Athens. One passes through a narrow porch, comes to a room fitted up with benches, a little dark, with low ceiling. A temporary arrangement, I am told; but there is plenty of youthful ardor inside. About thirty Greek boys are here reading Xenophon and Lucian, translating from the ancient into the modern dialect, committing fragments of the *Kyropaideia* to memory. With these heathen authors is coupled the Old Testament in its historical portions; Greek and Hebrew culture appeared together at times in a soul-harrowing mixture. There was the striving of Abraham, with his struggles and his sacrifice, with his unfinished and unfinishable condition; then came that clear, calm, harmonious development of soul and body in the famous *Education of Cyrus*, in which the citizen self-unfolded and self-contained, is formed to be a member of a free commonwealth, learns both to command and to obey, to rule and to be ruled, in fine to live beautifully and truly in an institutional, secular life, and not in a divinely capricious Theocracy. Both types belong to the history of our race and must be taken up into our culture, neither Greek nor Hebrew can be left out by us without one-sidedness; but on the slope of Parnassus there, nearest the top, what a dissonance they made in that Hellenic school!

As one looks into the bright faces, and casts his glances down the folds of their little fustanellas to the bare feet slipping freely up and down in the low sandals, one asks naturally which is the Socrates among them, and attempts to pick him out. Here I am certain is a young Aristophanes, for he is trying already to mock the manner and attitude of the stranger, simply for his own innate entertainment.

Such were the two schools and the two schoolmasters, whose acquaintance, once formed, will not be neglected. In the afternoon, I usually went to school myself, to the Hellenic school. There at a given hour was the lesson in the *Education of Cyrus*, always repeated from memory by the Greek boys in the original, and then turned into the vernacular. Thus they are trained to old Attic Greek and its forms, as well as permeated with ideas of ancient education. From such training comes the present tendency, so strong and rapid, of assimilating modern to old Greek; sometimes one will hear it predicted that Attic Greek will be fully restored in another generation. I too went for the purpose of being assimilated as much as possible; great was the pleasure of hearing antique Hellenic speech gushing forth from the lips of those school-boys as a vital thing, free from the rigid fetters of the dry formal pedagogue; many a vivid hint would come flashing down from antiquity like a sudden streak of lightning through dark skies.

Sometimes on pleasant days I would not find them at the school-house, but the neighbor's wife would tell me that the whole school had adjourned to the fields. Out I go in pursuit, following the direction indicated, come to a little knoll outside of town, which overlooks the Delphic vale in front, while to the rear of it rises Parnassus, snow-peaked and dazzling. There sits Loukas, the schoolmaster, on a stone in the midst of his pupils who cower around on the grass. He takes his book, it is old Lucian, and a choice morsel is read. Near by skips a brook down the mountain with music attuned to the old Greek speech mingled now with its sounds; far above is a herd hanging white on a precipice and calmly browsing;

just across one can overlook the top of Kirphis with its waterless hamlet, down the vale for many miles the olive tree-tops wave and dance and sparkle in the sun; thence too a song can be faintly heard, song of the maidens picking the olives, and at the same time uttering notes in sweetest concord with their work, with the trees around them, and with the skies overhead.

Thus the sojourner will spend delightful days at Arachoba, never failing of buoyant occupation. In the morning early he will hurry to the outskirts of the village and look at the people streaming down to the Olives — men, women, and groups of red-cheeked, white-gowned maidens. Into faces he will peer, not immodestly, but with friendly curiosity; he will be rewarded by beholding many a visage hinting of some vague ideal of which, perchance, he may have been in pursuit. He will watch the twin colors of the dress winding through distant by-paths all over the mountain side till they vanish amid the green foliage of the olive orchards. In merry squads they pass, sometimes singing; labor has the appearance of a holiday.

After going home and taking a frugal lunch of bread and wine, he begins a stroll through the Olives, which will extend for miles over the folds of the slope down to the Pleistus, stream of silvery flow amid the trees. On its bank he will lie down and rest before beginning the ascent in return. Every day he will find some fresh reward in his stroll — a new brook, a new landscape, a new acquaintance, with a little adventure, perchance. He will stop under the trees, where the people are picking the dark fruit from the ground; will himself help them pick for a while, particularly if he sees in the fair young face there before him glimmers of some antique vision.

Look far up the mountain to the vineyards; there a man in fustanella is working among the sunbeams; though he be only grubbing, the white folds, together with the total figure, have some harmonious rhythm which thrills the eye to this distance. Like an ancient statue endowed with life, it moves there, shedding a secret delight over the wavy hill-side. I dare not tell you how my heart beats when I behold that shape. It has something more than Art; it has the spontaneity of Nature, and one feels transformed into its sunny serenity at a look. These shapes have the power of dispelling all anxiety from the breast, of banishing all dark broodings of the soul; I cease to worry about my long delay at Arachoba, here I know is the spot, where of all the broad earth I belong at present. One can feel the change going on within, like Dawn pursuing Darkness over the sea. Thus I return home with bright images, to keep, I hope, forever.

But as you go toward the village in the evening, you will behold the young shepherdess reclining on a rock, with a crook in her hand, clad in the white and red garment, resting there in the golden haze of the setting sun. With the most exquisite grace she leans against a brown-lichened rock, amid her snow-fleeced flock grazing on the slope; you will be astonished to find how sensitive your eye is growing toward color and form in this atmosphere. At some distance let her remain from you, for distance, by enlarging her surroundings, gives more material of Nature to the vision, and furnishes a deeper harmony; you will note how that she is truly the center of the whole landscape, how that Nature simply culminates in her form reclining there against the rock, culminates by a certain gentle gradation from mountain, sunshine, herds, to the central human figure, how that she, in costume, attitude and movement has found the key-note of this Nature, and sums up harmoniously in herself all that is around her.

But she rises from the rock and begins to call to some one on the distant slope; what a trumpet in that voice! Buoyantly it rides over the vale and strikes the opposite mountain side; voice not shrill or loud, but far-echoing, like the Homeric herald's voice marshalling the hosts, or summoning the heroes. She shot the word from her mouth like an arrow; over the mountain it flew easily, one can hear it still whizzing past the summits or wandering among the distant peaks.

These Parnassian women are most obstinate workers — more industrious and skillful, it would seem, than the men. They pick the olives, grub the vineyards, attend to the children, and acquire a variety of household industries, such as weaving, dyeing, carpet-making. You will often meet the woman driving the donkey with its load of wine or olives, yet at the same time busily spinning with her distaff. In the rain I met her the other day with her charge, winding through the stony paths toward the town; still during that steep ascent, she kept plodding behind the donkey and twirling her distaff in the rain. The Parnassian woman, in my judgment, is physically as strong as the man, if not stronger, and from several cases that came under my observation possesses the ability to handle him, in case of necessity. Some fathers, I have been told, train their daughters to the use of the gun. They hunt the wolf now, but will fight the Turk, if they can only get a distant opportunity.

As you pass by the fountain on the outskirts of the village, the washers you will see, for they are seldom absent. Life seems an eternal wash-day, always striving to get something clean and white, often with terrific struggles, muscular and otherwise. Every fountain in Arachoba has these living nymph-like ornaments scattered along its banks or standing often right in the middle of the cold stream, with their ancient sculpturesque costumes, startling to the Anglo-Saxon eye, which has been trained so carefully to all concealment of form, which connects nudity and sin, and considers drapery to be virtue. Even after one has has got used to the stript marble in the galleries of Europe, this real nudity of the washers is striking, abashing at first. You have to go past them, for the road leads by the spring, otherwise you would hardly dare look that way out of respect for privacy. But you will find nought but innocence, innocence like that of Eve in Paradise, shame has not yet fully risen into consciousness; and you yourself begin to change within, to be transformed into that state of primitive innocence which is still the characteristic of the Parnassian world.

Often you will straggle into the wine-shop, the social center of the town; there the citizens gather to gossip a little and talk politics. All your male acquaintances you are sure to meet in that attractive place, and it is not too much to say that every man, woman and child in Arachoba knows you by this time. When you stroll for miles over the mountain, you are astonished to find that the lone shepherd there is aware who you are; he saw you on a certain evening in the wine-shop, and heard your story about that strange country of yours, where machines have learned to talk, where men go to bed in one city and wake up in another hundreds of miles away.

Conversation will not fail you, nor eager listeners. I recollect one evening the talk fell upon the Odyssey; Loukas was present, and Kontos, and other men of education. I unfolded the meaning of that book, its supreme significance, not only in the culture of Greece, but of the world; sought to reveal the purport of those fabulous shapes, Kirke and Polyphemus; endeavored to show forth the most universal character yet created in Literature, Ulysses. But consider the matter! Think of my interpreting on the soil of Greece to Greeks in Greek the greatest Greek work. Beyond this I cannot go, it is the last act of audacity toward the Olympians. The Odyssey is indeed the book of the West — the struggle of man toward the West — the book of enterprise, of man's mastery over the forces of the natural world, the prophecy, too, of his final intellectual triumph and repose — the prophecy of the Western world.

Again, one evening not long before my departure, they asked me what I was going to write about them, for they were never free of the suspicion that I intended a book. I replied: I propose to say four things about you with emphasis.

1st. That I found no brigandage in my journey, though I was afoot and alone. I have met men everywhere — along the road, in the fields, amid the solitary recesses of mountains; they could have made away with me and left no trace, yet I have never been molested, indeed have been treated only with kindness. Nor have I found anywhere the least public sentiment sustaining disorder or brigandage. I should say that a person is quite as secure here as in any other country on the globe; certainly there is not more danger in Greece to the honest pedestrian than in America, with its swarms of reckless tramps.

2nd. I shall seek to do justice to the ideal striving which I still find in your people. Aspiration you have, and a desire for improvement, though one may sometimes notice a lack of steady will; your ideal is not dead, above all, your political ideal; for I find you as keen theorizers on government as your ancestors. Nor has your character for dishonesty and sharp practice been justified by my experience, at least here in the country. The truth is, the Greeks have obtained their bad name from the superficial tourist who, being cheated by a hackman of Corfu or Athens, has at once proclaimed that all the Greeks are hackmen in character. Hackmen are, indeed, quite the same over the whole world.

3rd. For the study of antiquity Greece furnishes the best opportunity, better to my thinking than Rome. Here are still the two most perfect and significant remains of the old Greek world: the Greek language and Greek customs. Both are alive and in activity at this moment on Parnassus. The dry grammar and lexicon become at once a living source of speech and manners. Besides these one will find many remains — ruins of temples, walls, tombs; all of which have their true significance only when seen in their localities.

4th. There is still this Nature, quite the same as in antiquity, which hints at present of all that ever grew up here; it is the royal setting in which the past is to be placed with its splendid memories. Here you can behold the true background of the old picture, that which always suggests it and is in secret harmony with it; Greece today will thus complete and vivify the images of memory. Delphi and its character begin to be explicable when one sees this valley and listens to the whisperings of this Nature — of the mountain, the glen, the sea with blue eye peering through some opening between the cliffs.

Arachoba may be truly called the modern center of ancient Hellenism. The Hellenic customs and language are still here, the Hellenic landscape is seen on this spot in all its concentration; Europe has scarcely invaded the place. One saunters up and down the lanes, to the market-place, into houses, and may still think himself in classic times. He must take every opportunity of seeing the customs — the betrothal, the marriage, the festival, chorus, music. In proportion as he sinks himself into the spirit of these, will his visit be profitable and happy. He must wait, receive things as they come; this Greek life cannot be snatched up in a day and carried off in a note-book; it must be lived; sympathized with, enjoyed. Every day one will pick up some new thing, which fills out the image of the old and sinks deep into the emotions.

There are no ancient ruins at Arachoba; what stood here in antiquity is hard to determine, probably nothing of consequence. Local antiquarians speak of the foundations of a temple near the spring just outside of town, but I could never find them. Some outpost of Delphi this spot was, a little more than four miles from that sacred city. This is, then, a modern town where old Hellenic life has throbbed up in fresh energy, apart from its ruins, freed from its withered limbs, from decayed walls and temples. An idyllic green spot, the best introduction to old Greek life — such is the impression which these few days will leave; then grows the intense desire to proceed to the ancient town with its beautiful fragment of a vanished world. Arachoba is, you may say, an invitation to antiquity, to Delphi; it is the modern initiatory station from which you pass, when duly prepared, to the antique holy place, by a road bordered with flowers, the newest yet the oldest.

This freshness the town has for me, the freshness of a mythical, pre-civilized time which lies back of Hellenic life as we know it from books. A breathing soul it puts into what seemed long since dead; a soul into whose eye you can look deep, whose words you can hear in spontaneous utterance; a young new soul, though so old. It is indeed strange; the Greek infant which grew to manhood thousands of years ago, is still here and an infant; pick it up, clasp it to your heart, listen to its babblings for the sake of that which it is to become. The child is father to the man; its instinctive prattle often reveals clearest living fountains which later in life are profoundly hidden from the most piercing glance; in like manner this modern town makes old Hellas live anew with a childlike openness and freshness.

Much indeed remains to be seen and studied in Arachoba; I ought to stay till this scenery, these customs, this life sinks deep within me; but I am impatient to reach the goal of my journey. I would tarry here long, but the finger is always pointing down the road toward Delphi; thither let us now pass with a leisurely walk, for there is plenty of time and much to be noted. Flinging his mantle over his shoulder, and grasping staff and knapsack, the eager pedestrian begins his tramp once more.

Even the Greeks of the mountains are surprised at my persistent journeying afoot. The peasant meets me and looks at me, saying: "Why don't you take an animal?" Particularly, if he have such an animal to hire. "Why don't you ride like a gentleman?" The true answer can only be: O I am no gentleman, but one who knows how to walk as well as a mule. Whereat he wonders, noting the Frankish garments. The Greek gentleman rides, and has usually an attendant on foot who follows just behind the mule for the purpose of goading it into a walk, always a difficult, sometimes an impossible task.

But the delights of freedom and the pure pleasure of going afoot, are not to be bartered for a ride over stony pathways. The pedestrian, though solitary, turns aside and explores, loiters by the margin of a brook, sits down on a stone, from which he watches the flying clouds, or looks to his heart's content at a group of maidens, in red and white, half way up the mountain. The walk is no effort in this exhilarating atmosphere, or it is an effort which is made with such supreme ease that motion is a delight, a relief of the imprisoned energy. The body seems to rejoice in its own spontaneous flight, for it becomes now a pure reminiscence of the time when it was winged.

Thus we start for Delphi, seat of Apollo and the Muses, ancient well-head of prophecy and poesy. Can it be possible that we are so near that sacred spot, distant hardly more than an hour's sharp walk? One may well have some presentiment that it is not so near as it seems. The host takes me to the outside of the town and puts me into the road leading thither with a slight descent, along the side of the mountain. Above lies Parnassus, apparently not far; why not include it in the journey?

The heights are, indeed, enticing, as they lie dreaming in calm sunshine; there is, too, more than half the day remaining for the trip; accordingly the resolution is taken to go up to yonder first summit and see what may be revealed on Parnassus. Thence one may slowly coast along the ridge till he approach Delphi, when he can descend and enter the town. What are the difficulties, what are the precipices cutting off the way, what is the significance of leaving the straight path for the crooked one, are questions not pondered by the pilgrim now going to the shrine of the God of Light and Wisdom.

Without delay I diverge from the Delphic road, and follow a pleasant path which leads up through the vineyards. The vine-stocks are very small and low; the stony soil gives them its delicate nourishment in little drops, whereof comes the excellent wine of Arachoba. Then all cultivation ceases till the crest is reached. Here now I stand on the eaves of this immense mountain temple, intending to run around on the edge, imagining that I can get down on any side just as easily as I have come up at this point.

The view over the valley becomes more delightful, the air is more bracing, the world more conquerable; with new buoyancy one springs over the rocks along the mountain's eaves, looking down upon the earth below triumphantly. The sun is out to-day, and may now be called the shepherd of the sky, driving his fleecy sheep in scattered groups around the heavens, striking them once in a while with his golden rod. Then they flee, touched with his splendor; on a level with the eye they move up the Delphic valley smit with his sheen, while their shadows below race across the tops of the Olives or scramble up the steep sides of the opposite mountain.

Let us next pass over the crest and behold what is there. A new plain comes to view, a tableland slightly hollowed out like a shallow saucer, from which new mountains rise higher than ever. One of these mountains heaving itself upwards with enormous snow-drifts on its sides and with defiant pines thrusting their green heads through the deep white cover is Liacuri, highest peak of Parnassus, whose glancing summit has so long been beckoning us on the way to Delphi: now that summit becomes a point of intensely glistening crystal in the sun's glare. Ah, no; it is quite impossible to go up there to-day, or to-morrow, or the next day; often have I been warned against those smiling snow-drifts, not a guide can be found in Arachoba who would now intrust himself to their treacherous surface. So let us still skirt the crest around toward Delphi.

It is rough walking; there are no paths here except those made by goats, running in every direction; the pointed rocks turn their sharp ends toward you, till the whole earth seems a fretful porcupine with stony quills bristling outward. From point to point the traveler leaps with winged joy in his heart perchance, but with rapid loss of sole leather. The low thick brambles thrust themselves across his path defiantly and must often be pushed through by main force; sometimes they pluck from his garments mementos of his visit.

This table-land has quite a mysterious look, as if it knew some life all its own, quite distinct from the rest of the world. Yonder is a rich soil, and it is cultivated; the green crop is springing up in long rows; there is, too, a village of empty cabins, which has a sort of weird tranquility about it: not a soul lives there, yet we see every sign of habitation and employment. Though there be no human dwellers visible, something inhabits the spot and is now subtly active — if not human, then divine; rural divinities, half way between the seen and unseen, dance through the sunbeams a moment, then vanish.

Kalyvia or the Huts is the name of the place; the Arachobites come hither in summer, and lodge just under the snows of Parnassus, till the hot season has passed. Merry times are then said to be on the table-land of Parnassus. In the winter, as at present, nobody remains, not even the agriculturist who attends to the crop. In the middle of the table-land is a quiet lake, reflecting mountains; into the lake flows a good-sized stream, but where is the outlet? Not visible, wrapped in mystery; meanwhile there continues the silent whisper of spirits who people this high lonely spot abandoned to sunshine and solitude.

But it is time to begin the descent into the Delphic way below; for quite a distance I have been skirting the crest, running along the stony eaves of the mountain temple; let us, then, seek to come below again. A slant in the cliff offers an opportunity; about half way down that steep slant I pass when a precipice of many fathoms, previously invisible, opens suddenly at my feet and cuts off the next step. I look beneath, eagles are circling below and around me, often hovering near as if impatiently waiting for my body. Will they get it? I look up; then turning about I catch hold vigorously of a bramble and lift myself from that edge. This is not the way to Delphi, the shrine of the God is not to be reached thus. Back then; these steps from stone to stone must all be retraced, up-hill now. Thus I grapple and climb with painful respiration toward the crest again; far more difficult is the ascent than the descent of Avernus, as the poet remarks. With the aid of staff and of friendly bushes everywhere extending their helpful arms, I reached once more the ridge after an hour's desperate struggle, while the fierce Sun from above smote me with burning torches, and the sharp jagged rock blistered the bottom of the foot through the shoe-soles, now worn very thin.

Still, when one arrives at the comb and overlooks the scene after taking a good rest, he is unwilling to go all the way back to Arachoba simply in order to descend this hill. Hence he still goes on, painfully seeking for a place where he can get down, no longer so buoyantly leaping over the rocks which seem to be getting more spiteful and jagged than ever. At last a glance beyond the precipice reveals Delphi, whose houses lie in sweet repose along the slope; but it cannot be reached from this point. Here I stand on the cliff of Phloumbouki, ancient Hyampeia, from which the robbers of the temple were thrown down in olden times: such, I pray, is not to be my fate at the hands of the wrathful God — for that he is angry, is pretty evident from this day's experiences. The little village sits full of placid joy in the declining sun, but I cannot enter there, can only get a glimpse of it from afar. Still even the sight of it inspires fresh courage, and fills the soul with new dreams of hope. It must be reached to-day, if possible.

Let us then pass on, and see whether we can not in some way get down the cliff without having to go back. But here an immense gorge coming down from Parnassus cuts the comb in two, as if a straight slice had been taken out of the mountain. No longer can we skirt the brow as heretofore, turn back we must perforce, or coast along the edge of this new chasm. It is clear that the present gorge comes out near Delphi; possibly through it we may pass thither; such is the new plan that rises in the bosom with some uncertain flutterings of hope.

But what a spot! Desolation reigns on this cliff, nought which hints of such a being as man can be seen, nought which tells of his destiny, though Delphi be just behind the hill. A few goat-paths you notice, going everywhither and nowhither, truly capricious things, which give no help to the seeker for the path which leads to the Delphic goal. Needles of shivered rocks stick up; low, stubborn, spiteful brushwood grasps you by the mantle. Such is the product of this waste, not a flower, not a flock, not a solitary shepherd; only an eagle, and some crows flapping near till their wings fan your very face, seem waiting to pick your bones.

What are now the thoughts of the traveler on Parnassus, with thick mantle becoming very heavy in this sun, with knapsack irksomely dangling over the shoulders, with staff in right hand, — a staff of Providence indeed, which supports his leaps, lightens his sole-destroying tread through the rough rocks, catches him even when about to fall and helps him firmly to his feet again? He will say, as he turns around to the declining sun and wipes his brow: Let this be the end of traveling; I shall return home; I wish I had never started. Delphi is unattainable, the Mount of the Muses is a cheerless barren waste, producing only thorns and whinstone. I shall put back; would that I had stayed at home, where all was comfort and good roads, where there are no classic temples to reach and no poetic mountains to scale.

Such are the streaks of impiety which now begin to lighten through his head, without good reason I maintain. But here is a path leading down into the gorge hitherto inaccessible, a path practicable for the footman. Again hope rises out of the depths, wreathing herself in smiles; the traveler passes down into the narrow chasm with its two high perpendicular rock-walls, and at every step marks with wonder the growing twilight. He follows the Charadra or bed of the mountain torrent, now dry but filled with great boulders, washed and ground to whiteness by the descending floods of the ages. All the channel is waterless, but a beautiful cool spring gushes up, of which he will drink with reverence to the Nymph who has chosen to appear in this spot, so far away from the look of men, welling forth in solitude, in unadmired beauty, simply for the good of the lone shepherd or solitary wanderer. Arctodorema they call her, as I afterward learned, scarcely known to the inhabitants here; her sister Castalia is also in this same gorge further down, just at its mouth, but she is famed among men all over the world.

The wanderer will sit down on the edge and pat with his hands the waters which generously freshen him with new vigor and new hope. He would like to remain beside her pleasant, quiet visage, but it is no time to caress the Nymph when in pursuit of Apollo. So he hopefully continues his way through the shadowy gorge; it is a very narrow passage cut through the solid mountain of rock by the torrent during these past million of years. High on each side rise the walls in a straight line; a little ragged strip of sky and cloud can be seen as one looks up, with their outlines torn to shreds by the rocky points above; a dim mysterious light, fighting with shadows, timorously flies through the chasm. No sun reaches hither; but look ahead toward the end through the tortuous channel — there on a high rock a few sunbeams are lying; they encourage, saying that Apollo is still in his abode, that golden light will be attained at the termination of the dark, twisted passage. Such is the sign, favorably interpreted; onward, then, grapple the boulders, enormous, shaggy-sided, that lie in the white-glimmering channel; over them thou wilt climb darkly and wonder.

This is truly a Pythian defile, so one muses, looking up at the rock-walls cut by Nature into a thousand fantastic shapes; this is the passage of initiation through which the votary must go before he can look on the face of the God. Through such dark ways he must be mysteriously led, or must grope along by himself over chaotic masses; by these lofty walls he will be cut off from the world and inclosed in the very heart of Nature, here to feel her secretest throbbings, here to listen to her hidden utterances. Our primeval mother, Earth, was of old at work in this passage and still is; her the old Greeks worshiped at Delphi before Apollo came with his illumined face; one must still shudder at her wild orgiastic rites in this gorge, as he struggles through on his way to the temple of light. Dark is the passage and rudely chaotic, but ever yonder at the end of it can be seen some golden ray which bids us hope and hurry on.

But after passing down the gorge quite a distance and after many leaps and laborious clutchings, the wanderer comes to a steep descent right across the bed of the channel, a sudden pitch of twice or possibly thrice his own height. He scans it closely, this is manifestly a new problem; but by careful climbing and one long spring he calculates that he can get down the rock without much of a jolt; then he will reach that happy light now shining more golden yonder at the end of the chasm. He lays down staff and knapsack, takes off his mantle, that burdensome mantle which he proposes to throw over the steep first, thinking to leap upon the same to break his fall. Down flies the mantle and lights there below in the rift; he picks up the staff, about to fling it over, too, when, behold! his arm is caught, still upright in air, and held, held by a God. For it is a God who now whispers in his ear — I imagine it to be Pallas Athena, by her awful-gleaming eye, there in the dark abyss — and thus speaks in words of sharp rebuke: Fool! wilt thou cut off thy return? Seest thou not that this leap, if thou take it, can never be undone? Beware! what if there be another precipice in the dark and tortuous channel after this one, more deep and desperate yet, which thou canst not leap down? Then to all eternity thou wilt not be able to reach the goal where the sun is shining yonder; thou knowest not what may lie between here and there; once down this rock and thou canst not repass it, nor canst thou perhaps, go forward. There thou must remain, not to be rescued by the hand of man, caught in the grip of destiny, for I tell thee, these high rock-walls are the shears of the Fates, now ready to close upon thee, and into them thou art placing thy body. Cut not off thy return; back, then, while it is time; leave thy mantle to rot there in the chasm, better it than thou. A blessing thou wilt take back; thou art rid of an old hindrance; more lightly hereafter thou wilt climb thy way up the difficult steep.

At such admonition the traveler picks up staff and knapsack and turns around, hurrying up the gorge now growing darker than ever in the approach of evening. There will be no delay in his steps, though he has henceforth to climb upwards — a more difficult feat than to come down the channel. But in his heart he is glad, glad that he did not make that leap, having obeyed the voice of the Goddess. He soon comes to the sweet nymph Arctodorema, more laughing and delightful than before, as if she too was filled with some inner joy at beholding him unexpectedly once more. He leans over in a hurry and kisses her face fondly, almost tearfully, for it is not likely that he will ever see her again. Moistening his fingers and brow in her cool waters, he admires her lonely beauty sparkling cheerily there in the dim solitudes, and then turns away.

But look around once more through the chasm behind; the golden sunbeams which were shining in at the other end have departed, fantastic images of night are sporting there where the light rested, while the sides and hollows of the rock-walls begin to be alive with strange forms of monsters. Earth has let loose her imprisoned demons, and they now flit through the gorge; quick, up the slant, out of that rayless chaos; the entire way to Arachoba must be retraced with speed; long ago ought that to have been done. The sun is setting, soon it will be night on the top of Parnassus, as it now is night in the chasm. Still every step is made with joy, as the word of the Goddess comes into the mind — word spoken just as the leap was about to be made.

But do you know that the wanderer now seems to move more lightly, to be without something which previously weighed him down? It is the mantle, the oppressive mantle, which has been left behind in the dark rift; the whole day it was a heavy clog, at last it is gotten rid of; with the burden of its weight now, the return to Arachoba might be impossible. It has served its purpose; let it go; henceforth its possession could only be an impediment. It may also be added that the sole of the shoe is worn off, and the walker must now leap from rock to rock on his heels in order to spare the blistered balls of his feet: all with joy however as he thinks of what the Goddess told him.

Dusk finds him still toiling over the pointed stones and through the thorny brambles; no moon holds a lamp out of the sky to illumine his way, but Liacura yonder sends from her lofty cone a milk-white snow-light, rather vague but sufficient to help him find the path down the mountain. Nor will he lose the direction, having kept that peak in his eye all day. Thus he gets back to Arachoba after some misgivings, with its serpentine streets in Stygian darkness. One light only he beholds in the town, thither he goes and finds it to be his old friend, American Petroleum, vividly illuminating the oil-mill, and furnishing one beacon at least on Parnassus. A friendly hand conducts him thence to the house of his host the Doctor, to the great surprise of the family who had seen him set out so triumphantly in the morning for Delphi, but now witness him returning in no little humiliation. Then he narrates the adventures of the day, and in proof exhibits his shoes now fit only to be suspended in the temple of the God Hermes, as a votive offering, their work being done.

Thus I wandered on Parnassus, for this traveler of whom I have been speaking is myself, whom I have sought to conceal, partially at least, behind a third person, out of bashfulness; thus also many others have wandered before me, and will wander hereafter, since the mountain with all its impossibilities has some secret attraction for the world. Delightful prospects I could see in the distance, fertile fields with the promise of abundant harvest, pleasant streams running down the sides of the mountain and watering the vales; cold glittering snows I could behold high up above me on the peaks. But wherever I went, whatever I touched, was the rude bramble, the sterile rock; a rough inhospitable tract always bordered my pathway. When I sought to descend into the valley below me where were the Olives and vineyards, an impassable precipice cut me off; when I attempted to reach the home of Apollo, beholding it afar in the God's own sunlight, only wings which I had not could have borne me thither; finally, when I sought to go down the dark gorge to Delphic Castalia, fount of the Muses, terrific barriers, even monstrous sights, threw themselves across my path, till by the warning of the Goddess I turned back from the final leap.

Thus I strayed in capricious goat-paths that led nowhither, or pushed through desolate places with only a glimpse of the sunlit goal, yet with no possible attainment. What is the result of the day's experience? Clearly this: not by such a route canst thou reach Delphi, with its musical fountain and divine temple. Back, then, unravel the day and what is in it; undo the deed entirely, and begin anew, for there is a way thither, but not thus. Impassable cliffs, lonely sterility, dark chasms lie in this path, bitterly astray thou hast gone. Still keep patience and hope, twin sisters of the present and the future; hereafter follow thy honest and knowing guide, and wander not after thy caprices, which like goat-paths lead nowhither, running everywhither. Back, then, to the starting point once more with thy new knowledge, and do the thing over again, which has been wholly wrong from the beginning.

Such is life, or such at least is the wanderer's life, were he to make a clean confession; all has to be done over again, inwrought with the new experience. Take this day, if you wish, as the image of his eternity, and of yours, too. You shall strive to reach the goal, but you shall have to run the race again; when you have even attained the end, then you are fairly ready to start. But enough; there is a road to Delphi, for many have traveled it; the place exists, for I saw it myself; what more need one know? To-morrow morning I shall begin preparation for the journey; the next day, or the day after that, or still the next, I shall start on the straight known road; then, if the Gods find me swerving from that, let them smite me dead upon the spot.

I was curious to find out whether it was possible to have gone through the channel, if I had taken the leap. They told me that there were several descents after that which stopped me — one of at least two hundred feet. So I would have been caught between the precipices and imprisoned in the dungeon of Gaia, primeval Earth. Well was it that the Goddess Athena held my arm as I raised it to fling my staff over the steep descent; she indeed saves from the dark, deathful embrace of Gaia. Behold yourself there now; you can not go forward, can not go backward; what is to be done? Yell the weary hours away in the hope that some straggling shepherd may hear and come to the rescue; but in vain. Then sleep in feverish dreams the bodeful night away — and so on till the voice weakens to faintness, to silence, and the tired body lies down on a rock to its last rest. But do not shed a tear, the Goddess held my arm, and the dark monster, instead of myself, found only my cumbersome mantle within its deep-gaping jaws of adamant. Thus with a shudder I triumph; and you with me, I could gladly believe.

It rained the night after, and the rain filled my dreams with a new deluge. I am compelled to stay in the gorge, lying in its narrow bed; the showers descend, the waters begin to rush down the channel with boiling violence. At first I perch myself on a thin strip of rock outside the stream; then, with feet in water, I resist the current in a desperate struggle; but the cloud bursts on the mountain, which suddenly becomes a vast waterfall; the torrent sweeps me down and tumbles me over the precipice. Still I rejoice — I was saved because Athena held my arm. Such salvation comes to him whom the Goddess restrains from taking a leap into that rock-walled chasm in which there is no advance and no return.

Moreover, if I can read her divine decree aright, she refuses me as yet an entrance to the antique Delphic world; she has thrown me back even with violence upon modern Arachoba, where the life of antiquity is not a ruin but is still ruddy, being seen and felt in all the vividness of the present. Here, then, we shall stay, dutifully obeying her holy command, till she bid us start again for Delphi.

XVI. THE TWO WORLDS OF PARNASSUS.

There is a tone of rejoicing throughout the town this Saturday evening; the matron smiles, the maiden moves with a lighter grace, the old man tells a new story — everybody seems to be looking forward to some new joy; what is the matter? A festival to-morrow; to-night the people are allowed to eat meat, and great is their happiness. Sheep and goats are slaughtered in the public place before the chief wineshop; the blood of the animals runs down into the gutter and is licked up by the dogs, while the inhabitants look on during the operation. A deft butcher hangs up the flesh as fast as it is ready, when it is rapidly sold and carried away. Everywhere one meets with that quiet feeling of delight which says: Tomorrow is a festival. Lent is just at hand; before plunging into its sorrows and abstinences, let us enjoy once more our happy earth and its sunshine.

On the morrow the people go to church and drone after the priest the service, with many a gesticulation and genuflection, meaningless enough to the stranger; still it seems to satisfy the assembled multitude and make them happier, therefore let it be called good. St. George's, the new Cathedral is full to overflowing; Panaghia, the other church of the place, will not contain the throng. It is a day of festival, Heaven itself and all the Saints must be brought in to share the joy — for joy is here a religious matter. The women, as in the Byzantine churches generally, keep on the outside of the sacred railing, and remain together; in white-red costume, with faces peering out of the kerchiefed hair, with cast-down looks of sweet piety, they stand there massed in rows behind one another — a view very pleasing; to me, I shall have to confess, altogether the most attractive thing in the church.

The Greek is a great lover of festivals, and they are all connected with his church; in fact it is usually said that there are too many of them in the course of the year for a serious world. This custom of festivals is a direct inheritance of ancient Greek worship, which filled the calendar with festal days sacred to the various Gods; it shows too that Christianity sought to adapt itself to what already existed. Still further, the new faith had to adjust itself to the Greek character. Earthly joyousness goes hand in hand with devotion; religion has seized upon and promoted the gladsome side of man's nature, has reconciled itself with happiness. God gives to man festivals, and the duty of the latter is to celebrate them. How different is our Puritanism! There Sin forever stands in the background, Sin from the beginning of the world, Sin from Adam's fall in which we all participate. Each soul is born a guilty thing, let it never dare think of joy till it somehow or other get rid of a sin which it never committed. The innocent maid, pure as the angels, has done nothing, still her conscience is taught to accuse her; if she find nought of guilt in her heart, so much the worse for her; she is told that her heart is hardened in utter depravity. This Sin, standing in the background of Human Life, and casting a deep shadow over it with ever-threatening wings, has much resemblance to the Greek Fate, an amorphous black Power, which swayed mankind with a hopeless necessity and had supremacy even over Gods. Fate overwhelmed the Hellenic world, as we saw at Chæroneia, and became a terrific reality; now it is no longer an external Power, but has gone within the soul of man and become Sin; there it eternally threatens him with torment; still a dark angel it is, but at present it seeks to sway the inner world of conscience by its bodeful menacings. The Greeks, however, remained joyous, with black Fate always hanging over them; and let us too conquer our fiend, reserving our conscience for the guilty deed; for we distort it and corrupt it, if we plague it with the guiltless deed. Then for the happy victory let us have a Greek festival, in which we are glad, glad that we are born, glad that we live upon this earth whose heavy-pacing Time we are going to interpolate with many a bright holiday.

Shortly after dinner the people, especially the young people, can be seen flocking through the streets to a common place of meeting. That place is just on the outskirts of the town, and is known as the place of the chorus, being leveled off and kept free from obstruction. Young men have the snow-white fustanella with its profusion of folds dancing from thigh to thigh as they move; often a richly-embroidered dark jacket is put on over the fustanella; a red fez or ornamented parti-colored cap sets off the head. So the youth, proud, erect, of handsome figure, treads along with a gait like a strut, conscious of being worthy of the title of Palicari. A right festal figure, you will say, raying joy everywhere through the landscape.

But the maiden, the genuine Arachobitza, is also coming out, appearing in a new costume, which belongs to her town alone of the whole world. There is first the white dress, short, allowing the new shoes, tidily polished, to be seen; even the decorated stockings will entice a glance from the traveler, if he be somewhat of a prying turn. Over the white dress is worn in cool weather a woolen mantle, sometimes dark but usually white; then down in front falls the narrow red apron, reaching quite to the shoes; around the loins is scarfed the red girdle in warm embrace. On the head is a white close-fitting kerchief, quite concealing the hair except a thin crescent of it in front, but permitting it to fall down the back in a long braid. Nor should the metallic decoration remain unnoticed, varying considerably with the taste of the wearer, who seems to prefer coin to all other ornaments. The roseate face fading into the white fresh neck peers out in living contrast to the garments, and yet in complete harmony with their colors; sun-rise is in every cheek pursuing the milk-white dawn.

But a description of colors is dry and uninteresting, compared to the reality; only the eye can sport in these thousandfold changes, and dance over the multitudinous billows of living hues. Drunk with color our vision becomes to-day; it is a festival of sight. Let us try once more to seize the image by simplifying it: white is the background of dress, on this white is placed the vivid scarlet; then some dark spots dot the mass of figures here and there, like the passing clouds in a serene sky.

Nor must we forget the happy harmony between body and dress. The face gives the ground-tones of color for the costume; the red and white of the garments find their source and living relation in the red and white of the visage. On the other hand, the form of dress must be determined by form of body, which therein is concealed, but in a truer sense is revealed. Now the sport of these two simple colors over the human frame has something wonderfully joyous and vivacious in it; it is the merriment of a fond pair of twins, rolling and winding in each others' playful embraces, capriciously, but always giving out the same festal look.

But we must behold these colors in mass brightly

moving through one another in manifold changes. The whole town is present in the open air, either taking part in the dance or looking on with an instinctive delight in these hues and in their intertwining movements. Several hundred people are gathering, dressed in their peculiar costume, with the exception of half a dozen or so in European garments. All the women are apparelled quite alike, in the same fashion and same colors; the spectacle of the entire body of them, massed together on a slight elevation above the choral ground, makes the joy of the day irresistible. Then the colors are endowed with life and motion, forming a hundred graceful combinations every minute. I come down into the village from the hills above and gaze at the display of hues; these maidens, or rather colors, can be seen streaming through all the labyrinthine ways of the town toward the dancing ground. From the turn of this hill I can look down into the heart of the place and follow each bright form moving to that spot of greensward, moving from the town's heart in red streamlets, one may say. Add to these strong tints the beautiful day wherein Apollo puts every object as well as the entire scene into a mild yet joyous setting of golden radiance, and you have this touch of Parnassian existence. Groups of white forms of youths also move in sculpturesque dignity, yet with a light-hearted tread toward the same locality — all with one note in their heart.

Out of one of the streets emerges the band of musicians, composed of two men — one beating the drum, the other playing the caramousa, an instrument which has already been mentioned as snarling. This strange music rides heavily on the air, yet with strongly marked emphasis; it is no music in our sense of the word, it has no tune. But the dance begins to its beat; the circle of youths is at once formed, which the maidens join. After a short time, there comes a second band of music, with caramousa and drum; a second chorus is formed in a second circle alongside of the first. Thus the festivity opens, Joy is king of Parnassus.

These dances are not like our dances, and have in many respects a different purpose. The circle is formed by joining hands; two or three steps forward are taken, then backward, with a slight canter of the feet; then another movement forward and backward, and so on with manifold repetition. What is in the thing? one asks impatiently, perhaps. It is motion, love of motion with its graceful turns and undulating outlines; love of motion for its own sake and nothing else. In this respect these rustics show an inborn taste and natural artistic instinct which will surprise the observer from abroad; it will soon be seen that the dance is not a wild frenzy in which youth seeks to get rid of its own excess of animal spirits, nor does it ever become a maze of complicated figures in which the sense of harmonious movement is lost. Rustic is the dance indeed, yet truly Greek in spirit; the spectator who does not feel that spirit in it, must have little feeling for Greek Art. The simplest means are used to exhibit bodily perfection, grace of outline, and harmony of movement. At times the head dancer may leap and give a whirl, and otherwise perform some unusual gyrations; but that does not alter the character of the dance. Thus the old Greek chorus must have been, though infinitely more delicate and more developed in every way; the lyrist Pindar would rear this germ to beautiful perfection; but here is still the fresh rose-bud which once unfolded into the Parnassian rose, fairest of earthly flowers.

Another characteristic which strongly marks these dances is the extreme modesty and chaste manner of the female participants. Often they form a chorus by themselves, and when they dance in the same circle with the young men, it is not by pairs, but the youths occupy one half of the circle and the maidens the other half, while only the central couples join hands. Not prudish is this, but a delicate and perfectly natural touch of modest reserve. Nor do the women make any of the unusual movements, any of the fantastic leaps which are allowed to the youths, but they keep within the customary limits of the dance. They never spring with a violence which dashes their dress above their ankles, or seek to attract attention by unusual behavior. All is chaste simplicity, with a sense of moderation which the traveler wonders at among a rural population, yet all is filled with an inner quiet joy; existence is a holiday. One will be often forced to exclaim to himself: Yes, here is still the germ rude and undeveloped; here is still that same old artistic instinct, which shunned excess like death, and sought beauty in moderation, harmoniously balancing all the fierce contradictions of life.

As I stood there looking at the dancers, a young Greek whom I knew, caught hold of me and pulled me into the circle. At once the crowd shouted, "Bring him in, and have him dance." My two hands were held with a friendly persistence, and I not unwillingly danced along, though amid the titters of the pretty maids of Arachoba. I had watched the step, and thought it easy, but I found that it required some practice. Then I swayed backward and forward with my long overcoat, broad-soled shoes and European costume out of tune with the time; I felt the dissonance, mine was the sole inharmonious note in the company, still with a walk and a trip I went through all the movements. But they laughed at me, and I laughed at myself, dancing the Greek chorus with youths and maidens on Parnassus, under the very breath of the Muses. Still it must be done; the Greek journey would be worthless without just that inspiration from the Sacred Sisters.

Many a graceful turn will fall into the eye and arouse the feeling of festal delight; many a suggestion there will be of the ancient joy of bodily movement. To-day a Palicari, at the request of a friend, conducted me to his house and walked before me. The proud free stride, the care with which he moved his limbs to show their grace and dexterity, were a marvel; for remember that the outlines of his limbs were not lost in lopping French breeches, but in his close-fitting hose they revealed form and motion perfectly. Then the throw of the folds of his fustanella showed all the skill of movement, and shared in the proud bearing of his body, with a delicate play of their own. Thus he strode before me, entrancing me with his motion, for the stress which he laid upon his gait was certainly the result of intention, he was a work of art before my eyes. No such movement is possible in our dress, and probably no peasantry but this Greek one has such an inborn delight in harmonious motions. All the possibilities of ancient Greek sculpture are still here; the models even might be selected; yet it is but the germ, the primitive instinct, which, however, with cultivation, would again shoot up into forms of marble and poetry from this slope of Parnassus.

A friendly Papas I met on the ground; he invited me to enter a house with him which overlooked the choral place; people, simple and poor, lived there, but they served up wine, walnuts and sweetmeats with generous hospitality. Man and wife are over fifty years of age, yet they both say that they dance at the festivals. No old age has yet blighted their youthful feelings, or even their cheeks, eternal youth is in this house, like that emotion which ancient Greece herself everywhere inspires. I imagine that an aged person would feel young in this town to-day. People a hundred years old are not uncommon, walking still with a light gait, it is said; men over eighty years of age still go to their work in the fields. Old age this is, but without the lapse. The mountain air, bracing and pure, embalms life in that perfect gem, the body. This body, trained to harmonious movement, is the mirror of the Greek wherein he beholds his own soul; thus existence becomes to him spontaneous poetry, not written but lived, a continuous sculpturesque movement.

In such manner Old Age disappears in festal Arachoba — at least to-day. I go to the house of my host, and engage to dance next Sunday with his mother, who would elsewhere be humbled by her years. Indeed sometimes the Greeks are so deeply imbued with a love of youth that they quite forget that they are old. I have in mind a Greek lady, still beautiful and well preserved, who passed off her own daughter upon me as her sister. So at least was my understanding of the relation, till I was laughed at and corrected by an outsider. In the exuberance of Greek youth, she had quite forgotten that she was the mother.

As I was standing and looking with admiration at the chorus, identifying it in many ways with antique things, I was accosted by a man who asked me if I held the doctrines of Phoulmar. His manner, moreover, seemed to indicate that he thought the said Phoulmar to be a wretch, if not the Evil One himself. But who in the world is Phoulmar? I was puzzled to know what the man meant, when further inquiry developed the fact that none other was intended than our old German friend Fallmerayer, who has sought with such obstinacy to disprove the Greek origin of the Greeks. Now, if there is one invariable article in the creed of the modern Greek, it is that he is a lineal descendant of the ancient Greek, and that he in person is entitled to all the honors, dignities and privileges which belong to a descent from such high ancestry. But now comes a German pedagogue, this Fallmerayer, and with a vast display of erudition, tries to invalidate the claim. The result is, the name of Fallmerayer has gone into the provinces, has percolated through the layers of the people, and been changed thereby to the title of a sort of demon or Antichrist, a type of all that is hostile to the orthodox Hellenic race — in fine, the Greek devil. Accordingly I was at once questioned upon this important article of faith on the place of the chorus in presence of severe judges.

Of course I could give a favorable answer, for the whole theory was unsound from its basis, though with some scattered fragments of truth; moreover, it has been quite set aside in recent years by the labors of another German investigator; and is it not refuted by what I see before me? But that strange German pedagogue with his crooked idea! The idea is there in his head and is crooked; the whole world must conform to that idea, though the world thereby get crooked, too. So great is very often the significance of the idea to the German pedagogue, particularly if it be crooked. He pours into it all the treasures of books, all the buried lore of libraries, to the very dust and mould; no man on our earth can compare with him in erudition and multifarious reading. Wonderful, very wonderful he is indeed, but his idea is crooked and the whole universe gets twisted and gnarled in passing through convolutions of his brain, and has to be straightened out again, often with infinite labor. Thus mysteriously I met the shadow of my fellow guildsman, the Bavarian schoolmaster, on Parnassus, having become a veritable goblin there.

Thus it is with thee, O Fallmerayer's Johann Philip — and I curiously quiz, how will it be with me? But mark another offense: this very Arachoba he declares to be not a Greek word but Slavic, and cites several other names of places just like it between the Mediterranean and the Baltic. Now Arachoba revenges itself by considering him a brigand and an infidel. Still worse: he affirms that Arachoba means Crab Town (or more exactly Crab Corner, Krebseck); as if to insult the place with disgusting etymology. No wonder Arachoba examines suspiciously the visitor concerning his affinities with Phoulmar.

A fiery, fighting soul the schoolmaster had — he fought against Napoleon for German liberation, before he began this war against the Hellenic name; one feels his character in his style, for his words often leap forth red-hot, when it were better if they had remained cool. Intensity of utterance he has; withal he is a most impracticable, stiff-necked person, ready to measure swords with anybody, particularly on the Greek question. Still I like to think of the old schoolmaster who explored hitherwards before me; what a strange wake of light he has left behind! It is, however, a light, though a little sulphurous, and now grown somewhat dim in more recent light. Much that he has said was true, or the beginning of truth; he would have it all true, that was the difficulty; so the idea gets crooked. His own weapon of erudition has been turned against him; moreover the eye will confute him, beholding so often on this soil the old in the new. Such a difference shows itself to the eyes of the two schoolmasters visiting Parnassus.

But the dancing continues and the music. This music, however, is a problem. What doom will the startled human ear pass upon it? Notice the player on the caramousa, how he blows! Slowly he moves around the inside of the circle, keeping time and making gestures with his instrument in his mouth. Desperately he blows, turning red with the exertion, and inflating his cheeks with breath till his eyes seem ready to shoot from their sockets; Gabriel, the last and greatest trumpeter, will not more completely blow himself into that final blast announcing the end of all things. Now and then the player passes out of the circle into the surrounding crowd for a penny, though these pennies are not frequent. Long will he remember me by a small piece of silver which I gave him, a Danish coin, which had been put upon me in some of my exchanges. Marching around the circle with him is the drummer, slashing away with drumstick in one hand, and in the other holding a switch against the drumhead, thereby producing a crawling sound. A strange music indeed, yet it marks the time strongly — in fact it does more, it marks the movement of the body. This is then, the clew of the matter: music in the present case is wholly subordinate to movement which it must emphasize at important changes. It is not an independent art which can be listened to by people sitting quietly at the concert; it has no significance without the accompanying bodily motion, which it rudely hints and controls in a subordinate way. To portray the tossings and interweavings of all shades of the emotions — this is the realm of modern music, not of ancient; not even the Greek music of to-day has any such purpose. It is at most rhythmical, and thus we fall back to that love of motion expressed in the human body, which lies at the very foundation of all Greek Art.

Similar, too, is the song; it has a decided rhythmical tendency, and seems out of place apart from the dance. It is not the words so much as the movement, upon which stress is laid. Such was doubtless the ancient chorus — a harmonious combination of song, instruments and dance, of which only a few fragments of the verse have come down to us. The dance was to be a gallery of sculpture set to beautiful movement in the forms of fair youths; the ode, in word and voice, uttered the same as the dance, which found its completeness in the accompaniment of flute and lyre; so these arts were joined together in sweet concord which are now separated; the ancient lyric poet not only made the verse but taught the whole chorus in all its elements. Thus we find that this Greek music has its root in the antique and is not without meaning.

But another question is agitating all this time the traveler far more deeply: Where is the old Greek ideal? Often have the beautiful women of Arachoba been celebrated along his route; here they are now before him, hundreds of faces which he will eagerly scan, not without an inner exaltation. That which strikes him is the number of blondes he will see — not the flaxen blonde of the North, but the golden blonde of the South, with long luxuriant hair glistening in a soft glow like that of evening sunbeams, and pouring over the head and down the back a mild, yet frolicsome sheen of gold. The tender blue eyes melting in their own modest warmth are also here, to my astonishment, as well as the lily complexion tinged with the fresh morning red. Yet not all are thus, by any means; the most of the faces are of a dark tint, yet never brown-burnt. Nor are the features always regular, but the Greek profile one will see at times in surprising perfection; the forehead, the triangular nose with softly rounded angles, the line connecting forehead and nose are all here, to be marked by any careful eye.

What, then, may one affirm about the Greek type found at Arachoba? As I was engaged in the dance, I was at times brought very close to many of these faces, yet you must think quite short of absolute contact; it was a good opportunity to see them massed together and to glance into their eyes. On the knoll shelving toward the chorus stood a small amphitheater full of these roseate visages rising one above the other, and overlooking the dance. The eye will note the common type in all, though it varies from homeliness to beauty. These are laboring people, peasants; to-morrow they will be in the Olives and vineyards; even the maidens have to toil in the fields under the hot sun, though the location be high. A strongly marked handsome girl with all the traits of Greek beauty I have not seen to-day; it is the type which causes admiration, and each has that common type, not without some additional touch of grace or prettiness, if it be only the color. The traveler will enthusiastically declare it to be the handsomest peasantry, taken as a whole, that he has yet seen.

This is my conclusion: the ancient Greek type can still be observed on Parnassus, but it is undeveloped. The germs, the possibilities of the old Hellenic world are now existing amid these primeval mountains: such is the deep-grounded impression to which one always returns. The difficulty is that the primitive Greek germ is not allowed to develop itself freely out of its own nature, as it did in antiquity. Modern Greek culture seeks to be European, perchance, must be European; higher education is imported largely from Western Europe. The cultivated man from the University of Athens has lost his sympathy with the ancient customs of his fathers, and of his fellow townsmen: the cultivated woman throws aside her Arachobite costume as rustic, despises the rude chorus and music, reads European books, becomes European in dress, manners and thought; in fine, both man and woman lose by education their Greek individuality. Thus the germ of primitive Greek is choked at the start, it never flowers into culture, but is left to the peasant to retain in rustic rudeness and simplicity.

One can have little doubt that if these primitive manners and this primitive consciousness were developed from their purely Greek basis, the ancient Hellenic civilization would again appear. If the man would always seek to unfold these germs into flower and fruit, instead of grafting them into some foreign growth, if the woman of education would take this costume and add to it grace and refinement, instead of adopting the latest Parisian fashion, if she were trained as of old to form and movement, of which the rudiments are still to be seen in the chorus, the ancient Greek beauty might come to life again, and we might see the models of the old sculptors and painters. This is my firm belief: that primeval world, as it existed even before Homer, Hellenic or Pelasgic, out of which Greek civilization developed itself of its own inherent force, is still here on Parnassus, stranded upon the mountain, and thereby saved from the wreck of thousands of years. Fleeing from the swarms of invaders that overflowed the rich plains, to lofty and sterile fastnesses, the old stock preserved itself; but it remains a germ, and this germ, alive though it be now, is apparently losing its vitality. What hostility never could do, is done by civilization.

Still I do not think that the old Greek world is again going to appear in reality, or that its return should be desired; still less do I think that it would take the same relative position in the world's culture as in antiquity, when it became the teacher of the youthful race. Two thousand years have passed since Greece dropped out of the World's History, having fulfilled its mission; the stream of time is not going to turn backwards. But we must always explore its course and behold therein our happy early childhood; for after all, the individual man must pass through again what his race has passed through. Hence ancient Greece must remain the eternal school of the modern world, since its period takes in just the school time of our race. For such purpose modern Greece offers new aid; this must be our chief, but not our only interest in the Hellas of to-day and in Parnassus, where we now are.

Another reflection, already hinted at Chæroneia, will force itself now more strongly upon the mind of the observer: he will see here the possibility of ancient Greek poetry. Let the true singer again be born into these customs and be filled with their beauty; let the songs still sung upon this spot be made by a man of genius, illuminated with the culture which springs directly from this life; let the choruses now forming the amusement of rustics only, be unfolded by him into harmony, rhythm, grace — then you have the poet before you once more, quite as he of old arose on these hills. Let the person of wealth and leisure spend his time and thought in making the dance beautiful, and the marriage feast and the festival, taking his chief delight in rhythm and in exalted measure; let him support the poet who cuts these rough diamonds of the people into exquisite Greek form, then one can not help thinking, the ancient poetical world will spring anew into being. Such is the emphatic feeling which comes over the traveler beholding these original rude germs, being still the primordial forces of what Greece once became. With a little fancy and poetical instinct, he must feel that here he is brought into contact with the world which produced Pindar and his rhythmical odes; nay, he will come upon many a strain singing out of the background of old Homer's poesy. The original elements which summoned both these ancient bards into existence are still present and in action.

To-day there is a vast body of popular Greek poetry, having certain turns and thoughts universally diffused, though each village has its own version of the song, and often its own distinct song. The bard, too, is here still, as he was in the Homeric village; Arachoba has several, as I learn on inquiry, poets of nature, who will vary some old story with coloring of their own, just as the ancient rhapsodist diversified his one theme, the tale of Troy. Thousands of lines some of them can repeat from memory—a feat not unlike that of a Homerid. When I read to a small company a few Romaic songs from my Passow Collection, one of my hearers declared that they were not complete, and he brought me a man who added long interpolations — probably the Arachobite version of the same legends. Thus one is led to think that fragments of some Homeric epic may still be floating about on Parnassus, without any Homer as yet to smelt them through the furnace of poetic genius into one poem.

The popular song is of varied theme — of war, of brigandage, of fierce Palicaris; often of love, too, and even death and Charon. The voice of the singers has no great modulation; it is rhythmical rather, like Greek music generally, which really has no tune Herein there is a correspondence to the instruments already mentioned; but the true chorus is here, forming a union of voice, dance, poesy, varied with the flute or caramousa, and blending all into movement of body. Still the rude beginning, you will say, of those intricate harmonies which the lyrist developed anciently, and which a genuine Greek genius might still do to a certain extent, in spite of the rhyme, which belongs to modern Romaic song, and in spite of the accent, which probably existed alongside of quantity in the Greek metrical system of antiquity.

We see an internal conflict going on in Greece between the old and the new, which may be stated as the conflict between Europeanism and Hellenism. The moment the Greek becomes educated, he becomes European and is then chiefly imitation. The ancient Hellenic foundations are still lying in his very village, but he does not think of building upon them. That wonderful development of the primordial Greek germ into Greek Art, Poetry, Philosophy and into Greek political institutions, is not taking place; the educational energies of its people are absorbed in acquiring the culture of Western Europe. I do not affirm that this state of things can be avoided, nor that it is even to be regretted.

But in spite of the strong tendency to the new civilization of the West, there is a mighty conservative influence — it is the peasant, who still seems to be possessed of the instincts, not merely of his Greek, but also of his Pelasgic ancestors. It will be a long time before he is fully absorbed into the stream; these customs of his, driven to remote districts in the mountains where the brooks are always fresh and clear, will remain in their prescribed small channels, insignificant yet undefiled. In such places lived the last adherents of the old worship, the pagans so called, that is, the rude inhabitants of remote rural cantons. Indestructible as the mountains which protect them, seem these primitive seeds of Aryan beliefs and customs. Even Semitic Christianism has hardly been able to do more than gloss them over in their most retired strongholds. The ancient sanctuary of some divinity is now the shrine of a saint; the ancient festivals of the Gods have been changed to holidays of the church; the modern chapel is often built upon the foundations of an old temple; thus modern Greece, with superficial mutations, is still spiritually ancient Greece. Our

Arachoba, lying high up on the slope of Parnassus, seems to have suffered the least alteration; it is an ever fresh well-head of antiquity gushing forth on the side of the mountain. Hence to me it signifies the title already given: the modern center of ancient Hellenism.

Such are the twin worlds, the Old and the New, which the traveler will find at Arachoba, different, yet for the most part in perfect unison. Both he will dwell in joyously, and be attuned to both; indeed the marvel is that he cannot live in the one without living at the same time in the other. Here is the present with its throbbing life, full of healthy energy, limpid as a Parnassian brook. Yet it is of the aforetime, it has its source in the old fabled age, in the poetic world even before Homer. This feeling of twofoldness is given out of every thing here spontaneously, and with scarce a note of discord. The Old in the New we have noticed all along our pathway, sometimes with effort possibly; but now the one is the other, blent together in imagination and in feeling, not showing except by rigid search even a faint line of separation. Vision also begins to be double, as man himself is twofold, yet in harmony. If the view turns to an object of Nature, one instinctively sees what it hints; if it be some spiritual thing, it takes on of itself the form of Nature. Yet both are blended into a perfect unity, any division means violent tearing asunder of living members: meaning and form are one organism. The eye deepens into the spirit, while it remains eye, yet the spirit stays not with itself and broods alone over its unfathomable self, but seeks the eye and the outer world. Vision is a new thing on Parnassus, with a new virtue — once it sought but appearances, or beheld but its own phantasms; in it now the outer and inner meet in mutual concord and without disparagement to either.

To this double vision which at present possesses the soul, there will be added the third element, that of feeling. We have noticed how the image of sense has always the thought underneath, shooting through it rays of light, filling it with meaning; to these two, thought and image, will be joined the emotion, which makes both quiver like heart pressed to heart. Be it joy, or be it sorrow, it completes the man, making him musical too, because entire. Such is the trilogy of poetry: a thought, an image, a feeling, all distinct to a degree, yet all in one, and saying the same thing. But now the trilogy of poetry is realized, it becomes the trilogy of existence.

In such manner the Parnassian life rises to a universal significance. Two worlds should every human being possess in his own right, very diverse yet harmoniously interwoven at every needle-point. The one is that of common life, of prose, of practical activity — a necessary sphere, which makes itself felt by its very gravity. But the other is the ideal realm, which brings a solution to the conflicts of real life and takes away its grossness. Also it gives us the breath of freedom once more, freedom from the restraints, ceremonies, and conventionalities of ordinary existence. Poetry is indeed the world of freedom, it must break loose somewhere from the serfdom of prosaic life. Its wildness, its audacity, often its wickedness is but the protest of freedom, the desperate singlehanded sally of the ideal soul against a universe of beleaguering Prose.

Truly unhappy is the man who has not two worlds. Let him flee, if need be, to an idyllic life, and there build anew some refuge for the straightened heart. Such is one remedy, old as poetry, yet very insufficient for our modern time. Let him flee to Religion, also an ideal world, and for many good natures an efficacious remedy. Religion, however, has the tendency to throw its paradise into the past, and its heaven into the future; its ideal world always has been, or will be, never is. Strangely neglectful of the eternal Now is Religion inclined to be; it would be all-efficacious, could it fill itself with an everlasting Real Presence of the Divine. You and I must have our Ideal World now, if ever; this very moment must be raised out of Time into Eternity; and we say with grim desperation to our puzzled Priest who would fain give us help: We sigh not for the Past, we seek not for the Future — Now or Never is ours, by the Gods!

Thus our Ideal World makes man eternal, eternally

young; already we have noticed the buoyant youthfulness of old age on these Parnassian slopes. The spirit remains as fresh as the dew of the morning, being filled with an eternal Now. Ideally there is no growing old, springtime endures forever. Bad enough is it to see an old man old, yet it is tenfold worse to see a young man old, as is so often the case in these wearing days. But to preserve youth is not the prime object of the longing soul; youth is only the fresh ruddy image of endless duration, free from the cadaverous paleness of Time. To live truly the Now is not merely the prophecy, but the fulfillment of immortality. Lift up this temporal moment into the Ideal World and hold it there, and you have not simply proven, you have realized the life immortal: such is indeed its only proof. *Solvitur vivendo*.

Of all the bards who have said their sacred word to the human race, old Homer has the readiest faith in an Ideal World; he dwells in it, sports with it, is in earnest with it, smiles and weeps in it; the truth is, he cannot stay out of it but with an effort. The terrestrial struggle on the plains of Troy he wearies of, and must take his flight to Olympus; or if the case is desperate, he brings his Gods down into the combat among men. Two worlds he has, the Earthly or lower one, and the Olympian or upper one, intermingling, reflecting one another; such is the book he has transmitted, such assuredly was his life. He cannot tread on the ground without touching the heavens; all Nature becomes in him a divine reflection; even the acts of men, the products of human agency, belong not to this reality, but are terrestrial images stamped with the Gods. More than any other poet does he live in intimacy with the Ideal World; such, too, is his supreme lesson: he teaches us to lift our existence into an ideal realm, just as he elevates the struggles of men below into Olympus.

Thus sang the old bard, giving us to-day his divine nourishment, showing the two worlds of man, as none other since has done. But it is said, this scheme belongs not to us, our modern life is practical, material, that is the end of it. Still even we must be fed through the Unseen, through what is above us, which after all is some form of that Homeric Upper World. Not an easy undertaking will it be to transform turbid, roaring Mississippi into a clear Greek stream; a little pellucid Greek brook purling down the side of Parnassus it will never be. But even the Mississippi has something more than its terrestrial stream; through upper regions it must in some way flow back to its fountain head, else it would never flow below; that ideal current above is necessary to it also, according to the declaration of science herself. Even its vast waters would flow out, and the river run dry, were it not replenished from heavenly sources, from its ideal counterpart in the clouds, sending down its terrestrial stream.

Fabulous, too, that old Homeric world is called, a mere fiction spun from the imagination of the Poet. Fabulous it must be granted to be, and this is just its enduring value. Fable is truer than History; Fable is a Whole, including both the Upper and Lower Worlds; History is but a Half, embracing only the Lower one, and mostly but a fragment of that. Still to the prosaic Understanding how does it sound to say that Fable is truer than History? Quite the same as if one should declare that a lie is truer than the truth. Yet the realm of Truth is the Upper World, where it is reached by the Mythus; while below is the realm of the Senses, not to be despised I say, but whose whole end and purpose is to be stamped with the beautiful impress of what is above.

It is said that the Olympians have become the sport of the ages, mere playthings which amuse the children of leisure, toys not to be seriously regarded by the busy, earnest man. Such is the prosaic view of the old Gods; and indeed they have this side of sportfulness, which indicates the joyous serenity of their existence. But in their sport they image the Divine, with ease and joy they are the highest; in their play they are most earnest; in the world they are masters of the world, its Gods.

But on Parnassus one will not seek to be a philosopher; causes and consequences are not his pursuit. He feels the unity of the within and the without, he will not separate them in reflection. There is such a happy balance between heaven and earth, between Nature and Spirit, that he cannot disturb it; evil, indeed all deep disruption of soul has fled from the world. In this happy balance one will keep; no more pain, no more sin, no more philosophy, no more self-trituration of any kind. The senses and the soul rest in fond embrace; nought is there but harmony, that harmony between the inner and outer world called joy; man's existence is one of its delicious notes slowly dying away like sweet music in the distance.

Still you must not think that there are no jarring contrasts in the life here; but even harsh discords are strangely resolved into harmony. Here comes the fool who will be found on Parnassus as elsewhere in the world. I meet him going into the Olives, for he too gathers the fruit and presses out the stores of oil. He talks to himself, as he trips along; nobody pays any attention to him. He often bursts out into a hearty laugh among the Olives, such is the helpless joy of the fool. His existence is all to himself, but it is a merry one, a Parnassian one, though a fool's. He cannot share with others his delight, he is cut off from mankind by unreason, for it is reason alone which unites man to man, and makes each a participant of the other's life; but this fool has his own world, impenetrable, closed by triple walls of adamant. Still he laughs and talks and is merry, so much we see; but we cannot share his soul, or comprehend it, hence he is a fool — a miscarried human spirit, though it still strangely preserves its Parnassian birth-right of joy, when reason has sunk out of its being.

Passing up from the fountain where the bare nymphs seem to be sporting round the banks of the stream or wading mid its pellucid waters, you will be thinking of ancient statuary and its significance, which now begins to be felt in your existence. In some quiet nook you will meet Praxiteles, the sculptor, and you will eagerly inquire: How comes it, O Praxiteles, that thou hast made so many naked figures; therein I cannot fully reconcile myself to thy artistic endeavor. Was there any modesty, any morality in those old ages? Was there any religion?

For I confess, the nude nymph or the nude goddess is to me not altogether a holy object. Nor can I yet feel myself in harmony with the old games and gymnastic exercises revealing the undraped forms of contestants; and I have noticed often that the Greek, civilized but naked, contrasts himself proudly with the barbarian, uncivilized but clothed.

Whereat the old Artist answered tartly, with words echoing through the Olives: O thou religious man, thy deity made thy body, thy tailor made thy clothes; whose handiwork is the worthier, more beautiful, more to be revered, thy tailor's or thy God's? Thou would'st hide the divine work for shame; better it were to hide thy clothes, if thou art truly modest, as innocence is modest. The body is immoral, thou sayest; why dost thou carry it with thee all the time, cloaking thy immorality under garments, O self-confessed hypocrite? Abolish thy body as vice, like an honest man acting from conviction; then thou wilt find the outcome of thy morality to be self-destruction; man, to be good, must not be at all. O prudish, prurient soul, what has thy world gained by its fig-leaf but innumerable milliners' and tailors' bills?

But we Greeks, — continued he with voice melodiously growing tender — love the sweet body, such as Nature made and Art perfected; we rejoice to see it trained to all its capabilities, to behold it masterful in all movements — in the race, in the palæstra, in the battle. We like to see its deed elevated to ideal perfection and made eternal in marble; then it is the supreme of created things, is an everlasting triumph over matter; it is truly the manifestation of the Godlike upon earth to the vision of men. Such is its highest power: a continual utterance of triumph over all obstacles — a God.

It is not probable that any one of us will become as good a Greek as Praxiteles; nor is it necessary. Still we may throw ourselves back into his view, and live with it sympathetically. Manifestly he does not employ the sensuous body for its own sake, but for the purpose of expressing the Divine. He scorns to use it merely for tickling pleasure, but through it he will reach the soul.

The nude shape he chisels out of the rock but transfigures it into a God. He has two worlds, like Homer, the Upper and Lower; the statue stands below, but its spirit is above; to the Lower World belongs the naked figure which the gross eye beholds, but to true vision it rises transformed to the Upper World, whither it carries the beholder who therein becomes a worshiper. Thus the old sculptor, like Homer, helps us elevate our existence into an ideal realm, through the images of the Gods.

The faculty of double vision is the best, indeed the only true Parnassian gift; it beholds in the appearance what is substance; without doing violence to Nature it transmutes her into Spirit; in the new it feels the soul of the old. Such is the discipline of the traveler at the present moment, living in this mountain town of rural Greece; he is compelled to dwell in the Two Worlds, and to find his chief delight and occupation in their harmony. This relation between the upper and lower realms of existence may seem a mystery, possibly an intentional mystification; but here it is real, in fact it is the one overmastering reality. It may be unintelligible to hard-headed Prose; some minds seem unable, or it were better to say, unwilling to penetrate the truth of the matter. But to unfold the relation and harmony between the Upper and Lower Worlds has been in one way or other the attempt of all Literature worthy of the name. To speak the connecting word between the two is the superhuman struggle of the Poet; if he succeeds, then he has given something to his race, he has welded together the mighty dualism of the universe.

But the Poet's word grows dim by Time, his dialect becomes unfamiliar, and what is a greater hindrance, his consciousness passes away from his people. His gold therefore must be burnished anew, in fact it must be cast into the melting-pot, and coined over again into the current coinage of the period. Hence his interpreter arises with a clear duty; he too is to speak the connecting word everywhere, between the Old and the New, between the old Poet and the new Reader, in fine between the Upper and Lower Worlds. He is the true critic in Literature who breaks through the sensuous form and unfolds the spiritual element in the written word; he is the true Priest in Religion who helps us transform our life into an image of the Eternal in the Temporal. Both are interpreters and have a common realm: to show this outer reality to be a semblance revealing the inner spirit; both are to speak the connecting word which harmoniously joins the Lower and Upper Worlds.

But upon Parnassus to-day these two Worlds lie blended in a most musical feeling of unity. The one is so easily the other that we need no Interpreter; the third person placing himself between them breaks the melody, and becomes an intruder. There is the feeling of immediate oneness which can not brook the dissection of thought; it is that of a supreme work of art, transparent, raying its soul directly into the soul. Nor shall we allow any further intrusion into this intimate union, or any disturbance of this happy harmony, into which the twofoldness of man is melodiously transfigured, of which he longs to share as of his divine essence, and to which he seeks to elevate himself by many ways — by ecstasy, by poetic vision, by worship, by thought.

XVII. POLITICAL PARNASSUS.

Arachoba is just now in the midst of a hot political contest over the election of Demarch. True to their ancient instincts, the Greeks of opposing political parties cannot live together without fighting one another; in fact if there were no supreme authority outside of the town, I believe that the successful party would banish the unsuccessful one, and confiscate the property of its members. But each community is not autonomous now as of old; there is a central power of the State which keeps it in restraint. In no respect does the ancient political character of the Greek manifest itself more plainly than in these elections; the possibilities of those terrible massacres at Kerkyra and Argos are felt still; indeed, Arachoba furnishes at present many an excellent comment on Thucydides.

It was Sunday, and your traveler was sitting by the fire engaged in conversation about distant things, when an acquaintance rushed in breathless and announced that a fight had occurred on the market-place, confessed that his party had been driven off and compelled to take to their houses, and that he himself was one of the fugitives. I hurried out to see this new phase of Greek affairs, and was passing down to the market place, when a man ordered me and all others to leave the street and go home. Loukas, who met me, said that it was the Superior Judge, that he had the right to give such commands and that we must obey. There was still wild excitement, men were talking violently, women were rushing anxiously through the crowd looking for their husbands; imperfect obedience was rendered to the Judge on the part of all, myself included. But the fighting was over for that day, and the campaign had fairly opened in its first contest.

These struggles usually take place on Sunday after church. It is curious to observe persons uniting in the same worship, performing the same genuflections, making the same crosses over breast and forehead, and singing the service in the same dreary whine through the nose, and then an hour afterwards to see these very same persons trying to mash one another's noses as if not whining enough already.

The peasants are all collected in the village on Sunday, for there are no dwellings in the country; thus they are open to the fermentation of contact and to mutual friction. We think again of old Greek Aristotle, who defines man to be a political animal; such is still the modern Greek — particularly the animal. But assuredly his American brother will not be able to cast a stone at him, without the same stone's coming back and inflicting a greater bruise upon himself.

These fights I heard humorously termed *agones Olumpikoi* — Olympic contests. There was no little pride in them as exhibitions of prowess. The palicari is still unwilling to let his principle rest inactive without giving a blow for it; indeed he sometimes likes to give the blow without any principle. So, it is said, the old Greeks did at Olympia, they fought one another for mere sport; the same is true of us modern Greeks; we like to fight so well that, when we cannot get a chance at the Turk, we take a bout at one another.

The great issue at present is, then, who shall be the next Demarch? The opposing parties have set up two candidates, whose magnificent names are, Pappayohannes and Pappakosta. The principle at stake is not at all easy to fathom; it has a very remote connection with national politics; a little closer bond it has with some local issues — a clean market-place and clean streets were two of the things which were sometimes mentioned, and which predisposed the impartial stranger somewhat in favor of the party out of power. But the vital governing principle seems to lie in the fact, that the Demarch controls the appointments to about twenty little offices in his district. Pappayohannes is the present incumbent and candidate for re-election, of course; he has been compelled to set aside one hundred and twenty applicants, all of whom are now violent supporters of his opponent Pappakosta.

The wineshop, where the traveler will loiter among the people, blazes up in the hottest political discussion. There I meet Odysseus, that is Ulysses — a middle-aged bachelor, who has never found his Penelope, he says. A satirical rogue, at no moment wanting in banter which is tipped with a sarcastic sting; he has therewith a kind of squint-eyed chuckle; full of curiosity he is, too, about other nations. I seldom fail to find him in the wineshop, where he and I have formed a decided attachment. Whenever any thing of a new or exciting character occurs, Odysseus is always at my side with the question: *Einai tetoia eis ten patrida sas?* Are there such things in your country? — Thus the study of Comparative Politics, especially the Politics of Greece and America, seems just now to be his delight.

A loud supporter of Pappakosta enters, who had been an equally loud supporter of Pappayohannes at the last election. But he has changed sides; it is whispered that Pappayohannes failed to give him the position of Kerux or Town Crier, after having promised to do so. Now it is declared that Pappakosta will give him the appointment, and that the wily office-seeker this time has extorted the promise in writing. But it is wonderful how keen is the vision of this man toward the shortcomings of the present administration. Says he: Look at our filthy streets, a donkey can hardly get through them in muddy weather; incompetent officials burden the town; the public revenue is squandered; we have no road with the rest of the world. Elect Pappakosta and all these things will be rectified; then we shall have clean streets, paved roads, honest and capable officials. Hurrah for Pappakosta! — But you have changed; how is that? — Yes, he replied, I have changed. As for that traitor and demagogue, Pappayohannes, I elected him once, but he has turned out so badly that I am compelled to go against him this time; the public welfare demands it. — Such was the disappointed place-seeker at Arachoba, whose words seemed to have a familiar note, but were followed by sharp contradiction from friends of the incumbent, and the wineshop resounded with angry disputation. In the meantime Odysseus appeared at my elbow and asked with squint-eyed leer: Have you such things in your country? — What, men who change for an office? — Yes, Odysseus; there are such things in my country.

The women, though they have no vote, play a peculiar and important part in the canvass; they rush in and drag out their husbands when engaged in the combat. Herein they show a courage and strength which astonishes the stranger and makes him at first believe them to be angels of peace and mercy. Yet the women are the most violent politicians in Arachoba, as they are elsewhere in the world; they break off friendly relations with the neighbors of the opposite party; savage altercation between them takes place on the street, and at the pool, where many come together on washing-day, they fight and fight desperately, all for those glorious names, Pappayohannes and Pappakosta. White Parnassian robes become soiled in the dirt, soft blue eyes change to balls of shooting flame; golden-glancing tresses, reminding the traveler of fair-haired Helen, become sadly disheveled or are plucked out by handfuls and strown over the ground. Still, they will not allow their husbands and brothers to fight; if there is any fighting to be done, they are going to do it themselves.

The second Sunday the party of Pappayohannes, which had been defeated on the previous Sunday, determined not to be left in the lurch again, but to take every precaution for winning the day. Accordingly, just after church, the agora and the street which leads to it were filled with his partisans, who there surged to and fro, yelling for their candidate and defying Pappakosta. The house of the Demarch is on this street, and after many calls he appeared at a window, and made a speech in which he counseled peace and good order, with the advice that they retire to their homes. The crowd answered with approving yells, but with still greater disorder; it refused to disperse, but continued to vociferate and call for another speech from Pappayohannes. A second time he came to the window and counseled them all to go home and keep the peace. Bravo, hurrah for Pappayohannes, our next Demarch, they all shouted unanimously, but failed to stir from the spot, or to check in the least the unruly Greek member.

Bosh, said one of the opposite party standing at my side, this advice is mere sham; Pappayohannes himself is stirring up all the confusion through his strikers and secret agents. See that tall fellow yonder gesticulating in the midst of the crowd, I know him to be a paid partisan.

It is certain that the multitude kept increasing rather than diminishing, and kept growing louder, instead of getting quiet in accordance with the counsel of the Demarch. Nor did the Judge appear, as on the former occasion, and order the people home. The narrow street presented a variegated appearance; it was full of fustanellas and fezes, waves of white with crests of red. Old balconies hung over the street from the second story; these were filled with spectators. Outside the crowd, from the end of each alley converging into the market-place, women looked on, not without anxiety, ready to play their part in the approaching conflict. Thus the multitude surged and roared and hissed, calling for another speech and more advice from Pappayohannes. A man from the crowd touched my elbow; it was Odysseus with his satirical leer, and with insatiable thirst for a knowledge of Comparative Politics, asking me: *Echete tetoia eis ten patrida sas?* — Have you such things in your country? — Yes, Odysseus, there are such things in my country.

After an hour or so the adherents of Pappakosta appeared in force, and took up position at the lower end of the market-place. They built a narrow platform out of tables; on this platform two palicaris mounted and sang a song celebrating the glories of their candidate Pappakosta; by its quality, it must have been chiefly extemporaneous. They whirled and yelled and sang, accompanied by a heavy chorus of male voices massed around their platform; the recinato, too, put in appearance, and the drinking began. Merry Greeks they were, and always growing merrier; one of the singers poured wine upon the head of the other, as if they desired to be soaked outside as well as inside. This was indeed a sin against Bacchus — a profanation, thus to waste that precious juice of Arachoba, said to be the best in Greece. The God will punish you to-day for your contempt of his gift — such is the prophecy of the indignant stranger.

But the men of the other party are not idle. They erect a similar stand on the opposite side of the narrow street in front of a wineshop, where they go through with similar extravagances. The song in praise of Pappakosta they try to drown with cheers for Pappayohannes; then they strike up a lay of their own; thus the Muses still sing in rivalry on the slope of Parnassus, with incessant burden of these two far-sounding names, Pappayohannes, Pappakosta, Pappayohannes, Pappakosta. In this way the singers pass the time, under the inspiration of the Sisters and the Wine God, dancing on the table, rhapsodizing in rude verse, with good humor on the surface at least — an incessant bubbling from boundless seas of wild whimsicality. Nor must we forget the peaceful note; a shepherd has his pipe and seems to be lulling himself with its soft sounds amid all the din; with admiration I looked at him sitting there in the sunshine not far from the platform, enticing pastoral notes from his reed, and wholly absorbed in its simple tones, without paying any attention to the noise around him. He seemed to be dreaming that he was alone with his flock on the sunny hills.

Thus the traveler lounges about, observing; a lively Greek notices him among the crowd, and hands him a beaker of wine, saying: Here is to the success of Pappayohannes. But another rushes up with a cup of the same precious drops and invites: Drink with me to the health of Pappakosta. I answered: To Hades with both of your Pappas, I don't understand your politics; but I will drink both your cups with this toast — Long live Hellas; and I wish each of you to join me. They did so, grasping my hand; they were good Greeks, remembering that they had a country above party, if only reminded of the fact. So the three men emptied the four cups.

Thus for several hours I watched the human waves there, observing the endless bubbles rising out of those capricious waters, and then bursting into vacuity. At first I tried to count them, and mark them carefully, to see if they had some law of their own; but one gets tired of bubbles though they reflect all the colors of the rainbow. It was a wild riot of fancies, an unweeded garden of luxuriant oddities. Finally I grew weary of the play, concluding that there would be no Olympic contest that day, but only a farcical battle of animal spirits. I started home, but scarcely had I passed into an upper street, when I saw the group of women who stood at a distance, looking down to the market-place in great commotion, and beginning to rush for the scene of action. No pleasing sight were those anxious faces; mothers and sisters of the men below were there, but mainly wives with little children clinging to their skirts, with babes at the breast and yet unborn. A cry of anguish — and then a mother would clasp her infants and hurry off; it was enough to curse any election.

As I turned around and looked after a number of these women darting by, there was the following view: chairs were flying through the air, tables were broken into clubs, stones were hurled at random, and some forty or fifty neighbors were kicking, gouging, pounding one another with mutual zeal and edification. The Olympic contest has then opened at last; I hasten toward the spot, but the narrow street which leads to the market-place is choked up with spectators, and there is no Judge to send them home. Following a woman, I take another way far around, and have to ascend a hill to reach the place of combat. But here comes a mass of men and women rushing down the steep descent, with stones flying after them, and shouting, Run, run for life. I retreated a short distance with them, borne by the torrent I might say, but I am afraid that it was a clear case of panic. I soon turned about, however, no enemy pursuing, and went up boldly into the midst of the fight — a little to one side perhaps.

Stones and tiles were on the wing, somewhat; long knives were drawn and slashed about, wounding only the innocent air, as far as I saw; everybody was doing terribly, yet nothing terrible was done. "Leave here, leave here, O stranger," said one excited Greek who came rushing up to me with a stone in one hand and a knife in the other — which words of his were not intended as threats, but only as a friendly admonition. I laughed at him, and jested at his excitement, when he went away to meet the foe. The schoolmaster also warned me, beckoning to me from the distant window of a wineshop, the doors of which were locked to all save friends. His was the defeated party to-day, and he had been compelled to take to cover. But it was manifest that there was no great danger to anybody, least of all to me. Not a man there would touch a stranger, I knew; a stray stone might not be so considerate, but that would be an accident. So I stayed and saw the struggle ended, for it is not every day that one can see an Olympic contest on the soil of Greece itself. Two or three men with bloody heads are led off by their wives or friends; other combatants suddenly disappear; one palicari, the grand protagonist of the day, with long knife drawn, and with vengeance in his look, pursues the last retreating foe down an alley out of sight; the field is won, victory for Pappayohannes. The enemies had all fled to their homes or had secreted themselves; the market-place was in the possession of one party, with hurrahs and great jollification. Gunpowder, which had hitherto kept wholly out of the fight, now enters merely for noise, an old blunderbuss is touched off, and the Parnassian dells re-echo with detonations which must have put all the Muses to flight. Again the crowd shouts for a speech from the victorious Pappayohannes, who a third time comes to the window, counseling peace, and good order, and less noise. Odysseus, too, was there, participating in the general jubilation, for he was a partisan of Pappayohannes; with a squint-eyed chuckle he twitched my arm, shouting: Glorious victory, the day is ours; have you such things in your country? — Yes, Odysseus, there are such things in my country.

The crowd now began to disperse, it was getting dark, the combat was over for one week, and quiet rapidly settled down upon the market-place with the rising stars. The result of the battle, as I learned, was about as follows: three or four gashes, five or six bruises, two or three hundred cases of hoarseness. One irate woman was reported to have thrown from her door or balcony some water not very hot upon an approaching foe; she took this way of defending her husband and her party. All accounts agreed, that there were no serious wounds. The most painful that I saw was inflicted by a woman, who summarily led off a full-grown man by the ear, he in the mean time squirming and crying with bitter tears. I went over the field of conflict before going home; the platform had disappeared, shreds of fustanellas and torn caps lay around; but what touched my heart with sorrow was to see the fragments of the shepherd's pipe, the sweet pipe of peace, lying there on the stones where the shepherd had sat not long before, wooing its dulcet notes; the shepherd had disappeared, and the soft-tuned reed had manifestly been broken in the mad conflict of the day. Such was the outcome of the idyllic strain on Parnassus to-day.

As I was going to my quarters, I met a group of maidens dressed in their white garments with red apron and sash, in a back street overlooking the market-place. Evidently for the benefit of the stranger, they began a sham fight in mockery of the one which they had just seen fought by the men. They pretended to throw stones and to strike one another, shouting and leaping about with much banter and sport. It went off very well, till a big girl pushed over a plucky little red apron; down fell the snow-white gown into the dust with a broad sprawl, and was sadly soiled, quite ready for the wash to-morrow. The knee of the unfortunate maiden must have been slightly bruised too, one may modestly venture to think, by the way she rubbed it. But plucky little Red-apron was soon up and ready for an aggressive onset; this put a phase of earnestness into the contest, which threatened to bring the resemblance into complete reality, to elevate the counterfeit into the genuine article itself. But the whole matter happily went no further than loud mutual volleys of words.

At this juncture a man with a long venerable beard came along — one of the elders of the town — and thus addressed the company: Shame on you Arachobites and Arachobitzas! How will you appear before the world! Do you not see that there is a stranger here who is going to write a book about us, and scatter our names over the whole earth? He is a scribe, I have often seen him taking notes on the wayside and in the Olives; he will be sure to give an account of this day to his people; the Franks will think that we are still barbarians, no better than the Turks. How will the treaty of Berlin ever be fulfilled if he should write a book in which these reports about

Arachoba are published? Let us now behave ourselves.

At this time the news of the Treaty with Berlin, with all its hopes and new problems had permeated the remotest corner of Greece, and stirred the heart of the Greek people to its very bottom. Even the unlettered peasant rolled the strange word through his lips awkwardly, yet reverently, as if it were a prayer that would bring about the unity of the whole Hellenic race. But one thing I did not disturb; I left the old man with all his exaggerated notion about the importance of my book. I knew that never again could it by any possibility receive such a world-embracing compliment.

In the course of the evening I visited the houses of the leaders of both political parties. In the one there was joy and untold effervescence; a grand reception of the victorious heroes of the day was held; they continued to drop in, till a large company of men were assembled, talking, gesticulating, laughing, with many an anecdote of the triumphant day, and with many a taunt over the defeated foe. It was a veritable war-dance of the big chieftains; all the details of the fight were fought over again, in speech, action, and animated gesture.

The climax was reached when the hero of the day appeared — the grand protagonist, whom we saw chasing the last man from the field of battle. Proudly he entered, still bare-armed, with torn shirt dangling at the sleeves, but triumphant, with the laurels of victory invisibly wreathing his brow. He was greeted as he came in with a shout of triumph; he began to describe the event, and in the description of his own glories, he grew so excited that he again drew his dagger and slashed his enemies by the dozen, skipping about the room till he became more dangerous to his friends than he had ever been to his foes. Odysseus, too, was there, jubilating, throwing sarcasms upon the beaten party amid the merry crowd; feeling some one touch my elbow, I looked about and saw those inevitable eyes with the inevitable question: Have you such things in your country? — Yes, O Odysseus, very similar things we have in our country.

Through the darkness I sought my way to another

house where one of the leaders of the defeated party lived, with whom I was on friendly terms. Alas, alas! what a melancholy change! A number of chieftains were assembled there too, but they sat around in gloom; there was no light in the house save the pale flicker sent from the coals in the hearth, which made the white costumes look like a row of sheeted ghosts. Not a word those men uttered, not a sign of life they gave, but sat there in monumental silence. I wished to retire at once, begging pardon for my intrusion, as I thought that I was the cause of all this reticence; but I was detained by friendly assurances that there was no intrusion on my part, nor any secret deliberation on their part. It was the gravest, most tomb-like body of men that I saw in Greece — a very cemetery in the night. Where now is the Greek joy which once swayed so gayly Parnassus?

Soon from one of those sepulchral shapes a voice broke forth into bitter speech; it accused some of its party of cowardice, others of treason; reproaches of all kinds followed, with that most insulting taunt of being no true Palicari. The silent chamber of what seemed white monuments, was at once filled with a stunning confusion of voices; each pale ghost began to move violently in every limb; re-crimination pursued crimination, till a second Olympic combat appeared imminent. But the storm passed, and the happy Greek temperament broke into sunshine out of its clouds, at the suggestion of one of its leaders: "Next Sunday we shall whip them; let us prepare now." Hope at once arched the sky with her rainbow, each man smote his thigh vehemently, with a shout of applause, and they all adjourned to the next room for consultation, the question being, How shall we wallop our neighbors next Sunday after going to church with them, and take care not to get walloped ourselves?

I heard citizens repeatedly express their disapproval of these disorders; the Demarch himself implied in his speech, you will recollect, that he disapproved of them, when he advised the people to go home. As already said, political enemies charged the Demarch with being at the bottom of the disturbance; it was his method of conducting an election, they declared. What stranger can disentangle the truth? The real cause, however, lies deep in the spirit of the people; the latter are proud of their prowess and love of fight. True Greeks they are, delighting in Olympic contests, and determined to fight one another, if they can not fight the barbarian.

But this is not the end of the conflict. The next day, Monday, is wash day; early in the morning all the fountains of Arachoba are surrounded by a busy multitude of women, and by huge winrows of soiled garments. The white file continues to issue from every alley and by-path of the town, each woman bears her batlet and tub, often too a kettle for boiling the clothes; thus the squadrons gather with stout determined tread, and evidently mean business. That restless Greek tongue can not, of course, be restrained; usually it is the last wedding or the last betrothal which forms the staple of their talk, often with tinges of gossip more malicious. But to-day the new topic comes up first — the approaching election, and above all, the combat of yesterday.

At one of these places a servant belonging to the household of a leader of the Pappakostites met a woman of the faith of Pappayohannes, who was exulting in the victory of the preceding day, and triumphed defiantly over the bloody heads of her enemies. This was too much, there followed bitter words and then blows, or rather a tearing of clothes and hair. Other women ran up and took sides, and the combat became general. One wife with her distaff stood there spinning; this distaff is a long stick, which she brought down heavily upon the back of a sister. This sister was not without a weapon at hand; she picked up a wet garment which she was about to wring out, and flung it with water and all upon her opponent, who in her turn, the distaff now being broken, raised an immense Homeric stone (such as not two men of this generation could lift), but she did not throw it, and indeed was unable to throw it straight, but hurled a mighty epithet instead.

The combat continued to become more intricate. The large bat used for pounding the wash was raised by a sturdy

Amazonian arm; this caused an utter flight of all the enemy, when the bat fell harmless to the ground. The combatants, however, returned once more, they punched one another a little, pulled hair, and flung wet garments. But the distaff was the favorite weapon on Parnassus, as the broomstick is in this country; still the war was mainly one of words, all spoken in holy Greek, right under the seat of the sacred Nine.

Not the least curious to the spectator will be the names which he will hear interspersed among the blows of the conflict. Clytemnestra fights Penelope; the latter has still her ancient distaff, though she puts it to a use unknown in the Odyssey; Euphrosyne, that joyful name of one of the Graces, you will see engaged in the unpoetical act of upsetting the washed folds of one of her sisters, not a Grace, and dragging them in the dust. Look now at the white-flowing robes of the Parnassian chorus which were to appear next Sunday; with sorrow one beholds them, changed almost to weeds of mourning. Eurydike is here, having returned from ancient Hades to modern Greece, full of life, a beautiful maiden, blue-eyed, golden-haired still; nor can I, beholding her, wonder at Orpheus, who was so filled with the desire of possessing her that he descended to the Lower Regions with his lyre, and sought by music to restore her to the Upper World. Finally laughter-loving Aphrodite appears on the battle-field, not loving the laugh to-day but stern combat; bare-footed even, she runs along the stony highway, in angry pursuit of another Goddess, whose name is unknown, but whom we may call Here; thus to-day on Parnassus is repeated that ancient Homeric contest which was once kindled between the two Goddesses on Olympus. In this way, too, the old still manifests itself in the new.

There are at least a dozen of these washing places in Arachoba; at all of them were bickerings on that Monday; at several of them were scuffles, at one a pitched battle — bloodless, but not hairless. Sunday has to be fought over again; the victory, lost by the men, must be redeemed by the women of the defeated party. But the strange thing is, that the women will rush in and drag their husbands and brothers out of the struggle; so we must infer that if there is any fighting to be done, they are going to do it themselves.

Rumors of these various conflicts at the pools, soon flew to the men assembled in the market-place; party was forgotten, and loud was the merriment among the jolly Greeks. Partisans of Pappayohannes and of Pappakosta, who were trying yesterday to crack one another's skulls, adjourned together to the wineshop, and united in a universal guffaw over the Aristophanic battle of the women. Mark the roll of names: Plato was there in baggy breeches, Plutarch was there in white folds and red fez, heroic Achilles was present — indeed, is eternally present in Greece. With these heathens were many saints — Athanasius, Spiridion, my friend Loukas the Didaskali, or Saint Luke; emperors, too, lent their presence, Basilius, Constantinus. But the true monarch of the company was Odysseus, an inveterate misogynist, a man who had never found his Penelope, and who had a sort of crabbed humor in consequence of his failure to find her. He was now in his element, and began acting the feminine conflict; he grasped my staff and used it as the distaff in the fight; he mocked the language and attitude of the leading female combatants. The hilarity overflowed the wineshop into the very street where the passers roared; the threatened tragedy has turned not merely into a comedy, but into an acted comedy; to-day there will be no fight in Arachoba; the political collision has received a comic solution, Pappayohannes and Pappakosta are united in one brotherhood of laughter. Odysseus is the victor, the grand peace-maker; after he had exhausted himself, again I felt his touch upon my elbow, I saw the triumphant but squint-eyed leer, and heard the old question: Have you such things in your country?— No, Odysseus, we have not; the world possesses but one Odysseus, and he is in Arachoba.

Such was the lively whirl of local politics in the thrifty village of Arachoba; one might think its people were lost to all national interest in the narrow circle of their own neighborhood. But there were deeper currents which needed only a good opportunity to rise to the surface. The Greek is a politician still, local as well as universal; his political relations start with the little affairs of his own town; but they rise in natural gradation to the profoundest and most abiding struggle in History,—that between the East and the West,—whose bearers are at present the Turk and the Greek.

While I was at Arachoba word came that the Austrian and German embassadors at the court of Greece, with the British and Italian Secretaries of Legation, would pay a visit to the town. These gentlemen were making a rapid tour of inspection through the inland parts of Greece, combining some secret business probably, with momentary glances at the antiquities still remaining, and at the people. They had arrived at Delphi on their way back to Athens, and had spent there some hours in viewing the ruins of Delphic magnificence. Great was the expectation and curiosity of the Arachobites at the unusual visit; yet for no small portion of the citizens it would be attended with one decided pang. Pappayohannes, as Demarch and official head of the town, would reap the honors of entertaining such high guests. As candidate for re-election he was bound to make the reception a brilliant affair.

On the evening before their arrival the shrill-voiced herald, like that one of Agamemnon, was heard going round the town announcing the great event to take place on the morrow, with the request that the Arachobites should turn out and do honor to the distinguished visitors. But not a few of the town's-people resolved at once to go to their work in the fields, and not stick a new feather in the political cap of Pappayohannes. But the maidens who belonged to the party of Pappakosta, caused the chief difficulty; they determined not to dance with their political enemies at the grand reception. So there would be no chorus — the chief attraction of a visit to Arachoba. As the day turned out a fine day for labor, many of the men and women of the town were seen early in the morning hastening to the Olives and vineyards.

Still quite a number of people remained behind, and it

was announced that the visitors would arrive in the afternoon from Delphi. Not long after dinner the caramousa and drum resounded through the streets, followed by a small procession of patriotic villagers, who, after parading a little while and gathering up those who were still in town, marched out to the western entrance, there to await the approach of the guests. The schoolmaster and myself hastened out of the house to see the spectacle; as the line filed past our abode we dropped into ranks and went with the procession. The band was wisely dismissed by the Demarch, as soon as it had performed this service, for that music in European ears might have spoiled the reception and endangered the election of the Demarch. The embassadors might have continued their journey after hearing it, for it was not hard to mistake the music as the preluding strains of another sort of reception.

As usual there was a long delay, and much impatience was expressed at the visitors for their failure to appear on time. Groups of people dotted the hill-side, or were perched on protruding rocks; the pleasantest view was always the red and white bevy of maids in the distance. But the select company were gathered in the road at the entrance. The elders of the town were there: some had fought in the Greek Revolution, some had been present at the famous battle here or not far from here; others recollected the grand reception given to King Otho in his youth when he passed through this region; it was a day of fond old memories. The Judge who had ordered me home on that Sunday of Olympic contest was present; I had the honor of an introduction, when I mentioned the fact that I had seen him before, but he did not seem to remember me. Finally the little fat Demarch Pappayohannes was present, everywhere darting through the crowd, puffing, big with something which I afterward found out to be a speech; a fussy man, but capable and public spirited.

But the man who shone that day with a peculiar splendor was the Capitanos, thus familiarly called by the people. An aged son of Mars, yet full of fire and youthful energy with a springy step; he had fought in the War of

Greek Independence, and afterwards had served in the body-guard of King Otho, who conferred upon him the Order of the Savior. The badge of this order he now wore; he had also put on his old Greek uniform, tinseled and bedizened with barbaric splendor, yet dim with the dust of time. At his side dangled an antique sword, or rather scimetar, which he would draw and shake at the boys when they were noisy or came too near the road along which the grand cavalcade was to pass. He sprang through the company, fiercely looking around, ready to pounce upon the enemy, if that enemy were only there.

It was indeed a great day for the Capitanos. He fought his battles over again, and with that crooked scimetar of his he whisked off thousands of Turkish heads, to the intense delight of the assembled Greeks. Particularly he loved to give his version of the battle of Arachoba, when the Greeks under their chieftain Karaiskakis did actually capture some 5,000 Turks not far from the town, and at once proceeded to sever head from body. Then the monument that they raised was described by the Capitanos — a new kind of trophy, a pyramid of Turkish heads hewn off and piled up as high as Parnassus. The Capitanos pointed out the spot: there they were all heaped together. "How many?" "Pollas myriadas — many myriads," said the Capitanos.

But the chief event of that battle, as it comes from the mouths of the people, was the divine appearance of St. George, patron Saint of Arachoba. The mighty dragon-slayer was now needed to slay a new dragon spitting fire and death from these mountains; earnest was the prayer for his coming, and of a sudden he sprang out of the air in person to help his people in the hour of their affliction. There he was most certainly, in the midst of the fight, mounted on a white charger of enormous size, with shield raised and lance poised, quite as we behold him in the picture of the combat with the old dragon whose place is now taken by the Turk, also veritable dragon. Hundreds of eyes saw him skewering Turkish bodies on that lance and flinging them one after another high into the air, like sheaves of wheat from the pitchfork of the strong-boned agriculturist. In such manner the Saint went through that army; there lay the foe scattered all over the slopes of Parnassus; but when his work was done he suddenly disappeared. To-day the new Cathedral stands yonder in the upper town of Arachoba, overlooking our group; it is just about to be finished, having been built in commemoration of the divine event, on a spot connected, I believe, in some way with the great epiphany of the Saint.

So the good people of Arachoba believed and narrate in pious exaltation, not however without a little skeptical shaking of the head on the part of the illuminated. Even a Papas has been known to hint that it is probably a "symbol." " Do you believe it?" I was asked. "Certainly I do; St. George fought along with you, and of it there are many evidences. Far otherwise had been the story, if he had not fought for you and with you on that and other days. There would have been no free Greece, no flourishing Arachoba; there would have been no Capitanos here to-day to tell us the story. There are some days during that war on which he did not fight in your ranks; they read differently; hence I believe that he was with you."

Suddenly at this point we were interrupted with the shout: Here they come, here they come! Not far away a small cavalcade was seen emerging from one of the folds of the mountain side; it consisted of some ten or twelve persons mounted on mules and donkeys, with drivers afoot. The crowd hastened to the brow of the hill to witness the grand approach, and the legend of St. George dropped at once into utter oblivion; the women and maids rose up along the slopes, showing their Arachobite costume to the best advantage. Thus several hundred people were picturesquely grouped at various points within easy sweep of the eye.

The road from Delphi winds along the side of the mountain, clasping it close like a girdle; for a long distance it can be seen swaying up and down, through the depressions and over the ridges. The cavalcade seemed to ride like a vessel over the billows of the sea, as it sank into the little dells and rose out of them again. It was seen by the people at their work far above on the mountain and far below; soon they began to quit their toil, one by one, and find their way into the nearest path leading to the main road, by which they hastened to the town. After all, they could not stay away on such an important occasion for the sake of political partisanship. Some deeper interest throbbed in their bosoms than a village election.

The guests arrive and dismount, headed by the German embassador, while the little Demarch is pushing through the crowd to meet them and to receive them in the name of the town, full of perspiration and his big speech. Here occurred an interference of which I was the unwilling instrument. I was standing on the outer rim of the multitude which had gathered around, and I was doing my share of staring, when some one shouted, *Kyrie Zene, empros*, Mr. Stranger, forward. I think that it was Loukas who started that shout, let him be confounded, the mischievous schoolmaster. At once the cry was taken up by the crowd with looks all turned toward me, though I waved my hand in dissent. Two strong palicaris grasped me, each one holding an arm, and hustled me forward to the center of the group; there I was in the presence of the German embassador, to whom I addressed a salutation, to which he gave a friendly response, and we began to converse.

But this incident had entirely interrupted the course of the reception. The Demarch had not made his speech, upon which possibly was staked the success of his election. The little man elbowed his way through the bystanders, and with triple rows of sweat-beads upon his forehead said to me: two words, two words, O friend. I at once slunk back out of the crowd, ashamed of having been the means of disturbing the order of the ceremonies. Of course I was innocent, but I am in some doubt concerning those who started the shout.

It is true that there was not a man, woman or child in all Arachoba who did not know me, nay, who did not know much more of me than I knew of myself. I passed for a Professor in the Great Columbian University of

America to which the University of Athens was a mere drop in the ocean, which had 400,000 students or so, and covered a territory half as large as the whole of Greece. Though I always tried to stick to my honest title, that of *Didaskali*, or Schoolmaster, I never could get anybody to address me otherwise than as *Kathegetes*, or Professor, somewhat as it is in my own country. It was also taken for granted apparently that I could speak the native tongue of the embassadors; so the people thought that I should be the spokesman of their town, in which I had now resided for nearly three weeks, with many an evidence of delight. Such was probably the motive of this strange, but friendly outburst of theirs.

Still I have a lurking doubt that with two or three persons the affair was premeditated; I suspect that they intended to play one of their shrewd Greek tricks, making me the instrument of confounding the arrangements of Pappayohannes and possibly of jostling him out of his place at the reception. That would be a good political point and make a theme for many a jest against an opponent. Certain it is that the adherents of Pappakosta seemed to have had the chief hand in the matter. The whole thing is insignificant except as giving a slight touch of Greek political cunning and partisanship.

Still the reception was a success, a great success; the Demarch was equal to the occasion, and his speech was, I thought, admirable in every way, in feeling, style, delivery, but above all, in the fact that it was a true utterance of his people at that moment, an expression of their strongest aspiration. It was of course in Greek, and ran about as follows: "Honored Guests, Representatives of the Great Powers of Europe; it gives me great pleasure to welcome you to the town of Arachoba, a town not unknown in the annals of Greek independence. We make no claim to the refined civilization of Western Europe, but you will find us a simple and honest peasantry whose hearts beat warm for the welfare of our fatherland. It is our boast that we still possess many of those peculiarities which belonged to the old Greeks, whose works you study and admire so much. For they were our ancestors — there can be no doubt of it, though some have tried to deprive us of that honor. But we can make good the claim; look around you, and you can not help seeing evidences on every side. We, their children, pray that you will not forget us; recollect that off here in a a small corner of Europe the descendants of that people to whom Europe may be fairly said to owe its civilization are now living in poverty and weakness, and, besides, are deprived of their just rights. They are longing once more to rise into a new life, to be again a great Hellenic people. The ancient example still spurs us on by its eternal presence, for even in our town you will notice many a reminder of antiquity, indeed of old Homer himself. We pray that you will not deem it improper if we tell you the fervent hope of our hearts, and call to your minds the debt which you owe our fathers.

Greece now needs the help of Western Europe in acquiring a portion — it is but a small portion — of her just territory. The treaty of Berlin has acknowledged the claim, and adopted it as one of the provisions of Europe's peaceful settlement; but the Turk perfidiously refuses to fulfill his promise, and will continue to refuse till he be compelled by you. We ask your sympathy, for we well know how much you can do for us; we pray for your aid as Greeks who have transmitted to you the beginnings of culture and have always stood as Europe's barrier against the deluge from the Orient. We are also your fellow Christians; many of our countrymen have still to groan under the barbarian's yoke. By the ties of civilization, of religion, of humanity, we ask you to help us. By the feeling of nationality which you cherish most deeply within your bosoms, we beg you to aid us to rise to a nation. Arachoba is ready to show its hospitality to you, yet I would not have you go away without having heard her prayer, nay the prayer of all Greece, and of the whole Hellenic race."

At the conclusion of the speech, the people broke forth into rapturous applause; even the Pappakostites, of whom many had come from the fields, pronounced it excellent, being carried away by their enthusiasm for a united Hellas. Political discord disappeared in the common Hellenic note struck by the Demarch; in repeated cheers its vibrations were heard echoing over the billowy slope of Parnassus. They all then felt they had a country above their party, a principle higher than clannish allegiance; hateful partisanship everywhere dissolved for the time into the harmony of soul-uniting patriotism. Such is the true solution of those Olympic combats upon the market-place — they have vanished, at the sound of the golden word, into that higher unity which makes all Greek souls one throbbing aspiration.

A worthy speech, a genuine expression of the people's heart, proving the Demarch to be no mere village politician, but a man of Pan-Hellenic patriotism: such is the comment which the sympathetic stranger, not an embassador, will make. But it was utterly blank to the embassadorial intelligence, for that did not understand Greek, probably did not want to understand it. At the termination of the speech, the interpreter of the embassy dispatched the whole of it in two or three broken sentences of German, which the embassadors received with a truly diplomatic politeness and secretiveness. I do not blame them, it was probably the only part they could play, being without emotion, without any ideal, without color in their conduct, selling their political souls to Satan in the service of the home government. Personally I liked them, they were gentlemen, but I detest the system.

Such, however, was the volcanic question which suddenly burst up red-hot on that day from Mount Parnassus — in substance still that oldest question of Greece: Orient against Occident. Little Greece is seeking again to liberate and unite the Hellenic race; to redeem it from the barbarian is her prayer now as of old. There, too, she stands a bulwark against the Oriental man to-day as in the Persian War of Xerxes, ready even to make hostile reprisals on Asiatic soil as in the still more ancient Trojan War. Not now with a strong right arm do the Greeks stand there, it is true, but with something perdurably tougher — their spirit, their faith, their religion. Bodily they have submitted and are weak, but spiritually they are still as unyielding as were the old Marathonian soldiers. Thus the spiritual rampart remains yet, behind which Europe has lain and still lies in security — to be sure, not without some fighting on her part. No dragonading, no tyranny, no bribery has ever made the Greeks lapse to Mahommedanism, or other Oriental forms of spirit; through untold suffering they still remain firm — the adamantine wall which keeps out the Orient. Powerful Occident, so long protected behind that bulwark, both spiritually and physically, Greece now asks to disenthrall her politically — asks with fervent petition, but without much hope.

It is a consideration which must outweigh all others in the present question; this Greek spiritual realm the Turk has never been able to conquer. It is a barrier which he can not surmount, it stands before him high as heaven; he has assailed it with a rough, barbarous hand, has enslaved it, tortured it; but destroyed or absorbed it he has not, and can not. The salvation of Europe — one may certainly affirm, her security has been this Greek spiritual toughness; Turkey has always had to march West with the indigestible Greek stone in her stomach; with that unassimilated the Turk has never been able to make any lasting conquest in the Occident.

Still as of old the Greek looks across the sea toward the East in sullen defiance; here on Parnassus to-day the trump of war will draw every peasant from his hamlet, will nerve his heart to a supreme degree of energy and endurance for the Great Cause whose burden he has borne since the beginning of History. As you see him muster on the mountains, and train through the villages, you will feel that it is still the old Marathonian spirit, and you will think what a destiny has been laid upon him, the poor peasant — a destiny greater than that of his nation, the destiny of a new world. In the valleys the Greek may have become degenerate, in the cities, corrupt; but seek him in his mountain fastnesses, and you will find the same ring as of old in his actions, and the same instinctive readiness to take his place in the ranks, and do duty in the vanguard of Western civilization against the barbarous hordes of the East.

XVIII. RAMBLES OVER PARNASSUS.

You, my friends, as citizens of a free commonwealth have an interest in politics; I am certain you would like to hear how the election resulted. It seems that the opposition, reinforced by vast promises and by disappointed place-hunters, carried the day against our friend Pappayohannes; but the paved roads have not been made, nor has the market-place been even swept. Though there has been a complete change of administration, there has been no change in the condition of the streets, but for the worse; in fact Arachoba is said to be almost impassable at this moment on account of the mud in the thoroughfares.

It is also stated that the number of applicants for the offices has just doubled; and Pappakosta, the new Demarch, is still wrestling with this problem — how to divide twenty places among two hundred and forty persons, and to give each a place. But the saddest lot befell the applicant for the position of town-crier, whom you will recollect to have changed sides so patriotically; in spite of the written promise given him by the new Demarch, in spite of all his political work, he did not get the place. Unhappy man! Now he is reported to have changed again, having returned to the fold of Pappayohannes, ready for a new election, with a still sharper eye for the evils of the present administration. My letter from an Arachobite friend recounting these matters, concludes with an animated apostrophe: "O ye office-seeking Greeks! why work so hard for a dishonest penny when an honest one can be gained for a tithe of the effort! Why so true to falsehood, so faithful to treachery! they can never reward you even in money for your labor, not to speak of your lost manhood, lost in such filthy work! Yet if you merely prostituted yourselves, it were endurable, though bad enough; but you are poisoning the life-blood of the nation; you pervert the State, which is man's chief instrument in raising himself to a universal life, to your own individual purposes of gain and ambition, making it as selfish as yourselves. O ye office-seeking Greeks, you will yet ruin our beloved Hellas."

But we have quite forgotten the embassadors whom we left some time ago right in the middle of the street, unprovided with food and shelter. A serious breach of etiquette toward those high dignitaries; clearly ceremony is not the strong point of our traveler. But let us hasten back to them, still standing amid the applause of the people, who cheer the Demarch's speech, till the sound seems to crawl up the sides of snowy Parnassus to the very peak. The large company, piloted by the Demarch, soon started to make the tour of the town afoot in order to see the few curiosities and to enjoy the picturesque views from the heights. After the strangers, who marched at the head, stretched a long straggling crowd of white fustanellas, like the tail to a comet. I followed, too, somewhere in the tail, a spectator; but again friends caught my arm and said: "Go forward." "Why should I go forward?" "To talk to the embassadors." "But they have an interpreter who speaks Greek better than I." "Never mind, we wish you to tell them about us and about Greece." Such was the urgent demand coming from the people there, I may say; I took it as a call to represent them to the foreigners, and at once I obeyed. But why they wanted me to be their interpreter, they did not say, nor can I tell, unless it was the very strong interest which I had shown for their life and manners during my stay of several weeks. They must have felt that I would not treat them unsympathetically, nor misrepresent them, nor be put down with a sneer. Accordingly I went forward, worked into the conversation, and told the embassadorial party what I knew of Arachoba somewhat as you hear me tell it now.

"What do you find here to keep you so long, here where there are no antiquities?" asked the German embassador. I replied: "The two most splendid and perfect monuments of the ancient world — the Greek language and Greek customs. Both are fragments almost complete, of the old stock, yet both are alive still and green; neither can be adequately obtained from books, but only by living contact. Ruins they may be called, but Italy and Europe cannot match them; nor can they be carried away from this soil and set up in museums. The truth is I am engaged in a sort of excavation, not of death and ruins, but of life and manners."

The origin of the modern Greek, too, came up for discussion in which I maintained the Greek origin of the Greeks, at least of these of Arachoba. The honest dealing of those sturdy people I praised; their sincere yet poetic life I tried to describe. I recollect that the embassadors never took sides, neither affirmed nor denied what I said, never changed their impassive color; every one of them seemed to be waiting for orders from the home government. I sought to point out certain Homeric customs still common in Arachoba; the blank faces appeared to answer me: Upon that point we have no instructions from our ministry. One thing I did admire in them — it was the stoical perfection with which they could endure being bored. World destroying dullness, star-sparkling vivacity were, I should judge, quite the same to the embassadorial mind; and why should they not be to men who get their souls sent by mail from the home government? Their indifference did not disturb me much; the thought darted through my head to touch them with a political theme, which was very near to me and to my Arachobite constituency: namely, the attitude of the European powers toward Hellenic-unity. I was saved from this last impropriety by the Demarch who came in, announcing: Dinner is ready. At once the stark embassadorial countenance changed, lighting up with the rise of the new suns, and saying with great brilliancy: Upon this point we have instructions from the home government. They disappeared through the door of the dining-room, at a run, that was the last I saw of the embassadors; and the chief thing about them still remaining in the memory is, the embassadorial cut of the coat-tail.

It was one of the curious episodes of my European journey — I reflected after I went home that evening —

that just here in the rural town of Arachoba I should meet the first embassador, and be brought into personal relation with diplomatic gentlemen. I had passed through capitols full of such people, but I had avoided all courts and all ceremonies, for witnessing which some diplomatic intervention is necessary. No minister of my own country had I met, not even a consul. Now at a town out of the way and inaccessible to a vehicle, where few strangers are ever seen, these diplomatic dignitaries had come to me, and I was present for the first time at a kind of reception. Thus what one studiously avoids comes upon him in places where least expected — as if chance loved once in a while to indulge in an ironical jest. The modern History of Europe leaves an odious impression of diplomats and diplomacy upon the mind of the reader, who will be inclined to shun the thing in all of its manifestations.

Nor can I avoid interweaving some discordant reflections upon the American Diplomatic Service in Europe. The whole system ought to be abolished, and the business of the Legation, like any other business, be put into the hands of a competent agent. Anybody can now travel from one end of Europe to the other without recourse to an American official; I never found any use for my passport even. The minister at present serves chiefly for the introduction of American women at court, for which there seems to be as yet no urgent international necessity. Still the pressure must be something awful, if we may judge by certain cases known to travelers, in which the American colony of a European city has been turned upside down to get the girl of the period, daughter of the haberdasher almighty, presented to royalty. Let us abolish the whole business; it is an old-world bauble with which we have nothing to do.

Diplomacy does not belong to America nor is it an American need; it is a child of European necessities. For Europe is an intimate family of nations with contiguous territory; each of these nations may find it worth while to have a representative always present at the capitols of the other nations, in order to promote domestic harmony and prevent domestic quarrels; thus it is a domestic arrangement purely. Just as it was necessary for Europe at one time and may be still, just so unnecessary it is for us. Did America have anything to say at the Berlin conference? Nothing — and justly so, she does not belong to the family, and had no business with the quarrel. Nor does the minister attend to any really important transaction at present, he cannot be entrusted with it. Witness the Geneva negotiation; we sent a special agent to look after that affair, as we must do in all such cases, if the work is to be properly done. Doubtless the minister is given something to do abroad, but often it had better be left undone, and always the special agent will do it better. The truth is, in our system confederation of states has taken the place of diplomacy; and in any system the unity and brotherhood of nations ought to be elevated into law, and not subjected to the caprices of the diplomatic weather-cock.

But if the effect abroad be nothing or positively bad, the effect at home is much worse, it corrupts the whole elective system. Foreign appointments have fallen to the nature of political bribes, with which the successful President rewards his supporters. Politicians, having become intolerable in their own community are sent off for a time, to be forgotten at home, but to disgrace their country abroad. Recently distinguished literary merit has been rewarded with diplomatic appointments — just the thing to which it has never been trained, and for which it is specially disqualified. A good poet is not likely to be a good diplomat; but he is not a disgrace, and that is a gain. Recall the ministers resident, give us competent consular agents to do the business, the best legal talent for the international questions, and abolish the Diplomatic Service with its senseless aping after things European. Much has Europe to give us, but this thing belongs to her exclusively.

Yet Diplomacy is clearly doomed in Europe too. It is a very unsatisfactory way of securing the unity which belongs to the European Powers. A faint recognition of the oneness of Europe lies in the fact of Diplomacy, but altogether too faint for the spirit of the age. Its heartlessness, its treachery, its infernal system of lying, its injustice have made it hateful to honest men at all times, but now its inadequacy is the most serious ground for complaint. This international life must be raised out of the realm of caprice, and secretion and deception, into the clear open day of law with its universality; in other words it must be made institutional in the highest sense of the term. For an international spirit has arisen and demands full recognition and an organization — distinct from, yet not hostile to, but complementary of the national life. In that spirit man lives with his age and not alone with his nationality, he leads a universal life.

Diplomacy is thus superannuated, it hangs together with standing armies, national jealousies, war. There must be an organized Europe, a United Nations of Europe as there is a United States of America, with supreme authority, and an independent existence outside and above its several members. This is not to destroy nationality but to preserve it, to assert the primary principle of the nation to be the right to its own individual life. This should be the first article of that higher European Constitution: no Nation shall be destroyed. Such a consciousness once universal in the people, and realized adequately in institutions, dispenses with armies, with wars, with diplomacy — it solves the European Problem of the present. But think of old Blood and Iron taking my advice or any advice: so lie on and fight on till the time be ripe.

Upon Parnassus one may have the privilege of dreaming of such a European confederacy, and of Greece being a member of the same. Then there might be some fair adjustment of her claims based upon a recognition of the Hellenic people, as a member of the European family. Recognition is the divinest attribute of the soul — recognition that thy neighbor is what thou art. It is the foundation of all that is true in man, of all that is right in the world, of all that is holy in heaven, for God is the supreme recognizer. If a people could see that a wrong done to another people is a wrong to itself, if an individual could see that an unjust act to the neighbor is the worst injustice to himself, this would indeed be a new-created world. The only true life for the State as well as for the man is the universal one, springing from recognition, from that insight which banishes all selfish limitation, and by which one beholds true self-hood not in himself alone but also in his neighbor. Such recognition, realized in an institution, will yet give the Federation of Europe.

I am well aware that the practical statesman, as he delights to call himself, has far other standards of conduct. Thus he will speak, always laying the emphasis upon his practicality: "You pedagogues, professors, pedants, avaunt with your dreams of old Greece! Go stick your noses into your Homer and Plato, there indulge your fancies; don't come around us practical men with your visionary sentimentality begotten of your reading in the ancient classics. Are we to abandon our interests in the Levant on account of your admiration for Sophocles? Statesmanship is a practical science, it has nothing to do with your fine theories concerning national rights; as to your rhapsody about recognition, I don't understand it, I don't believe there is such a thing." Let the man alone, he is building his own hell-fire, only through it can he and his class be purified and prepared for the better world.

But we shall now take our leave of diplomats and diplomacy; on the whole it is a discordant theme in this region, but it forced itself upon our attention, sending its dissonant thrill through Parnassus. Arachoba settles down to its customary life, resuming its songs and its task; an industrious town, one will say, yet not feverish with over-work, not always desperately clutching for gain. Politics arouses the people at times, but the atmosphere is one of golden tranquillity, a repose even in effort, a happy moderation both in toil and in rest. Here reigns that harmony between the inner and outer world called joy.

My friend, the schoolmaster, has often invited me to cross over Parnassus to the towns on the northern side of the mountain; something worthy of being seen is there, he affirms. Accordingly with gun on his shoulders he starts out taking me along; he hopes to fetch home a hare or pheasant, though his choice of all game would be a Turk. Yet he is one of the gentlest of men, a believer in universal peace, after the next war with Turkey is done. For several hours we toil over ridges and through defiles; strong mountainous scenery shuts us in on every side, yet utterly desolate. Some feeling of terror there is here, nature speaks with the voice of a Titan, that voice is certainly felt, if not heard. The mythus will seek to give expression to this feeling; the need of such an utterance can still be strongly experienced by a walk among these towering shapes; no scientific knowledge of geological formations and causes can possibly take the place of that primitive voice of the mountains.

The schoolmaster tells me of the supernatural powers which are still thought by the people to dwell here. He called them Nereids, who, however, no longer stay in the sea, but haunt the mountains, with a particular fondness for caves. The Korykian Cave near one of the summits which we passed is their favorite resort, whence they strike the children in the village. One will see the Arachobite mother dressing her baby, and throwing on its little shirt some powder which will keep these wicked sprites at a distance; cases having been known in which according to popular legend, infants have been snatched up by them and carried off to the mountains. Thus the modern Nereid has made a wonderful change of position; having risen from the depths of the sea, she has perched herself on the top of Parnassus.

We begin to descend the other side of the range, and reach a small town which still lies high up in the mountains; this my friend tells me, is his summer residence during vacation; while the hot season lasts many people come from the plain below and reside in this cool little nest among the rocks. It is a pleasant spot, with fountains, fruit trees, mills, cascades; but it doubtless possesses the capacity to become wearisome. We visited several citizens, among others the schoolmaster of the place, who is in luck, having just brought a young bride into his house. Fortunate schoolmaster! Could he but teach his own success in such matters, what a school would he not soon bring together in that lofty Parnassian village from the ends of the earth! We went to another notability of the place, the wife of a shepherd. A strange husband she has; if he comes home and stays in a house, he gets sick; so he sleeps under the stars among his sheep, leaving his wife and children to live under a roof in the village. In such manner we pass from house to house, everywhere enjoying hospitable welcome, with bread, cheese, and roast lamb, floated by rivulets of recinato gurgling on all sides.

To-day is again a festival; caramousa and drum have already begun to send up their notes from the choral place, whereat everybody shows some uneasiness in the feet. Thither, accordingly, we all adjourn; on our way we come upon dances led by the song, and composed wholly of women, both the young and the grey-haired. Years seem not to make people old here, and life is a continued festival, with some work-days thrown in for the sake of variety. A new set of songs one will notice, too, yet with the old theme which remains ever new — Love; then other elements of Greek life play in — the brigand, the papas, the Turkish dog which they all would like to eat alive. Strange to say, I heard the love affair of Margherita sung by Parnassian maids, who accompanied their song with a dance, which must have stirred up the ghost of Father Goethe.

The chorus is quite the same here as at Arachoba and need not be again described. But the traveler must make honorable mention of a youth, the king of dancers, who performed a great many new variations to the delight of the assembled multitude. How he leaped and whirled and plunged and shook himself! The most surprising movements he went through, extemporaneously it was evident; the folds of fustanella surged around his body like troubled waves crested with sea-foam. At a certain crisis he kicked off his red moccasins and danced in his bare feet. He sat down exhausted finally, with a look of disappointment in his face, probably because he had not succeeded in leaping out of his own skin.

The costumes produce no such effect as at Arachoba; nor are the women so handsome. The acquaintance at my elbow gives the reason: the women in these parts have to work in the plain during the summer, when they become tanned by the sun, and often diseased with malaria; while the Arachobite women labor out of doors during the winter only, and when summer comes, are occupied with in-door work, particularly with weaving. Still the speaker thought with the same opportunity, his townswomen would be more beautiful than the Arachobitzas, wherein he revealed a slight touch of jealousy. Thus that Greek resident sought to claim beauty as native to his town; though he probably would not make an expedition for it, as his ancestors did, across the sea to Troy.

As I stood looking at the chorus, a man touched my arm, and thrust into my face, when I turned towards him, an enormous wolf-skin stretched on a pole, crying, Pentari, pentari. The skin came from an animal which he had killed somewhere on Parnassus; this mountain is still infested with wolves which often in cold weather descend upon the flocks. When any one kills a beast of that kind, he fetches the skin to the village, and exhibits it fastened upon a pole like a banner; with it he goes around at the time of some festival where the people are assembled, and is entitled to a small contribution from the inhabitants on account of the general benefit conferred by killing the monster. The pedestrian will not feel himself exempt from this small tax, for that same wolf, running at large might have fed on him during his solitary rambles over the mountains. Wild boars are still reported to be on Parnassus, lineal descendants of that one which wounded Ulysses, and produced the most famous of all scars known in legend or history, the scar of recognition in the Odyssey.

Yet another scene. Suddenly a man darts through the crowd having a drawn knife, and brandishing it with angry shouts; the chorus breaks up, all the men rush to a common centre, women huddle to one side affrighted. It is manifest that this is no part of the dance — what, then, is the matter? It turned out to be an old grudge between two shepherds on account of a she-goat. The young fellow, a hot-head, flamed up seeing his adversary dance with so much joy at the festival; he drew his knife and rushed forward, but friends stepped between, and held him, though he tugged stoutly to be released. Still I cannot think that the youth's thoughts were very bloody; there was too much display in his attempt, he too plainly sought to be stopped. If you wish to kill your man, step up quietly to him and run your knife into him; if you wish to be stopped, make a terrible ado. So I gave to the young shepherd the credit of considerable theatrical talent; the dramatic muse of Parnassus still imparts her gift to the humblest dwellers on her mountain.

The chorus commences anew, but we start for ancient Lilæa, or rather for the modern town built near it and situated at the foot of the mountain. Scenery is varied and at times approaches grandeur; there are deep gorges and high precipices; a few vineyards hang on the slopes, wherever they can find a little soil; herds one will pass through. The shepherdess carries her household slung across her back, in a kind of bag, with a little head peeping out, sometimes two. Most beautiful is the atmosphere, perfectly transparent, yet with a golden haze resting on the distant hills. Every look at them becomes a tender poem; but the passage over the road, horrent with sharp-pointed rocks thrusting themselves out of the mountain at you, is the dreadfulest prose. The mule winds about through them as if they were a nest of vipers rearing their heads from the earth and hissing; a straight path through them is impossible. Such is the horrible discord under our feet, but distance reduces it to the sweetest harmony, for yonder soft blue hill-top is said to be as prickly as our present way.

The Greeks, with me, seem to have little appreciation of this landscape, yet it would be a great mistake to think that it produces no influence upon them. It is a kind of education; its result comes out in the way of poetic temperament, in the way of costume and of manners. Direct admiration of scenery you will not notice, but this Nature certainly attunes the heart to a musical idyllic existence. The expression of it, therefore, is not in words, but in life — altogether the best expression. For the love of scenery is to a certain extent artificial, or at least the product of an artificial society seeking with effort to get a fresh breath of Nature; that effort is too often perceptible, and causes a jar in certain glowing descriptions.

Still the modern love of scenery is genuine; what is the ground of it? It is a reaction against Law; everywhere in civilized life Nature is chained down by Law, and made subservient to the uses of men. Let us see her free again in her own spontaneous outpourings; — so we go to the country, to the hills. Civilization makes Nature a slave, Natural Science forges the chain. The Great Mother loses her volition in the cities; we wish to see her acting of her own accord; this has given rise to a literature which undertakes to describe Nature in her freedom. It is a true field for the writer, but there is the danger of a florid extravagance, and the still greater danger of sentimentality. Science has disenchanted Nature of her poetry; we seek to recover this poetry by sentiment, which is a true thing, but is liable to gush into the sentimental, which is an untrue thing.

To us Nature is not alive as it was to the old Greeks; it is now a sort of a stage; we call it appearance, scenery, that is, stagery, some pageant gotten up by a mechanical contrivance for the amusement of the spectators. Such are too often the descriptions of Nature in the Novel, in the book of Travels; artificiality, often affectation, makes them anything but refreshing. The forms of Mythology which represented Nature to the Greek, have also become stagery; Pan and the Nymphs are often as affected as Nature herself. Now what is the matter? It is clear that these forms must, in all true Art, represent the spiritual; if they are filled with that, they remain eternally fresh and young; if they lose it, they become a kind of theatrical machinery introduced externally for mere effect, they become stagery. Nature has a soul in all her manifestations; he who can catch that faint efflorescence of the spiritual in a landscape, and transmit it in words or by color, is the Artist. But he who can give her merely outward forms without at the same time imaging what is within, may be a good mechanic in words and colors, but his work is and must remain soulless; Artist we cannot name him.

Two new classes of Artists we moderns have called into being, and in whom we have a right to rejoice: landscape-painters and landscape-poets. Far otherwise is the attitude of the simple-hearted pastoral man toward Nature; he cannot say to himself: "Come let us admire this scene, then let us give a description of it." He elevates the natural appearance into the mythus; the tree even becomes a divine object with a God in it, still more the mountain and the running stream. Every physical object changes into the expression of the spiritual, indeed of the divine; thus all Nature is transfigured under his vision, and he himself is no longer this natural man simply, but becomes a mythopœic being, filled with the whispers of the Muse, who is singing perpetually of these wonders around him; he becomes a mythus himself.

But we have already reached the town at the foot of the mountain: here, too, rises the sound of music and song — it is another chorus. Four or five villages appear in view; also from these in different directions the same sound of festivity can be heard, marked by the low dull thud of the drum. Truly all Parnassus has become vocal to-day with melody, rude but genuine; we can scarcely utter the literal fact that the mountain is the seat of song without rising into the mythus. In some such way that old designation of Parnassus arose, which, once the simple expression of truth, has now become a fable.

From the inhabited village we pass to the ruins; here lies the old Homeric town which contributed its contingent to the Trojan War, as duly noted by the Poet; it, too, could throb with fierce ardor for the recovery of Helen; the traveler will tingle with delight as he looks on the walls which held such a people, will be kindled anew by their example. Is there not a common bond between him and them — the old dwellers of this spot three thousand years ago? So he feels, so you may feel; a brotherhood of aspiration it is, very different is its outer manifestation, but one in soul. Not much is recorded of the town in Gceek history; it lay off here in its quiet nook, enjoying its songs and its tranquil existence; but that single fact is enough to preserve it forever; many a city far richer, far more active and populous, will vanish into nameless dust, but this little spot, marked by the headwaters of Kephissus, will never lose its name; all because it marched forth valiantly for the recovery of Helen. Something eternal there seems to be in that action.

Two sets of walls will be noticed at a superficial glance. The one, inclosing a small conical hill, is the wall of the acropolis — massive, cyclopean, piled up to endure forever. This was, doubtless, the Homeric town, girded with those heavy stone blocks; the sacred part, which must be most strongly built on account of its divine duty — hence it is preserved almost complete to-day. For these huge stones were brought together with untold labor, not to protect the man, but the God, guardian of the people. Something adamantine in these Homeric towns; their fame and their stones endure together; indeed, the cyclopean wall has many a touch of a line of Homer; strong, simple, most sincerely built, and of a primitive grandeur.

But the other wall, which is of considerable extent, and includes a part of a high hill is of later date, doubtless of various later dates, if we may judge by the difference in the masonry. It speaks of a large, prosperous city; of manifold calamities; even of a decaying false civilization; for portions of this wall indicate pretentious flimsiness, tell a falsehood quite like a human tongue.

Let us then turn away from it and notice this hill-side, where the ancient theater doubtless was; seats are still visible in the undulations of the ground, though they are covered with earth. Fragments of stone, wrought parts of some column still lie in the soil, quite in the same spot where the pitiless barbarian left them after toppling them down, one imagines. People, too, one will put here, in the mind's eye; if stone suffered such ruin, what must flesh have endured? Read it in the pieces, in the broken pillar, in the fallen temple. Flesh indeed is the bearer of the same spirit as stone; both are smitten by the same blow, quite in the same fashion, when the thing they represent must be gotten out of the world.

Passing beyond the two walls of ancient Lilæa, one of which we see to be adamantine truth, the other of which we feel to be something less than truth, shading itself down into absolute falsehood, we strike into another strong and true thing, namely, an old road paved with large thick stones, evidently once used for wheeled vehicles. It is a strange appearance; no such road is to be found now in all this region; even the macadamized Great Road which we left long ago, contrasts unfavorably with this stout enduring way, still marked with creases from ancient usage. Let us follow such a road, for we have faith that it will conduct us to some spot worth visiting.

The way leads to a little temple which overlooks the golden grain-fields of the valley; mark its delightful position; build it up anew from its ruins, then walk among its columns, glancing across to the sunny hills opposite: such a view is an act of worship. A few steps further will bring you to an immense spring which gushes up from the earth and is at once a river, roaring at midday like a bull, said the old traveler. Here is another small temple or chapel, built over the fountain, or very near it, sacred to the nymph, we may suppose. A piece of a marble pillar lies in the bed of the stream, with end jutting out of the ooze above the surface of the waters which gurgle around it caressingly as if rejoicing that it is still their own. In the fountain, indeed, is an utterance of ancient faith, a worship of the blessing which leaps forth to sunlight out of the dark earth; this faith has built the temple. On a slight elevation beyond the fountain is another ruin, more extensive and better preserved; it is claimed by some to have been the temple of Demeter, Goddess of the harvest, she who smiled specially upon this plain. To her the Lilæans reaping their grain gave thanks; it did not come of itself, there was a divine power in it worthy of adoration.

Thus at some distance from the town must have stood a group of temples sending gleams from white column and pediment far over the valley in a joyous serenity; Greek temples clustered together with a sort of mutual delight, recognizing each other's beauty, all reposing on the hill-side in the sun. To-day we seek to restore them to their ancient completeness, and to find out what they spake over this valley to all its dwellers; we also try to call back the worshipers, in festal procession moving up the paved Sacred Way to this consecrated spot, asking them: With what in your hearts do ye come thither to these shrines, O people? An answer is given, but hard to render again in words; somehow in this manner it runs: "Look across the sun-filled vale, and blend in thy soul its two qualities, a calm repose, yet a joyful exaltation; turn about and glance up to Parnassus; lofty he towers above, yet amid all his elevation, he shows a restful supremacy, like a deity above the struggles of the world." Such is the hint felt to-day in the situation, by the stranger; felt so deeply by the old Greek that he embodied it into a God, and gave to the same his adoration; and the image of the divinity wrought piously by the hand of the ancient artist, sought to reveal just this ideal culmination, and raise to the same height the soul of the worshiper, blending repose and ·exaltation.

Such are the ruins of Lilæa which must have been once a large, wealthy city, with abundance derived from this plain, very fertile and well-watered, said to be ten miles across, on the average. Now it is malarious, not drained to any extent, and but partially cultivated. People have to flee from this spot in summer, and go up the mountain; a very different appearance it must have presented in antiquity. These ruins give the image of everything here, of agriculture, of culture of all kinds. Yet there is struggle toward the better; behold these excavations which are an attempt to get back something of the old and combine it with the new; thus there is heard a low whisper of hope even among ruins.

If you listen carefully, you will hear another sound, the tramp of armed men coming down the mountain from the direction of Delphi. Stern is their tread, stern their look; one will think that they have some strong purpose in their hearts, into which their whole being is sunk. They file along the paved way and enter the sacred inclosure where the temples stand; quickly they pile arms and take their evening meal. Spartans you at once discern them to be, about the most pronounced type of men that have stamped their figures upon History. Iron-souled men in every way; but behold their leader who embodies in triple intensity his people's character. To-day they have marched from Delphi over Parnassus; it is altogether the most notable body of men that ever marched in these mountains, that ever marched in the world. Who are they? Whither are they going?

Across the valley from these temples is a hilly ridge, not high; it has a gentle slope along which lie sunny villages; the summit reposes peacefully in a soft curve against the blue sky, then turns down out of sight on the other side. Behind that ridge is the Pass of Thermopylæ, thither these Spartans are going with their leader Leonidas; work they have there which they are plainly resolved to perform. The pass is a marshy tract at present, yet with the old springs still gushing up, from which it derives its name. The ancient description of the locality by Herodotus is quite minute; streams and sea-coast have changed, but the main points of the topography can be identified to-day.

Most famous of the world's heroic deeds of sufferance in battle was enacted here; it has become the symbol of all patriotic sacrifice, and an inspiration to the same in men. Yet not this alone; these people had in their action a deeper purpose than nationality; unconscious it was doubtless, still it was felt from afar and strengthened them; it was the whole Occident, our Western civilization. The heritage of the world's development they fought for, like those at Marathon; they gave their lives for it, and this is the meaning of their fame; for you and I must honor the blood poured out thousands of years ago for what is truest and worthiest in ourselves. Often has the deed of Thermopylæ been told us; but its repetition cannot weary, indeed furnishes a light perpetually renewed; it rises into the heaven of History like the sun which returns every day with the same radiance, and causes no weariness, but gives needful illumination. Such are all great deeds, furnishing a yearly, monthly, or daily light, according to their luminous value.

Of rock the men were who stood there, like the mountain under which they fought; an utterance as of granite they have, indestructible; their deed is this first most emphatic expression of freedom: it is better to die than to be enslaved. That alternative, now the most common of the world's commonplaces, was then the world's new problem: Freedom or Death. It was settled at Thermopylae, settled in its most terrible phase — Death, quite to the last man. The people who can truly make this choice have already won; whatever becomes of them, it is clear, that they will not be the slaves of a conqueror. Thermopylæ, on account of its tragic termination, has wrought more impressively upon men than Marathon, with its victory; the sacrifice strikes deeper into the heart than the triumph.

So much we may grant to Thermopylæ; but was it a wise act? To stubbornly die rather than to retreat when it is wisdom to retreat; such is the question which even heroism cannot put down. There is no doubt that if the policy of Leonidas had been carried out during the whole Persian war, it would have been gloriously unsuccessful for the Greeks. The Spartans died bravely, it was a good example; but if the example had been followed, there would have been no Greek world, no Europe, probably no record of Thermopylæ, their greatest action. But there was a far better example, Marathon, which showed equal courage and devotion, stamped with success, the radiant child of wise endeavor. A glorious death is well, and at times must be; far better, however, is a glorious life.

The deed of Thermopylæ, therefore, lacks intelligence; such a judgment can hardly be avoided. The epigram says, that in obedience to their country's laws the Spartans perished; but like all epigrams its point is more striking than its truth. It is impossible to think that a Spartan law forbade the general to make a retrograde movement in face of the enemy. Dozens of cases in this war contradict the very notion of such a law; witness the movements of both Eurybiades and Pausanias. But if there could have been a law of that kind, Thermopylæ was the very narrowest interpretation of it, the hide-bound Spartan interpretation. The deed of Leonidas is, therefore, tainted with unwisdom, with an unwisdom which would have destroyed Greece. Heroic sacrifice it was, but not filled and burning with reason, which makes the great sacrifices of the world examples of action, even objects of worship. Still Thermopylæ is the great Spartan deed, the type of Sparta, showing in one burning point her character, both in its highest worth and in its narrowest limitation.

It was well that a man very different from Leonidas and a city very different from Sparta arose to control the destinies of Greece: these were Themistocles the man of Intelligence, and Athens, the city of Intelligence. Mighty is the transition from Thermopylæ to Salamis, the two battles are two distinct epochs of the World's History, two diverse stages of human development, the two typical deeds of man. The Prometheus rises with his new idea, seen both in the individual and in the city: the thinking Titan, in authority under the ruling divinities, in thought over them; but he must control in the end by his intelligence, if the Gods themselves are to endure. Mark the man and his deed; in that scene before the battle of Salamis it is brought out how his intellect over-arches all, both Greeks and Persians; friend and enemy; how he forces the Greeks to remain, and the Persians to fight when and where he wishes; thus he easily spans both sides, though he is but a subordinate on his own side; veritably an Olympian deed. It is true that he is not held by any formal law, as Spartan Leonidas, nor indeed by any moral law, as Athenian Aristides; he is above law, he changes it and makes it for his own purpose; he is the law-giver now, uttering it from his world-historical judgment-seat. Thus he is the savior of Greece, because the man of intelligence, and not merely of heroism, or of moral devotion; above the religion of his time, too, he clearly places himself, for it was he who interpreted the doubtful oracle of the God into clear daylight, and bade the Athenians betake themselves to their wooden walls. An unparalleled, heaven-scaling man — look at him!

In such manner we run along in the groove made for all time by the Father of History. Read the Seventh Book of his work; it is a Spartan Book, culminating in the battle of Thermopylæ, with the death of Leonidas and the Three Hundred. A tragic book, with a profound sorrow like that of a world passing away; with a terror, too, as if the Gods were quitting the earth. But the Eighth Book is an Athenian book, and recounts the doings of Athens and Themistocles at the battle of Salamis. What a change in the spirit of Time! Amid all the calamities of invasion and of flight, amid even the crackling fires of burning Athens, there is the continuous undertone of victory, the certainty given by intelligence. The Spartan Book shows valor in a supreme degree, but coupled with spiritual blindness, or at most a stern adherence to formal law. It shows what the outcome of Spartan leadership must be, and Sparta is now leader of Greece; the whole struggle promises to be a Thermopylæ — death. It is therefore a fearful, fateful Book; of dark foreboding; Greece is a tragedy. But a new spirit enters the following Book; it is no longer the old law or custom or religion which crushes like destiny; there is asserted the supreme validity of the new principle, Intelligence. Athena, Wisdom, is the Goddess; no wonder that the Athenians after this war erected to her a new temple which, in its ruins, still smiles over Attica the smile of that ancient triumph.

The transition from Thermopylæ to Salamis means, however, something more than the defeat of the Persian; it means also that the Spartan is no longer to have the guidance of the Grecian future. He has shown that in his hands Greece will perish; the Spartan ideal, Leonidas, is dead and cannot come to life again, being slain at Thermopylae. If the Persian was defeated at Salamis in the victory of Athens, so was Sparta; she had to be outwitted and conquered by Athens, as well as the Orient, if Greece was to fulfill her destiny. Mighty is the task to conquer the enemy, still mightier to conquer the friend.

Another transition, quite parallel, was taking place, though more gradually. As the political supremacy was transferred from Sparta to Athens, so the spiritual supremacy was leaving Delphi and passing to Athens; Delphic utterance was soon to become Athenian, whereby as Literature and Philosophy it will be eternal. The Oracle itself is to declare that Socrates the Athenian philosopher is the wisest of men, wiser than itself. A prediction of its own end; instinctive wisdom is to pass over into self-conscious thought. But in the Persian War it still asserted itself as the great spiritual center of the Hellenic race.

But our Father of History is still Delphic at heart; the oracles run through his work and can in nowise be separated from its texture without destroying its spirit; they are an organic part of it, indeed they are its very soul. I would not have it without the oracles; they show the consciousness of the time better than anything else; they are the spiritual groundwork of the people, as they are of the Historian's book, and of himself too. It was a Delphic time, and we must throw ourselves into it, and be it, giving ourselves up to it, just as that old Greek world did when it came to Delphi to consult.

Still the spiritual scission was taking place, the break in the Greek consciousness was widening into total separation, when the oracle could no longer keep in its sway the intelligence of the age. This dualism, too, is found in the Historian, strangely; he laughs at the ambiguous oracles, yet he trusts them; he seems in many places to have lost his implicit faith in the old myths, yet he cites them at other times with credence; then he rationalizes, interprets, distinguishes them, separating the true from the false. Such is our Historian, truest image of the Time, himself as well as his book. Partially a child of the new light, for a period resident of Athens, an admirer of her deeds and character: yet fundamentally he remains Delphic; his Athenian culture, though genuine, does not pierce to the core of his life and transform him; in his heart he is Delphic and belongs to the whole Greek world, rather than to Athens specially. This is the best reason for loving his book today; it is true in a much deeper sense than being merely veracious — it images the soul of the Time. Watch the struggle of the profoundly honest man; behold him fall back upon the Oracle, after trying to rise out of it; see him relapse into the mythus after seeking to elevate himself above it by some reflective process. But after wandering discontentedly for a time, he always returns to the true Hellas of his age, to the unconsciously poetic world of Mythus and Oracle. Thither we, too, shall seek to return with him.

Such was the old struggle narrated by the Father of History, fought between Greece and the Orient under these hills at Thermopylæ; a desperate struggle resounding from sea and mountain still, and which will resound forever. Yet what is now the struggle? What do I hear on every side of me this moment? It is the echo of the same conflict; the Oriental man still threatens Greece, holds in bondage Greek brothers: the talk, the cry, the song is to-day: We must free him, let us march! A local election is taking place with dissonance enough; but beneath all the discordant sounds can be heard the one voice of Greece in unison. From these villages rises a note in perfect harmony with that rising from ancient Thermopylæ; it is still the note of conflict between East and West — deepest, most abiding conflict in the World's History, celebrated in mythus by Homer, narrated in history by Herodotus, sung now in barbaric measure by rude voices in every Parnassian wineshop. Thus the old and the new blend in a fierce martial strain to-day over the ridge of Thermopylæ.

But it is time to rid our thoughts of this never-ending struggle of peoples, and return to our old Historian whom we love so well because he is Delphic; we wish to fall back with him into the instinctive utterance of the human soul, into the oracle, into poetry. He has made a path to Delphi upon which the pilgrim can travel back to the ancient shrine; he leads to the deep Greek fountain heads, which spring up to sunlight on the side of Parnassus. Long have we been hovering in prospect of the holy town, serving an apprenticeship of preparation; but the command now is to go, and on the morrow we shall pass thither out of this modern life, seeking the sacred spot for some word of musical, possibly of divine import: this is, in fact, just your worthiest pursuit and mine. There, too, is the spring of the Muses, welling forth from unseen depths its unconscious music; some record of the visit it may command. The final order is given; to-morrow we shall certainly go to Delphi by the straightest road.

XIX. THE DELPHIC ORACLE.

Long have we loitered at Arachoba, to some purpose it may be hoped. The town represents the old in the new more adequately than anything we have yet seen; it gives the feeling of old Hellenic life still blooming as in the days of its youth. The ardent pursuit with which the journey started, has to a degree been rewarded; shadowy images have been filled with flesh and blood; truly we may say that a deep satisfaction is the result of our stay. Hardly did we expect so much at the beginning; a great deal of what was previously a dream, is now a reality; but there remains one step more to be taken, in order to complete our journey.

The longing now arises to see the old, not in the new but in itself, so far as there are any remains of it which we may be able to restore in imagination. Off yonder round the slope lies Delphi with its ruins of an antique world; quite different from Arachoba, we may suppose it to be, yet in a strong undertone of harmony with the modern town. There some image of antiquity, not in its germ as we saw here, but in its perfect development, may be hoped for, even amid its dust; such at least we are now going to seek for as the finality and culmination of our journey.

Not again shall we hazard the lofty way over Parnassus on which we were so utterly foiled before; but we shall take the directest road, and then hereafter from Delphi we may venture into the high table-land where the Muses have their seats. With deep interest does the memory of that day now arise; just above me is the ridge along whose comb I wandered looking for a place of descent. I can behold now the lofty eaves of the mountain temple from below, and see myself there again, wandering along the edge. Utterly impossible is it to descend. A glance up at those cliffs causes a shudder to run through the body, they seem monsters which man cannot control; let no mortal dare explore their secret ways. Yonder is the spot where I undertook to come down; from below it plainly shows the seductive slant to a steep precipice; just at that point I came to the edge with rolling stones under my feet, when I turned and caught a bramble, which saved this Delphic journey from the eagles. Still those birds are hovering around the spot; let me exult that I am here below; to-day I shall not wander from the straight path.

Nature, one can here feel, has her uncontrollable aspect which inspires fear; many a demon seems to be lurking in her rayless caverns ready to rush out and swallow the wanderer. Of old these mountains must have had terror in them, till they were tamed; that was indeed just the problem — to tame them. The Greek grappled with Nature in her wildest forms and reduced her; such at least is the main burden of all his song: triumph over Nature. But I certainly do not triumph now, looking up at the summits; too well do I recollect how Pallas Athena turned me back in the gorge. To-day I have no ambition to grapple with the mountain; first I must see what Delphi has done, perchance she mastered this Nature and will furnish to others the weapons for its subjection.

But this road from Arachoba to Delphi, what shall the exalted mood say to it? A revelation it is, or the beginning of one; this is the famous Delphic vale which wrought upon the pilgrim as the initiatory passage to the great temple. The way descends gradually, winding in a wavy line around the side of the mountain over seams and ridges; one looks far below and wonders, then he looks up and adores. The vision is drawn out to an unusual breadth, you have to see beyond your common ken if you see at all. The eye seems pressing outwards as if seeking to lose itself in a happy harmony with this Nature; yet at the same time it turns inwards, subtly beholding there too the image, the spiritual counterpart of this outer world.

Look down the slope afar, there behold the olive orchards — a moving sea of green with many a ripple and wave, and even with grand oceanic swells over the ridges. At last the trees, silver-starred, reach their limit at the Pleistus, small meandering stream at the foot of the far-sloping mountain. In the distance a patch of sea, blue, with shimmering crest, steals at times into the vision suddenly, then hides again among the hills. Kirphis mountain is just yonder, with the sun resting upon its ridges, almost on a level with my path; between here and there lies the deep vale. Cannot one fly across and alight on the other side? One cannot help thinking of flight on this spot, looking from mountain to mountain; it were so easy to sail over in the air and drop on the opposite crest. The feet grow light and lift of themselves, till one looks down to see if they have not little wings like those around the ankles of the herald Mercury. A strange feeling as one goes to Delphi this morning — a tendency to fly, which comes of light heels, and possibly of a lighter head.

As we pass along the road, ancient foundations come to view; here must have been some one of those temples which the old traveler saw, as he came from the East, at the entrance of Delphi.

Athena was here, Athena Pronaia, to receive sacrifice from the pilgrim before he approached the Delphic recess; shrines to the heroes who assisted the Delphians in their defense of the city against the barbarians, were somewhere here; those heroic forms were once seen as divine prodigies appearing on horseback, and routing the foe with utter terror; thus the God protected the center of Greek civilization. Note these huge boulders rolled down from the mountain above — what do they mean? Are they the identical stones which the God hurled upon the Persians as they approached his fane? I believe that they are the same, being mentioned by the Father of History; at least to the eye of faith they will answer the same purpose.

Moreover we are passing through the cemetery of ancient Delphi, on all sides along the road reposed her illustrious dead. The old pilgrim had to make his entrance into Delphi through the monuments of her Great Men; they were to live in his memory before he could behold the actual city, the mighty work of theirs which endures when they are gone. Some sepulchres are cut in the mountain wall high up yonder, quite inaccessible now; others are hewn below the surface of the earth; but most of them seem to have been stone coffins, which are lying scattered through the Olives. All are broken, a few have sculptured figures upon them, and many fragments of finely chiseled limbs lie about the field. Just like Greece it is, just like Delphi; beautiful, but in ruins, — a broken sarcophagus. I admire the custom which the ancients had of burying their dead along the highway at the entrance of the city; thus we pass through the history of the place and all its previous years to the present moment, revealed in the monuments of its worthiest examples.

The Sun was out when I started, shining in full splendor at Arachoba, the new Greek town; but often his face has been dimmed by thick-coming cloudlets hurrying past the eye toward the East. The heavens are full of them, flying in many battalions up the valley overhead and at my side; look at them, trailing across the sunlit skies and dropping into the low vale down to the tree tops. But in the West they have massed in dense columns, and are moving forward like black walls, creased with fire. Now it is raining at Krissa, the lines of water drop from the heavy clouds to the earth, they are coming up this way and will soon meet the approaching wayfarer. Darkness increases as I enter Delphi, the abode of the God of Light; when I turn an angle of the mountain, there lies the little village, called by the modern name of Castri, wrapped already in nebulous gray folds of falling showers. I hasten to that roof on my left, half hid in the limbs of old olive trees; it is the Metochi or cloister, now tenanted by a single monk who receives the stranger with generous hospitality.

To the rear of the building is a low-roofed porch looking contemplatively down to the Delphic vale and toward the sea. There one will sit and behold the rain; before him are all the wonders of Delphic scenery now danced over by light and shade fluctuating with the depth of the clouds. The mountain rests in the background, lifting at times its nebulous cap and catching a few sunbeams on its head. But the storm comes along, and with one dash wipes off the radiance from the summits, or perchance it is the wind-cloud blowing it out like a candle. Then the mountain soon relumes, piercing the skies and bringing down the sun on its sides to glow more brightly than ever; but the illumination lasts but a moment only, with redoubled effort the black demon outspreads his wings, enveloping the whole landscape, and the new light is extinguished under triple folds of night. Such is now the Delphic contest between day and darkness, seen from the back porch of the low-roofed monastery.

The traveler sitting there will exclaim to himself: Thus has Delphi received me, in storms hinting of something beyond; I gaze through the darkened air into flashes of sunlight over the summits; that, assuredly, is Nature's suggestion of hope. So the mind looks through present clouds into gleams of future clearness; so may I look through this Nature which is dark enough now, into that which sprang from it, which is clear Delphi resting in sunlight. This is indeed the Delphic mystery: to behold the oracular city of its own innate force springing out of the obscure earth upon this hill-side, and reposing in the light of the God.

Some such view we must at last get, if our visit is to mean anything; though we have to stay long and question this dim spot, it were better to wait patiently for the answer. We must hear the oracle, uncertain, ambiguous at first; but finally we shall understand it, for the God must reveal himself in order to be a deity. This problem then looms up in the Delphic foreground above all others, has been looming up during our entire journey: What is the meaning of the Delphic Oracle? Such is the question which, intensified by this darkened scenery today, haunts us at every step, troubles every thought, waylays every image, intrudes itself into every bit of landscape. The deep gorge, the vale, the very stones seem to propound to you with an enigmatic look: What is the meaning of the Delphic Oracle?

You will first take a glance off into this Nature before you, with its immense variety, power and concentration; it must come foremost in the image, being the primitive setting of the Oracle, and suggesting it: for what is the whole country with its seams, chasms, valleys, but one vast oracular recess, out of whose mouth Earth, Mother Gaia, speaks and reveals her innermost secrets? According to ancient legend Earth had the first Oracle upon this spot; here is that Oracle still, ready to deliver its response, and uttering the dark prophetic word of Nature. Moreover you will notice that the sun rests on these summits, and rambles through these dells with a peculiar rapture, chasing the shadows, fighting them with a sort of triumphant joy, conscious of victory like a God. Dark Prophecy belongs to the spot, but so does Light; once they were warring elements of Nature, still they are such on certain days, even to-day; but they were anciently made into a spiritual union. Prophecy and Light became one in Apollo, God of Wisdom. Such was the old Delphic Mythus wrought by the Poet and sung at the festival; fragments of it, under several forms have come down to us.

But we must not think that Nature made the Delphic

man; the latter made it quite as much. He seized it, formed it into an utterance of what was deepest in him, and thus created an image of his spiritual being; for it is spirit that is in him and driving him to seek expression. Here was doubtless his earliest expression, in this dark oracular Earth whom he questions, wishing to know. The rude response of Nature is given; but it has to be transformed into clear utterance, and he does the work, which thus becomes beautiful; so Art leaps forth, newborn, transfigured from these rocks. You can still imagine it springing up like a flower on this hill-side — that old Delphic world with its culture and beauty breaking out of the bosom of the earth, Mother Gaia's bosom, and spreading its fair petals in the sunshine. But that is not all; in the image of Delphi we can behold entire Greece unfolding into its glories; the whole soil of Hellas transmutes itself into a garden, whose typical flower is the Delphic one.

The visitor cannot help thinking that this was an ancient seat of instinctive wisdom which broadened out so as to include quite every Grecian land. The Hellenic race must have found its first elevated expression here. Wise men dwelt at Delphi and were in some very intimate relation with the entire Greek kinship. Not a provincial oracle by any means was the Delphic one, but it uttered prophetic words for the Greco-Asiatic, for the Greco-Italic stock; from Lydia in the East, from Rome in the West, very remote relationships of the Hellenic peoples, its decrees were sought and respected. Deep and dark down into the very roots of the Aryan race does the Delphic influence extend, blossoming forth to the Sun on the slope of the mountain.

But chiefly as the center of the widely scattered Greek communities, as the profound tie which bound together remote colonies in Asia, Italy, Africa, must we regard this influence. In the Delphic Oracle the Greek race felt its oneness from the most distant rim of settlements; and the Oracle in turn planted itself upon this oneness, promoted the same, gave it expression. Harmony the Oracle sought to bring into this mass of seething Greek energy;

peace between the people of Greek blood was upheld by its holy responses; but chiefly it maintained Hellenic civilization against barbarism. All this came from a deep-seated feeling of unity in the Greek race, felt in its full intensity, and, as it were, bursting forth from the earth here at Delphi.

This was truly the divine attribute of the Oracle, the unifying power exerted upon these, early Greeks restlessly centrifugal; it held them by the deepest and subtlest tie, the instinct of brotherhood. Hence it was holy, it healed the wounds, it made Greece whole; it, giving voice and authority to the common bond of kinship, stopped the murderous hands of kindred, or furnished otherwise relief to the troubled states. It was the point of union of the Hellenic world, thus it was worthy of worship. What is holy, asks Goethe, but that which binds many souls together?

> Was ist heilig? Das ist's was viele Seelen zusammen
> Bindet; bänd' es auch nur leicht, wie die Binse den Kranz.

In the God and his responses the Greeks felt their common brotherhood; and the God too felt it, and gave it utterance. That utterance was the golden word of unity, harmony; such was the universal purport of the Oracle. So from Delphi secret threads went out over all Hellas whose aspirations and fears and calamities pulsed back to this spot as the heart of the whole people. The most sensitive part of the great Hellenic body was at Delphi, and received impressions from every member, which were then to be attuned to the one Hellenic soul. To keep each community in harmony with the rest, to have the whole before the eye, and to adjust the warring parts to the whole — such was the function of Delphi.

The Oracle is, therefore, a voice, voice of the Greek God, telling what is best for Hellas. For has not this Greek people a voice as of one person, and a reason back of that voice? There is, indeed, one Hellenic soul in which every Greek participates; it is his greatest truth. upon this truth the Oracle plants itself, having in its vision the whole, not the part simply; no individual end as against the universal one can it favor without losing its divinity. Conceive the widely scattered limbs of Greece to be one body, give to this body a soul, endow the soul with a voice — that voice is the Oracle uttering the truth of Hellas to Hellas.

Every Greek, therefore, had the Oracle within him, and at the same time without him; his true self-hood is not merely his own self, but is universal, and reaches up to his God. But in what form is this Universal to be uttered? That is the supreme difficulty for a people not yet arrived at a self-conscious expression in thought. It must, accordingly, assume impure forms, starting from Nature — from exhalations, convulsions, ecstasies, and rising into the dream, the vision, the oracle. An honest attempt, but inadequate; often so inadequate that it seems mere jugglery. But never forget the truth in it: it is a sincere effort to express what is universal in the Greek soul; still the expression is imperfect in form; therefore this form must be finally cast away. Hence, too, the Oracle is often ambiguous; it will be consulted upon matters which do not lie within its province, and which it can have no feeling about; what response can it give? Only an ambiguous one, which must be interpreted by the person who receives it; thus the Oracle says: Determine this matter for yourself, it is not my duty to decide for you. Ambiguity, therefore, throws back the decision upon the responsible man. Still there were many oracles whose purport was plain; these were the true voice of the God, not the shirking ambiguous utterance, which is the seed of death in the Oracle.

The wise men of Delphi can hardly be called far-sighted statesmen consciously furthering the great plan of Hellenic unity. Still less are they to be considered as a band of cunning priests living from the deception of mankind. They performed a true function for their people; they saw in vision and uttered instinctively what should be done for the totality, since all Greece had her center of emotion in the Oracle. It was a vision enraptured, prophetic — it was the feeling of what was best for the entire Hellenic stock. Conscious ratiocination there was probably not much, it was the instinctive sympathy with the whole, setting on fire the Imagination and breaking into rapturous utterance, at times very enigmatic, but at times clear-sighted enough. Purified were these prophets often till their instincts reflected a true image of the innermost essence of Greek spirit; not as an operation of reason, but as the gift of immediate insight.

I am well aware that the common Understanding scouts this process, that modern science with its syllogism of experience seeks to explain a half and to throw away the other and better half. Inaccessible is the Oracle to a mind solely working in the categories of Formal Logic or of Inductive Process, though there is a logic which recognizes it fully, and says that the oracular power must exist as a phase of human intelligence. A cunning priestcraft is the explanation commonly given, priestcraft based at times upon wise policy and foresight, at times upon selfish gain — still always a form of priestcraft: such is the explanation of the Understanding. I do not believe it; the Oracle uttered truth, the prophets saw truth. Woe had it been unto them, if they had uttered falsehood to their race.

Indeed any explanation, so called, of the oracular process is likely to be unsatisfactory. The thing when explained is no longer oracular; to be oracular it must remain inexplicable. Explanation seeks to identify the known and the unknown through some middle term; but the intuition of the Oracle has no middle term, it is immediate, it is the direct vision of the object without the mean of the reasoning process; if the mean be found, then it is not the oracular process. But that which we can do and have already done, is to state the content, the purport of the Oracle; this is the unity of all Greece, its universal principle, seen and uttered instinctively.

Animism is now the favorite word of explanation; the Oracle is traced to an original tendency in man to see ghosts. Turn about the statement rather; ghosts are called forth by the Oracle, not the Oracle by ghosts. That universal spirit of Hellas is first in the Greek man, and takes on many forms; among others, those of ghosts, visions, oracles. The highest form, however, is the self-conscious, self-clear reason, in which the universal spirit sees itself purely and comprehends itself. But so far Delphi never went, — nor have we yet; therefore, let us snap the thing off with a sentence: Animism cannot explain the Oracle, the Oracle rather explains Animism, in one of its phases.

The Pythia's wild ejaculations were put into form by the priests; it is manifest that these priests had the most important share in the utterance. They were seers, too, they saw what the totality of Hellas demanded; the merely natural effect of the earth's exhalation upon the Pythia was a chaotic babble like that of Gaia herself; but they reduced it to order, indeed they threw a Greek harmony into her wild and whirling words by an hexametral rhythm. Every oracle, therefore, went through the whole Delphic process; it began with the dark shapeless suggestion of Nature, and was elevated into the form and expression of spirit. Such was the true function of the priest: to bring the known out of the dim recess of the unknown, and to transform it into an utterance for man. In the same way the Greek everywhere enters into Nature and transforms her; the priestly duty is in perfect consonance with all that is deepest in Greek spirit. Noble was the function of the God, in all ways divine; hence its authority rested in every Greek soul. Foreign wise men were also celebrated at Delphi, and their sayings were set up in the vestibule of the temple. Wisdom was here, instinctive, spontaneous; the people of Delphi knew their own position and called their town the navel of the world.

Such was the early genuine Delphi; but it did not remain thus. It had aided the unity of the Greeks in the wars against the Persians, and in such action was true to itself. But the time came when Hellas was split in twain, and the Oracle had to take sides with Greek against Greek. During the Peloponnesian war it favored the Spartans against the Athenians; thus the Oracle was rent in the grand disruption of Hellas; the unity upon which it reposed and to which it owed its influence was destroyed.

Delphi no longer felt for the whole of Greece but only for a part; it ceased to command the worship and the confidence of the Pan-Hellenic world. At that unhappy period it was no longer holy, it did not unite but rather dismembered. From this time Delphi declines.

Still it shows the inner scission of the Greek consciousness. Athens, the intelligent half, breaks loose from Delphi, and marches forward to a self-conscious utterance in philosophy; Sparta, the backward half, remains Delphic and clings to the utterance in prophecy. Still a new utterance has arisen; our Socrates, whom even Delphi pronounced the wisest of men, is really the new Delphic Oracle, and supplants the old one. The inner spiritual unity of Greece is lost, in true correspondence is the outer political unity, sunk now in strife and hate. But those early days when this hill-side was the organic center of the vast energetic Greek body, the heart to which and from which throbbed all the hopes of the Greek race, are the glory of Delphi, and form the period with which the sympathetic traveler still seeks to place himself in harmony.

But the rain has passed over, and the sun is rapidly driving the broken clouds out of the Delphic vale, which wears now a laugh of triumph. Let us leave the cloister; this brook at our side comes from the fount of Castalia, bubbling forth just at the mouth of yonder gorge. Pass by the musical spring for the present, and enter the gorge; it is the identical one through which some time ago I undertook to reach Delphi, when Pallas held my arm. Follow the chasm as far as you can, till it grows dark and full of shadows; something of awe you will feel at this remarkable work of Nature. No wonder that Gaia, Mother Earth, had her first rude Oracle upon this spot, one will think in this very cleft perchance. Something indeed she says here, vague, wild, chaotic; you share in some struggle of forces pent up and as yet undeveloped. An attempt at utterance one feels rather than hears — a deep, speechless throb which dimly foretells the day of utterance. At times one is quaked by the rugged pulsation; it is Trophonius in his cave once more, but not destined to stay there. A shape in the rocks above stretches out like a mighty arm, then it assumes a monstrous half face; Atlas it seems to be now, with stooped shoulder, bearing the earth-ball of Gaia herself. Chiefly the deep rift, sliced down into the very heart of Gaia, as if to lay open her first secrets — that is the marvel; the heart you will call it, rude, made of rock, with dim fantastic shapes bodied into it; still the heart throbs, and you feel its pulsations trembling through you.

Go up yet further; ancient steps have been hewn into the solid rock; in old days one could ascend this wild rift and feel the might of its deity. The walls of the gorge are very close together. The place is darkened as it were for some awful presence. Notice again the cliff above, Nature is there making a huge, seamed, uncouth face, yet distinct as the stone itself; she is making many faces at you, the stone changes to capricious grimaces. Now it is Pan, followed by his rude choir, chasing over the rock walls; it is the realm of wild, disordered fancy; it is the world of caprice which the human soul must pass through, and then leave behind in the dim recess.

You will therefore not remain with Gaia, nor did Delphi remain with her in the dark chasm, with her dark suggestions. Out of the dim cavity the Oracle too must come into the realm of Apollo, God of Light. Not without a struggle did the God obtain the prophetic spot; he had to slay the serpent Python, couched in this gorge and ready to devour too often the followers of the dark chaotic oracles of Mother Gaia. Such is the legend which hints the great Delphic transition; a far-off adumbration of ancient pre-historic struggle one can discern in the mythus; or, if you wish, it may be taken as an utterance of all struggle out of Nature to the Higher. For the God of Light must slay the serpent Python lying in the dark chasm and guarding the primitive oracles of Mother Gaia: all culture demands it; Delphi has given her own greatest change in the advent of Apollo, and the slaughter of the serpent, woven into a Delphic fable, which is born into your soul upon this spot.

But as you pass out of the gorge into the light, here is Castalia, fount of the Muses. It is a new world; note how all has been transformed, how Nature at once leaps out of Chaos into things of beauty. A basin with steps in it holds the fair flowing water; a temple rose over it in antiquity; statues stood in the niches above. The gorge was suddenly transformed: this is the grand Delphic transformation. Wash in the spring; it purified the ancient priestess that she might give a Delphic response; then it became in its own beauty a weighty utterance on this hill-side, nay it became the inspiration and symbol of all beautiful utterance for all time; Castalia is still invoked as the source of the Muses, melodious givers of song.

And, strange to say, the traveler feels the new influence, he cannot keep himself from becoming rhythmical; his body moves with a novel stride which he cannot account for, his feelings are attuned to an unaccustomed music, he has to march to an unknown irresistible harmony. A Delphic change is going on within — a rhythmical attunement of soul; life and nature are moving together in a Greek chorus. Behold the situation of the town resting in the mountains in the form of a theater overlooking the vale, overlooking the world. Yonder was the temple; its foundations still peer forth; it too repeats the same harmony as Castalia, the whole mountain side echoes the same harmony rising from every ruin of the old city.

Here, then, we shall stay; clearly we have come to the great goal of our pilgrimage. These Delphic harmonies must be traced in their details, still more they must be felt often and be allowed to sink deep into the soul. This is not the work of one day, nor of one week; certainly there is no task in life which is to be done before this; eternity itself would seem to be lost unless filled with these divine harmonies. The melodious secret must be sought and taken up into existence, if possible; we must know what that secret is, or find out that we cannot know it; such is our first Delphic duty. At least this rhythmical gait must walk itself into exhaustion, and this keen musical feeling must become blunt in its own excess of enjoyment, ere we shall be willing to quit the presence of the Oracle.

Such is the fragment of the first Delphic day, glorious enough; but where can one find lodgment in this village, now so small and poor? The monastery cannot be a congenial abode for a Greek-minded person; though very hospitable, it hints of too much which is discordant with ancient Hellenic life. On my way from the Castalian spring, I meet a good old man, grey-haired Paraskevas, who tells me that he is in search of me, having heard of the arrival of a stranger. He offers me a share of his hut; he has blankets to spread on the floor to keep his guest warm, he will make the cot alongside of the fire-place, he can furnish a frugal meal of black bread, beans and wine, with some meat occasionally. A generous offer; never will the traveler forget aged Paraskevas, veteran of the Greak Revolution, now passing his sunset at Delphi. His abode lies in the sacred inclosure of the old temple; ruins peer forth from the soil on every hand; walls with inscriptions run before the very entrance of his door. A few steps from his threshold lies the drum of a column; upon it one can sit down and overlook the Delphic vale. A bargain is struck for an indefinite time; I can easily foresee that my stay will not be short. Food and shelter thus come to me providentially — the rest of the Delphic repast will be furnished by the Gods. It is a new feeling indeed, a mild, hopeful joy at this fresh intimacy with the antique world. I enter the hut with a slight stoop of the head, and lie down beside the hearth to rest for the night: to-morrow the days of Delphi will begin.

XX. THE DELPHIC TOWN.

The history of Delphi is a history of the spiritual life of Greece. The social and political changes of the country took place elsewhere, but their inner significance is best imaged in the mutations of the Delphic Oracle from its early importance to its cessation. It was the intense spiritual center; to it the fresh Greek problem was always presented for solution; it had to give some response, often uncertain enough. Over a thousand years we know that it was consulted, and probably much longer. During that time its history would be the best reflection of the Greek consciousness, had we anything like a complete record of its eventful moments.

Now can we get an image of the old town, an image true yet not detailed, which will tell its own meaning? Not a mere picture of the fancy, I mean, but an image which is an utterance of the real thing at Delphi, which in its own visage reveals what lies back of it and created it. Such an image becomes laden with profound significance, with the very profoundest, of a nation or age, and speaks as nothing else can. Thus, too, great monuments ought to speak; thus they do speak, if read aright. Delphi is full of ruins; they are still an expression of that old world — in fact just the true expression of it, if they be made to tell their secret. Such is now our vocation: to compel their utterance, if we can; accordingly let us begin during these sunny days to ramble among the stones of Delphi, and listen to their broken speech. Not with the pains-taking research of the antiquarian shall we make the round, but chiefly solicitous about the thing said or intended to be said by the monuments. Can we hear the voice of the Delphic stones and put it into words? It is not a slight task, but it must be attempted.

The sojourner will, therefore, settle down to his occupation, perceiving that he has no small enterprise in hand. Chiefly let him feel that the work is not to be done in haste; indeed, forcing of any sort will spoil the whole result; leisurely loving assimilation is the only method of reaching the Delphic heart. It is not with him a subject of erudite search, of antiquarian lore; still he must organize his studies, which will naturally fall into certain divisions; he will consider the Delphic town, now represented by ruins, in its various parts. These ruins he will dwell among, listening first to their separate voices;

then he will seek to find the common note in them all. He will also cast a glance every day into the physical background of the town.

Already we have had much to say about the aspect of Nature at Delphi; yet we have by no means said enough; it must never be left out of the vision. Nature is indeed the oldest monument of Delphi, and the best preserved; little change has come over it since the beginning of the Oracle. It has its own ancient note still, that is the keynote; it whispers the same to-day as yesterday, and vaguely hints wherewith it is to be filled. The most indefinite perchance, still it is the most enduring of Delphic memorials and always in the background.

What strikes the observer at once is the immense variety of Nature within a small space. Earth seems to have centered all her diversity at this spot, and therein to have attained a sort of universality just here; no wonder then that she was the first divinity of the ancient Delphians. You behold mountain and plain, sea and valley, with the eternal interplay of clouds and skies; all the seasons with their various vegetation are within eye-shot; rudest aspect of rocks with mildest repose of fields sport through the range of the same glance. Such is the intense concentration of Nature, yet ever in movement too, like Time itself. But there is no confusion, on the contrary everything has its chosen place, and the whole moves forward in quiet harmony. Day by day you will watch the landscape, study it with new wonder, till the feeling of it sinks deep within you, and you will exclaim: This is indeed the center of the earth. So the old Delphians felt when they showed in their town the *omphalos* or navel of the world. That was but an utterance of their faith, and it still may be taken as the utterance of Nature to-day.

Yet it is strange that the ancients had no landscape artists in our sense of the term. Small bits of scenery seem to float through those pictures of Polygnotus in the Lesche, but there were then no painters of landscape, nor any writers of landscape, such as we have now in excess. Shall we say that anciently there was no love of Nature on these hill-sides — love of Nature for its own sake?

The truth is, the ancient Greek man had more of it than we have and he lived more near to Nature; in fact he was too much a part of the same to distinguish himself fully from it. To stand back and admire Nature, demands separation from it in the admirer; not so free from its immediate influence was the Greek as we are, it is in his soul more deeply. Therein lies the very source of his art: Nature was not separated from spirit, but in a most intimate, triumphant harmony with it.

So Nature becomes filled with Spirit, and is transformed from her primitive rudeness, being made into the image of mind. Thus Art springs up, for Art is Nature transfigured. This transfiguration of Nature is the most beautiful, if not the most important, step in the history of mankind. It took place on this hill-side, for the Delphic city is the center and outgrowth of the surrounding nature. Here are the ruins, the remains of that ancient transfiguration of Nature; let us traverse them, and try to hear what they report.

Delphi lies on the mountain slope in a small depression of a semi-circular form; the site has often been compared to a theater. You will say, after some inspection, that the town rests in the very eye of the landscape, is its eye's apple in fact. The peculiarities of the Delphic territory are concentrated at this point, ready to burst forth into new forms. The city springs from the unwonted travail of the earth; buildings rise up from the slope, telling even in their ruins the Delphic secret. Let us go through them in order.

(1.) *Gymnasium.* Still many remains of this building are visible; it was upon the site where the Metochi or cloister now stands. Thick walls of cut stone appear, inside of which the chapel is at present; scattered about are fragments of columns, of architectural ornaments, of reliefs. A broken world, yet capable of being put together again — for it was not a caprice, but a severe, even logical development of forms. This structure was a principal one of the town, indeed of every Greek town, an integral element of communal life. What then was done here?

This was the place of education, we may call it the Greek school-house; yet very different things were taught there from what we teach in such a place. It is the house of training, but the first thing to be trained in man is his natural part, his body. Such is the primary function of Greek education: to transfigure that physical element which belongs to him, then he can pass beyond his body and reduce nature. Thus he elevates his own frame into a work of art, making it transparent with his own will, the beautiful implement which not only subserves but also clearly images his intelligence.

From this educational basis sprang much which belongs peculiarly to the Greek man. First of all, health, the harmonious working of the members of the body; it thus becomes truly an organism in which there is no jar. Health he had and cherished, for health is harmony and attunes the world to harmony. The Greek leaves everywhere the impression of health, no dyspeptic outbursts and no hysteric jerkiness, but health. The Greek Literature has this glory of health; struggle, despair, death, it has — but the death is a healthy one. Therefore, if he keep his Greek harmony, he must train the body, to which then he may attune all. Here is the training-school, first step of Greek education, yet never laid aside — for old as well as young practiced gymnastic exercises. From the body this health went over into the mind, from Nature into Spirit; and as spiritual the Greek training is a persistent fact of the world.

But not for health merely was the gymnasium built here, not for physical education only; it was rather that man might make himself a beautiful object, his body become a perfect thing of its kind. Let it be developed for its own sake, let the germ be unfolded into complete being — then the body will be beautiful; behold it! So every Greek man sought to make himself the bearer of a perfect thing, though it be the body merely. Not only this; he loved to behold that perfection in others, loved to look at the most beautiful man. Hence the Gymnasium was a place of gathering to behold beautiful forms, organisms working melodiously with a delight of their own.

See the youths wrestling, and the eager spectators! The eye becomes trained to form, sensitive to graceful movement. But watch that other man intently gazing there with inner ectasy. It is the Artist, he is to shape a statue of Hermes; now he beholds the God divinely floating over land and sea in yonder youth. Thus the Gymnasium became the inspiration of plastic Art. No beautiful man must perish, the artist must rescue him from death; so we read of 3,000 statues of athletes in the inclosure of the God at Delphi to be protected by Apollo as long as his worship endures. The Gymnasium thus found its utterance in Art; its training ended in bringing forth the beautiful plastic work, in which the Greek beheld himself in a divine mirror.

Far different is the training here at present; the monastery stands upon the site of the old Gymnasium. Not the transformation of body now, but its laceration, its destruction; it is given us to be crucified. An ugly thing it is, to be disguised in black garments which reveal no form; a worthless thing, to be punished forever for something which it never did. Quite the opposite to what one anciently saw on this spot: joyous youths leaping up in radiant shapes, children of sunlight, white as day. But let us not live now in a modern Kastri, but in ancient Delphi.

(2.) *Stadion.* If the Gymnasium was the place of training, the Stadion was the place where that training was put to the test. Thither we may now pass to the upper part of the town; thence we overlook the ancient city, overlook the vale, and from one part catch a glimpse of the sea, with Arcadian summits lying beyond in the blue distance. Seats cut out of the solid rock can still be observed, rising upwards, row after row; let us fill them with the mass of ancient faces gazing there. What were they looking at?

It may be summed up in a word: struggle. A trait of abiding intensity in the old Greek was to behold struggle, the beautiful struggle. The Gymnasium prepared the body into an instrument of grace and dexterity, that was the first struggle of training; but who among these many youths and men has the most perfect bodily instrument? It must be settled by contest; thus arose the games and their rewards. Practice leads to conflict; the end is beautiful victory; the result of training is shown in the outcome of the contest.

With deep participation they looked from these seats on the struggle, and therein beheld an image of human life. Man begins with struggle, his whole existence is struggle, important if the struggle be desperate. Thus the value of existence is measured by struggle. The contestants stood in the Stadion, with forms developed by training; they had made the preparation, so that every movement was skill and beauty; it was the beautiful struggle which the spectators gazed at; such, too, they were to make of their lives. Struggle it had to be; let it not be frantic, spasmodic, extravagant, but regular, moderate, beautiful. An ideal principle always lurked in these games, quite as much as in the conflicts of a tragedy.

Harmony, therefore, we see even in struggle. Now this harmony is to find expression in a more tuneful way; hence the poet enters. He celebrates the victor; he throbs with exultation as he beholds triumph in the beautiful struggle. He sings Kallinikos, beautiful victor; not the rude superiority of brute force, but the victory of nature trained, of beauty. For this the paean rises, and includes Heroes and Gods; for have they not done likewise, and are they not Heroes and Gods just by virtue of beautiful victory, over wild beasts, monsters, robbers, over giants and Titans? Our Delphic God had his contest with Python, ending in victory which gave us Delphi: anciently the fight was described in music with flute, harp and song.

But the struggle did not end in one strain; music too had its struggle. For many were the musicians ready to celebrate the beautiful victory; who can make it most beautiful? Next then we must have a musical contest, in which a struggle is thrown momentarily into harmony itself, only to end in a still newer harmony. The hillside re-echoed with harmony, life was to be melodious, and to seek a melodious utterance. The poet is, therefore, the last expression of this harmonious world. He too has had to be trained; he has had his struggle with rude nature out of which he has lured his strains; then comes the poetical contest ending with him also in beautiful victory. Thus the Stadion rises to a grand musical swell, culminating in the song and triumph of the poet who is here the lyrist or sweet singer of odes and hymns to the victors.

(3.) *Theater.* Still there is struggle or the representation of struggle, but it is of a new kind. Deep conflicts of soul now enter, and possess the realm of Art; these are to be represented in all their strength. It is no longer the beautiful struggle of bodies but the beautiful struggle of principles, of exalted ideas; Nature has risen to Spirit. Such is the transition from the Stadion to the Theater. Behold Antigone and Creon; they are not the bearers of a physical conflict but of a spiritual conflict; each has a right, and these two rights grapple like two athletes, not to the outer eye but to the inner vision, with an agonizing intensity. The unseen realm is now drawn into struggle — become a vast arena whose mighty combatants are thoughts, body-controlling, world-conquering. An ideal element always lay in the bodily combat, but it was obscured by flesh; in the Theater the last shred of rude nature is thrown off and the struggle becomes wholly ideal — two athletic thoughts wrestling for the control of the universe.

The Theater, therefore, manifests struggle in the Upper World, while the Stadion manifests struggle in the Lower World. Yet even the latter bears the faint impress of the former, and therein finds its chief glory. But the theatrical representation is wholly the work of the poet; its combatants are his creations; they fight entirely under his command. For the poet's realm is peculiarly this Upper World, in which he dwells, and to which he leads the spectator from below. Thus there arises upon this spot the Dramatic Poet, portraying the collisions of principles and resolving them into a final harmony, which is the nature of beautiful victory.

But among dramatic poets there is a struggle — struggle to represent this sphere in the most adequate manner. There must be a contest and its prize; who among these makers of harmony is most harmonious? A temporary dissonance, but ending in sweetest concert with beautiful victory for the poet. Thus the struggle in its twofold phase, in the dramatic work, and in the dramatic contest, has ended in harmony. No wonder that a fountain of song was eternally welling up at Delphi, and in all Greece; here is the veritable fountain now gurgling at our side, which has become the type of all poetic fountains.

(4.) *Castalia.* Doubtless the spring at the mouth of the gorge is the ancient Castalian fount dear to the Muses. The earthquake of 1870, which destroyed Delphi, filled the spring with a mass of broken rock from the mountain above. It has now been cleared out, and the form of the site can be observed accurately. Six stone steps descend to the rectangular basin of water; leading to these steps was a pavement of stone. Niches hewn into the solid rock, now sacred to St. John, show the places for ancient images. Behind the basin is a passage cut through the rock which leads to small chambers, the innermost sanctuary of the spot. The whole was doubtless covered with a small temple; column and frieze engirdled the waters; still a few architectural marks will be noticed.

All is laid out in the happiest proportion, though only the foundations remain. There is a simple harmony speaking from these hints. Here one sees in the strongest light what the Greeks did with nature. Around Castalia on all sides are rude fantastic shapes, jutting precipices, chaotic ravines; at once they drop into symmetry, nothing is capricious, the phantasms become filled with harmonious law. No contrast could be more direct or striking than the one just here. Behold the two — Nature and Art — set alongside of each other in the gorge; thus the world becomes harmonious, man too — and Castalia is veritably the inspiration of such an existence, the abode of the Muses.

Thus the contrast rises into an act of worship for the ancient man; he could behold what he was, what he must make out of himself. The example for the eye and the heart of the pilgrim was here; the ceremonies within the little temple said the same thing, also the statues in the niches above. Fancy the beautiful things once on this spot; the whole mountain seemed to be passing into the new transformation; the suppliant entered the shrine with such a lesson, the natural spring is changed into a hundred rills of marble beauty. Nor can one forget the long white folds of the priestess descending into the pool ere she sits upon the tripod; the utterance of the fountain in one form or other she must give, being herself transformed and beautiful.

Of Castalia the modern traveler will drink daily during his sojourn; the image of its old form will spring into his mind, its purport too will not fail to suggest itself like a face under the water. The fountain beautified by Art, and raised into a symbol of the transfiguration of Nature, will be quaffed: such is the true poetic draught. Equally needful will it be to go back into the dim gorge and there behold the image of an immense head in the rock with long mane-like hair — the man of nature who is to be transformed into the beautiful statue. Dark is this descent, full of shudders possibly, but the faithful pilgrim has to make it, and to be purified.

The earthquake, too, will become in his mind a sort of a typical thing, in its attempt to overwhelm Castalia. The bruises of the falling stones are marked everywhere upon the basin; still she appears again in beauty. Such earthquakes have been frequent at Delphi, both of the real and spiritual kind; chiefly the latter. Above all, those tides of barbarians, from the oldest to our own, from Persian to Turk, have come like an earthquake; ages of ignorance and of prose have buried Castalia out of sight, but someboby will be forever bringing her to light again. Thus every occurrence seems to adumbrate a meaning below the surface. Castalia elevates all reality into a type; whatever happens to her becomes a poetic deed, revealing underneath the truth of ages. Veritably, therefore, it is the spring of the Muses. Just as the body was trained in the Gymnasium so Nature was trained in the fountain, to reveal her spiritual visage.

Into what a different world from that of the dark prophetic recess does Castalia lead you! In it nature is trained to beauty, to the mild bearer of spirit; the rough sides of the mountain fall into harmonious proportion in the chapel and temple; out of the naked rock spring happy shapes representing what is divine; the fountain itself is changed from a wild spontaneous gush out of chaotic masses into the calm pellucid basin of marble which now holds it. Such was the Greek world imaged in Castalia herself; such too was the Greek religion faintly adumbrated, whose more complete manifestation we may now consider.

(5.) *Temple of Apollo.* This was the central point of Delphi, we may say of all Greece, at one time, namely, its instinctive, prophetic period. But its deepest foundation rested upon training also, training of the mind, to which we have ascended from training of the body. Wisdom is the result, hence that old inscription seen in the vestibule, *Know Thyself*. Castalia, however, had done this too in her rise out of nature; but now mind comes to worship its own principle in Apollo; mind is the God. The divine has truly appeared, and spirit adores spirit in all its manifestations. These we shall hastily trace in their connection with the temple.

It is clear that the world of Art revealed itself primarily here in antiquity. The ancient pilgrim, rounding the spur of the mountain behind which Delphi lies, looked up as he came from the East and beheld, what? First the temple, one of the finest and largest in Greece — the Greek temple with white column, architrave and metope; Apollo, God of Light, was perched aloft in the pediment; this was the first object falling into his eye. Then around the temple were grouped the smaller buildings, treasuries, porticos — each one an architectural gem; all gathered around the heart of Delphi. Thither he would pass through a forest of statues, over 3,000 in the time of Pliny after repeated depredations of the temple. Nero alone is said to have carried off 500 works in bronze. Famous paintings too were on the walls of the sacred edifices, notably those in the Lesche, hereafter to be mentioned.

Art, then, is the revelation; the early religious instinct comes forth in forms of beauty. Thus there appears to the outer sense the Greek world; here it is revealed, revealed in Art. On this hill-side is the bloom of Greek life; this Delphic work we may call its fairest coronal flower. As one looks up and sees all that beauty restored, he asks again, how did it happen to spring up just here? One cannot approach Delphi to-day, without feeling the might of Nature, that she is doing her best to utter the spiritual element which lies back of her. Such is the variety of her forms, and their intensity too, ready to rise into the new transfiguration at the touch of the sympathetic hand of skill. Nature declares herself to be a Greek artist with all her shapely figures bursting forth to the sun on this hill-side.

But the anxious inquirer could not be content with the sensuous glory, he must go deeper and seek the dark roots of the fair flower, roots striking deep into the Delphic rocks. In other words, from Art he must pass to Religion. For is not this the most important question: What is Time bringing forth for me and out of me? Time, as the elemental principle of our world, has all concealed within its dark chasm; the eager pilgrim would fain have himself brought into sunlight from his own obscure depths, as beautiful Delphi has been brought into sunlight out of dim Nature. So he enters the temple and inquires of the God there, who himself has risen into this beautiful revelation. The Priestess springs upon the tripod, the strange prophetic vapor rises from the unknown depths of the earth and inspires her; thus she seeks to bring the dark unseen thing to light, which is her holy act and her loyalty to the God. Her lispings are written down in poetic form by the priest, sometimes a distinct utterance, sometimes very indistinct, but even then commanding the consultor to put his own meaning into the response, and thus to take his own deed upon himself.

Therefore we have even at bright Delphi the obscure symbol of man's ascent out of darkness; necessarily an unclear thing, though very real. Within the sacred walls was a deep cave, to which very few found admission; the glorious temple with all its fair works was built around a dark recess of Gaia; if the consultor would know his own origin and what is to be, thither he must descend and listen. It gives the process of Greek culture and hints what every Greek man has to go through, giving him an impressive symbol of his regeneration, whereby it becomes his religion, the deepest principle by which he lives.

Art also at Delphi has expressed this dualism of Greek life — its Upper and Lower Worlds. In the famous painting by Polygnotus in the Lesche was the Trojan war, that grand struggle of Grecian civilization with the Orient. The profoundest duty of the Hellenic world, its duty to be the barrier of the West against the Oriental man, was therein expressed vividly to the vision. The Greek of every age could read in that picture his supreme call, could behold his ideal. But there was another painting in the same place: the descent of Ulysses, the wise man of Greece, to the Lower Regions, and what he beheld there. Thus the wise man must do, must go back into the primitive dark chasm of things — such is the inner descent which was imaged by the painter, but which had to be performed by the worshiper.

There was also the sacred fire kept forever burning, and the sacred hearth of the God, the primitive spot which binds to unity human feeling. Subterranean caverns or chambers were built under the temple round the fount of Cassotis, whither one might go and catch the first rude lisp of mother Earth. The Earth is indeed the primal Totality, and will reveal the Totality — for has she not in her bosom, all that is to be? Let the priestess be absorbed into the Earth, and feel the faint oscillations, or whisperings perchance; then let her utter them. Often Gaia does seem to forewarn and to reveal deep secrets in that way. In some such manner the worshiper tried to get back of the fair life at Delphi, the world of temples, statues, treasures, to reach what lay behind them and brought them into being, and to appropriate the same unto himself. The beautiful life must be mine, it is that which I worship; let me transfuse myself, now a rude thing of Nature, into the Delphic image, by passing through the same process.

Very far back was the Delphic worshiper led; there were hints of that remotest form of worship, the fetish. The sacred stone upon which the first Sibyl sat and uttered her responses was pointed out in historic times, still an object of reverence. Then the stone of Cronus, which Rhea gave him instead of the infant Jupiter, was there; this infant grew up and overthrew the old Gods, the Gods of mere Nature, and instituted the new glorious epoch of which Delphi is the highest manifestation. Let therefore the ancient relic, the symbol of the mighty revolution be preserved as a holy memorial. Chiefest of all is the Omphalus or navel stone, marking the center of the earth. Jupiter sent out two eagles, one from the East and one from the West, and they met upon that spot; such was the divine proof. The stone had the two images of the eagles upon it, as the account runs. Very old indication of the importance of Delphi, this is; the place is a center, an intense physical center first, then a spiritual one — in fact the one images the other. We have already noticed the primitive oracle of Gaia; the first rude attempt to grasp the Universal, for is not the Earth the first All to the natural man? Thus the worshiper was led back deep into the origin of things, and deep into himself. The two stones, one of the formless fetich, the other the marble statue of Apollo, showed the Delphic transition.

In the ceremonial at Delphi, we may therefore notice several stages of primitive worship, each of which was a descent of the soul into itself as well as a going backward in historic time. This correspondence of the growth of history with the growth of the single soul, of what is universal with what is individual, is the great fact of religion; each human personality must be what its race is; nay, must ideally go over what its race has gone over. The worshiper beholds in these rites a rise out of that which he himself is and an elevation into the divine; it is to him, therefore, the most vital of all processes.

Thus the world or its history is nothing more than a man, — the universal man, developing himself according to his own spiritual law, with which universal man the individual man must place himself in harmony in the act of worship. The World-Man let him be called; he too is seeking to unfold himself into reality, whereof the Greek time is one great phase. To this World-Man correspond infinite individuals, reflecting him as their Highest, adoring him, going back through his primordial stages, for his way is their way. Thus was every Greek in the Delphic time, an image more or less complete of the World-Man then; this was indeed his very essence, was that which made him Greek.

In one way or another every individual has to pass through the development of the World-Man, of his antécedent historic realities; such is the education of the race to-day. One must be all that the World-Man is or has ever been essentially. Merely individual development would be worth little, if there was not in it at the same time a universal development, if the World-Man did not shine through it and transfigure it. Each person must grow over again what mankind has grown over; on the wings of his race he rises out of savagery to the front of his own time; such is true education, such, too, in another form, is worship. Thus the Delphic worshiper in these rites lived over again the life of his race, and rose with it into the clear happy sunlight of Delphi.

Mythology too has imaged the same course of things as the ceremonial. The legend says of Gaia that she was here first, then occurred changes; Themis, she who establishes, had the Oracle after Gaia, before it passed to Apollo. Then the slaying of the serpent Python marks the advent of the new God. Dim adumbrations in legend they are of early changes, early advances; the mythus always pictures the ascent of the spiritual from the natural; indeed it is just the forms of nature filled with the contents of spirit.

(6.) *Pylaea*. This is the supposed site of the Amphictyonic edifice — the political instrumentality of Delphi. The Amphictyonic council sat here, it was the political framework which protected Delphi; a sort of federation it seems of surrounding tribes, whose object was to defend the God, to preserve him as the sacred center of Hellenism. One highest purpose alone it could have — that was to unite Greece, to make these little communities harmonious; all Greece was to be a Delphi, many Delphis, beautiful flowers springing up from rocky slopes. The oneness which the whole Hellenic race felt in its God the Amphictyons were to make institutional, to elevate into the State.

But this could not be, this was the limit of the God, the limit of Greece. The unity which she felt in her deity, she was unable to realize in her political institutions. Her oneness remains an emotion, an aspiration, a dream, an oracle. Not strong enough to realize her common brotherhood — such was her weakness, and with it the brand of destiny. The Delphic Amphictyony as a political contrivance is utterly fragile, shows in fact the limitation of Greek spirit in all its nakedness. Thus the bare stones of the Pylaea are deeply significant — they mean the ruins of Delphi, temples and all; that Hellenic unity in the God never became an abiding fact in the world. The town had no adequate protection from without, which is furnished by the State; Greece never translated, never could translate this Delphic feeling of oneness into one government for the whole Greek kinship; the religious unity was never realized in the secular policy, which, therefore, never had any true center. The stones of Pylaea represent more than Delphi, they are the image of entire Hellas.

Not all the ruins of Delphi have we here reported, nor is it necessary. There is one Hellenic note in them, they sing in unison, when they are once introduced into their company. That note of unity is what the eager sojourner is eager to hear, and to carry away in some form, if he can; many times during the day he goes out and listens. But not always can he hear the music; it has its day, its hour, its very minute; it cannot be wooed at will, it cannot be held by violence. But after many attempts, after long sitting amid the tumbled stones, after a loyal surrender to the influence, it will come, come unexpectedly. The Delphic unity, that of the whole Greek world, will rise up a living thing, a creative thing in the soul, will be yours, though your utterance of it be faint and fragmentary as Delphi itself.

XXI. THE DELPHIC NOTE BOOK.

APOLLO, says the legend, stopped at Delphi in his wanderings over the Earth, and set up his temple. He found here the miracle of Nature which sought expression through him, and which he was to fill with his own soul. Erecting his shrine, he began to form these hills and with them to transform man; thus the spot became a radiating center of light, a spiritual sun, and prophetic therein of all that Greece was to be. Like Apollo of old the pilgrim passes to Delphi; he may lightly run over the rest of the Greek territory, but at this point he is stopped by Nature, who is still full of spiritual suggestion, and dumbly prays for a voice. If he goes on he will be drawn back; he must think that here is yet some utterance of the God, that here is some service to be performed by one who wishes to transfuse himself into harmony with the old divinity. So the pilgrim will seek to do over again at Delphi in image what the God did in reality.

——The rocks, the bushes, the mosses you behold growing on the side of the mountain; but if you turn your eye beneath, you see them reflected in the waters of Castalia; indeed you will take in both image and reality with one penetrating glance. You will also behold your own face among the green shrubbery mirrored in the translucent depths; nay, you may observe your own eyes beholding all this varied imagery in the fountain.

One must always be able to see double at Delphi, see not only this glorious Nature, but its reflection in Castalia along with the image of the beholder: wherefore the Muses' fount is it, if not for that?

—— The harmonies of Delphi mainly flow from the happy union of Nature and Soul. Whatever we see suggests some strain, strikes the chords within; still more, whatever we feel and think, drops at once into vibration with the outer world and therein finds expression. Can you wonder that a person becomes deeply attuned amid such surroundings, and is absorbed into their musical mood? It is a necessity of air and sky, of mountain and valley, of the vineyards and Olives. Then back of the Present lies the Past which fills it and sets it throbbing; every object is laden with the old transfigured into the new; the antique world welling up into the modern life and scenery gives the rhythm, in whose sweep all is embraced and harmonized. But it is not the jingling of words of like sounds, not a merely external tintinnabulation; it is rhythm, harmonious modulations of the whole world revealed here, resembling those of the sea with its ever-recurring sweep of long waves, that come on like Fate, yet with many a little capricious water-curl playing over the surface.

—— There is something which one seeks to live with intimately in the artistic instinct of the Greek. His eye must have been a wonder, broadened into touch, deepened to soul. It lay on the way between the inner and outer worlds, both of which dwelt in that hostelry, imaging each other in a transparent happy harmony. The Greek did not turn wholly within and brood over his own formless, fathomless depths, nor did he abide without, sunk in a mere life of the senses. Whatever from the outer world passed into that true eye of his, was filled with the inner world; and the inner world in brotherly harmony took some kindred outer shape in which it revealed itself and became beautiful. A small poem in the Greek Anthology, often about the humblest daily matter, has an eye which seems to have quite gone blind in modern life; an eye clear-seeing, clear-imaging, an eye in whose translucent depths Nature and Soul meet, embrace and wed with eternal marriage-song.

—— The sojourner will often long to go to the white summit of Parnassus, which every morning rises enticingly before him, but he will be warned against snow drifts, and the danger of getting lost, even of being overtaken by wolves. Still on some fair day he will set out and traverse the cliffs to the table land; there among the deserted huts he will sit down at the foot of lofty Liakuri, and look up at the snow-line and the pine woods beyond it; he will be unable to restrain himself from the ascent; he must go up and see what is going on there. He passes the border and sports in the snow, smells the fragrance of the wetted pines and rouses the hare from her cover. But spring has set in, the frozen sides are melting, every rill is full and hurries off to the Olives and vineyards, where the fruits of autumn are to be nourished to bloom and maturity. Flowers spring up in the wake of the retreating snow-line, driving it further up the mountain; the bees follow and the butterflies, often flitting gaily over the frost as an enemy conquered; then comes the shepherd with pipe and song, bringing his herds to the freshest herbs of the season; all are in hostile pursuit of the snow, and will soon push it into its inaccessible fastness on the summit of Liakuri. Thus icy Parnassus seems to loosen in the spring and thaw itself into rills, into flowers, into song, making a vernal harmony which will be always humming in the ear of the wanderer as he rambles through the mountains.

—— Many are the flowers that grow on Parnassus — but there is one which you will select, a small blue flower, and feel to be the fairest of all in her tender beauty. The slope is now full of her mild eyelets; the whole mountain rather is one flower, a maiden you will say, whose every glance changes to a flower, and remains fixed in its blue tenderness looking up at you, at times with a dewy tear on its lid. So Zeus transformed Kalokaira into an Oread, whose glances were held fast on the mountain side and preserved in a pretty flower. Indeed, we all have seen blue eyes in which each look was a sudden flower, and whose life was a flowery dream flitting away with the moments. This modest wee flower, slightly hanging the head as if to shun the stranger's gaze, springs up in the stoniest spots amid the hardest rock, sometimes peers out of the surrounding snow; tenderness, then, is strength. I pluck one carefully out by the roots with the earth clinging to them, and think of transplanting the same to my home, if it be possible — that delicate Parnassian flower, yet so stout-hearted that neither coldness nor sterility can subdue its smile of tenderness.

—— Through a distant opening between two peaks one beholds an arm of the sea running out into the blue Corinthian waters which in placid repose lie amid the dreamy hills, whose outlines express a calm symmetry. Still further in the background are the Arcadian summits, swimming in the horizon, which closes the aperture through which we are looking. Over all is spread the haze which still further subdues the ruggedness, the striving of the peaks; Nature has seemingly put it into her picture for the purpose of tranquillity, and then added to it the mild golden light of Apollo. Happy serenity, not even the struggle of contemplation it suggests, but a glorious reconciliation of the beautiful world before us softly throbbing in silent harmonies.

—— From the hill-side one looks at the veil of haze suspended above from the blue welkin, dropping down upon the mountains, resting gently over the valleys — looks long and wonders what it means. A bond of union it is, first of all, uniting sea, summit and skies, transfusing them, you may say, into one melodious concert of Nature. A divine thing, therefore — being that which unites, not that which separates, bringing into harmony the disjointed and jarring members of the rugged landscape. A visible outward sign of their union it appears, corresponding to their inner oneness, yet in its transparency revealing their distinctness. Then, too, peace it means, peace scattered over hill and valley, peace attuned to the soul of man. Reclining under the trees of the orchard we glance up at the mountains in light blue veil;

it is the suggestion of serene sweet repose for the highest heights; wherever it lies, there is tranquillity; even the rough restless features of the hills are softened in the breath of its quiet. Not a tone of tumult we hear now, hardly of activity; repose has settled upon the summits, and they cease to struggle upwards, content to rest in their new divine harmony. The traveler, too, becomes one with the landscape, whose music sweeps through him; he is himself transmuted into haze as he lies under an Olive, and gazes up toward the blue heights, feeling within himself the oneness of the Delphic world.

—— As the sojourner descends from Delphi, at the head of the village he will enter the Olive orchards. The trees will attract his notice by their subtle sparkle set in green, by their loads of fruit, by their old hollow twisted trunks, by their fresh sproutlings. The Olive is truly the holy tree of the Greeks still, one may well call it the favorite of Pallas Athena. Meat grows upon its branches, it furnishes vegetable and animal food together — the most universal of fruit-bearing trees. Now is the season for picking the olives, and this is the main occupation of the village. The young folks are here — maidens full of mirth and love, singing throughout the orchards. When the stranger comes near, they attune their voices, for they see him and instinctively try to lure him with their most enticing gift. And he is lured, since he will go up to the group, or perchance stand still at some distance, hesitating to expose himself to their gay mockery. But when he sees one of them alone with the parent, thither he will pass and help gather the berries, for this is his harvest too.

—— Often he will wander for miles through the orchards, loitering along streams of clear running water, through deep clefts, past mills turned by mountain streams. Often he will sit down under a tree, take out his note-book and try to put in words the view and its mood — somehow or other those words will fall into a sort of a rhythm as if playing at verse mid the Olives. The maidens in the distance empty their baskets of fruit, and the slow donkey toils up the rocky winding pathway through the trees, the mountain opposite rises steep and bare, perforated with curious caverns, homes of the nymphs. He will go through the chasm darkling, he will come upon ancient foundations of cut stone, he will see the beautiful shrine or temple arise once more to the sunlight, and perchance in an unguarded moment he may catch a glimpse of fantastic Pan and his rout disappearing in the distance among the trunks of the trees. This Lower World will not persist in his view, but transfigures itself into another and Upper World, which is the enduring fact of Delphi; all Nature seems on the point of turning mythical and becoming a poem.

—— Only every third year, it is said, is a good year for Olives; two years they must rest ere they again bear fruit. From the great earth they draw up but slowly their juices after the fatigue of the season of bearing. Still, in these vacant years, they are not idle; new wood they deposit, the old trunk they inlay with many a fresh fiber from which comes the youthful life which produces the fruit. The body of the tree, nay, its vegetable soul, must be renewed to reproduce itself; it is the new life which begets the new life. Note these little channels running everywhere through the orchards; they bear water to the Olives through many a rill, forming crystalline nets stretched out on the hill-side under the trees whose trunks they entwine in a thousand meshes. They carry the fresh streams of Parnassus to the exhausted rootlets, renewing the old stem and nursing the sproutling; for it is the new tree only which yields the new olive, the aged stock has to become young again. Whence come those streams? From the tops of Parnassus they flow, or well up from unseen sources within the mountain, watering the Olives.

—— Every three years only the Olives produce, then they repose to gather anew their youth. Thus too the Poet or Maker: after exertion he must rest for a season till he become young again, with new tissue, whence he may draw adolescent freshness and beauty. Born over again must he be after the work of creation; the throes of utterance waste the youth of his spirit, the dew of the soul is dried up in the fire of conception. A new life, then, he must have — a life softly stored away in his brain by the years, that he may be veritably young whatever his age. Many a rivulet from Parnassus, too, must water his fruitful orchard, till youth's sap rise into the ancient fibres in place of weariness and decay. Many a day of sunshine must be taken into each tree till it be stored full of happy gleams; many a breath of air from Parnassian heights must be inhaled, till the new transformation take place, with all of which the Muse must mingle her melodious strain. Each thought is a birth, each line of the Poet must sing itself into being. Age is impotent, the new word springs from the new life, throbbing after reposeful periods into utterance like the triennial yield of the olive.

—— The olive tree was very old, hundreds of years possibly had fled past it, often with fire and sword; still it stood. Its limbs were everywhere filled with berries, but the corrosion of age had touched the last fibre, though no one knew it. I looked into the top of that tree, it laughed with a youthful delight, wide-spreading was its crown, richer than ever was its yield of fruit. An enraptured vision it seemed; standing there in the sun it dreamed of eternal duration. A light wind came down from the mountain, the last thin fibre snapped; still the prostrate monarch had the joy that he never grew old, that his last was his richest burden.

—— Here, take in your hand this olive, the rind is a dark rich brown with shades of red; graceful is its form, and there is lusciousness in its look. It is full of meat holding little sacs of oil; the globules will exude if you only brush the surface. But at the heart it is red, red around the stone, with decided warmth and richness in the color — a genuine hue of the heart's passion, you will say. Press it, there follows a gush of oil; the heart at once gives forth all its essence, and seems glad to yield up its secret wealth to this gentle pressure of a sympathetic hand. Even bruised and broken, it reveals more generously the rich stores of its heart.

—— In the paths that lead through the orchard are

shown many of these berries; they fall helpless from the limbs above into the road underneath where they are trampled upon by the men passing that way. There they lie in the dirt, crushed, disregarded; the rich oil is trodden out into the dust, a dark greasy spot is all that remains of them. Stirred by some storm or possibly by a light wind only, they fell from the paternal branch; now they are lost forever, nobody will pick them up, nobody will touch them, men will simply tread on them again, heedlessly, till they be buried out of sight, trampled into their grave. I do not deny that I avoid stepping on them, pity them as I see them lying there with all their oil spilled. Such are the crushed olives which one will see on his pathway even in Delphic mood.

—— One will curiously think of an ancient crushed olive, noted at Delphi for her gift of five hundred spits to the God. It is a puzzling donation; why spits for such a purpose — why so many — why just she, fair Rhodope? But leave the matter to the antiquarian, and listen for a moment to the scoffer. "Les prêtres paiens ne se montraient pas plus difficiles que les prêtres chretiens pour ces sortes d'offrandes; ne sont ce pas les grands coupables qui ont toujours enrichi les Eglises?" (Larousse, Enc.; Art. Delphi.) Wicked Paris! That view of the Delphic world we shall not take, whatever be the solution of Rhodope's problem. Was it a wild piece of mockery, or a genuine act of piety? We say the latter; in deep sincerity the crushed olive gave up its offering for restoration; I can see a longing of that sort in those trampled most deeply into the dust at my feet.

—— When the olives are gathered, then the busy hands pass to the vineyard in order that Bacchus may rejoice in their work. They loosen the earth round the roots of the grape vine, that it may distil the bright drops, drawing them into their little vats in the fruit. A soft bed for the God we prepare in the ground, and by our caresses we shall entice him to rest with us. Thus we change the kind of our labor; our thoughts, too, change; our songs change. These are filled with the glories of Bacchus and the hopes of the autumn. I, too, change with the others, a touch of the madness of the wine-god I feel, as I think of the rootlets sipping at a perpetual banquet or dipping up the dew from the soil for us and storing it away in the grape. They are all little Hebes — cup-bearers of the God; note how each one carries his little tear-drop and lays it away in a small cell for me the coming autumn. All are working for my behoof, I see. Not unrewarded shall ye be, my little gnomes; to your glory shall I drink, and even may make a song, if the coy Muses be not frightened from the revel.

—— Notice the old stock of the grape vine, it is a character. Dozens of years has it stood, bearing its annual crop; crook-backed with its burden of labor, it still puts forth young sprouts which are hung with grapes. Twisted and squirming with the struggle of life, it is yet green, and rejoices in youth and the sun. Often it has been cut by the pruning knife; wounds it has received all over its body in the hard battle of existence upon this hill-side; still from its scars it sends forth new blossoms which yield the richest and most plentiful fruit. Age cannot wither it, seasons cannot quench the gay works of its rejuvenescence. Truly the plant of Bacchus, the beloved stripling divine, thou springest from the earth; no wonder thou makest us young when we partake of thy stores; it is but thyself which thou impartest to us, and even to the old man thou restorest the days of his youth. Thou wreathest the brow of the God with thy leaves, elevating thyself to a divine participation; for whatever cuts off Time from his dominion, confers immortality, and is to us mortals a deity.

—— Look at old Yankos at work in the vineyard; how he lops each vine with a quick turn of the head, making his iron-gray curls spring round his brow in chorus! Do you not like to see his white folds dance about his body? Speak to him and hear his answer; his is a mountain voice, attuned to this lofty air, and made for talking from peak to peak. Thus his words are few and far-echoing; filled too with a sort of natural music. He never stops his work while conversing; his very life is to prune his vineyard. It seems at first a pity to cut the green twigs, but only by trimming, Yankos says, will the vines be prevented from becoming mere leaves and branches, and be made to bear grapes. Foliage, Yankos does not wish, but fruit. On the stock he leaves two small buds, which will produce all the wine for the next vintage; the sprouts on which grew last year's clusters are cut away, they have now grown old and fit only for the flame. The young shoots alone can produce the true nectar, young shoots from the old body. Then the juice makes young whoever sips of its drops; but the vine must be trimmed, trimmed by the careful pruner into perpetual youth. Look at Yankos again, he is no longer old, he is so sunk in his work that he grows young with his vineyard, transformed by his art into one of its products, or rather into sudden gleams of youthful Bacchus.

——— One of the chief Delphic delights is to trace the ancient foundations of dwelling-houses, still marked by grooves in the rock where it was cut for the base of a wall. Steps hewed out of the stone lead in many a winding passage over the steep hill-side; you will mark the place of each house. Here was a location chosen anciently for a dwelling by some skilled Greek eye for the sake of the glance down into the landscape below. I try to look from the spot with that eye, examine the scenery; I seek to become what the Greek owner was, to feel what he felt, as his look swept through the valley to the sea, then turned about and rested upon the snowy peak of Parnassus. From each of these sites you behold new combinations of landscape — always something new is seen though the separate objects be familiar. Thus one may still enjoy the old Greek's view, build his house, sit with him, and look at Delphi with its temples, listen to him reading Homer, fill the court of his house with flowers and colonnades. But the conversation is hushed as the white-robed daughter glides past through the columns on her way to her apartment. Not a word she says, her face is almost hid, still from behind the cover the dark eye sends a single gleam, and one glimpse of that perfect line joining face and forehead is left as a precious boon to the stranger, the most delightful memento of Delphi.

—— The old temples, too, the traveler will build up again and place in their locality. The pediment will be filled with marble myths, friezes will be drawn around it, showing some conflict of heroes, or some noble festival of mortals. In the evening when twilight falls upon the modern hamlet, he will hardly see the hovels yonder, but the whole site of semilunar Delphi will become white with colonnaded rows, with groves of lofty statuary, with sculptured fables writ in stone better than in words. Lines of pilgrims arrive from the sea, march in procession to the shrine of the God, bearing rich offerings; the world is beauty, life is an eternal holiday, joy rises into worship.

—— Extensive excavations have been made at Delphi, it is the design to make still more extensive ones, for much is supposed to be buried under the village. But why should we dig here? Why do we of this day dig everywhere in classic lands — dig for dear life to get possession of a few fragments? This is truly the age of excavations; a strange impulse it seems; we must find out what our ancestors were, even if they be monkeys. So we dig into the past, into old soil, seeking for aught which we have not. Ah, something has left us, and we feel the void; the old Greek world had what we have no longer and are searching for. We seek it, and well may we seek it; we long to complete our life with theirs, so our salvation cries out: dig, dig; restore that culture, that beautiful existence in its best phases, though it be but a fragment. Man is not entire till he be all that his race has been; therefore let us mount to the sources or dig down to the remains of our former selves. The heroes of the day are excavators.

—— But is it not strange that what man broke in pious zeal, he now piously restores, patching together the smallest chips, more precious than gold, of heathen idols? Aye, the conflict is over, let the enemy rise, help him to his feet. Yet the sensible traveler would not wish to reverse the wheels of Time; just what Delphi is now lay in her own deed and character, she has received nought but what had to be, namely her own action in its consequences. Delphi foretold her own fate; when the seeress predicts the destiny of her own nation, she must have that prophecy turned back upon herself. So, too, O Delphi, one reads in these ruins thy greatest oracle, beholds it therein fulfilled. Nay, this excavation one can see in thy wisdom, this rejuvenation lies, too, in thy foresight. Men cannot do without Delphi — even thy ruins are prophetic; to-day still thou givest responses, nor is thy oracle yet dumb, nor will it be while these fragments lie in thy soil.

—— Yet even at Delphi there are marks of a time before the Delphic era — of a primeval time which breaks through the Greek aeons and reduces them to children of yesterday. We look at the immense chasm worn by the Castalian brook out of the solid rock; in antiquity there were steps cut into that rock right where the torrent abrades the channel. Two thousand years old or more are those steps, yet unworn almost: millions of years then must have fled over Delphi before the advent of Apollo or the slaughter of the Python upon this spot. What an epoch is counted out to you by this gorge worn by water which in two thousand years scarcely rubs off the mark of the chisel! Greek Delphi is old, at its antiquity we sometimes wonder; but what is it compared to Nature? The reign of Mother Gaia is that primeval epoch not forgotten in Delphic legend; she was sovereign of the rude chaotic world before the rule of Apollo. But even he with his city is now a shadow on the hill-side; yet behind his shadow is another of numberless centuries resting upon this chasm — the shadow of old Mother Gaia.

—— Thus one lives back at Delphi, or just as well lives forward. Time, the final God of limitation, who seeks to put his fetters upon the soul to the last, is dispossessed of his sovereignty in the Delphic world. I am above time, I live thousands of ages in a moment; all the past lies in me, I am the germ of all the future. All centuries move through me when I know myself: I have no limit in Time, the soul is not bounded by it; small as I am, yet I hold the All; I make Time and refuse to be made by it. Strange that man should surrender his soul, immortality's dower — should imagine it to be a creature of Time and hunt for his origin in Time; thus indeed he reduces himself to the thrall of Time. So at Delphi I am what it was, before it was, and will live on after it through the ages. *Know Thyself* was the Delphic maxim; not without truth was the answer of the satirical rogue: "What, know myself! You ask me to undertake too big a subject." A big subject indeed, quite All, Time included, if understood aright.

—— Yet Time has his trophies at Delphi — the tombs which lie on both sides of the village, east and west; these are not to be neglected. One sees a large opening hewn out of the solid rock of the hill and enters; places are there for the ancient urn and the sarcophagus; possibly, too, these were seats for the living, who still tried to retain the bond after death. What does this untold labor mean? Some name of importance we may read, for the tomb cut in this rock is made to last forever. A struggle for immortality mingled with sighs it is; painfully hewing it out day after day smites the laborer with his pick — millions of strokes merely for a tomb. Why make the fortress of death so strong? Can mortal arm ever take it? Here, too, lies a sculptured shape — a likeness, we may suppose. Chiseled in the rock, most lasting of materials, it seeks to be eternal, but will that preserve the fair body? Such are the immortal longings cut in the Delphic rocks, enduring some thousands of years. No, Apollo says, immortality comes not thus; seek it rather in that other Delphic monument: *Know Thyself*.

—— There is, however, stout denial here as everywhere; an enemy to Apollo has shown himself, still shows himself in the heart of Delphi; it is a God, Seismos, the Earthquake. Pass along the shining cliffs, you will see the convulsions of the Titan fixed in the stare of the sun. Layers of rock overlap, wrench, struggle, edge against edge; it is indeed a mighty protest. A huge wedge is driven into the mountain aslant by the God's maul; chips and pebbles lie in the seams. A great Titanic arm has tumbled the earth into confusion; a voice says that discord shall reign. But when we come down to the town, we see the conquest of Apollo and his people, for they have hewn and shaped into harmony even the rocks of Seismos, and all Delphi is the perpetual song of triumph over the dark God. Still Seismos is angry and threatens in these overhanging cliffs; Phloumbouki leans over fair Castalia with savage glance, ready again to precipitate himself into her bosom, as he did anciently and yesterday, and hide in dark caverns her gladsome waters.

―――― Still another protest, very different from that of barbarous Seismos, can be heard upon Parnassus; it is the voice of the new Prometheus who has again risen, and is in conflict with Zeus. The old Greek life is still here in the new, but it has fallen into a struggle with the newest — with the modern culture flowing from the West. Thus the world-conquering Titan is bringing his new fire from heaven to the Greek, and great is the upheaval which is threatened. Dim notes of the conflict can be heard at Delphi to-day, coming out of the distance like the doom of Fate; but we shall shut our ears to the discordant sounds and listen only to the Delphic harmonies.

―――― Even on rainy days Delphi is not without some divine guest — fire appearing in its primitive home on the hearth. It is strange how we all sit around it, and look into it steadily, as if bound by some demonic spell. Only once in a while is the silence broken by a fitful word, but the gaze is not broken; the white Palicaris sit there with rough bearded faces flared upon by the light. Behold the thousand forms that the blaze takes, yet one form underneath — a varied utterance, yet one thing uttered; it is a God there forming, playing with forms which appear and disappear in the breathing of flame. Vulcan is in the fire, and is at work with heavy respiration; it is his element, but these fleeting shapes he, the God, will make permanent, fixing eternally what is divine, in his Olympian smithy. Mind and light fraternize, in them the inner and outer become a mysterious one, speech too calls them one. The soul is fire, said an old Greek philosopher; certainly their kinship is near, and they fondly embrace through the eye; they form the first bond of friendship between the inner and outer world.

—— That of which the stranger will not grow weary, is the ever-changing play of the sun, clouds and mountains. Such variety within such a limited space, yet in most magnificent proportion, he has not seen elsewhere; he will gaze till his very soul seems to have taken its abode in the eye. The blue dome is striped across with many a white fleecy band, the sun shifts over the summits, shadow and sunshine race in sport down the hill-sides. Then a hole in the clouds allows the eye of Apollo to peer through, whence he illumes for a time the tops of the mountains, setting them in burning splendor; over the leaves of the Olives full of silvery sparkle stretching afar down the slope he passes, with a golden shower often lighting up a group of maidens who are singing among the trees. So I saw him to-day hold through an aperture in the clouds a long gleaming tube of solid sheen, fixing it for many minutes upon a group of white and red forms, as if he too delighted in them like a common mortal.

—— The Parnassian maiden refuses the European dress, with its variegated dullness and parti-colored patches. Only a peasant girl she is, but the white garment falling in immaculate folds is still her favorite drapery. Not always immaculate though; she has to work in the fields; but such is her inborn instinct. Indiscriminate formless play of colors is not her poetry. Two simple colors she has, white and red; in happy contrast, yet in complete harmony; white innocence blushed through with the dawn of love. Hardly dare we call it the symbolism of colors — it is the simplest nature, the purest instinct — the freshest, most unalloyed utterance upon these hills, uttering the complete music of passion and of chastity in the human heart.

—— Often the people of Delphi spoke of Zálisca as a wonder worthy of being seen. After some directions given by Basili, I set out for the abode of the nymph, who was represented to be always sitting in her grot somewhere in the deep gorge of Pappadeia. Alone I pass through the Olives down the mountain to the mouth of the chasm, and begin slowly to creep up the channel through which is flowing a strong bright brook of water. The walls of rock get steeper and higher, the gorge grows darker, the stream leaps wilder. Still, here not far from the entrance is an ancient foundation, a small fane, one may conjecture; it is the introduction to the wondrous ceremony. Still further up in the chasm were other stones of a second structure. Some ancient passage, we imagine, full of solemn beauty; the little chapel was here with white column and statue. But look above, there is Nature's enormous temple carved with many a fantastic frieze and walled up to the clouds. In this spot, too, the old Greek sought to make Nature transform herself into Art, and placed here his beautiful work, which thus became divine, the habitation of his Gods.

Clambering over the second fane, now overgrown with weeds and briars, though flowers spring there, we come to the grot of Zalisca. Leaping across the wild cataract of the brook, we reach the open door and look in; there is indeed the home of the nymph, singing in a still sweet voice like Calypso. A clear basin of water lies in the cave, into the bottom of which jets gush up whirling the sand; the ceiling is decked with thousands of gems and figures; heavy fret-work hangs down wrought of stone; while outside many a vine trails over the doorway and embraces the mossy rocks. But the special glory of the day was the illumination made for me personally, I am fain to think, by Apollo, who passed over the gorge to the south just at mid-day and shone for a few moments. Just as I came to the door he threw his torch inside the grot, when it was lit suddenly with a thousand lamps, the ceiling was filled with rich drops of color like a new starry heaven, the waters became transparent at a gleam, revealing the fair form of the nymph, as she lay there in natural beauty. I confess to have felt the shudder which comes from the presence of divinity.

Several times afterwards I went to the grot of Zalisca, always with a kind of awe and with a secret feeling of some ceremony. I felt myself being ushered through certain rites into the abode of the nymph, there to look upon her face. Thus at Delphi does one go back into the dim symbolism of Nature from the beautiful outer world of Art, of statues and temples; into the dark mystery of religion he must grope from the clear sunshine, seeking to bear the light of Apollo with him. Zalisca's stream is said to be supplied from the lake on the Parnassian tableland, conducted hither by a channel underground, whose waters gush up into the lap of the nymph. For it has been noticed that when the Parnassian source has been dried up by drouths of summer, Zalisca is widowed of her buoyant stream, and no longer sings in her grot with the gushing waters. But when Parnassus again sends forth his thousand rivulets, Zalisca receives the fresh endowment and begins to pipe her songs once more in her grot with new-born joys.

—— The traveler, in his solitary walks, will excite wonder through the village; at last some inhabitant will address him: Often I see thee walking alone through the town, often wandering through the Olives as if to shun the glances of the world. Thy head is bowed toward the ground, and thy lips keep moving; always with some shape thou seemest to be talking, which I cannot see. Ever alone and alone; at times, too, thou makest a gesture in some earnest dispute and speakest aloud to an invisible thing,— what ails thee, O friend?—Whereto the traveler replies in a questionable way: When I talk to the nymphs, I love to be alone; they are shy and refuse to speak in the presence of another man or woman; only to one will they sometimes give a word — sometimes not even to him. They are nude, too, and modestly shrink from showing their fair white forms to vulgar gaze; but for me solitary they disrobe. Hence I in my walk seek no companions; the undraped Muse flees from the view of the stranger. I would not come to Delphi to see thee and talk with thee; many like thee I could have at home; the inhabitants of another world than thine have lured me hither with hopes of fellowship; when I can be with them, I must abandon thee, though thou, I well know, art my good friend.

—— You will notice new beauties in Castalia with every

visit; some ancient trace you will see, which at once suggests the perfect beautiful thing it once was. Thus to-day the old spouts ranged in a row played for me suddenly, where before I had seen only some meaningless holes in the stone. But the chief suggestion for one who stands and gazes long at the fountain, is in the mild upwhirl of the sand; as if it were the source of all poetry, he eagerly asks, whence come the bright waters? — From dark formless depths; many gloomy cavernous passages the stream traverses, where the old Gods, Night and Chaos, sit enthroned; deep in the bowels of the mountain it winds, receiving a drop of coolness here and of flavor there. Who will trace it, who can dig it out of the entrails of Parnassus? No analytic pickax and spade will do it successfully; leave it alone, let it gurgle through its dark channel; when the appointed time comes, it will leap forth to the sun in transparent beauty, and quench our thirst with its refreshing waters.

Scum lies now on the surface of Castalia which the pious traveler will skim off by means of a branch with a bushy top. Unseemly weeds, too, bedraggle the translucent ripples; these, also, he will pluck out, in part at least. Mosses gently waving under the surface along the bottom of the basin he will leave standing, for they yield calmly to the soft pulsations of the welling streams. Innumerable small jets throb from the bottom and lightly whirl the sand, not enough to disturb the clearness of the water, but sufficient to show its incessant activity under the crystalline surface. They come up like the bubblings of inspiration; underneath, from deep unseen well-heads they send forth fair cooling drops, yet the fount never grows turbid in its tireless endeavor. Some message the waters bring to the sunlight from obscure depths, but the moment they are touched by the rays of Apollo they drop back into transparent repose, so that the surface is never troubled. But mark, beneath the calm waters the eternal activity can ever be seen in the thousand little cones of bubbling sand, and this real fountain is transformed under the very eye to an image of the Muse.

—— Even the donkey is a poetical beast at Delphi and

drinks from the Castalian rill as he enters the village. He marches up and sips unconsciously, backward and forward move his ears in a kind of chorus, loud resounds the music of his bray over Parnassus. More serene, too, becomes his obstinacy, often he refuses to budge from the sweet song of the rivulet, in whose waters he is fain to lie down, trying to meditate the Muse in her native source. He buries his broad nose in the stream, moves his long ears — longer here than elsewhere on the face of the globe I think — and he brays his prolonged hexametrical modulation: the traveler may well wonder whether he, too, hears the nymph.

—— I tried, in one of my moods, to dress Castalia in rhymes, but the nymph spurned the jingling garments. Some musical longing, an inner melody, one always feels at Delphi; indeed it gives the mind no peace till there is found for it some adequate utterance. For the soul frees itself in the voiced wavelets of air, and therein finds happiness; it must be rocked upon them and soothed by them, moving in deep correspondence with them; it is an instrument struck by this Delphic Nature, whereby it vibrates and rings in perpetual pulsations. But Castalia refuses the modern crinkle-crankle, the superficial jingle of sweet sound. She said: Give me the old drapery, or something like it, for that reveals the fair form even under its cover; beneath its delicate folds movement will show itself in a thousand echoes. Give me the old music which harmonizes the body into its cadence, and does not dissolve the mind into dulcet, formless sound. Rhythm is my being — spurn the jingle.

—— Too well I know, continued the nymph, my white folds do not please you moderns. They are white and impassive, to you they seem without color and without feeling. Nor can you gaze at my step with delight, for I seek the quiet graces of mere movement; your wild dance stifles the ease-breathing chorus. Nor does my music please you, controlling simply the motions of my body; hexameters you banish with their long free stride. Travelers come and see me, then go home and traduce me: even the Greek of to-day, though he praise and be proud of me, casts off my folds and follows your fashion.

The true-hearted visitor answered: Truly hast thou spoken, O nymph, but I shall drink of thy waters with a new joy, and all day wander along the stream as it flows through the Olives. I shall dance too in thy chorus, taking delight in thy measures, though I, a stranger, move awkwardly, and cannot acquire the full grace of thy step and motion. Even thy garments I shall dress me in, and attune my gait to thy rhythm, though all Parnassus laugh at the strange figure. Nay, though I be alone in my devotion, and though men mock thee and me, still at thy shrine I shall worship.

―――― Last night I paid a visit to the fair Flower of Delphi, Louloutha, having been invited by the father. We ascended the outside stair to an upper story, where an ancient balcony hung over the street. When the company sat down by the fire, the wine was brought, she filled the glasses, I never saw anything more winningly done. She is truly a Delphic appearance; with blushing smile she withdrew to the window, when she noticed that she had attracted attention. Her eye curious, yet modest, would casually look up, then drop down, meeting the glance of the stranger. A Greek maiden, and just at the Greek period of the maiden's life, she lives in that happy golden world which hovers between what she knows and what she does not know. The woman is within her, yet she is not aware of it; in thought she is a child, but her actions speak innocently of something deeper than thought. What art thou, O Louloutha? Childhood is past; concious womanhood is not yet present; truly the Delphic period of thy sex. There is the conflict seen in her which forever makes the maiden interesting to man, makes her more than herself, raises her into a type almost worshipful. She is not, yet is; she will not, yet will — the opening rose which more enticingly reveals the redness within by half a disclosure. We behold in her the happy musical oneness between the inner and outer world which is the soul of Greece, of all Greek work. She indeed stands for much.

She is called out of her retreat by her mother, and resigns herself tremblingly to be looked upon by a man's eye with favor; innocence it is, yet a gazing out upon an immeasurable sea; a presentiment she becomes of all that she is to be. She seems to look down Time and transmit herself as an image to the future; she will be again, often again. At another glance she remounts to the past, she appears the transmitted image of the ancient Delphic world; she has been before, often before. Of her own accord she brings a quince and pares thin wafers of it into the wine, which thereby receives a new delicious flavor from her hand, indeed from her soul. I sip the beverage slowly, and seek to engage her words or at least her looks; not a syllable she uttered, yet she gave all she had; it was the old Delphic heart which still throbbed in her young life. Long I talked to the father while she listened, but really I was talking to her — the lovely image of Delphi, to me the fairest, freshest appearance of the Old in the New.

—— Nor shall I forget the last time I went to see Castalia, most generous nymph, who for so many weeks had met me with a smile every morning, and had refreshed me with a cooling draught every mid-day; who had thrown back to me so joyously innumerable Delphic images from her transparent depths, to remain mine forever. I reached down and trailed my fingers in the water; therein I could not help seeing my own visage more clearly reflected than ever before, as I thought of departure, asking: Shall I behold her again? The question at first caused the tears to start; but soon I was at peace with myself, for an assurance came from a voice within: I know I shall behold thee again; there can be henceforth no permanent separation; often I shall visit thee and drink; during my entire life thy image shall not go from me and thy mirrowing depths shall abide with me. — As I went toward the fountain, I was full of the melancholy of parting; but as I left it, bearing the last reflection of itself within me, I was buoyed with the presentiment of return, indeed of many returns.

XXII. THE DELPHIC FAUN.

After lingering some days at Delphi, the traveler will feel a strong desire to wander over the mountain back of the town, and see with his own eyes what may be there, and not hear it merely from others. Already certain strolls have been taken in that direction, but now a whole Delphic day must be given to the task. The high plain lies above in sunshine, and the summits in snow; a struggle, too, is going on between the seasons with alternating line of victory marked on the slopes. What then lies behind Delphi? is the question to be answered by this day's walk.

In the ascent one will first pass through the ancient Stadion, and will fill its seats with an ever-rising sea of faces; in company with that multitude he will listen to a chant or lyric measures in praise of the victor, or in praise of the Hero or God. That song speaks of the aforetime when man and deity dwelt together; still it seeks to bring back some image of the Divine to the eager throng. The hill-side overflows with the music; it is Delphi seeking to sing its own origin to itself, to explain the miracle of its own harmonious existence. The hymn goes far back of the town and throbs in unison with the rise of its temples into musical utterance. But having viewed the happy festal procession, and having caught the soul of the hymn, we turn our look up the steep.

There is an ancient pathway cut into the solid rock, winding through these huge stony splinters; little landing places you will observe in this path overlooking town and vale; here too are marks of an old foundation chiseled upon the mountain side. The house which stood on this spot commands a particularly fine view; the bright ribbon of Pleistus is quivering far below through the valley; over the long waves of olive tree-tops we behold the blue Corinthian waters bending gracefully behind a hill out of sight; in the foreground lay anciently white colonnaded Delphi. The view was a poem; it was an image of the Greek world, with its setting of nature and its Delphic soul in the center. From this center the landscape vibrates melodiously to-day. Pindar was the man who put this melodious vibration into his lines; here then we may place his house when he sojourned at Delphi.

It is still early in the morning, and the sun has just risen to a horizontal line with the summits above Delphi; the God is hurling his golden fires against the top of the crag, shooting them as if from the muzzles of millions of unseen muskets. One turns about and looks, after mounting to the crest; a cataract of sunbeams now pours over the heights of Phloumbouki into the lap of the little village, which rests strangely transfigured in the blaze. View it again, though often seen before; then face about and enter this high plain.

Not a human being is visible, nor does this seem a place for a human being; still the wayfarer appears not to be altogether without company. There is a kind of intoxication in the air, and some little sprite hovers about that is handing him the beverage. Who is it? I cannot tell, but I know that I am not alone. The path winds along to a mountain lake, silent, imaging quiet peaks; the little lake gathers the springs of Parnassus, and melting snows; through the dark earth it seeks an outlet, and breaks forth at last into that grot of beauty below Delphi, where we beheld Nymph Zalisca sitting on her throne; from her hand the stream dashes down into the plain, watering many an olive tree in its course, till it finally passes into the azure serenity of the sea; thence some drop of the mirroring Parnassian lakelet washes every shore of the earth, even to our own.

One will skirt its banks a short distance, throwing into its waters now and then a pebble which it swallows with an audible gulp; thus it too is a sort of being endowed with a voice and furnishes company. The town of empty huts is next reached, Kalyvia it is called, and used for summer residence. There is still a noise in its deserted streets, the silent hum of absent villagers; the air is yet vibrating low with the voices left here last summer, and will continue the vibration to eternity, — for how can that sound, once set a-going cease? Words, left to wander, never wholly vanish; let us beware of the wrong word; to the new spiritual ear of the speaker it will be coming back to his Last Judgment. Still one hears the faint speech of men swinging in infinitesimal wavelets on the air with many a strange commingling of antique voices. What they say cannot easily be told; they leave, however, some strong impression, which attunes like a prelude.

The path forks; which road now is to be taken? There is no voice to tell; there is no form of flesh and blood to give body to these uncertain sounds of solitude. One will look through the huts for some guiding word; he will be disappointed, and must fall back upon himself. Shall we turn round? This side of Delphi has become familiar; bright it is and very noble; we have seen it spring from the mountain in beautiful forms; but can we not catch a glimpse of the obverse side? Many hints we have had already of some strange hidden world upon these heights and amid these lofty woods; without delay, then, let us continue the search.

So the traveler selects a way for himself, allured by a pleasant glen of pines which promise good company; up through the fragrant conifers he winds slowly, giving full control to the unseen guide. The path is hardly visible, footsteps have at times passed this way, rarely the track of the donkey can be noticed. Once in a while there is a trace of the woodman who has left his chips and lopped branches as a friendly salutation to the lonely wanderer. Deep silence, overglowed with weird sunlight holds all the trees in a dumb, yet attentive posture; look at this muffled pine, he is listening, but to what? The wayfarer will stop and listen too; not without a slight shudder lest he hear something which is permitted only to the trees to hear.

The sunlight falls pleasantly among the green tree tops, and comes dangling in patches to the ground underneath; these ragged golden patches are favorite resting places for the eye, possibly too for the nimble spirits of the woods, which seem to flit out of them at the intrusion of a human glance. One looks up the whole slant of the mountain against which the sun is shining; what sport is there? Sunbeams and needle-leaves are wrestling with changeful victory for the possession of the entire slope; nor can one help seeing that other beings are there who dance for joy through the lights and shadows of the combat — a chorus of Hamadryads living in secret sympathy with the trees, and forming the people of that city called a forest.

Not a living person is met, scarcely a trace of humanity is seen, still the persistent fact is, that the wayfarer is not without some society. At first he is unconscious of any presence, but after walking a little while through the woods he wakes up to the knowledge that he is not alone, and he wonders who it can be that is following. A slight terror is felt at that unseen companion who skips away behind the trees as soon as one tries to look at him; the voice, too, vanishes when one stops to listen to what it may be saying. A small panic is experienced in the breast throbbing audibly between two held breaths, as one hearkens again; this panic is sent by the God Pan, who dwells in the forest, and punishes in such manner those who intrude upon his sylvan solemnities. The old Greek, passing through this glen to-day, would have seen the deity with his whole train of nymphs celebrating their rites, and would have heard and remembered their song, would have sung it himself at their next festival.

Several miles we thus pass up a gentle slope, pine-clad; the forenoon sun is always getting higher, till at last he pours down his beams quite parallel to the trees, and smites the traveler straight upon the head. The latter comes to the ridge which divides the range and begins to descend gradually; here is the turning point to the other side of the Delphic slope. This is the snow-line too, now driven by the sun higher up the mountain, like a retreating foe. Just here is the battle-field: many a little path of melting snow, as if mortally wounded and bleeding to death, is seen in covert places and lying under protecting rocks and bushes. The pedestrian, somewhat thirsty, will snatch up dripping handfuls of it as he passes, and hold it to his parched lips, whose thirst, however, refuses to be slaked by such a draught.

Nor can we omit to notice the vast quantity of loose stones that are strewn everywhere along our path, as if some Titanic sower had scattered them like seeds of wheat over the grainfield. Here upon Parnassus, says the legend, Deucalion and Pyrrha were left the sole survivors after the flood; here upon this very spot, perhaps, that curious casting of rocks took place, whereby Mother Pyrrha, throwing these stones behind her, begot the destroyed human race anew in a great hurry, for each stone sprang up a full-grown man. Such a feat is indeed possible only upon Parnassus — to change the rock to a living man; but the touch of Pyrrha is no longer to be found among the Parnassian women. Still the consoling reflection can be made that there are enough stones left here to re-establish the race a second time in case of flood or other calamity.

We now enter a small cultivated plain; very small, but a few hundred yards in length and less in breadth; this is wheat growing upon it in little green blades, and yonder are three huts. A mysterious tract; abrupt mountainous cliffs snow-capped hem it in with a sort of fond look down into it; shut off wholly from the world it lies in the lofty bosom, veritably snow-white, of Parnassus, not far from the top. Not an inhabitant can be seen, not a child at play before the door of the hut; it, too, is completely deserted, and over it hovers that audible silence sending through the new comer its panicky shudders. There is no doubt that one has a feeling of intrusion, he has come upon some band of dwellers unexpectedly though he behold nought; he has interrupted some ceremony by his human presence. Look up at the mountains now; they threaten, filled with shapes whose chorus below was scattered by the stranger's sudden advent. Let us go past those huts, perhaps they contain somebody of our kin; the road leads a little distance in front of them; one door stands slightly ajar, but there is no human appearance or apparition. With a still greater panic, which will be taken as a warning of the God Pan, one will hurry by without stopping to investigate those huts or their contents; he will not defy the divine admonition, nor does he care to meet face to face that strange-speaking companion who still flits at his side. As he emerges from the plain he looks back; the dissonance caused by his presence is vanishing, the harmony of that little world seems restored as he departs, and the nymphs with rude satyrs begin again the dance; this is the home of their revels.

Thus we continue the unusual journey behind Delphi; it has brought us into contact with a new set of beings, with glimpses into a new world: What can it be? Never mind; we are going on. Here we enter a deep dark cleft where mid-day turns to twilight; above the head the mountain overhangs and threatens to cast itself, down upon the puny wayfarer, as he looks up at the lofty ledges swinging in the skies. What is a man here? The might of the mountain overwhelms this petty individuality; a person is naught, and may be thankful if the giant will only let him pass. What if the old deity would loosen his hold upon one overhanging rock? Here, too, is a voice that speaks and takes on a shape corresponding with the utterance; it is not that joyous mysterious voice which comes from sunshine playing amid the pines; not that deeper voice of interrupted solitude over the plain; this is the secret mutter of the mountain holding back convulsion and fierce outbreak. A hoarser, more terrible voice; listen to it rumbling amid these rocky bowels, and form an image of the monster, then pass on.

I have, however, repeatedly thought of turning back, having seen enough of the other side of Parnassus. But there is some demonic power which entices forward— these new and changing utterances furnish alluring company to the hesitating tourist. Yet they have a strange law; they are loudest when you do not hear them; if you listen, they vanish upon the air. It is a ghostly company indeed; they stay at your side if you do not try to think who they are; you can see them skipping through the sunny landscape and fragrant pines, if you do not attempt to look at them; you seem to know them best when you do not know them at all. Such is the riddle with its enticement everywhere; the dark glen, the light wood, the sudden precipice start it into life; even the panic with its shudder allures. Fine views break from the distance at intervals, like harmonious swells of music from beyond; that other world behind the visible one is the strong abiding fact, and leads you irresistibly into its unseen domain. I had better turn back, but the truth is, I am infatuated, and so go on, not being really in possession of myself.

As I come out of a little patch of trees and reach a far-extending mountain slope, I hear a noise quite faint. It is a new tone in a new locality; a few steps further and I hear it again; I listen, it can be heard continuously, and not vanishingly. This is, then, a real sound, belonging clearly to this sensible world, and permits itself to be caught and held by the outer ear. It creeps around the mountain side, growing clearer and more definite as I advance; what can it be? I conclude that the sound comes from running or falling water, though I cannot see anything of the kind. A moment more and I am standing on the brink of a brook hid among the grass and stones, flowing down the side of the mountain, which is not steep enough to make a cascade, but sufficiently slanting to produce a strong rapid rush of the current. Moreover, the slant is even and very long so that the stream darts down in a straight crystalline band almost from the top to the very foot of the mountain, making a wild melody with the pebbles in its course. Clear, sparkling, beautiful, springs the rivulet; a silvery ribbon, which one might think of picking up from the slope where it lies. I lean down and put my hands into it; but it will not suffer itself to be lifted except by palmfuls to the hot temples and thirsty lips, which are now freshened with a new life.

Its music, too, you will hear after sitting beside it for a while; there is a rise and fall of sound, notes higher and lower, form a kind of tune which gives a certain melody to the solitude. A natural harmony, though rude; still it is a harmony and brings all the surroundings into unison, so that you may well say, this is a musical spot, where Nature breaks forth into melodious expression. Another fact you will mark, as you sit and listen; the stream has a key-note, around which its other notes move, and to which it is attuned: Niagara, too, has such a note, and the Ocean itself. So we hear the primitive musical instrument of Nature played upon by the unseen hand — whose shall we call it? Little difference does it make, so we catch the music and cause it to play within us.

Thus the weary wayfarer greets the brook as a friend; its babble will soon banish all panic from his breast, and its look, as it joyously dances down the side of the mountain in the sunshine, will refresh him quite as much as a draught of its waters. After sporting with it a while and enjoying its melodious ripple, he will feel like turning up the slope to the fountain head of so much music and mirthfulness. A pleasant saunter along its edge will bring him to a piece of ground spreading out like a fan, on which hundreds of little sources gush up, and soon unite their streamlets into the brook. Here is an ancient trough, hewn out of stone and covered with moss and rust; other dressed stones lie about, which the imagination at once builds into a shrine of the spring-nymphs. It is a sacred spot, joyous, useful too, singing an eternal hymn; not without reverence may one still regard it.

In the midst of the gurgling well-heads is a smooth seat, a single stone upon which one may sit down with the little company around him. There is solitude yet, but no shudder comes; the sunlight, the pines, and the brook are in complete harmony and attune the soul peacefully to their strain. But hark! what is that new sound? Amid the notes of the purling waters was suddenly mingled a human voice, or what seemed such. Then it vanished into the sound of the brook and was forgotten. But soon it returns and speaks more plainly than before; what does it say? That I cannot tell; but so much is manifest: these are words, not mere unbroken sound;

they are articulated, wrought into the chain of human speech; they seem the words of children talking near by, so real that I look up to see them. I try to hear them again, but they refuse to come back at my bidding, and gradually I get to thinking about other matters. But presently the talking is heard once more — a conversation as of question and answer; yet when I am fully awake to it, at once it stops. This startles me, and the panic slightly returns; there is no human shape present, yet there is articulate speech upon this ground. Moreover it balks my will, it cannot be heard by effort, only in the unconscious world does it speak to me; it selects the moment of utterance, not I. Clearly it belongs not to my self-conscious life; a strange unaccountable thing in the brook, which fascinates — possibly a divinity. Can it be the nymphs of the stream who are thus chatting together, and are they realities?

This is the voice that the shepherd hears, that the old Greek heard when he fabled of Naiads speaking in the fountain and enticing men; it is a veritable voice. I would like to hear it again, but it will not speak, however much I listen. Gradually the mind drifts away into the distant mountain haze, and is lost there, forgetting the nymphs. Suddenly the voice speaks once more, now just at my feet; I have it, I catch a little of it, and drag it into my conscious state. One small ripple tells the secret, it continued to prattle when it ought to have kept silent. It is the water which articulates at certain intervals; these thousand little cascades leaping over the pebbles form the chain of successive sounds at certain moments, and then break off; moreover these sounds may be loud or low, like the rise and fall of the human voice, with manifold modulation.

The peculiarity of the noise rising from the flowing water is this articulation or linking together of sounds like the speech of man. Then it ceases after babbling its meaningless words upon the air. The brook being very shallow and wide at this point rushes over innumerable little obstructions, and forms these short watery vocables in succession; thus it seems to talk, to utter for a moment syllabled speech. In a higher or lower key, in the tone of children and grown people, in question and response, quite all the phases of language are to be heard; then the new tongue loses itself in the continuous gurgle of the brook. It is a brave struggle; the waters try to speak, and sometimes do articulate, but they soon drop back into their indiscriminate babble, and the new words are drowned in the rushing current. The brook certainly attempts to talk, and you cannot help listening.

Such is the language of the nymphs, not put down in the works of erudition, and being without grammar and dictionary. In the welling sources, in the long glide of the crystalline stream down the mountain is hidden a voice; the old mythus speaks that voice, and it can be heard to-day. I now recollect that this is no new experience, that I have heard this sound before along the brink of stony brooks, that in former days I have turned at some word of the rill to see who was talking. But never till now has the matter risen out of the Lethe of unconsciousness; for one must be unconscious at first in order to hear the voice; when I sought to catch it ever so slightly, it was already gone; through that dark world alone will it come to daylight.

But what do the nymphs say? you ask. It is simply an articulate sound, the word laden with spiritual meaning it is not. Yet it speaks to the soul in subtle harmonious suggestion; it has many a curious modulation, there is a certain character in its sound too; it has a note of persuasion, as if it sought to entice the listener into its watery bosom, and sport with him down into the valley, were not his body in the way. It can have the sound of anger, then it breaks into laughter; but its chief note is the low sweet note of love. It is no wonder that so many of the ancient worthies were enamored of nymphs; these assume a positive shape to the imagination with their caressing tones; the unconscious world bursts into expression, and the old Mythology becomes a vital thing once more. Thus one loiters the time away in golden idleness; he is entranced by the new world, and would fain drop away into a dream of the brook; it is a spell which changes the man into a stream, which transformation has been hinted in many an ancient fable.

Such is the natural word, aspiring, struggling to fill itself with a soul and thus attain unto speech: but it cannot cross the unseen barrier, it always falls back into the brook after leaping for a moment above the surface. The heroic struggle of Nature to rise into a higher being we may consider it; some aid it seems to pray for; is there no one who can catch that helpless floundering word, hold it, and make it eternal? Yes, there is: his name is the Poet; he seizes the dim suggestions of Nature and flings them out of the brook, he wins them from the trees, he captures them from the mountain; a strange magical sort of man dealing with invisible spirits whom he makes visible. His words are still the words of the brook, the tree, or the mountain; they have the sound of the waters, the fragrance of the flowers, the sport of the leaflets; but they are on his lips transfigured, and receive a soul which holds them up from falling, and which is the fulfillment of their former aspiration. The word of Nature which the Poet hears and utters can never drop back into the undistinguishable elements, but it becomes winged and soars into ethereal spaces, imaging the things of Heaven.

But it is time for the wayfarer to depart; too long already has he dallied with the nymphs, listening to their revelations. He turns away with many delightful calls in his hearing, for the whole stream has now become vocal, and has admitted him into its inner sanctuary. A tender farewell has to be given; with a final draught and gentle plash of the hand he takes his leave of the musical company, though the receding voices sound long in his ear and try to persuade him back.

He returns to the small peak-girt plain where the huts stand empty with one door slightly open; but now the door is shut, shut tight, there cannot be a doubt of it. No living object is visible, though the former influences are felt; guess me this riddle? Indeed the door is fast; hands have done it — what hands? There is some power at work in this deserted spot; we felt it when we were here before; at present it is even more perceptible. Let us hurry forward; Pan touches again, sending stronger shudders than the previous ones; we shall not tarry in his domain for fear of some further punishment. It was he who closed the door to hide his revels from mortal eye; the shaggy deity has refused to reveal himself, being so unlike the fair nymph of the spring; the panic is the sole reminder of his presence. But he belongs to that unconscious world also, into which the Mythus strikes its roots and draws its nourishment; we must form, too, his image, as he vanishes amid the trees.

A new path shows itself into which one enters without further thought. The woods still appear overlaid with patches of sunshine, and the unseen company is never absent — in fact, I am now getting used to their presence, and they no longer flee from me as they did at first. I feel myself becoming a denizen of their world. My glance does not seem to drive them out of the sunny spots as it once did; the shudder, too, has quite left me. Moreover, the feet seem lighter, the side of the mountain is no longer so hard to climb; I verily believe that I am partaking of their nature. It is certain that a transformation has taken place since morning, a new relationship has been established with a strange order of friends. Imagine me walking along through the forest alone, yet in cheerful companionship, scaling the high rock with ease, unburdened by a single thought, dwelling wholly in a free unconscious world with its own inhabitants.

A new side in human nature wakes, unsuspected before or regarded as a dream or delusion; stranger still, a new side in external nature comes to view, in perfect correspondence with this human phase. The chasm between man and the world outside of him seems filled; a new bond has arisen, indeed a new being who joins the two into a harmonious whole. The senses are open to the keenest delight and possess the sharpest intensity; thought, however, sinks into their ocean and disappears; existence seems but a dream. Such you will become, if you wander through the Greek woods over Parnassus on a sunny day; you sink away into a new kinship, which, suspected and shunned at first, changes to a secret confiding intimacy.

But this is not all. We have found a new life, and it is to be embodied into a form; if we possess the Greek instinct, we shall discover the image for our conception; indeed, the image is its true expression. This new life must find utterance now, must have found utterance long ago; of its own accord the shape rises up and walks into being at my side. It is no effort of mine, I do not make it, it appears when I have the ability to see it. Not at the time did I identify it, or try to identify it; I could not then reflect — it was the pain of Hell to think; but now I can look back at the appearance, and tell you my judgment concerning it: it was the Faun.

But wake up and behold this real thing: a large hole in the mountain not far from the top. Hither, our path has led us deviously but with certainty all day; it is the famous Korykian cave. The disturbed eagles fly angrily a few feet above my head; another bird, unknown to me, mingles with them, gifted with a scolding voice, of which I now get the full benefit. I reach for my tapers, which I brought along, suspecting that I might have to conduct you through dark places. In spite of the sunshine, the journey has been somewhat nebulous at times, but now we shall have to take our little lights and grope about in the secrets of the cavern.

As I turn around a short angle, I come suddenly upon a person who is lying on a rock, propped up with his elbows and finding some hidden entertainment in the objects of Nature inclosing him around. A glance reveals that it is Dimitri, with whom I had a very slight acquaintance at Delphi; to-day he is taking a short stroll over Parnassus all alone, for the mere delight of the solitude. He pretends to have a little errand, he is going to catch some rare beetles for a professor of entomology at Athens; he knows the very spot, and the only spot where they are to be found. He has a crook in his hand which he employs like a lengthened arm; his whole satisfaction is to lie on grassy banks along the brooks, to roam the forests, or to dream the hours away reclining on a stone in the sun. He avoids the vineyard where there is work in trimming the vines; he shuns the Olives where he has to stoop so often in picking up the fruit; but he runs off from Delphi and wanders alone here on Parnassus, where he seems to find his true kindred.

Dimitri is indeed a strange character. At Delphi he is in ill repute on account of laziness; but judging by his agility at times, by his readiness to clamber up the steepest rock for a trifle, by the unnecessary steps or rather skips that he takes in a day, I cannot call him lazy, though it is manifest that he will not work in the harness of the Delphic world. Look at his clothes; they are the garments of civilization, but they do not sit well on him, his body seems in a sort of protest against them; at every movement it cries out to be left alone or to be girt with a simple, goat's fell. His cap falls over his eyes and blinds him, till he takes it off and goes bareheaded; then he can see, and I believe smell, with the keenness of a wild deer. He carries no mark of age in his looks; his face never loses its dreamy smile when he is among the mountains; he can laugh the moments away lying on his sunlit rock and never think of the lapse of Time. The Faun has now become a reality in him; I do not deny his close relationship to this locality, to this day, and to myself at this moment; but chiefly, my unseen companion follows me no longer, he now leaves me to the seen presence of Dimitri.

He offers to conduct me through the Korykian Cave, which with such a guide must reveal all its secrets. This cave was well known in antiquity, and was celebrated by poets as the home of their poetical beings; it was visited by our traveler Pausanias, who has compared it with other famous caves that he knew of, and has pronounced this the most wonderful of all. He tells us, too, that it was sacred to Pan and the Nymphs; an inscription found upon the spot in recent times commemorates the same fact. Thus we have arrived at the very house of those strange existences which have been flitting through the forest and over the mountain during the entire day.

We enter the door and walk down into the first chamber, a large presence-chamber. The ceiling is arched above, and is said to be forty feet high in its highest part; it has an imperial magnificence; one looks up at the clusters hanging there as if it might be a fairy palace. On the ground lie small circles of stones heaped up and blackened with fire; they date from the time of the Revolution, when this cave formed a retreat for the neighboring villagers from the Turk, as it did for the ancient Delphians in the time of the Gallic invasion. Still the walls are begrimed with the smoke of those fires, and of the torches of visitors. One marches into the unknown darkness carefully; again there is felt a touch of the panic as one enters deeper into the obscure cavern. But behold Dimitri; he needs none of my tapers; he seems at home, at one moment he is at my side, at another he springs away into some unseen corner as if to give a caress to a nymph, or to greet an old acquaintance.

As soon as the eyes get used to their new duty, a striking series of objects emerge from the darkness on every side: the statuary of Nature formed of stalagmites. There are several groups along the wall arranged as if in a gallery; then there is a large group that stands entirely free, to the rear of the chamber. The most remarkable is the Mother and children, suggesting Medea clasping her infants. But the tendency is to masks, to faces of wild caricature, which pass gradually into the rock. Mocking satyrs may be distinguished, and one of them the visitor will be inclined to call Pan, who now appears fashioned by Nature herself and dwelling in his own mountain temple. Such is the primitive gallery of sculpture, suggesting all which Art is hereafter to reveal of this unseen world.

Nor must we forget that in antiquity there were, besides these natural shapes, the statues of Pan and the Nymphs set up in this cave, genuine works of the Artist. Thus we attain the completed Greek conception, and we behold the direct transformation of Nature into Art, seeking to express the invisible powers of this region. Pan still runs over these summits and through these glens — he, that magnetic link connecting man with the secret energies of Nature. One feels him and his influence in the solitudes, and forms his image — such is the first stage; then he bursts into visibility in these rude shapes of rock, which, however, fall back into impotent formlessness, till the hand of the Artist reaches out and helps them rise into complete being in the statue, in which the suggestion of Nature is realized and transcended. This, we recollect, is quite what the Poet did for the natural words of the brook.

But accident now shows the culmination of the series in a living being. There he stands alongside one of those rude figures of stone, gazing at it with a far-off wonderment — my companion Dimitri, the living Faun, beside the rocky Faun. The resemblance is astonishing, almost appalling; you ask, which indeed could have been the model? The broad nose, the hairy forehead, the look of jolly animality are common to both; even the drapery is similar: as Dimitri's body seems to disappear in his formless garments, so the outlines of the figure vanish in the formless rock of the cavern; both, too, appear equally besmirched by the smoke and dust of time. He looked at the stony image with a strange fascination, he had evidently selected it of all others in the cave from some secret affinity. I glanced at each imaging the other, and said: "Why, Dimitri, that is you." He gave a wild snort of angry terror, and darted with his taper into the next chamber, whither I groped dubiously after him.

Between the two chambers is a kind of curtain, partly suspended from the ceiling — a wonderful piece of tapestry which hints of Nature as the primitive weaver. On all fours one has to climb now, through moist dark passages; in the rock, up which one crawls, is a little spring which freshens lips and temples. A little eye of a fountain beaming in the dim light of the taper — it seems to have life, even love in its glance. This room is gorgeously furnished, with fine incrustations over head, where hangs many a sparkling drop of translucent stone. A large conical column in the center is inscribed with the names of visitors — all nationalities, all languages, all periods seem to be represented — a grand column of fame, upon which, after some trial, I totally failed to grave my name.

My guide, the living Faun, now conducts me to the small chambers in the rear — bedrooms of the Nymphs one may call them without fear of being successfully confuted. These apartments are not easy of access; it would seem that their fair occupants did not wish to have their privacy disturbed in this last refuge. To enter the first room, Dimitri flings herself down on the floor and crawls through a narrow aperture, taper in hand; he seems to shrink in the act, like a witch going through a key-hole. I follow his example, but the stone above fits so close into the small of my back that I am caught, and can neither get in nor out. Dimitri laughed; Pan, the satyrs, and all the dwellers of the cave, seemed to be laughing in a universal echo with him at the poor mortal caught in trying to enter the Nymphs' bed-chamber. But there is Faun enough in me to shrink also and wriggle through; this day's experience has not been for nought. It is a friendly room, somewhat dark, fit for the obscure mysteries of its inhabitants. More interesting than ever Dimitri is getting to be; he now seems at home as he squats down in one corner; he is in bond with the hidden influences of the place, and he has an air of familiarity, begotten not of knowledge but of fellow-feeling, indeed of kinship. After showing the secrets of the spot, more by his actions than by his words, he suddenly sprawls and glides through the aperture, as if it were the only door he ever knew. "You lizard," I cried, and crawled after him. But ah, that close-fitting stone! It seized me again with a tight span around the waist, so that all the india-rubber in me was required in order to squeeze through. "Dimitri, no more holes of that sort, I tell thee; I have seen enough of the Nymphs to-day, at any rate."

But he insists with unusual urgency upon conducting me to one chamber more, which lies high, in a sort of upper story; he scrambles up and pulls me after him over the slimy rock. More delighted than ever he looks; he turns to me and says: "This would be a fine room to which to lead home a bride." *Nymphe*, in modern Greek, means a bride, and the word at once connects him with the invisible occupant of the chamber, the Nymph. He throws himself down and rests a moment, looking up at the stalactites with a rapt eye which sees spirits. I look, too, at the ceiling; a little mask laughs out of the stone above, then slides into indistinguishable rock with the rest of its body. The moment I see it, it turns to crystal, but I am quite sure that Dimitri saw it alive, and that it recognized him with that little titter still visible in the stone. Again glance at the pretty face above; it is Dimitri's bride. I nudge him, waking him up from his revery; unwillingly he turns away, and, giving a kind of salute, he slips down the side of the cavern.

It is time to pass out; we go by the conical column with its roll of names; we come to the little spring, gathered drop by drop till it amount to a shellful, by some busy unseen benefactress; it offers now its last draught. We reach the royal antechamber again, with its statuary and spangled ceiling. But there is a change; I felt the unpleasant shudder when I came into the dark place; now the masks are familiar, even merry, they have become reconciled to the presence of the stranger, and salute him. Darkness also seems to have changed to light; the stealthy tread toward dim uncertainty has been transformed into the sure, easy walk of familiarity. I now feel at home in the cave, and in accord with its inmates; several times I pace through the accessible chambers, and give myself freely to their suggestions. Dimitri, too, has changed toward me; at first he was shy, and did not let himself out, but now he treats me with strong affection, almost with fawning at times.

Here one beholds the influences which are at work in these mountains, formed into shapes, and placed in a temple by Nature herself. What lay previously in the vague unconscious realm, now seems to find a symbol, a sensuous representation and an abode. After such a long wandering walk with its many new experiences in the forest and upon the mountain, one feels that he has found in this cave an utterance, dark and uncertain, still an utterance, which by main force springs into fantastic shapes in the attempt to reveal itself. Nature's fancy may be seen in its thousandfold workings, which call up a corresponding activity in man; still it is but Fancy, the Fancy of Nature sporting capriciously with its own shapes.

However this may be, the Korykian cavern has one prominent ground of interest: it is the best place to observe how Greek Art is hinted even in its minutest shadings by Nature. These are still the works of Nature, but it is Nature struggling to be Art, needing just a touch of the hand of man to preserve the persistency of her forms and carry them out to completeness. Alone, she is unable to bear forward her shapes to a full representation of spirit; they swoon back into rock, half made, with perhaps an arm only, or a face looking out from the stony wall. The suggestion is certainly given by Nature, but she is impotent to attain to the spiritual; we wonder that she comes so near to it, but still falls short; with an eager shining face she looks and points to her supreme end, but cannot reach it.

Here is Architecture in all its germs; behold its decorated inclosure, its richly hung ceilings with hint of column and structural proportion, as well as of ornamentation. The cave has a striking resemblance to the Greek house; it suggests the very plan upon which the buildings of Pompeii are erected. Indeed Pompeii with its Hellenized Architecture is seldom absent from the mind as one passes through the various parts of the cavern. This is the typical form of the Greek house; such is the thought which one carries away. In a still higher degree have we the hint of Sculpture; the single figure, the group, the gallery, have already been noticed. These were the first models, let the Artist now appear, and set the encumbered form free from the rock.

And the Artist does appear, and set the form free; the statues of Pan and the Nymphs stood anciently alongside of the half-revealed shapes in the rock. The old worshiper came here and saw the transition with his own eyes; he beheld the complete figure of the sculptor rise out of the stony swaddling-clothes of Nature, and become the bearer of a spiritual purpose. Therein, he saw, too, his own supreme end; it was to make this material existence of his an image of the soul; he too, was to undergo transformation like the stone before him. This, then, was a temple of worship wherein man could behold some phase of his transfiguration; even Pan, goat-footed though he be, has a true utterance; his sculptured form is a spiritual presence, revealing that spirit which is felt everywhere throughout the forest and mountain.

Numerous modern legends are connected with the cave. The Arachobite mother thinks that it is the home of the Nereids who kill and carry off her infants. The puzzling etymology of its name has given rise to the following legend taken from the mouths of the people. A number of maidens resolved to retire from the world and devote themselves wholly to the service of the Virgin. They took this cave for their cloister, whence it is called *Korykion antron*, that is, maids without men, *korai dicha andron*. It also bears the name of Sarantavli, the Forty Halls or rooms, from the belief that forty monks once took up their abode in the cave, and closed the rooms behind them, where they have remained ever since, and are still expected by the peasantry to come and free the orthodox church from the hateful sway of the Mohammedan. In the midst of the mountain they remain at prayer, monks in their deep monastery of stone. Hence, to-day, there are so few chambers, some half dozen only, the rest being closed till the great day of restoration. Thus the cave still is a religious abode, but of a very different kind from the ancient one. A monastic character is now given to it by legend, whereas anciently it was full of the fresh breath of Nature, of the joyous worship of Pan and the Nymphs. In such manner the ancient and modern worlds have left their image even upon the Korykian Cave; but Dimitri is the true central figure of it to-day, being the living presence of the Old in the New.

In going out of the cave, we pass by that strange statue of the Faun; Dimitri will not now look at it. I called his attention to it; still again he turned away with a shudder. But previously he preferred that shape to any other in the cavern, it had a deep fascination for him, which is now changed to abhorrence. He has seen his own image, he has cast a glance into his own spiritual being, he has become self-conscious to a degree. It is but a glimmer of the world within, still it is torture, it is horror. Never before has he had a reflection, one may think; never has he looked upon himself and asked the question: "What, then, am I?" Like an animal, which turns away from its own image in a mirror, or snarls or snaps at it when seen in the clear brook, he is terrified as well as angry at his own appearance. "Dimitri, be not afraid," I cried; " dare to face thine own ghost and become a man; that image is thyself, look upon it, and thou art already above it." I grasped his arm, and led him to the figure, feeling him tremble; I was now his guide, he was no longer mine. He looked at it with unsteady, blinking eye, as if trying to gaze into some intense light which vision could not endure. We turned away, he skipped no more, his joy was lost, he had come to a dim knowledge of himself; he was transformed, the Faun began to disappear.

We pass slowly down the hill-side over the tableland toward Delphi. Dimitri has certainly lost a portion of his buoyancy. Sometimes the Faun in him returns, he frisks over the fields, bounding out of the path, and reclining a moment against a stone. Then he would walk slowly in the beaten way, sunk in thought, considering apparently that strange image of himself. But he would wake out of reflection at another moment, would run and fetch a curious pebble, flower or insect, and watch with a puzzled gaze how they affected the stranger. We reach the summit over Delphi and behold the level rays of the setting sun shot straight against Phloumbouki; into that round ball of fire the Faun looks with delight and wonder, his face shows a kind of worship; the luminary sinks in a blaze, Dimitri turns to Delphi with a saddened aspect, as if it was the last time that he, the Faun, was to look at the setting sun; to-morrow he must behold it with other eyes. Without a word he slid off into a by-path of the village;

it was probably his unhappiest day, and he owed it to me, who had brought him to look upon himself.

Imagine now with me the future career of Dimitri. There has been a conversion in him; he has been revealed unto himself, and thus rises out of his former condition. I predict that he will lose his friskiness, that he will begin to go to the Olives and vineyard, that he will adjust anew his drapery, that he will no longer spring alone over the mountains, but weighted with his cares and thoughts, he will pass heavy-paced to his day's labor. He begins to realize the Delphic oracle: *Know Thyself;* he starts to-morrow with the burden of a new world upon his shoulders. To the unconscious race of beings he belongs no more; he renounces the company of Pan and Nymphs — he is now Delphic. But how great the difference between me and thee, O Dimitri! I seek to fall back into that instinctive soul of pure Nature, which is my Paradise, whilst thou must strive to get out of it, since it is thy Hades. I would fain live there days of thoughtless existence, drinking of the first fountains whose melodious waters heal the worn and dusty heart; but thou must rise from faunhood to manhood, taking upon thee the burden of thine own image, a seeming shadow indeed, but heaviest of sublunary things.

XXIII. THE RELIGION OF BEAUTY.

That was indeed a wonderful epoch in Universal History when Religion and Beauty, when the spirit and the senses were united in a supreme world-embracing harmony. A most important epoch, too, it was; life became musical, its extremes touched and sent forth the thrill of sweetest notes, existence seemed a fountain of melody, welling up into song. The two great struggling principles of the human soul are the sensuous and the spiritual; war, eternal war, has been declared between them, till this state of man is an everlasting field of battle, with the fight renewed hour by hour, and victory daily lost and won. Once, however, there was peace, universal peace between the two conflicting elements; a peace uttering itself in the noblest strains of song, in a joyous activity, in a serene worship. It is hardly more than a point in the sweep of Time, but that point gave expression to the harmony of the Universe; it was a music of the spheres in melodious conjunction; Religion was the worship of Beauty, and Beauty was the inspiration of Religion.

Whatever be the kind of religion, there are in it two factors — the worshiper and the worshiped; the Man and the God. In some separation they at first are, vast and deep; they stand off against each other, indifferent and often hostile. To bring the two sides together and make them harmonious, is the supreme act of worship, indeed of life; accursed is the man who has fallen out with his Gods. Such alienation is the unhappiest of all mortal states, the darkest and deepest chasm of the human heart. The harmonious relation between the Human and Divine is the eternal verity of religion, the final test of its value for man; and we always ask, what discords of soul does this religion overcome, what melody does it reveal and utter in its worship, what reconciliation does it give between man and his God.

We would not say that there are no dissonant notes in the Greek world; there are such and in abundance. But in her worthy period, they seem to vanish into melody; they pass over into sweet sounds which have been perpetuated in her song. Discords there are, but they do not remain; indeed deepest music springs from discord overcome; the deeper the dissonance, the deeper the resultant harmony. The faculty of changing disruption of soul into equable well-attuned health, is peculiarly Greek; dead and meaningless is music without tension, simplest reed pipe is more; song as well as worship must show victory over struggle — the reconciliation after the conflict.

Accordingly we shall ask in the main two questions: What was the Greek God and what was the Greek worshiper? To comprehend the relation between these two is the final highest act of the Delphic sojourn; in it all the manifestations of Hellas center, from it they ray out in every direction. We must transform ourselves into that worshiper and adore the God with him, seeing and feeling what he saw and felt; thus we shall perform for ourselves a sacred act in the appreciation of the Divine as it was manifested to some of the noblest souls of our race. For us, too, the Gods existed, if we be but willing to make them our own.

The first fact of the Divine in its Greek manifestation, is that the One breaks up into the Many, religion becomes polytheistic. This is the most important consideration; not too much can we wrestle with its meaning. Multiplicity instead of unity is now the Divine Word; that is, there is a descent of deity into the world, an embodiment in manifold sensuous existence. There is a dropping down into the multiplicity of Nature: God is no longer the One, Jehovah, far above all finitude, dwelling in heavenly sublimity. As such He is pure ethereal spirit, freed from the earth and the earthly; an enormous unbridged chasm lies between Him and the world. But the divine soul has descended and taken possession of the sensuous world, has filled it in all its variety; thus the Divine has become many divinities, which hover below among men in some fond longing for their society.

So the old Greek felt when he went to worship; this deity has come down to me, has even my bodily shape; indeed a divine form may dwell in the brook, in the grove or mountain. He did not think of throwing away the sensuous side and elevating himself to the purely spiritual essence; that sensuous shape lies deep in the nature of the God, and through it alone can man come into relation with divinity. Thus all Nature is lit with the Divine Soul, all the works of man are instinct with it, and man himself is to be its completest revelation; the world of Beauty springs into existence, being one too with the world of Religion.

The ineffable abstraction of deity thus becomes individual — nay, a real, tangible shape. Gods are individualities, each with its own limits against the other; such is Greek spirit everywhere, imaged in the Greek territory, in the Greek State, in the man, finally in Olympus itself. All proclaim, the divine substance is now individualized in the history of the world; in the Gods the Greek man beholds the image of his own profoundest being and aspiration. The essence of himself they are, of what he is, and must be; he must realize them in his life, and for them suffer death. Greek polytheism means the rise of the individual as an abiding factor, not only in the World's History, but in the complete culture of every human being.

Such was the stress laid by Greece upon the individual — she loved him, fought for him, worshipped him, transfigured him at last to a God. Thus she made him eternal. The immortality of the individual is the gift of Greece to the race. Every statue of marble is an attempt to immortalize some phase of this spirit — some deity, some hero, or perchance some man. In certain countries of the East were previous hints of this doctrine, notably in Egypt; but its fruition could only be in Greece, where individuality is grasped as the primal germ of man's spiritual nature, as divine and eternal. The body will pass away, but the individual spirit is an everlasting thing; so the Greek body, the Greek State, Greek Olympus have long since disappeared, but their spirit lives to-day, being immortal, and therein a true prophecy of itself.

The Greek Gods, therefore, descend into the world and become many; but they must not be considered as mere natural objects or forces of Nature. They still remain spiritual, are beings whose essence is intelligence in some form. They have a physical side, but even this physical side is to be filled with the divine soul, is in some sort to be a revelation of the deity. Yet the natural element must be present in the God, it is not a mere external sign or symbol, it is inseparable from the divine manifestation. The two worlds, the physical and spiritual, touched in the deity and were transformed into a new world of harmonious forms, that of Art.

It is true that the Greeks spoke of an antecedent time in their own development when the Gods were quite sunk in Nature, hardly more than physical appearances. But such Gods must be put down, the old Gods of Chaos; hard was the struggle, this primal struggle of Greek spirit. It has been narrated by the poet Hesiod, and has already been considered in our journey, of which it is a very important part; it is the song of the rise of the spiritual out of the natural. Many of these old Gods were hurled down to gloomy Tartarus out of the way; others were still tolerated in certain dark corners of life, as the Furies; others continued to flit in the little by-ways of Nature, as the Nymphs; but the true Greek world belongs to the new Gods, the Olympians.

Still the Greek religion remains polytheistic. It has purified itself of gross natural forms, it has elevated itself to spirit, but not to the unity of the Godhead. That can never be, the beautiful world of the Gods would then perish, there would be no Religion of Beauty. The happy mean must be preserved which delights in the revelation of the Divine through the senses; the war is not yet opened which is to drive out of the world the last remaining sensuous element, and smite to pieces the beautiful Gods. A dim mutter of it may be already heard in the background, still the Greek remained joyous even amid his forebodings.

The Gods are, therefore, many; Hellas would not be Hellas, if it had not many individuals in its Pantheon. Still, in spite of them there is one Divine essence in which all the Gods participate; does that deep-lurking thought never hover before the consciousness of the Greek? When he speaks of the Gods, their unity comes out in the very instinct of his speech; he must consider them as having one thing in common, namely divinity, else they could not be Gods. Yes, he must feel that unity lying back of his present conception; the One thus will start up before him, or float dimly in the distance. There it is, an ineradicable phase of human spirit; spectral it may appear to him, still it is a reality.

Such is, indeed, all intelligence in its innermost movement, though thwarted by man's perversity. Let him assert the Half, it will insist upon being the Whole; let him, as at present, assert the Many, in the very assertion it will hint the One. Strangest, deepest of all human facts, the fundamental one of all mind; it is the key-note of history, of man's development, the source of all movement; this it is, that the human spirit will not rest in a one-sided phase of itself, but demands its own completeness. Behold the process: a party arises which lives for a period by asserting a part, which may be well enough at such given date; then it dies of a lie which is usually this, under many forms: our part or party is the Whole. Upon such an assertion it acts, ignoring or seeking to destroy the other part or party; this destruction of the other may indeed take place, still the Half cannot make itself the Whole; the very attempt is self-destruction.

Of old this movement of mind was known to the Greek thinker; its most abstract phase is touched upon in his discussions. Plato called it the Dialectic, and its development of some given theme a Dialogue. Truest of all things for the Greek mind was Plato's Dialectic of the One and the Many, now often deemed a mere play of ingenuity; but in that play an entire world was involved. Therein the philosopher reveals the very soul of his nation in its purest essence, and at the same time shows a new stage of its development; he casts away the old revelation of Art as sullied too much with the senses, and exhibits Greek spirit viewing itself in its own stainless mirror of Thought. But Plato lies beyond the precincts of Delphi.

So we look eagerly for the traces of this feeling for the other Part, for the One, in Greek polytheism. Soon we come upon its faint suggestion and begin to recognize it; behold it, a dim far-off specter, ghostly in every sense. Many are the Gods, but there appears a shadowy hand behind them which holds them, or is already in some deadly struggle with them. Read Homer, the first and greatest Greek, creator of the Greek world; even above his Zeus a dark necessity seems at times to hover, formless, uncontrollable, swooping down into the Olympian household and upsetting the plans of the Gods. At other times this dim power seems one with the might of Zeus, who thus becomes the one and supreme divinity. A veritable specter to the mind of the Greeks, standing back of their world; so it must remain while their time lasts. But that specter will advance into the foreground and develop into the solidest reality; we saw it come down upon Greece at Chæroneia, and sweep away the Olympian world. In many forms it hovered there in the Greek background; Fate the tragedians called it, and represented it as the outer unknown realm which inclosed every Grecian man and the Grecian State, thus making it the dark, awe-inspiring setting for their tragedies. Homer rather subjects Fate to Zeus, by conceiving both to be one at bottom; yet even he is full of premonition of that which is to come; developed Hellas will be over-arched by that impenetrable brazen sky of Fate which at last will fall and crush all that is beneath it.

In such untoward way the One appears to the Greek world, spectral, fateful, threatening. Moreover it was conceived as formless in the main, while the happy Greek Gods had forms, beautiful forms standing in the clearest daylight. That supreme One cannot be formed, cannot have limits put upon it. No one can get the full consciousness of the Greek worshipper without this amorphous fatality eternally hovering over him, even over his Gods. It was the shudder he felt in his joy, it was the everlasting threat suspended over his life, his world; it was the God above his Gods, it was the One behind the Many and controlling them. Polytheism begets Fate.

Yet the strange thing to us is, that this condition did not produce unhappiness, but joy rather. The Grecian man accepted the event in full; if it occurred, that was enough, it had a supreme right to be, whatever may have been his will in the matter. The fact is the divine reality with which he will not quarrel even if it kills him; thus he retains his mood in spite of the Tartarean ray of Fate casting long shadows upon him and his world. Indeed he was more joyous than we can possibly be, just for the reason that Fate lay outside of him; thus he could internally free himself from its pressure, and remain serene, even mirthful. But we moderns have taken up Fate into ourselves; we have made it internal, and thus destroyed it; such is the Christian solution. Still we have its responsibility, its weight within our souls, where it must be fought and put down every day with struggle and sorrow.

This necessity is, therefore, the highest divine attribute; it must accordingly appear in the Greek Gods themselves. Mark its transition; it is the supreme influence of the Greek Pantheon, hence must enter every deity; hardly of that Pantheon it is, yet it cannot be excluded. Is not the conception of God one of power, indeed of all-power? But here is the supreme power; Fate is that highest might in which each Greek God must participate, if he be a God. This is his one divine element among many human elements, this constitutes his unity with divinity; take this away, and the Gods are merely human, are indeed no Gods. But as above all chance and partaking of this necessity, they are deities.

Thus Fate, the supreme One, descends into the God. Now can we find this characteristic in the divine expression? Let us glance at the statues, and mark the main feature of their faces; a feature which they manifest in common. A look of the eternal, unchangeable, a look of Fate they all have amid their variety; human forms they possess, but transfigured to something above; they partake of an existence which is not transitory and temporal, which reaches even beyond themselves into an unseen world. They all have that look above, the look of Destiny; this is indeed the essence of Classic Art, and which no other art has or can have — that divine look above, the look of Fate. So we see the element of necessity manifesting itself in the divine and becoming its attribute, declaring, Thus must the God be and not otherwise. A gallery of antique sculpture has such a look even through Roman imitation; its chief interest is, that we may behold all these chiseled shapes having the one look, the look of Destiny.

The statue of the God, though a reproduction of man's

physical body, has in it something far more; indeed, the fact that it is not a copy of the human form, makes it what it is, namely a work of Art, a manifestation of the Divine in a sensuous shape. Mere imitation it is not; the distinctive thing is thus left out, which is the look of necessity, the serene elevation above the temporal. The actual man of flesh and blood has in him and around him the element of accident; his physical being is on all sides exposed to mutation; the transitory is the very stamp of his life. The child of Time and Place, the sport of Chance, the victim of externalities — such is the individual man by nature; but in this statuesque formation, or rather transformation, the phase of accident is stripped off, the caprices of Nature are gotten rid of, he is created anew by the Artist, every part of his frame has the image of necessity peering through the physical setting, the human form is transfigured into the Divine one.

Such, then, is the work of the Artist: to transmute the finite into the eternal; it still seems the earthly shape, yet everything earthly has been removed, made pure by Olympian fire. To have the eye which can see the true in these fleeting members, and embody the same in a marble shape which speaks of aught more lasting than marble, which has the look of Destiny itself, belongs to the Artist, the God-compelling man, not Artist so much as Priest, as Revealer. The natural thus becomes the bearer of the spiritual, which is its supreme purpose in the world. Note again that the work of Art is not the copy of some model; then the merely accidental features and natural elements would appear; it is the transformation of these into the image of the necessary, of the divine. So the Gods of Greece looked in their true realization, when they were the creation of faith, of the Religion of Beauty. That look above is the Idea, filling the soul of Seer, now the Artist; with it, every limb becomes transparent and reveals the God. Later in time this faith was lost, Realism entered and the Ideal vanished from the marble Pantheon.

The great religious teacher of Greece, therefore, was the Artist, and his doctrine was the Religion of Beauty.

not as an affected dilletantism, but as a profound, soul-inspiring faith. He revealed the Highest unto the worshipper with a sacred zeal; through his work alone the divinity was manifested. His gift was imagination, creative imagination, for he created the Gods, that is, revealed them. Recollect the statement of the pious old Historian, Herodotus, who says that the poets Homer and Hesiod gave to the Greeks their Gods; the same was true of Phidias the sculptor. The imagination catches the look of Destiny and fastens it into a face; thus it transmutes the human to the divine, nature to spirit; it fills the shape with the Ideal and makes it a work of Art. Yet to the Greek it was more, it was a God, a revelation of the world-governing power, and worthy of being worshipped; thus Art and Religion were inseparable, and there arose the Religion of Beauty. The great Revealer, too, was the Artist, who was truly the High Priest or the Interpreter of the God to men; as Religion and Art fall together and become one, so do priest and artist.

Such is the twofold development of the Greek Pantheon; the Gods descending into the sensuous world for their manifestation become many individuals, each of whom participates in the divine essence, and thus looks back to the unity of them all. It is the One, this glimmer of the true God, threatening Olympus from the outside like Destiny, yet reflected in the face of every Greek deity. But the multiplicity remains the enduring fact, without it there could be no beautiful world, no Religion of Beauty; with it Delphi alone becomes a beautiful world of these transfigured shapes, into which the Artist has put the look of the Divine One; thousands upon thousands they stand here, statues forming an Olympus of their own. Nature, too, comes to the front with her transformations; every object of hers is changed to an image, if not of marble, then of poetry, even more lasting than marble.

We may now turn to the second religious factor; the worshipper, and seek to enter into his feeling and thought as he approached his sanctuary. Worship is the act of the finite man elevating himself into harmony with the Divine; he feels the God dwelling within, and thus passes from alienation to unity with the Highest. The work of Art is the revelation of Divinity; in it deity descends into the world, and is reconciled with the world. Before the statue the worshipper appears, and is to make the harmony expressed in it his own, the harmony between the senses and spirit; thus his life will be in musical concert with the world around him. For that image of stone is to become internal, the worshipper is to transform it into spirit, to transform the hard marble; he is to make the God indwell his soul. Temple, too, is to go within him; hence it is built with such care and beauty; the finite man is raised to be the true temple of divinity.

As the Artist reveals the God, so the worshipper takes up the revelation and makes it his own, makes it himself. The one forms the beautiful object, the other transforms himself into that beautiful object, and thus is his own Artist, with his own life as material. Such was the true Greek worshipper, he also had to be Artist, to be poet in his worship. The image before him must rise out of its natural form into its spiritual suggestion; devotion was a poetic work, an act of imagination; still further, he must mould his character into that conception; thus he realizes in himself the nature of his God, and becomes a Maker too. The shape of stone before his eye is not of necessity an idol; it is rather a radiant image which flashes into him the divine manifestation; it is the supreme artistic model after which he is to fashion himself. The Greek Divine Service was an act of the poetic imagination; worship was a poem conceived, if not sung; therein was the worshipper elevated into the presence of the beautiful God, into whose image he was to transform himself, and be a living embodiment of the Religion of Beauty.

We must expect to find the character of the Greek Pantheon imprinted upon the Greek man who adored its deities. There was the polytheistic side; festivals, games, theater, song and dance, all in honor of the God. The rich, sensuous life of the Greeks unfolded in this divine multiplicity to its fullest bloom. There was, too, the Olympian sportfulness, for many are the Gods, and they cannot all be in earnest; they must limit one another and be like mortals, though they claim to be Gods too. There is an irony in them which is always ready to burst into open mirth; they are indeed a happy company. Yet there is the unity behind them, the dark background of Fate which threatens them all, in which however they must participate; thus joy passes into earnestness, and both are joined in a supreme serenity.

In the Greek sacrifice, too, the same principle prevailed; some object of value was surrendered, swine and cattle were slaughtered to the God, but therein were enjoyed, for the sacrifice was a scene of eating and drinking; the God was chiefly honored by man's happiness. This is not our notion of sacrifice, this is not renunciation, the surrender of the whole life to some divine behest, accompanied with want, hardship, even death. To the Greek such a renunciation would be a terrific dissonance; between the divine and sensuous life there must be harmony, which finds its true utterance in worship. Polytheism is this descent into the realm of the senses which it fills with song, sacrifice, festival, — in fine, fills with beautiful Gods, and reconciles, for a time at least, the Upper and Lower Worlds.

But that outside power still remained and made itself felt in everything — that external might of destiny. Every Greek will was to a degree paralyzed by it, and would not act without a sign which came from the outside power. There was something external to him which he knew not of, it was the Divine which showed itself in an omen, it was the Fate which lay back of his life, back of his Olympus. He had not in himself the complete circuit of his deed. Behold the flight of the eagle, it furnishes the missing link without which he cannot act, it is the messenger of the hidden power, whose very essence consists in not being understood. Any object of Nature might express that unknown realm, which lies outside of his purpose; the rustling of leaves, the brook, the bird, animals, unconscious human speech. Thus an external accidental power entered into every Greek deed, as it was a constituent part of the Greek world.

It is in the drama, however, that we find the strongest expression of this external power. It makes the poetry of the Greeks tragic, as well as their world. Fate enters and sweeps off the individual who acts, particularly the heroic individual. His deed lies in a realm which is surrounded and controlled on all sides by this incalculable destiny; he defies it, grapples with it, like a Greek athlete, and is flung out of existence for his daring. A wrestler with Fate is the Greek tragic character; manfully he steps forth to meet his combatant, the dark and formless, issuing from the bounds of the Greek horizon; the spectators look on with quakes of terror, for they feel in the end of their hero their own end, the end of Hellas. It is that same Destiny which we saw threatening Olympus.

The great historical character, Themistocles, Alexander, has the same element in him; like the Greek divinity he is the victim of Fate. He, too, is a tragic character, his end is unhappy; heroically he struggles with his problem, but it contains the portion of Destiny which overwhelms him at last. Yet this is not all. Fate descends into him, as it descended into his deity, and becomes a part of his innermost nature, in fact his divine, eternal part. The Great Men of Greece are plastic figures, as the Gods are; they have that look above, the look of destiny; they seem beyond mortals, into whose form they have come down, they are still our exemplars of lofty individuality. Their high deeds show this fateful influence, which, while it smites them from without, at the same time possesses them within.

In some such way we bring before ourselves the two leading facts — the worshipped and the worshipper — of the Religion of Beauty. There was the recognition of the God by the Man, and of the Man by the God; the two touch in a kind of ecstasy and become filled with endless musical vibrations. How comes it that the Greek soul was so melodious? is the ever-recurring, never-answered question; to the last a person is dissatisfied with any abstract solution, however complete, and longs to turn his ear to the music itself. We know that this sensuous life when filled with the divine spirit throbs in pulsations of harmony, which are the source of all true song; we know that the God embodied in forms of sense becomes the supremely beautiful, and giver of joys which make life one continued festival. Therein we may dwell for a time, in imagination at least, which we are aware is the soul of Greek worship.

Another question we must ask of this religion, the gravest of all questions: For the heart alienated from the God, what way of restoration could it show? What peace could it offer to a being who has become conscious of a separation from the Divine, perhaps of a fall therefrom? For man, even the Grecian man must have experienced at times a scission from what keeps the Universe in order, from what is truest above and here below. To overcome that deep disruption, and to set the jarring soul in concert with itself and the world, is the prime task of every Religion, and of every worthy system of Thought. The bright Greek temperament falls into discord, into sorrow, possibly into despair; what rescue? The Religion of Beauty has a path of escape, a by-path, not clear, not fully revealed, but unquestionably helpful.

This is the domain of the Mysteries, Eleusinian for example, which, true to their name, have remained mysterious to this day. But so much may be said of them: they were separated from the open public worship; the beautiful world, product of imagination, revealed in Art, was abandoned; a deeper, more awful rite was craved by the soul. Initiation was required; it was something which did not carry its purport on its face; symbolism entered which seeks to convey a meaning from beyond; the simple harmony between spirit and sense, which is the principle of Art, is split asunder, and Art is no longer its own explanation. The way of purification from the natural and the rise to the purely spiritual, by symbols, is the mystery — a mystery indeed to the Religion of Beauty, indicating its limitation as well as its final overthrow. Yet even thus the mystery is reached, not through suffering but through vision; after all, the individual, serenely viewing the wondrous image of transformation, is not assailed, but has his joy, and so Art makes itself valid in this last Greek refuge. Some glance into immortality was also given, doubtless, in the Mysteries; since to behold it is the last purification of vision. But their great doctrine was unquestionably that unity of the Godhead, which in the public religion had dropped into polytheism; some adumbration of the One, the spiritual One, must have been given, and thus Fate, the tragedy of the ancient world was to a degree softened, if not overcome, by the Mysteries.

But the plainest view of a mastery over Fate, was given by the great Athenian tragic poets, who thereby indicated that they were not fully satisfied with their Art, or at least saw beyond its limits. Look at blind old Oedipus, who was so often whelmed into wrong by that dire external power, and heroically took all the consequences as his own; at last through much suffering the insight of freedom comes to him, he declares his innocence and is absolved from guilt, being received to the Gods. Still stronger is the example of Orestes, as portrayed by Aeschylus; after long wandering and sorrow, he is purified of crime sent upon him by Fate, and is restored to a new guiltless life by institutions which pronounce him free; thus he is not taken to the Gods for salvation, but is rescued in this lower world. Deepest prophetic gleam is this, not merely into the future of the Greek religion, but of all religion, which is to be truly realized in secular institutions. In such manner the ancient tragic poets seem to break with Fate, casting far ahead in Time and demanding some reconciliation, though Fate was the ground-work of their Art and of their world.

Such was the lofty view of the Athenian bards, true prophets; a glimpse into the atonement which was to be, an early message was theirs of that religion of suffering through which comes the final reconciliation. They saw that mind must heal its own wounds, if it be universal; sorrow purifies the soul, which therein reaches a new transfiguration. Some such word they speak, must indeed speak, for the poet is the herald of the new time which bursts out of the old. But with that word comes another change; the Religion of Beauty, which had made its world so harmonious, separates into two hostile armies, and the war between the spirit and senses opens; therewith the Greek music is brought to a close.

XXIV. THE GREAT TRANSITION.

The traveler will pass Lent at Delphi, he will witness there the ceremonies of Easter; a new note, deepest, most intense of all, thus mingles with the old Delphic music and brings it to a conclusion. He is upon the ground where the last great religious change of his race was accomplished with long, desperate struggle; the whole people still celebrate this change with surprising vividness and faith; it is the time of strong sympathetic renewal of the event and its memories. Yet there is one point of identity: as the ancient Delphic man went through the history of the God in his worship, so the modern Delphic man enacts the life of the new deity. It is the last transition; we must seek now to make this transition too, and our task is done.

Much have we spoken of Fate in the Greek time; let us at once go back to it again, and move with it, for it is the driving principle of the mighty spiritual change of the old world. Already we have marked the ancient worshiper at his devotion, and have seen how he felt that Fate behind his many Gods, the spectral One which hovered over his existence, and entered into the very soul of his divinities. But by this act of worship he too participates in the One in which the Gods participate; he thus rises with the Gods above the Gods. The Greek religion always pointed to the One higher than itself; the Greek worshiper, as he rose to intimacy with the Divine, beheld and followed the indication. The Greek faith prophesied its own end, the prophecy was heard by its children, who must in time manifest its fulfilment. Such is the preparation going on in every Greek heart by worship.

Then comes the terrible reality, which we have already noted; Fate realized descends upon the Greek world, first in the Macedonian, then in the Roman conquerer. This was the bitter discipline of Greece, its intense suffering; the Roman sway was Fate realized, no longer divine and threatening Olympus, but terrestrial, having come down to earth and taken its abode there. The suffering, however, was not of Greece alone, but of the whole world, which Rome reduced to its iron sway and held fast in its clutches by its iron organization. The world is lost, its Gods conquered, dead; Fate is supreme in reality, the most real thing of the age.

But what has become of this Fate which stood outside of Hellas with its dark minatory glance? It has come down into the world, and no longer stands outside of the same; it has now become internal and thus disappears, for it is the nature of Fate to be external. It was therefore destroying itself when it was destroying the world; when it descended from its high threatening position, it could threaten no more; its own realization was its own end.

Such was the subtle inner movement of history; Rome was the minister of Fate, fulfilling its behests, but therein destroying it; that dread external power no longer controls the world which is now ready for freedom, for the new Word. The Roman discipline has been the scourge of the peoples, but it has conferred the greatest blessing upon the race; it has put Fate inside the world, by conquest, organization, law. The soil is indeed ready; for mark now the ancient worshiper, particularly the Greek worshiper: he, in adoring the Gods, adores the One in which they all are divine; he, too, is putting Fate within himself in the act of worship. Thus the man is doing for himself what Rome is doing for the world; each individual is passing through the same process which the universal soul of the age is passing through. Fate both as regards the world and the individual, is becoming internal, and is thereby ceasing to be at all.

Untold has been the suffering; direst agony through war, slavery, chiefly through death of the Gods, without any new divinity to take their place. But liberation is at hand, could the world but see it; that is indeed the next problem, to make the world see it, to bring the mighty change home to the soul of man and thus save him. The person now comes forward who is to reveal the new fact, reveal it not by word merely but by action, by his own life. That simple history of him is in reality the World's History; one individual embodies in his own life the spiritual life of the race, and is truly the image, the very Son of the Highest.

He came just when Rome had accomplished her mission as minister of Fate, she had conquered the world which was now to be redeemed, that is to be presented with the boon of freedom, of inner spiritual freedom, freedom from Fate. Thus destroyed mankind rises up transfigured, and there is a resurrection after death; the dead world slain like Christ by Fate, has received a new life, with Fate overcome forever. Fate in slaying the old world has slain itself, and therein begotten a new world whose principle is not Fate but Freedom; this is the glad Evangel which is now to find utterance in word and deed, and thus bring hope and salvation to the perishing people.

Deep and subtle is this inner movement of history which we have been tracing, very hard to be understood by the humble unlettered man. But it is to be revealed, revealed to the very senses of the lowest human being, who therein can participate in the great rescue. It is embodied in a man, this is the grand fact of incarnation; the profoundest thought of history takes on flesh and blood, lives a human life, seen and read by all men in the crimson letters of the heart. Greatest of all events is that one, the incarnation; an individual can elevate himself into being the very soul of his race, can live for all, can die for all; can make his life both the past and the future. The incarnation is the utterance of the World's History for every man, even the humblest; whereby, if he truly behold and believe, he is redeemed from Fate.

It is a beautiful morning, the traveler rises with the

customary joy in his heart; he will go forth to look at the Delphic vale and worship according to the Religion of Beauty. But sober faces meet him everywhere, it is announced that Lent has begun, and henceforth there must be fasting, prayer, religious exercises at Delphi. A time of sorrow has set in; Parnassus, though bright as ever upon its summits, must now be wrapped in spiritual gloom for many days. What calamity has befallen you, O Delphians? Death, death that occurred some eighteen hundred years ago; this death must still be wept, celebrated by sorrow, abstinence, penitential acts; the whole land is to be draped in memory of the Great Sufferer.

It is indeed a striking change from the joyous world in which we have been living. Suffering, not Beauty, now demands adoration; the chorus stops upon the Parnassian slopes, the betrothal, the marriage, often the daily tasks in the fields are suspended, festivals become a curse, mirth a sin. Food is not to be taken as usual; no meat, no olive oil, not even eggs; we are to suffer death, or some approach to it, because of that death so many centuries ago. Some deep necessity lies upon the world to suffer over again in soul what its Heroes have suffered; thus we are redeemed and saved from the bitter reality of their sacrifice. It is a strange phenomenon, doubly strange upon Parnassus; what does it mean?

This outer semblance of mourning means death, but it is an unusual death — that of God. Awfulest word for human lips, awfulest thought for human soul, that deity can die; a heart-piercing contradiction that makes the man shout in the pain of hopelessness. There is no conception like this for utter woe, when it truly enters the feeling, that God can die, has died: torment, carnival of distress, Hell that now is, to the heart which receives the wrenching struggle. For is not the whole spiritual universe in a conflict with its own essence — a war between the Finite and Infinite in which the latter loses and you too are lost? Such a pain now comes over the Delphic world; the people too are seeking to die, or at least to approach the gates of eternity and peep in. All the people share in this deep distress, not of one person, but of a world, not of a man but of a God.

One will often hear of the *pompa* or grand procession in the night before Easter. At midnight the sleeper will be aroused by the tolling of bells; the quiet village is already alive with a multitude, and the streets, usually so dark, are illuminated by many a bonfire. From each of the churches the procession starts and moves through the town, every soul muttering in low voice, *Kyrie eleéson! Lord have mercy!* This is the key-note, that of intense sorrow and supplication for a world which is perishing. A throng of boys come first, shouting in shrillest cries of lamentation, *Kyrie eleéson!* then the dead Christ in rude image is borne by priests on his bier lighted with tapers; after it follows a long line of men with muffled heads, each carrying a torch, and repeating continually in a low prayer, *Kyrie eleéson.* The procession completes the circuit of the town, and certainly makes an impressive display; from this humble spot of earth, wrapped in night, there arises but one voice to the heavens: *Kyrie eleéson!*

For it is a display, though the participants are deeply in earnest; the death of the Saviour is acted out in complete representation, being thus brought home to the very senses of the people. In the church service, too, there is this element of theatrical exhibition; it indeed takes the place of all theaters, which we must remember were, in the mind of ancient man, sacred to the God, and hence places of worship. The old theater has, partially at least, passed into the modern church. The great tragedy of Christ, the sum of all tragedies, being the image of man's tragic existence, is exhibited in decided colors, must be exhibited for the people. Nor can the audience remain mere spectators, they must take part, and every man has to enact in himself the mighty sacrifice of deity. Listen to their song; it is the chorus of a fallen world, supplicating for pity and redemption — *Kyrie eleéson!*

The ancient world was indeed tragic, the ancients knew it to be so themselves. The great plays of the Dramatic Poets revealed it most plainly; all the heroism and greatness of antiquity rest upon this tragic background. But now there is a change, resurrection has come and eternal life; salvation it is also called. Before the simple-hearted people the life and death of Christ have been given, he has been acted out in full for many days; they have taken him into their very being and have been transformed. But the grand culmination enters, the drama of human existence is not now a tragedy, man is saved, and the end is restoration. Here we have old tragic Heathendom represented with its fatal termination; but also we have the transition out of it into the Christian world, into the new life; this is not and never can be the victim of Fate, whose last shout of anguish is now dying away with a faint echo in the darkness: *Kyrie eleéson!*

But what is this which the traveler suddenly beholds? Men embrace in wild rapture, crying, *Christos aneste!* — *Christ has arisen!* The dolorous time is over and the question settled forever — *Christos aneste.* Friends rejoice together, enemies are reconciled, the stranger is greeted with fresh welcome; it is indeed a new world — *Christos aneste.* On the streets, in the wineshop, at the hearth, they dance and shout that the old time of sorrow is gone — the time of Fate — *Christos aneste.* Uncontrolled is the joy; they kiss, men and women; that is, the men kiss the men, and the women the women; not the men the women — at least not to the vision of the watchful traveler, who is, however, borne along irresistibly in the stream, and shouts with the rest of the people: *Christos aneste.* Such is the happy solution of the great tragedy; the world bursts into a sudden comedy, at times ridiculous enough, but always deeply genuine; joy cannot be held down by propriety, but breaks out into a universal laugh; it is the grand drama of mediation in which all are saved in that glorious last act: *Christos aneste.*

After the first jubilant effervescence, the crowd disperses to amuse itself till daybreak, when the roasting of the lambs will begin, and the grand barbecue take place; for the season of fasting, of death, is now over. A large company adjourns from the church to the wineshop, a very easy transition in Greece; hot punch is served up, games are played, songs are sung, while we are all watching for the chaste light of Aurora to creep over the top of Parnassus. But she delayed, and I grew tired of watching so long under the window of the intractable beauty; I slipped away from my more determined companions, and went home for an hour's repose. Still there ascended from the village, as I threaded its dark alleys, the notes of mirth and song, whose burden was that universal shout of jubilation: *Christos aneste.*

It was high morning before I was awake, my room was full of smoke, and I sprang out of my bed, thinking the house was on fire. I slid into garments, and raked my articles together into the knapsack, not forgetting this note-book; every moment I expected the flames to break through the ceiling or door, for the smoke was thickening to suffocation. I raised the window, ready to leap out; voices I heard in the yard, the schoolmaster's baby cried in the next room, female coughing resounded through the apartments. What was now the reflection of the traveler? Fate has, then, not been put down so completely, but appears again, savage, inexorable, on this very morning of the day when we are celebrating our victory over him. Besides a rain has come up, and is moderating the joys of the festival with torrents of heavenly tears.

Still the fateful threat must be some illusion, a mere comic show; I can hear the laughter of the people outside amid their prolonged fits of coughing. Just then the schoolmaster, my host, rushed into the room, half-choked, and explained the situation. The Capitanos, our next neighbor, had built a huge fire in the yard for roasting the lambs. The rain had driven him to bring the fire under the shelter of the porch, whence the draught had sucked the smoke into every room of the house. No danger; it was all smoke and no fire this time. My room had become uninhabitable; I rushed out to the porch, but the smoke there was still denser. Thence I fled into the open yard, but it was raining by the bucketful. Meantime the Capitanos was heaping on grape-vines and the smoke was increasing. Holding my breath I ran back into my room; but this, too, was full of murkiness with tormenting demons in it; surely old Splayfoot is in pursuit of me, and will get me on this Easter morning for my many sins. A fateful situation: outside is drowning, inside is suffocation; how can poor mortal escape? At last I compromised between the two infernal powers by hanging my head out of the window under the eaves, and leaving my hams and sides within to be smoked. Think of me, sympathetic fellow-mortals, hanging there, trying to save my bacon — *Kyrie eleéson*.

Finally our fire-fiend, the Capitanos, had his bed of coals ready, the smoke cleared away, I was released from the new grip of destiny, and we all rushed out of the house into the open air; even the rain had ceased, and the glorious sun had come out of the clouds, as if he too was going to celebrate Easter with us, vividly imaging the great restoration, and chiming with a refrain of sunbeams — *Christos aneste*. But the Capitanos is now our hero; he is in the splendid humor of success, as he rakes together the large pile of live coals burnt from grape cuttings, which give a special flavor to roast lamb, a slight delicate tip of Bacchic ecstasy. The Capitanos, too, is not without his wish for immortality; at every important stage of his heroic achievements he calls out to the stranger present, whom he considers to be some wandering Homerid: "Take a note of that, Didascali."

But it is time to begin the roasting. The entire carcass of the lamb is spitted on a long pole and held over the coals; the turnspit, who is none other than our Capitanos, keeps turning till it be evenly done throughout. There he sits in his court, watching the progress of the work, once in a while stirring the coals, speaking in loud commanding tones, conscious of an heroic deed; for did not the old heroes do something very similar to what he is doing? Women, children and stranger look on in wonder, often placing themselves in the fragrant wreaths of fatty incense which rises up from the steaming carcass gratefully to the Gods. The children roast little pieces, such as heart and liver, for themselves, and devour the same like young lions; it is now many weeks since they have tasted flesh; "it seems a hundred years," said the wife of neighbor Patroclus, who had dropped in for a moment to kiss our hostess. "Have you such things in your country?" asked the Capitanos. "Yes, we have there roast lamb, but we have no such heroic roasters as I find here," was the reply. "Take a note of that," said the Capitanos.

Somehow thus, the traveler reflects, were roasted the far-famed hecatombs at sandy Pylos by god-like Nestor when prudent Telemachus paid him a visit. Not a hundred bullocks now, but one little lamb composes the sacrifice; certainly a great diminution in quantity, very important to the hungry man; but the classic eye will here see again the Old, though so much diminished, in the New. Meanwhile a Greek neighbor, Patroclus himself, not his wife now, comes into the yard, approaches and kisses me, exclaiming, *Christos aneste*. That sudden osculation came down upon me like a stroke of Fate; my refractory lips would not respond to his, but instinctively muttered, *Kyrie eleéson*.

From every inner court one could see the smoke arising from the fires early in the morning. A friend passes and takes me with him to make the circuit of the town. The same thing is going on everywhere — roasting of far-famed hecatombs. In one place fifteen lambs were held over an enormous bed of coals by fifteen jolly young fellows, who offered us full canteens of heart-lightening recinato, and sang in unison a Klephtic song against the Turkish dogs. Sweetmeats and cakes were handed around by the women, who saluted me gracefully with their *Christos aneste*, but without the kiss. It is a joyous festival; the happiness is increased by the gratification of the appetite for animal food; the Lenten restraint, so oppressive, has been removed from the world; the very body breaks out into joy and claps its hands, shouting, *Christos aneste*.

When I returned home, the Capitanos had the second lamb over the coals, which still glowed with a festal ardor under the dripping carcass. "Whose hecatomb is the fairest in the town?" he asked. There seems to be no little rivalry in this matter, and I was glad that I could answer with truth: "Thy hecatomb, O Capitanos! according to my judgment thou art, of all the men on Parnassus, the true hero in lamb roasting, the very Achilles."

Holding his spit in one hand, and reaching his other hand into my coat pocket, he drew out my note book and held it up to me, saying: "Take a note of that without delay, O Didascali."

But the roast is done, and the eyes which have been watching it so long, are ready to devour it literally at a glance. We all light upon that lamb like eagles and young eaglets — men, women and children ; soon the bones are picked clean of every fiber, and the second lamb pretty well clawed up. What delight the penitential body expressed to taste animal food once more! *Christos aneste* — we can have flesh again. The bean diet is past, it represents a dead world, *Kyrie eléson!* Many people were hurt by the fast, health was injured, spirits were depressed, it was a kind of death. But now it is over. There is to be henceforth a resurrection out of it; joy has returned, melodiously attuned to that new Parnassian keynote, *Christos aneste.*

But hark! the drum, the drum, and with it the festal squeak of caramousa; it is the music of the town marching to the place of the chorus. Best of all we can now resume the song and dance; no sooner is the appetite satisfied than the poetry breaks out. From the lanes and the houses the young people are pouring forth, and the old, too; like bees they gather to their hive, which is the choral ground, there is the true Parnassian honey of song and festival. For many weeks there has been no chorus ; great has been the deprivation ; everybody longs for the stately-stepping pomp and the grace-breathing measure. Quite as much hunger for this the people show as for animal food; it is indeed a part of the grand resurrection. The stranger will follow the music, and note with fresh delight the chorus ; greater zest, a new life it seems to have, bursting forth in the spring like a flower ; still it is the same as we have already seen and described. Therewith we have completed the round of our journey, which has returned to the former world of festal joy and idyllic repose. With this last march to the choral place, it is manifest that our Delphic cycle has closed.

—— Thus the Greek peasant celebrated the sufferings

and resurrection of Christ; he does so with an earnestness and intensity of adoration which sweeps the indifferent observer into a strong communion of feeling with him, both of sorrow and of joy. He, the humble, often letterless man, seeks to be crucified and resurrected anew, as if his salvation depended upon his deed; and who will dare say that his salvation does not depend upon his deed? He is acting over again his nation's life, he is freeing himself from the death of the old Greek Gods, from the death of the old Greek world; he is redeeming himself from Fate. Each man is passing through the trials of his race and enacting its history; which if he do in truth, he can never fall back into that ancient fateful world of his ancestors, but comes forth fire-purified, and rises transfigured into this new life where is his home. Most profound is his instinct in this matter, one can feel; the Great Example he must appropriate, or perish; it is that which bears him out of heathendom and saves him from destiny. With such a bulwark in his soul, no external power, not even the Turk, has destroyed or can destroy him.

In this way every peasant becomes a conqueror, conqueror of the ancient world which was so long wrestling with despair because it had seen its deities perish. Imagine its condition! What is highest and most sacred in a people is blasted by a destroying breath — Fate overtakes the God. There is a feeling of hopelessness, of utter misery, often giving away to demoniac frenzy, often turning to a bitter scoffing wrath against all holy things. Most melancholy of human actions is the one vouched for by Polybius, speaking of a Macedonian naval commander: wherever he anchored, he built two altars, one to Illegality, the other to Impiety; to these he sacrificed, and he worshiped them as divinities. God was indeed dead; the awful thought must have been burnt into the very soul of the time. It cannot endure; the supreme question with every sincere man must have been: How can such a world be reached in its despair and saved? The prayer is for the New Man, the New Example, who will conduct the race out of the old into the new life.

Into such an unhappy world the New Man descends, suffers what it suffered, undergoes what the Divine had undergone. As the old Gods died, so he dies. Thus he enters the heart of the time, makes himself one with the time. He meets Fate, and in his suffering he stands for all who are victims of Fate; truly he died for the whole world, for Greece, Judæa, even Rome, all of which nations were overwhelmed by that outlying might of Destiny; for this Greek peasant, too, threatened still by Fate, who now seeks by fasting and much ceremony to pass through the life of Christ and in this way to make it his own.

The New Man comes into the world, is the world in all its finitude and suffering. His death is the final identification of himself with his time; he elevates himself into the type of his race. This is the great action, greatest of all conceivable human actions, so great that it is divine. What mortal can so identify himself with his fellow-man that he in his suffering can become the bearer of theirs? It is still your problem and mine; every act, every word of ours we must seek to raise into a type which is no longer for us merely, but for many, yea for all, if possible. Who can make his life, or his speech that universal poem which utters the hearts of his people, and therein relieves them of destiny and fills them with hope? Yet far more than a poem is this, rather the basis of all poetry for all time; that person is the hero who endures for us and for all. He who can make himself the bearer of men's souls is the only true Great Man; he is the man of profoundest thought as well as of action. The mightiest fact in the World's History we must recognize to be this fact of Christ; it means that mankind have now a mediator and can escape from Fate; through him the old is transfigured into the new. Yet not for a few, but for all, even the humblest; that is the miracle of greatness, he died for all, whether they acknowledge it or not; there is not one of us who could have gotten out of the old world — we would be there now, hemmed in by Fate like the antique man — if we had not come through the passage opened by the Universal Man.

Though by death he identified himself with a perishing age, he did far more, in fact the supreme thing; he carried the age out of death. For what is it that dies in him? Nought but the mortal, perishable; it is the death of this finite sensible form which he assumed — the death of death, the fate of fate. Christ died, but under that finite manifestation is revealed the Infinite as its very essence; even the mortal cannot be without immortality as its deep-hidden foundation. The old world, tragic, fateful, is thus led out of its despair and transfigured; and the Divine rises up anew and asserts itself the most enduring of all things; through death is the resurrection. The hackneyed words of creed thereby become endowed with living breath, indeed with the very soul of the World's History: he arose from the dead, appeared to his friends, was transfigured and placed on the right hand of God. In fact Faith must be filled and vivified with the history of the race, if it rise above a hollow barren formalism, or be aught more than blind credulity.

The grand transformation is to make every individual a bearer of the Divine; to have him manifest the death of Fate. He beholds it all in the story of the Great Sufferer, beholds it in image; into this image he is to transmute himself and be rescued. Such is the true imitation of Christ: unless you make yourself divine and resurrect yourself every day, you are a lost soul. The life of Christ is the History of the Divine Idea; the world has gone through that process, is going through it still; you, too, must travel the same journey; it is that which can make your daily struggle the victory of living.

In such manner the Greek peasants on Parnassus have sought to impress anew the image of the great rescue upon their hearts for many days. Therewith we have made the transition out of Delphi, indeed out of the ancient world. A new joy has arisen, not the old Greek joy exactly, which was immediate, the direct outpouring of a strong sensuous nature; this present joy comes after sorrow, it is the joy of the new life attained through suffering, the joy of the triumph over Fate. This is the return to the Divine from which the world had been alienated; there is now the absolute certainty that Fate can never again imperil the race, that it is dead with the old heathen Gods.

But a new responsibility has come with the new time; Fate has indeed gone within the man, yet it is to be conquered there, where it is conquerable now; every person has to fight over again within himself that mightiest battle of the World's History, the battle against Fate; every mortal man must fight and win, and thereby become immortal. Only in this way can he be a child of our modern time, which is itself the offspring of that ancient conflict. He must conquer his freedom from Fate himself, therein he makes himself an image of his Great Example. So says Delphi to-day, quite obscurely, it is true, and with strong nasal twang of the priest; still this is now the Delphic utterance.

But there is another utterance, far more distinct, far more complete, and to many of us far more congenial; it is that of the literary bibles of our modern age, speaking in words pointed with fire, melting with infinite tenderness, revealing the profoundest depths; — those bibles written by Dante, Shakespeare, Goethe. They all declare the golden word of atonement, of redemption from destiny, of a rise out of the finite into the eternal. They all say in substance: Transfigure thy deed and also thy word; raise them into a typical thing which is the only truth. If thou doest, do for all, let thy deed be universal; if thou singest, sing for all, let thy joys and thy sorrows be those of thy people, of thy race, if thou canst; if thou diest, die for all, as the true follower of that one Man who died for mankind and was God.

www.ingramcontent.com/pod-product-compliance
Lightning Source LLC
Chambersburg PA
CBHW031948290426
44108CB00011B/718